D1121729

Living the Fishing

History Workshop Series

General Editor

Raphael Samuel, *Ruskin College, Oxford*

Already published

Village Life and Labour
Miners, Quarrymen and Saltworkers
Rothschild Buildings: Life in an East End
    Tenement Block 1887–1920
East End Underworld: volume 2,
    Chapters in the Life of Arthur Harding
People's History and Socialist Theory
Culture, Ideology and Politics
Sex and Class in Women's History
Fenwomen: A Portrait of Women in an
    English Village

Routledge & Kegan Paul
London, Boston, Melbourne and Henley

Paul Thompson
with Tony Wailey and
Trevor Lummis

Living the
Fishing

First published in 1983
by Routledge & Kegan Paul plc
39 Store Street, London WC1E 7DD,
9 Park Street, Boston, Mass. 02108, USA,
296 Beaconsfield Parade, Middle Park,
Melbourne, 3206, Australia, and
Broadway House, Newtown Road,
Henley-on-Thames, Oxon RG9 1EN
Set in Bembo 11 on 12pt by
Rowland Phototypesetting Ltd
Bury St Edmunds, Suffolk
and printed in Great Britain by
St Edmundsbury Press
Bury St Edmunds, Suffolk

Library of Congress Cataloging in Publication Data

Thompson, Paul Richard, 1935–
    Living the fishing.
    (History workshop series)
    Bibliography: p.
    Includes index.
    1. Fishermen—Great Britain—History.
    2. Fishermen's wives—Great Britain
    History.   I. Wailey, Tony.
    II. Lummis, Trevor.   III. Title.   IV. Series.
    HD8039.F66G778 1983   305'.96392'0941   83-3053
ISBN 0-7100-9508-2
ISBN 0-7100-9519-8 (pbk.)

Contents

Preface   xi

Glossary   xiv

Part I The means to a living

1   Fishing – a way of life?   3

2   Fishing communities and the developing exploitation of the sea's resources   9

Part II Capital and labour

3   Trade unionism and industrial conflict   49

Close-up: Lancashire by Tony Wailey

4   Strike – the Fleetwood trawlers, 1920   70

5   Community: life in the inshore village of Marshside   75

6   The old ethic and the new – inshore village within a trawler port   90

7   The aftermath of defeat: the paradox of rebellion and organisation   99

Close-up: Aberdeen

8   The nemesis of steam capitalism   110

Part III The economy and the family

9   The penetration of capital and the family boat   149

10   Women in the fishing   167

Close-up: East Anglia by Trevor Lummis

11   Luck: longshoremen, smacksmen and driftermen   182

12   The Protestant ethic, the family and the economy   203

Part IV Community and individuality

Close-up: The Moray Firth
13   The moral order of free enterprise:
          Buckie   227
Close-up: The Western Isles
14   The chiliasm of despair: Lewis   264
Close-up: Shetland
15   A choice of destiny   308
16   Ahead   359
          Note on methods and sources   365
          List of informants   369
          Abbreviations   372
          Notes   373
          Select bibliography   385
          Index   397

Illustrations

between pages 174 and 175

1   Whitby fisherman and woman by Frank Sutcliffe (Sutcliffe Gallery)
2   Norfolk longshoremen at Sheringham (Peter Frank)
3   Marshside shrimpers (P. Gilchrist)
4   Buckie Yardie
5   Buckie mother and girl (Moray District Libraries)
6   Baiting lines at Portsoy (John Mair)
7   Skipper Wharton at sea (Fishermen's Mission)
8   Skipper Wharton at home with his wife in Lowestoft (Fishermen's Mission)
9   Trawl fleeting: unloading the catch (Fishermen's Mission)
10 Fleetwood trawler (Fishermen's Mission)
11 Gutting in a rough sea (Fishermen's Mission)
12 Aberdeen trawlermen at work (Fishermen's Mission)
13 Aberdeen trawler aground (John Adams)
14 Portknockie harbour: sail, 1890 (Moray District Libraries)
15 Portknockie harbour: steam, c. 1908 (Moray District Libraries)
16 The Geddes family's drifter
17 Skipper Pirie of Buckie (Moray District Libraries)
18 Crew of *Star of the Sea* (Moray District Libraries)
19 Joch and Lass Bruce of Buckie
20 Landing catch from *Transcend* (William Stewart)
21 Net factory at Grimsby (Hull Museums)
22 Coopers at Lowestoft (Peter Frank)
23 Buckie hunger march, 1920 (Moray District Libraries)
24 Two Buckie herring girls (William Stewart)
25 Herring gutters at Stornoway (Peter Frank)
26 Herring fleet at Barra
27 Raiders' crofts at Coll

28 Mission service at sea (Fishermen's Mission)
29 Shetland sixereens and sail drifters (George Washington Wilson Collection, Aberdeen University)
30 Shetland boats in Lerwick harbour
31 Salmon fishing at Bauline, Newfoundland
32 Abandoned Grimsby trawler in Aberdeen
33 Whalsay purse netter

Preface

This book has grown out of a variety of research projects over the last ten years with the help of many different people. My own work goes back to my first visits to Shetland in 1970 and to Lewis and the Barra Isles in 1971 with Thea Vigne, interviewing as part of our national 'Family Life and Work Experience before 1918' oral history survey for *The Edwardians* (1975). Trevor Lummis, who had also been part of our research team, then went on to his independent study of 'The Family and Community Life of East Anglian Fishermen', while I developed my own interest in the Scottish fishing communities, beginning work on Buckie with the help of Thea Vigne and Alun Howkins in 1973, and subsequently on Aberdeen. In the meantime Peter Frank, a colleague at Essex, had set about his own study of the fishing industry in his home town of Whitby, again using oral history. Finally Tony Wailey, who had gone to sea from Marshside and began work on the history of that community while at Ruskin College, came on to Essex and completed as a project for his degree the research on which his essay here is based. The idea of a joint book came naturally from our many discussions together, and was reinforced by a special History Workshop, 'On the Waterfront', organised by Raphael Samuel, in which we all participated. In the event, chapters 4 to 7 of this book were written by Tony Wailey, chapter 11 by Trevor Lummis, and the remaining chapters by myself; but if its final shape is primarily my responsibility, it is nevertheless the fruit of a collective enterprise in which the critical comments and continuing encouragement of Peter Frank, Trevor Lummis and Tony Wailey especially have played an essential part. And we would all wish to thank most the generosity of the men and women of the fishing communities who talked to us about their lives and shared with us their knowledge of the past and ideas about the future. Without their help this book could have been neither conceived nor realised.

I should particularly like to express my own gratitude, both in terms of practical help and in suggesting ideas and discussing interpretations, in Shetland to John Graham and Brian Smith, and in Fraserburgh and elsewhere in the north-east to Andrew Noble, himself both a historian and full-time fisherman on a purse netter. I have similarly been especially helped in Buckie by Richard Anderson of the Fishery Office, in Lewis by Judith Ennew and by Norman Macdonald, writer and crofter of Tong; in Scalpay by Jean Mills and in Aberdeen by Deborah Rolland; and more generally by Eric Cregeen and many other members of the School of Scottish Studies in Edinburgh. I also owe a special debt for stimulating discussions with Orvar Löfgren of Lund in Sweden, and Rex Clarke, Raoul Andersen, Neil Rosenberg and their colleagues during my visit to Newfoundland. For other valuable suggestions I should like to thank Fañch Elégoët of Plouguerneau in Brittany; Sven Ek and Birgitta Frykman in Göteborg; in Norway, Brit Berggreen and Ann Louise Christiansen of Oslo, Edvard Bull and Dagfinn Slettan of Trondheim, and Johan Foss on the isle of Fröya; Robert Storey on Barra and Vatersay; A. M. Morrison of Stornoway, James Slater of Portsoy, George Strachan, Malcolm Gray, James Coull and Paul Dukes of Aberdeen, Barbara Robertson of Edinburgh and John Barnes of Cambridge; Peter Gould, P. J. Edwards and Jean Marshall on Grimsby; for locating records, J. K. Bates of the National Register of Archives (Scotland), and for permission to consult their firm's records, Richard Irvin and Sons. We are grateful for financial assistance to the Social Science Research Council, which funded the two first-mentioned projects at the University of Essex, and to the Fuller Bequest which helped with some later expenses; to Stephen Hatch, Deborah Boyle and Caroline Broadway for other interviews in Shetland in 1970; and for transcribing interviews, to Janet Parkin, Sue Maclennan and Sue Mayes. For comments on the final manuscript as a whole, we are especially indebted to Natasha Burchardt, Raphael Samuel and John Saville. I would also like to thank Alun Jones for drawing the maps.

Lastly, I must thank John Buchan and the crew of the *Lunar*

Bow of Peterhead for the culminating moments of my own exploration of a different world. I shall not forget those autumn nights off the far north-west coast of Scotland, when, surrounded in the blackness by the lights of two dozen neighbouring boats, we twisted and turned after the mackerel shoals; and how, beyond Cape Wrath where Loch Eriboll opens to the sea, just as the grey clouds turned bloodshot with dawn and sunlight picked a silver glitter from the stark cliffs and the granite moorland slopes of Ben Hope, we knew that a giant shoal was in the water below us – shot for them and found them . . .

Paul Thompson
September 1981

Glossary

arles   engagement money given on hiring to bind a worker to an employer

badger   shrimp potter or salesman

beatster   net-mender

bloater   whole herring lightly smoked over oak logs

bond   duty-free drink and other goods carried by boats working outside a certain area around the British Isles

bothy   hut or one-roomed dwelling; accommodation of unmarried living-in farm labourers

broo   unemployment pay, dole

but and ben   kitchen and parlour of a two-room house

coble   fishing boat with flat bottom, deeper rudder, square stern and oblique squarish sail

cod trap   stationary net trap with doorways, set in inshore waters

coper   boat supplying spirits to deep sea fishermen (Dutch 'kooper', dealer)

cottar   landless cottager

cran   volume measure of herring: roughly 750 fish or one-fifth of a ton

croft   small agricultural holding

culch   shells collected to be laid down as the base of oyster beds

deckhand   ordinary fisherman ('deckie')

dory   small, flat-bottomed boat

drift nets   nets joined to hang vertically like a curtain from floats on the sea's surface, with weights below, let out to drift in the current

farlin   long wooden trough from which herrings are gutted

fourareen   four-oared boat

fry   portion of fish from the catch given to crew for home consumption

guernsey   thick, close-fitting, knitted wool shirt
hairst, hirsting   harvest, harvesting
jigger   lead replica of a fish with hooks, dropped and jerked up and down on a handline
keelboat   larger boat with a definite keel, in contrast to the coble (Yorkshire)
kettle nets   U-shaped walls of netting staked on foreshore as tidal traps
kipper   split herring smoked over oak chippings for about ten hours
laird   lord, landowner of land
landowner   of boats: an owner who does not work at sea
lazy-bed   six-foot wide potato bed built up of soil dug from adjoining trenches or carried from elsewhere
leep   basket for shrimps strapped on the back
lie-day   day off work between trips at sea
line   *small line* or *hand-line*, baited ashore with shellfish, and dropped vertically to catch fish in mid-water or on the bottom; *great-line* (from Dutch 'grutline') or *long-line* baited with fish at sea, and strung out along the sea bottom
longshoreman   inshore small boat fisherman
mattie   early herring, non-spawning (from Dutch 'maatjie')
muckle   great
nett   amount remaining after deductions
nobby   small flat-bottomed boat used in Lancashire tidal estuaries
peerie, pirie   small
piltock   young saithe or coalfish, one to three years old
poundage   wages or bonus based on ship's earnings
pull away   customary small percentage of catch deducted by trawler owners before the remainder was put on the market
putter   form of hand trawl, a bow shaped net fixed to a long wooden shaft and pushed by hand through the water (Lancashire)
quine   woman
red herring   brine-soaked herring slowly smoked over oak-dust to a deep red-brown
reek   smoke

ring net   net used to encircle herring shoals in enclosed waters: originally as a beach seine, but later offshore, commonly worked by two boats (in the nineteenth century incorrectly called 'trawling for herring')

risk money   bonus on wages introduced during wartime

scattald   common rough pasture

scotch cure   herrings gutted and pickled in barrels of brine

scutcher   wooden herring scoop

seine net   net designed to enclose shoals of fish which has developed in several distinctive forms: first (and earliest) the *beach seine*, run out from the beach in a semi-circle (generally from a small boat) to hang like a curtain from surface to sea bottom and then hauled back on to the beach; second the *seine* or *Danish seine*, worked at sea and hauled onto a boat, a cone-shaped bag net dropped to the sea bottom whose ropes are laid to encircle and as they are hauled frighten flat-fish into the net – boats using this net are known as *seiners*; third the *purse seine*, like a very large ring net, shot out to encircle a shoal with floats keeping the head-line to the surface, while the weighted bottom of the net sinks around the shoal and is then pulled together under it and closed like a duffle bag by a wire through its rings, and finally hauled by a power block, a winch system of hydraulically powered rollers – boats using this net are known as *pursers*.

shanker   shrimp catcher

share money   earnings by owners and fishermen calculated as a share of the boat's nett profit

shiller   shrimp seller

siller   silver, money

sillock   young saithe or coalfish, under one year old

sixereen   six-oared boat

smack   single-masted sailboat, rigged fore and aft: in East Anglia, a sailing trawler; in Shetland, a large fishing vessel: crew, *smacksmen*

stocker, stocky   fish not the main object of an expedition and if caught regarded as a perquisite of the crew, either for use or for resale

tacksman   middle man who leases land to sublet it in small holdings

trawl net   bag-shaped net dragged along the sea bottom: *beam-trawl* net, kept open by a beam; *otter trawl* net, with twin boards kept apart by the force of the water; *light trawling*, by boats of under 80 feet length; *pair trawling*, a single net towed between two boats

trimmer   fireman

trip money   small fixed payment on completion of each trip

voe   sea creek

willens   branches of scrub woven into baskets

yawl, yoal   small fishing boat fitted for rowing or sailing

Part I The means to a living

1 Fishing – a way of life?

'It's no fish ye're buying – it's men's lives',
Sir Walter Scott, *The Antiquary*, 1816

This is a book about fishing communities. We are concerned
with both the past and the future; with how men and women
have shaped their lives around different kinds of fishing, how
they and their communities have met the drastic changes of the
last eighty and more years in the fishing industry, and what
chances they have of survival now. In writing it we deliberately cross the boundaries of sociology, anthropology and history. And our conclusions point beyond our particular subject
to the future of all of us: for if we are right, economic and social
development depend as much on the situation of women, and
of children, and the history and consciousness of communities, as on matters of capital, cash and profit, of today's and
tomorrow's market.

The image of the fishermen conjures up deep feelings:
Biblical resonances of Galilee, echoes of childhood hymns,
nostalgia for the last true hunters plying a trade that goes back
to the very origins of humanity. The mind's eye fastens on the
life ebbing from hundreds of tiny harbours and creeks around
our coasts. We think of heroism in the face of winter danger, of
the sea itself, and the struggle of mankind with the elements.

Take one of Frank Sutcliffe's rightly famous photographs of
the Whitby fishermen at the end of the last century. What does
it represent? No doubt in his patterned woollen jersey, huge
leather seaboots and wide-brimmed wrinkled sou'wester,
with his distinctive gait, arms held out as if for balance, or a
pipe clutched in swollen hand, such a fisherman could be
picked out anywhere. But does this distinctive dress also
indicate a separate, long-standing tradition, a stable way of life
maintained despite all the changes ashore, and perhaps only
now at its end? John Dyson opens his recent book *Business in*

Great Waters by presenting fishermen as 'a race apart', among whom regional differences – in contrast to the rest of the population – were unimportant 'because their way of life allowed them to transcend these differences'.[1] We would disagree. Fishing has been an unstable occupation for centuries; for, in order to survive the constant changes in the sea's resources and the demands of society, generations of fishermen have had to seek new grounds and new markets, learn new techniques and new attitudes. It is these very differences, between communities and over time, which we believe are the fascination of fishing history. The world of Hull – of Jeremy Tunstall's *The Fishermen* – or of Fleetwood is emphatically not the world of Shetland; indeed, they could hardly be more sharply contrasted. Certainly something of a common universe of ideas has arisen among fishermen alongside the common aims and technology of the industry. But similarities in equipment or dress do not have to imply a uniformity in attitudes. Such stereotyping can only obscure what is, in our view, the essence of the story: how fishing communities have had to adapt and fight to survive.

Fishing as an occupation does not automatically push men towards a single, simple view of life. On the contrary, it pulls in very contradictory directions. Why, for example, have some fishermen proved dogged – if often defeated – trade unionists, while others are so fervently anti-union, at a time when all have been increasingly at the mercy of big capital? Why has the growth of big business interests in the fishing industry not been matched by an equivalent growth in class consciousness among fishermen, as it has among miners, dockers, railwaymen or factory workers? Through their communities, generally isolated and cohesive, dominated by a single industry, well aware of their special economic interests and the ways in which they are exploited and undervalued by the wider world, fishermen certainly experience a powerful communal solidarity. And this is reinforced by mutual dependence on workmates in an exceptionally dangerous occupation. But work also divides fishermen, for they are scattered at sea in small units with scarcely more than a dozen to a crew working aboard boats which may be in port all together only for brief moments two or three times a year between fishing seasons, are very likely individually owned, and certainly actively competing against each other for their catch of fish. All this generates suspicion of almost any form of collective action, from co-operatives to trade unionism. And the exact balance of attitudes is shaped within the context of each local economy and social structure.

The same is true of the fishing family. Why are some fishermen lampooned as drunken wife-beaters, while others are known as 'family men', with strikingly 'progressive' attitudes to women and children? These drastic variations can again be seen to be rooted in the economy and the work context. Fishing takes men away from their homes, often for long periods. This makes conventional family life difficult; and at one extreme may lead to the blunted affection and callousness which Jeremy Tunstall portrays among the Hull trawlermen. Yet their very absence can bring fishermen to recognise a special dependence on the labour and economic management of their wives, while in looking after themselves at sea they may acquire cooking and cleaning skills which make them unusually considerate husbands. Again, only the local context can show why the balance falls one way or the other; how far attitudes to women and children are interconnected; and the extent to which the economy shapes the way in which children are brought up – or vice versa.

With religion too – itself intimately bound up with family attitudes – the way of life may again push one way or the other. No doubt the dangers of an occupation at the mercy of the elements draws men towards religion. But work at sea also takes them out of sight of ministers and congregations, outside the hold of institutional religion; and the unjust changes of fate, and the unpredictable irregularity of their earnings, have as often driven fishermen ashore to the public house and superstition as to the church or chapel pew. And the fishermen's religion has its own special, complex relationship with the local economy. A religious revival, for example, may be born of economic desperation, yet in time, with changing circumstances and opportunities, it may itself provide one of the means towards renewed prosperity.

The variations which can thus be found between fishing communities at first seem perplexing, and certainly defy any over-simple general theory of social change. They make nonsense of 'modernisation' theory, with its sharp contrast between societies slumbering in 'traditional' immobility and poverty, and 'developed' societies which have earned their present affluence through adaptability, acceptance of the logic of science, the cash nexus and individualism. Modernisation theory of this kind is a perspective of profound influence in world economic and social policies today. But fishing communities, which have lived for at least 200 years on the basis of a volatile market economy and developing technology, demonstrate without any doubt that there are other paths to prosperity, in some cases firmly based on the *re-creation* of more 'traditional' attitudes, such as work organisation round the family boat rather than wage labour. Such facts do not fit more easily with any straightforward Marxist interpretation, which would expect the progressive commercialisation of the fishing economy to have led to the 'proletarianisation' of the fishermen, their reduction to class-conscious wage labourers. Such a view would have looked plausible enough sixty years ago, but not today.

We need new theories: interpretations firmly rooted in the variety of fishing experience. And there is a logic in each local story on which we can build. This is why, after setting the general context of the social economy of fishing in the first three chapters, we turn to close studies of the conflict of capital and labour in local communities. Next we take up a second set of more general themes, on the relationship between the family, ideology and the economy. These are in turn explored in three local 'close-ups' of community and individuality, each with its markedly differing economic fate. And finally, at the end of the book, we come back to the wider perspective, and look ahead.

The constellations of economic, social and moral structures and beliefs which we shall discover not merely characterise each community, past and present, but in a vital sense help to determine their future. And we believe that in the history of particular communities we can find the key to the paradox of fishing in Britain today. Fifty years ago it was the great company-run trawler ports of northern England like Fleetwood and Hull which seemed to hold the future of fishing in their hands. The smaller inshore boats were everywhere on the way out: ageing boats, each year fewer seaworthy, more laid up to rot; men forced to scratch a living as best they could, and – in the towns – queue for the chance of a job. Who would have guessed that today, Fleetwood would be on the verge of bankruptcy and Hull facing virtual closure, while the prosperous crew of a purse seiner from the remote Shetland isle of Whalsay – which by the normal logic of 'progress' ought to have been driven out of business decades ago – could afford to lay up their £½ million ship for a week, in order to take in the hay harvest on their crofts?

Figure 1   Beaching a rowboat at one of the best Lewis harbours of the 1870s, Port of Ness; on the hill, a woman carries a creel on her back.

2 Fishing communities and the developing exploitation of the sea's resources

Let us go back to Frank Sutcliffe's photographs of the Whitby fishermen. You can pick them up in stationer's shops right round the country nowadays. But why? What do they convey? The message seems simple enough: an image of a way of life now past, which was more stable, closer to nature, buffeted by the elements perhaps, but not at the mercy of the market as we are today. A life of poverty, but equally certainly of continuity. And a visit to Whitby might well seem to confirm that impression. Here surely, walking up from the harbour where there are still fishing boats active today, we can see a link in a long tradition? After all, Whitby was already 'a great fischar Toune' when John Leland the antiquary visited it in 1536; and still today Whitby's hundred fishermen work from sixteen 'keelboats' and a dozen 'cobles', now fitted with motors, but their basic shapes evolved centuries ago to meet the special needs of inshore line-fishing off the Yorkshire coast.

Yet a closer look reveals a less straightforward picture. Many of Sutcliffe's photographs were not of Whitby itself, but of other nearby coastal villages. The booming prosperity of Whitby as a ship-building centre during the Napoleonic wars had almost killed its fishing. In 1816 the town could count a mere 9 fishermen in a population of over 10,000. The village of Staithes, with over 300 fishermen and 80 boats, was by far the biggest fishing station on the north Yorkshire coast; while Runswick and Robin Hood's Bay had another 40 boats each. Yet within two generations, the pattern was being reversed. By this time it was the Staithes and Runswick men who were being lured from fishing by the opening of ironstone mines in the hills behind the coast. Whitby, on the other hand, cut off from coal and iron, was shrinking as an industrial centre, so that fishing now looked a more attractive alternative. Its larger population, swollen by summer tourists, offered a much better market than the smaller villages. Its fine natural harbour, cut by the deep cleft of the Esk between its cliffs, was well looked after once the town council had taken over from a neglectful Harbour Board. The villages had no harbours at all, so that their men and women had to haul the cobles up the beach to safety. Consequently, already by the 1880s Staithes men were keeping their larger boats in Whitby, although they still 'returned to their village homes' when fishing from the smaller cobles. But before long the most active fishing families were moving permanently into Whitby, helping to reconstruct the fishing community there; while fishing in the smaller stations was being abandoned. The Robin Hood's Bay men had gone over to work in the merchant marine by the 1880s; the last Staithes yawl had stopped fishing by 1914, although some fishing lingers on; while at Runswick, it finally ceased in the 1950s.[1]

What seems at first sight to be a continuous tradition thus emerges as a broken pattern, moulded by the vagaries of local industry, markets and resources, and held together above all by the living threads of migrant families. And if we look round the coast of Britain, we find again and again a similar story. In Stornoway, for example, the principal fishing port of the Western Isles, the present fleet has been built up from near extinction twenty years ago. Again Lerwick, Shetland's capital, had scarcely any native fishermen before 1900. The small boats at the quay today may suggest an immemorial tradition to the visiting tourist, but to the townsmen they represent a relatively new intrusion, a colony of 'Scotties' from the declining inshore villages of north-east Scotland, who migrated here in the 1900s. In Barra, southernmost of the Western Isles, you can find the descendants of families drawn there by the later nineteenth century herring boom from as far apart as Aberdeenshire and Ireland. Conversely, there are descendants of Scots herring girls who settled in the English east-coast ports as far south as Yarmouth. And the rise of the great trawl ports from the mid-nineteenth century sucked in labour from all directions: apprentice boys were brought from the great city workhouses, Norfolk and Suffolk families moved with their smacks to the Humber, and Humber and Tyneside skippers moved on north again to find boats in Aberdeen. In Harwich today there are families who can trace their origins back to the once-prosperous fishing communities of Greenwich and Barking which supplied London before the mid-nineteenth century, and whose relatives have moved on to Hull or Grimsby. Fleetwood drew its crews from as far away as the Hebrides. Right round the coast, so far from being locked in a world of immemorial stability, generations of fishermen, encouraged by the very nature of their occupation, have been constantly on the move, their communities in flux.

Undoubtedly the pace of change has quickened in the last hundred years. Yet it would be wrong to see this pattern of movement as simply a special effect of the great economic transformation of the industry since the mid-nineteenth century. Certainly that provided the immediate context for the growth of the communities whose story we tell in this book. But to understand its true significance, it is necessary to look back further, briefly, to make two points.

Firstly, the intervention of large-scale commercial interests in fishing goes back many centuries. Certainly a marginal element of subsistence fishing has normally persisted side-by-side with commercial fishing. But because of the perishability of fish, the resources needed for curing, the uncertainty of fish stocks, and the technical sophistication which has to be acquired, active fishing has been primarily for the market: fresh fish for direct local sale, and cured fish for sale, through merchants, much further afield.

There has indeed, been a continental European market in fish for hundreds of years. Iceland was an important source for dried fish for Europe in the early middle ages, when merchants from East Anglian and Yorkshire ports were already financing boats for the long, dangerous voyage which this trade demanded. So were French and Basque merchants; and the latter were also sending boats to the Bergen and Lofoten fishing off the north Norwegian coast – picking up their curing salt from Portugal on the way. As late as the 1740s, Yarmouth was sending 200 vessels a year to the Icelandic cod fishery. But from the early sixteenth century, with the discovery of America, it was gradually succeeded in importance by the

Newfoundland cod fishery. This was a ruthless merchant enterprise operated from the western ports of Europe – such as Bristol, Poole and Greenock in Britain – to supply the Mediterranean dried-fish market. It was a seasonal fishery, conducted in an appallingly bitter climate. Up to the eighteenth century it did not even have the advantage of a permanent base, for while the British government provided some naval protection against attacks from the French and other rivals at sea, it attempted to prohibit the settlement of the colony, so that each season the migrant fishermen had to fight each other for facilities. They caught the cod either close inshore with fixed traps, or out at sea by line or 'jigger' rods from 'dories', tiny two-men boats which could be launched into the open ocean from the big smacks. The catch was dried aboard the smacks or ashore. The cod were abundant, and the enterprise highly profitable; enabling the merchants, when the Newfoundland outports later became settlements, to establish their iron grip on the colony's economy. Even after this the seasonal migration of European smacks across the north Atlantic continued into the twentieth century, working a virtually unchanged primitive technology. It still dominated the distant water scene right up to the 1890s. Only then did the North Sea white fishing succeed in its place.

Meanwhile, much more briefly, some of the east-coast ports had developed another specialism in the late eighteenth and early nineteenth centuries – whaling. This again was of necessity a large-scale enterprise. Hull and Aberdeen, Peterhead and Whitby all became notable centres. But with the falling price of whale oil, whaling from Yarmouth had ceased by 1810 and from Whitby by 1827. It continued much longer from Peterhead – and also from Norway; indeed, for a few years in the early twentieth century there were small Norwegian whaling stations working in Shetland and Lewis. Some of these enterprises therefore lasted for no more than a generation, others far longer. But again there could be no doubt that each of them was wholly commercial, depending on the continuity of profit for their very being. Thus it has been for hundreds of years within the context of an industry powerfully shaped by large-scale organisation, and a competitive international market, that inshoremen have sought to make their own living.

Secondly, there are not many small independent fishing communities proper, of the village type, which can be traced back before the eighteenth century. It is true that from quite an early stage each of the larger towns commonly had a fishermen's quarter, or a village on the outskirts, supplying it with fresh fish, such as Newhaven to Edinburgh, and Greenwich to London. As population grew, there was room for a cluster of specialised villages of this kind to develop in a very few especially concentrated areas like the Thames estuary or the Firth of Forth. But these fishing stations tended to prove relatively short-lived, due to pollution, over-fishing, and the easy availability of alternative work. And even if one takes today's major fishing ports, only Lowestoft could claim that it has a longstanding fishing community of significance.

If this is true of the main population centres and ports, it applies still more to the relatively sparsely populated coasts between them. Before the eighteenth century it was rare for fishing to provide the mainstay of a coastal village, because it was not easy to find – or supply – a regular fish market, and there were more direct ways for the community to meet its needs, through farming and artisan craftsmanship. One might take as typical of this stage the economy of the Kentish coast. An eighteenth-century report described the people of Thanet as:

> amphibious animals, who get their living both by sea and
> land . . . equally skilled in holding helm or plough,
> according to the season of the year. They knit nets, catch
> cods, herring, mackerel, etc., go voyages, and export
> merchant dyes. The very same persons dung the land,
> plough, sow, reap and carry in the corn. They work hard
> and live hard and are truly industrious.

On Thanet, Ramsgate was soon to become one of the leading sail trawling communities; but on Dungeness the 'amphibious' style of life remained typical even into the twentieth century. Here the marshlanders were able to combine small-boat seine netting from the beach with wage work on the farms. They also had the produce of their smallholdings. For house-building they would pillage wood from wrecks. Steve Prebble from Dengemarsh remembered how they would use 'an old boat turned bottom upwards for a roof', and if it was well fixed, 'rigged up properly right round, you could see the water going up, blowing over the top of the house' from the sea. The neighbouring farmers also fished from the beach, using stake nets, known locally as 'kettle nets'. They were all part-timers; and there were cases in which a man might be at various times throughout the year, kettle-net fisherman, itinerant herring or potato salesman, ditcher and draincleaner, haycutter and thatcher, sheepshearer or thrasher.

Along the Norfolk and Suffolk coast too, where the Norwich city market had encouraged specialised villages much earlier, there were still within living memory many independent-minded men who would switch from fishing to farm labouring according to season. Smallholders would become horse-and-cart fish-hawkers round the villages for the autumn fishing season, and farm labourers take berths on the boats after the hay was cut, hoping to earn some real money at last, *'if he was lucky'*. These men from the farms tend to remember fishing for the fighting, spitting and dirt aboard, the lazy skippers: 'You earned your money at that time o' day. That's *Hell's Playground*, they say. But it toughened you up.'[2]

By the 1900s in East Anglia such seasonal deckhands were merely supplying a reserve of casual labour. In the northern and western islands of Scotland, however, the *normal* pattern remained a combination of small farming (crofting) and fishing. Indeed right up to the present, there is only one thoroughly specialised fishing community in Shetland – Hamnavoe on Burra Isle, which took on this character only in the 1890s; and two in the Western Isles – Eriskay and Scalpay, both rocky, infertile outcrops which were settled, as a result of the mid-nineteenth century clearances of crofts from better land, by people who had little choice but to fish or starve.

In Scotland the oldest true fishing villages are to be found on the north-east coast. Here Buckie was settled in the seventeenth century. It was one of an almost continuous string of coastal villages from the Moray Firth to the Tay, which grew through the eighteenth century from the landless rural lower

class of the farming hinterland, often ex-smallholders deliberately resettled by landowners. Several fishing villages were
originally laid out by entrepreneurial landlords who provided the men with boats along with their homes, in return for
a half share of their catch. The north-east villages are thus not
survivors of an ancient way of life, but on the contrary, a
manifestation of the social changes wrought by the agricultural revolution – and a response to market opportunities.

There was little work on the north-eastern farms except for
living-in servants, and the people of the fishing villages had no
crofts of their own. From the start, therefore, these were
communities of full-time fishermen. And necessity soon became a principle. It was an old saying in the Moray Firth, 'The
corn and cod dinna mix.' Apart from fishwives tramping the
farms selling fresh fish, there was little contact between the
farm and sea communities, and almost no intermarriage. This
was partly for economic reasons, for the help of the women
was an essential in mending nets and baiting lines as in
hawking the catch. In Crovie, now abandoned for fishing, one
can still sense the atmosphere of these villages up to the
mid-nineteenth century, just a row of low single-storey
houses, in which nets, lines, ropes and sails were all still
prepared, closely hugging the shore on which the family's
sailboats were beached; and behind them, green hillside. Here
a score of families made a hard, bare living, trading haddock
and herring for potatoes: a community of poverty hitched to
the fringes of the economy. These first true fishing communities represented social disturbance rather than tradition, a
response of the disinherited driven to the margins, and still far
from secure. They had much to gain, as well as much to lose,
from the economic transformation of the fishing industry in
the nineteenth century.

The most sudden and spectacular element in this great
nineteenth-century economic transformation was undoubtedly the rise of a new white-fish trawling industry based on the
North Sea ports. Behind it lay both the gradual evolution of
fishing technology, and the immense social and economic
changes in Britain as a whole which opened up the possibility
of a new national market for fresh fish.

Most of the inshore communities had fished with lines or with drift nets. Cod, haddock, ling, plaice and other species which live on or near the sea-bed were taken with baited hooks either on hand-lines, or on long-lines strung out along the sea bottom, sometimes for up to six miles with as many as 5,000 hooks. The labour involved in preparing these was obviously enormous. Drift nets, hanging in long rows from the water surface, were used to catch fish which swim near the top of the sea – herrings, mackerel, pilchards and sprats. There were some local variations, like the 'circle net' with its base rope held ashore, the antecedent of the 'ring net' worked by Clyde herring men in their sheltered sea lochs; or 'stow nets', huge bag-shaped nets streaming in the tide from anchored boats in estuaries like the Thames, the Wash and the Solent. Most elaborate by far were the tripartite Cornish pilchard seine nets, worked by whole 'companies' of men, financed by local export merchants, from the sixteenth to the late nineteenth centuries: a six-oared seine boat to carry the main net, two smaller 'followers' to close its openings with stop nets, 'huers' on the cliffs and a 'lurker' boat to spot the shoals, and 'tucknets' to scoop the trapped fish out of the main net into baskets. But in general, fish caught themselves.

The trawl net, on the other hand, dragged along the sea bed, could be manipulated, and thus gave man a much greater advantage over his quarry. Some form of trawl net can be traced back to at least the fourteenth century. But it was the Devon fishermen of Brixham in the eighteenth century who probably devised the key improvement which made the 'beam-trawl': the forty foot beam of wood to keep open the bag net behind. Tickled off the sea bed by the ground-rope, few fish of any type or size in the way of the trawl had much chance of escape. It made for an immediate, startling increase in catching power. Some of the Brixham men moved with their new technique up the west coast. Others by the 1830s had settled with their families in Ramsgate. And then onwards to the Humber.

For it was above all in the Humber that the new technique was to converge with two more key factors: new grounds, and new power. Before 1830, according to the later evidence of one Grimsby smack-owner, there was only a single fishing vessel based on Grimsby, and none at all at Hull. But in the winter of 1837 the accidental discovery was made by one of the Brixham migrants, just off the southern end of the Dogger Bank, of the Silver Pits – a ground of unprecedented richness: 'the nets were hauled up bristling with fish trying to escape through the meshes, and such enormous catches were made as the most experienced fishermen had never before thought possible.'[3] This proved the making of the Humber fishing; for it combined with the opening of a national market for the growing urban population, through the building of a steam railway network. Hull, with 40 trawlers in 1845, mainly from Brixham and Ramsgate, would have been able to go ahead, if it had had suitable facilities, but it was without a fish dock, and its railway head was a full mile from the quayside. So in 1848 the Great North Railway took over the Grimsby docks, opened the direct rail link to London, and set about building the vast Royal Dock with its great Italian tower, still the town's principal landmark, especially for the fishermen. By 1869 Hull had answered with its Albert Dock. Both ports boomed. Hull by 1877 had 440 smacks, Grimsby 505. In that year the railway carried 44,000 tons of fish out of Grimsby's docks.

The urban market which could take fish on this scale was to expand steadily, not merely as the population grew and the railway network became complete, but with new forms of consumption. This was important, because much of the fish scooped up by the trawl net did not fit customary notions of what was worth eating; indeed it looked positively unpleasant. It could only be sold if well cut up, often under a false name, or a deceptive new euphemism like 'rock salmon'. But with the rise of the fish-and-chip shop in working-class districts in the late nineteenth century, an alternative market for cheap white fish to the fishmonger's was created. By 1914, when Grimsby was sending out 13 full fish trains every day, there were some 20,000 fish-and-chip shops in England and Wales.

In the meantime perhaps the most radical change of all had come: the application of steam power to the boats themselves. It was William Purdy, master of a Tyneside paddle-tug, who decided to experiment during a slack time in 1877 with fixing a trawl net to his tug. So immediate was his success that, within months, some forty tugs were trawling out of North Shields – and catching three times the landings of the local line-fishermen. Line-fishing was in fact to survive commercially for many decades for the high-quality fresh fish market; and even sailing trawlers were able to continue for many years in the shadow of the steamboats, working the nearer waters which, through over-fishing, were not worth the time of the higher-powered boats. Ramsgate still had 152 sailing trawlers in 1914, Brixham 193, and Lowestoft 265. But it was the steam fleets which were growing. And they were step by step improving their technique. From 1880 the early paddle-driven steamers gave way to screw-propellered boats, and 'otter trawl' was devised, both pioneered from Scarborough yards. Next came the twin-drummed steam winch for hauling the nets. Then, searching further and further afield for better grounds on which to use its increasingly expensive equipment, in 1891 the first east-coast steam trawler fished off Iceland. The era of modern distant-water fishing had begun.

Communications, and later capital resources, gave an immense advantage to the small number of ports which had led the new white-fish industry: above all Grimsby and Hull on the Humber, Shields and Aberdeen to the north, Fleetwood to the west, Milford Haven in Wales – and not far behind them, Lowestoft in East Anglia. Of them all, only Lowestoft had been of any significance in 1840. The others rose as spectacularly as later they were to fall. Now Grimsby, with over 500 first-class steam trawlers in the 1900s and 6,000 men, was the premier fishing port in Britain; Hull only a short head behind. Either alone could easily outstrip the entire national steam-fishing fleet of Germany, Britain's strongest international competitor in the new industry.

The rise of trawling had created at the same time a new set of social relations for fishing: the characteristic relations of modern industry. The early steam trawlers cost roughly a hundred times as much to build and equip as a secondhand inshore boat; and before sailing a steam trawler needed coal, ice to preserve its catch on the longer voyage, and provisions for its crew. The leap in costs was so sudden and drastic that the change could not have been brought about from the resources of the inshore communities. Steam trawling had to be created by shore capitalists, and it bore their unmistakeable stamp.

At the top of the new system was a small group of owners. In all the trawling ports most of the boats were company-owned, even if companies were quite small, from a very early stage. The biggest owners not only worked boats, but invested in coal and ice supply, marine engineering and ship-building, and made as much of their money from these ancillary activities as from trawling itself. The fishing industry did not create millionaires, but it could bring substantial fortunes. When Christopher Pickering of Hull, and Richard Irvin of Shields and Aberdeen, died in 1921, each left over £250,000.

Between them and the crews were the skippers. In the old fishing communities skippers and crew worked side by side, and were similarly rewarded with a share in the boat's takings. But on the trawlers they were deliberately separated from the men, in the hope that they would drive the boats harder. They alone – at least in the early decades of steam trawling – were given a share. They were encouraged to believe that they might themselves in turn become owners: and a few did indeed do so. Moreover, in the best years their earnings could undoubtedly be far above those of even the highest-paid skilled workers in industry. Hence they also became to an increasing degree socially separated from their crews. Ashore, they began to move their families out from the deckhand's streets to more select parts of the town. When they went out there were some who would sit with their wives in the theatre dress circle rather than the stalls, drink with other skippers in a hotel rather than a fisherman's pub, or meet up at their own skippers' clubs.

At the bottom were the men – and very much at the bottom. Most of the skippers had been born into fishing families, and drawn in from other ports. The owners needed their skills in seamanship and finding fish; and if possible a mate and third hand of comparable character. But with the other men it was different. The trawl ports had expanded so rapidly that they had to procure hands as best they could. In the first place this meant paying straight wages, in the hope of attracting men away from alternative labouring work. There was a precedent, for the big 'well smacks' which supplied the London market with fresh fish from the end of the eighteenth century had been crewed by wage-earners, with only the skipper on a share. In London there was already competition for labour. But inshoremen elsewhere saw their own self-employed independence as part of the essence of fishing. As one old Northumberland line-fisherman put it in 1878: 'All classes work on these trawlers. They are not fishermen, they are paid wages for their work.'[4] But it went further than this. The owners, failing even through this to persuade enough adults to man the smacks, fell back on the draconian method of recruitment which had been used before to create a workforce for the first great northern textile mills of the industrial revolution. They turned to the masters of orphanages, reformatories and workhouses in the inland towns, and persuaded them to bind their pauper boys to sea as apprentices in the fishing boats. Originally apprenticeship had been intended as a form of training under the protection of the ship's master. But now it was reduced to a system of cheap labour backed by severe punishment. Ashore, some apprentices were housed and fed by the master, and others were given the comparative freedom of boarding out. But at sea all were forced under constant threat of violence to work incredibly long hours, and in frequent danger, for a financial pittance; and if they deserted, they could be imprisoned. The system was used, to a varying degree, in Brixham and Ramsgate, Lowestoft and Yarmouth, and above all in the Humber, where in the late nineteenth century half the trawler crews had come in this way.

Inshore fishing offered a far from easy life; but work in the trawlers, apart from bringing a more regular income, repsented in almost every way an intensification of hardship and worsening of conditions. The smacks went increasingly further out to sea, gradually moving northwards, into colder, rougher weather. They were therefore away for much longer periods from home and throughout the year. This made the primitive accommodation – no ventilation below, only shelves to sleep on, no sanitary facilities, nowhere to wash – much less tolerable.

Distance introduced technical difficulties too. The fish had to be kept fresh. One early tactic had been the eighteenth century 'well ship', in which the fish were kept in water tanks. Another, which – along with the use of ice – was pioneered by Samuel Hewett in the 1850s, was working in fleets, with carrier boats sailing the catch back to port. This enabled the main fleet to stay still longer at sea. The peak of the fleeting system was in the 1880s, when there were fourteen main fleets at work, the largest being Hewett's Short Blue Fleet of 170 trawlers. It was Hewett's collapse in 1900 which at one blow was later to end Yarmouth's significance as a trawl port. Fleeting at Grimsby was ended in 1901, but it was carried on for distant water fishing from Hull until as late as 1936.

Fleeting further increased the already serious danger of fishing under difficult weather conditions, for the catch had to be taken to the carrier in the small vulnerable ship's boats. The death rate through accidents among trawlermen was appalling, seven times that of inshore fishermen. From 1884, when accident figures are first available, over 2,000 men and boys were lost in ten years. In 1894, the worst single year of all, 494 fishermen were killed – one in every sixty in the country.

For those who were injured rather than killed, there were no medical facilities at sea before 1882, when the first Mission Ships were equipped to provide the fleets with doctors, tobacco sales, and the spiritual comforts of sermons and hymn-singing. The crews had to gut the fish on deck, in order to stave off decay. This again contrasted with the practice of the inshore boats and herring drifters, which landed more frequently, so that preparing the fish could be mainly the responsibility of the women ashore. Gutting at sea greatly lengthened hours of work, which during active fishing became virtually incessant. It also aggravated the sea boils, cracks and poisoned hands caused by cuts and chafing from the fish, hawsers and nets, the salt, and intense cold. Trawlermen were marked by their bent, mutilated hands.

Exhausted, driven relentlessly by their skippers, the men vented their exasperation and anger on each other, and especially on the boys. Some trawler lads were given 'cruel, debasing and disgusting treatment', an official inquiry of 1882 concluded: and 'short of ill-usage, much "horse-play" of a rough character'. There were a few instances of murder; and many more of repeated thrashings, of boys fed only on the crew's leavings, or forced to stay on deck night and day. 'They were rough old boys, boy they were rough at you,' recalled Sam Larner of his first years on Yarmouth trawling smacks in the early 1890s:

> a real old bulldog breed they were, they didn't care for nothing, neither God nor man, they didn't. . . . Now and again you'd find a kind man among them, but some of them were cruel – you weren't allowed to speak. . . . They'd chuck a bucket of water on you to shake you . . . put the rope onto your backside if you got into trouble . . .

Cruelty was undoubtedly exaggerated by drink, which the crews could take to sea on the trawlers. When the original supplies were exhausted, more could be bought from Dutch 'copers', floating grog ships which supplied the fleets until 1893 when their trade was legally banned. No wonder apprentices bound to the trade fled when they could. The Grimsby records from 1883 onwards show that a full quarter succeeded in absconding altogether; and a third of those who stayed on served part of their time in prison.

Trawling capitalism, in short, had created a new kind of fishermen: a workforce of wage-earners who clearly saw their own interests as sharply distinct from those of their employers. And this drew them quickly towards the characteristic attitudes of the industrial working class in the towns as a whole. Already by the early 1880s the trawlermen had shown their capacity to unionise and to strike: and the owners to fight back. It was the beginning of a prolonged struggle; and over the next two generations the trawlermen were to experience more setbacks than victories. But there can be no doubt that over that period, wage-payment, work experience and fifty years of erupting conflict with their masters brought them to a consciousness and culture which was essentially urban, industrial and working class. It was a culture with its own special strengths and failings: but these men – 'hardworking, hard-drinking, tough in language and in love', in the novelist's phrase – were by then incontestably both fishermen *and* working class. Indeed, looking back to an evening in Grimsby

in the early 1930s, one has a picture which could almost have
come from one of D. H. Lawrence's own Nottinghamshire
mining towns, but for one last phrase:

> The glare and warmth of the many public-houses, the
> cheerful brightness of the cinema, the rough horse-play of
> the lads and girls in the Market Square while the band of
> the merry-go-round blares out its tunes and whistles
> shriek, these are the realities, these are the things that count
> for them. Tomorrow night they may be at sea again.[5]

Here were the men who still seemed to hold the future of
fishing in their hands. What could the inshoremen do?

There can have seemed little hope in the later nineteenth or
early twentieth centuries for the inshoremen's continued survival. From the mid-nineteenth century onwards most fishing
stations right round the coast steadily declined in competition
with the few growth centres, squeezed by falling prices,
higher costs if they were near to industry, or inadequate
transport if they were more isolated. Again and again complaints could be heard like those of the Caithness men: 'The
boats are going more into the hands of what are locally called
capitalists, . . . and the fishermen are of opinion that they are
gradually becoming hired hands.'

In principle, three remedies were open to them. These were
protection from the trawlers, subsidies to compete with them,
or to find an alternative specialisation. All three were to some
extent applied. The first two, however, ran directly against the
grain of the prevailing economic philosophy of the era.

Certainly nobody took seriously the inshoremen's demands
that trawling should simply be banned. This was the call
which they put strongly before the Royal Commissions of
1863 and 1878, in terms which anticipate the conservationist
measures at last being imposed today, when the North Sea has
been all but scoured of fish and its herring utterly destroyed.
The indiscriminate trawl nets, it was said, were cutting into
the renewal of the fish stocks by destroying spawn, fry, and
young fish: 'I have seen large quantities of small fish, haddock,
codlings, which are young cod, and such like . . . thrown

overboard [and] quite destroyed.' But there was little scientific evidence at that date to back up the inshoremen's opinions.

Equally serious was the difficulty of disentangling genuine conservationism from attempts to assert local communal property rights over the sea. The freedom of the seas was one of the cornerstones of Britain's position in the world economy, and a principle not lightly to be tampered with. But it was not a universal principle accepted by all maritime countries, nor had it always been so in Britain. Swedish law recognised the customary rights of farmers on the Baltic coast over inshore waters adjacent to their land. Around the Quebecan islands in the Gulf of St Lawrence sea territories were divided between parishes and rights to fish inherited through the family. In the early nineteenth century the fishing banks around the Scottish Barra Isles were annually apportioned by lot – a 'system of marine runrig' – and similar local customs for allocating 'berths' for cod traps were recognised under the Newfoundland fishery regulations of 1890. Where the catch had to be cultivated, as with oyster fishing, even in Britain continued regulations witnessed the protection of local rights – although not always clearly enough to prevent sharp conflicts, like the incident of the Essex coast in the 1890s when the Tollesbury boats, spotting Burnham smacks dredging the culch on which their common oyster bed was laid, boarded them 'armed with shovels' to fight them off. But these were hardly attitudes which governments wished to encourage. When inshoremen demanded the banning of trawlers, it seemed all too clear that they were as much concerned with defending territory as protecting fish.

There was nevertheless a lurking sense that the inshoremen might be right about fish stocks. A small concession was eventually made. From 1889 trawling was banned within the three-mile limit; and some of the larger indentations like the Moray Firth, were also closed to home, although not to foreign, trawlers from 1892 onwards.

It was the more isolated communities who suffered most from the kinds of difficulties which could have been mitigated by subsidies. Lacking capital, they were increasingly forced to work with outdated boats and gear, and could have been greatly helped by a government loan scheme for boat purchase. But although brief experiments were made in this direction for the Scottish crofter-fishermen in 1887–91 and later for the herring fleets in their inter-war crisis, it was not until after the Second World War that a wholehearted application of such a policy was to prove effective. Again, foreign practices varied. Faroe's first government loans scheme came in 1904. Norway set up its State Fisheries Bank in 1921 to offer loans to working fishermen; and from 1938 gave fishermen's co-operatives a monopoly over the first-hand sale of all fish landings. The doctrines of laissez faire economics have proved too powerful for British governments to respond imaginatively to the requests of fishermen for assistance of this kind.

There were fewer objections to the provision of better harbours, which had strategic as well as economic justification. In fact through the Fishery Boards and local authorities some government aid for harbour construction was given as a regular policy. But there was little of this money, and it had to be spread very thinly. How it was disposed could determine the life and death of a community, for there was always a tendency for the more peripheral villages to be gradually abandoned as the active fishermen and their families moved closer to the most viable local port. And along the more exposed cliff-coasts there clearly could be no future without harbour construction. An extreme case is offered by the plight of the fishermen of Church Ope, on Portland Bill in Dorset, on the eve of the First World War:

> The cove is in process of being filled up by the rubble and waste which are tipped over the cliffs from the neighbouring stone quarries. . . . So serious has this filling up of the cove become, that the fishermen have now abandoned it. They prefer to use an ugly ledge of rock a mile or so to the north east of the cove, where they have erected a crane, by which perilous means their boats are, in all weathers, launched and lifted again to a small flat area above the reach of ordinary storms, a proceeding which has, we regret to hear, been since attended with a serious accident. The catches are carried on the fishermen's backs over a rugged path to the railway station some two and a half miles away. That the fishermen should be talking cheerfully of

installing motors . . . or indeed, that two motors are now being installed, speaks volumes for their grit.

Grit alone would not suffice to save such a fishery from extinction.

A more general problem for the more isolated communities was their lack of good cheap land transport. A prosperous fishery up to the 1930s required a railhead, as close to the quay as possible, with a fast service to an urban market, and coal available at cheap prices. One of the worst problems for the fishermen of Devon and Cornwall was their distance both from population and from coal. The railway system, although privately run, was government-regulated, but no intervention in the fare structure to help the more distant regions was attempted. As a result, by the 1900s the most pervasive decay of an entire regional fishery to be found in the whole of Britain was in the south-west. The old major deep-sea ports of Brixham and St Ives had once been among the leaders of the national industry. Brixham failed to convert to steam trawling, although its sailing smacks remained active into the 1900s. St Ives by the same time presented a scene of unmitigated melancholy, its men 'despondent and disheartened', their abandoned luggers 'moored up with old chains and rotting ropes to the rusty railway lines of the old broad-gauge along a grass-grown quay'.[6]

Yet even for such disadvantaged communities an alternative to economic despair could sometimes be found through a sensitive adaptation to particular local economic opportunities. There might be chances of combining fishing seasonally with other work, like the holiday trade. Probably the Devon and Cornish fishermen who managed best in these difficult years were amphibious fishermen like Tom Woolley of Sidmouth, with whom Stephen Reynolds the writer made his home in 1907, and so vividly described in his book *A Poor Man's House*. Tom picked up his living from spells in the Royal Naval Reserve, boat-hiring to visitors, carpet-beating and cleaning, or pushing a wheelchair, as well as drifting for the herring or mackerel shoals, prawning, lobster potting or line-fishing.

There were also more specialised adaptations, often again frequently linked to the growing economy of leisure of

Edwardian Britain. Thus several Essex coast villages, like Wivenhoe and Brightlingsea, became centres for high-class luxury yachting, so that fishermen could take seasonal work as hired crew on the yachts. Other inshore communities developed shellfish trades, especially where there was a nearby luxury market, like London for the Colchester and Whitstable oysters, Cromer for the north Norfolk creeks, Blackpool for Morecambe Bay, and Southport for Marshside.

None of these solutions, however, could have saved more than a scatter of inshore communities. What really transformed the inshoremen's chances after the 1880s, and lifted their communities into the twentieth century, was the herring boom. It was only through the remarkable development of the herring fishery that the seemingly inexorable suction of the future into the dominating trawl ports – the logic, it indeed seemed, of the capitalist process – was to be blocked, and ultimately to be set in reverse. For the herring boom gave the inshore communities three more generations of living. It saw them through the steam age.

Until the 1950s the herring shoals moved each year with the Gulf Stream, some appearing off the north-west coast of Scotland in early summer, others later on off the north-east, and yet others reaching the narrows at the southern end of the North Sea in late autumn, as if in one vast annual encirclement of the British Isles. Unlike white fish, sought out through exploring and combing the sea bottom, the herring was caught swimming to the surface in drift nets, hanging like immense lengths of curtain to wait in the paths of its moving migratory shoals. The shoals were dense, but not easy to find. Although their movements were seasonal, they were always somewhat arbitrary, and it is only quite recently (too late) that they have been fully understood. The herring shoals gathered either for feeding, especially in the early summer as the plankton grew in the light, or for spawning; once 'spent' or spawned, the shoals dispersed. Different groups of herring spawned at various times of the year in different parts of the sea. The fish provided rich food, but deteriorated rapidly. Herring fishing was thus inevitably chancy; and to succeed on any large scale required a method of marketing big catches over brief periods from a succession of different localities.

Originally, the fishermen had simply waited for the shoals. They were most easily found trapped in a sea inlet or passage. This was to the advantage of the Clyde fishermen, who eventually built up a fresh herring trade using the 'ring net' worked by two boats to enclose shoals in the sea lochs. And the first great herring fishing was during the later middle ages, in the straits between the Baltic and the North Sea. For several centuries it was one basis of the prosperity of the Hanseatic ports. Later on the shoals moved northwards, first allowing Sweden in the late eighteenth century to become the leaders of the herring fishery, giving way in turn to Norway in the early and mid-nineteenth century. The East Anglian ports, especially Yarmouth, were in another strategic situation, and here again the herring fishery went back to the middle ages. But off most of the British coast the herring's appearance was too irregular and brief to be treated as more than a lucky bonanza for seasonal fishermen.

From the early seventeenth century for almost two centuries, the North Sea herring industry was dominated by the Dutch. They discovered that salted herrings lasted much better if gutted immediately, before being barrelled in salt brine. This was quicker and cheaper than smoking, and the barrels were easy to transport. They were thus able to provide a cheap winter food in the continental towns for months after they were caught. The Dutch built up a mobile fishery, with a fleet of 2,000 sailboats mainly based on the British east coast ports from Shetland down to Yarmouth, but bringing their own curers, who worked aboard the boats. This enabled them to keep their secret, and hold control of their immense export trade to Eastern Europe.

The traditional Yarmouth trade had been in the export to Mediterranean countries of slow-smoked 'red herring'. During the Napoleonic Wars building up the fisheries became part of Britain's naval strategy, and generous bounties were offered by the government for boat-building and herring-curing. The Dutch secret was finally identified by J. F. Denovan of Leith. It was renamed the 'Scotch cure', and the newly formed Scottish Fisheries Board was thereafter able to guarantee reliable standards through its graded crown brands. Later on, there were to be important innovations in smoking herring too. Kippers, split smoked herring, were an invention of the 1830s by John Woodger, a Newcastle man who settled in Yarmouth. The whole smoked bloater was invented by another Yarmouth curer at about the same time. But it was the Scotch cure, because it allowed a much quicker handling of larger quantities of herring, which provided the key breakthrough to success in large-scale fishing. Quite soon leading Scottish landowners and merchants were combining to construct fishing harbours and housing at Wick and Helmsdale, to intercept the summer shoals in the far north. And the new enterprise was launched at a moment of natural fortune, when the herring began to invade the inner firths of the Scottish east coast in especial abundance. Hugh Miller described how in 1819 he was taken for a night's fishing in a Cromarty boat, and the whole firth 'so far as the eye could reach, appeared crowded with herrings; and its surface was so broken by them as to remind one of the pool of a waterfall. They leaped by millions a few inches into the air . . . living myriads of creation.' On the west coast the irregular, deeply indented coastline always made the appearance of shoals in particular sea lochs occasional and arbitrary. Off Shetland, the shoals provided a brief boom in the 1830s, and then were lost again as they moved further offshore. But on the east coast, up until the 1870s their visitations were sufficiently consistent to provide the local basis for an international industry; and by the time that the shoals began to move offshore again so that the fishermen needed larger boats to find them, they had laid down enough resources and commitment to follow.

The growth of the industry had been startling. The number of barrels of herring cured in Scotland rose steeply from 90,000 in 1810 to over 400,000 ten years later, and on to 600,000 at the mid-century, finally taking the lead from Norway, with one and a half million in the 1880s and two and a half million in the peak year of 1907. In England there was a more gradual rise to around half a million barrels in the 1880s and over one and a half million by 1907, overtaking the Scottish figure immediately before the war. But a third of the English herring landings were from Scots boats, and cured by Scots curers.

British cured herring was originally sold as cheap winter food for the growing home population, and also exported to Ireland and to the West Indian slave plantations. When these markets failed, with first the emancipation of slaves and then the Irish potato famine and emigration, the British began to take over from the Dutch in Eastern Europe. Dutch and also German herring fleets remained throughout the period important rivals. Nevertheless, by the 1850s Britain was exporting 250,000 barrels to Europe, and by 1913 3 million. Even between the wars, though markets never fully recovered, in the best years British exports still topped half a million barrels. On the eve of the First World War, with four-fifths of the herring catch sold abroad for £6 millions, the herring industry was a big export business.

Through most of this long period, despite the complex, far-flung market which they served, the ownership of both English and Scottish herring fleets nevertheless remained in the hands of the fishermen themselves. Steam trawling was an unencumbered, fully fledged capitalism, directly serving a growing urban home market; but the herring industry was above all an export business, a merchant enterprise dominated by men whose skills were in extracting profit from bargains rather than as employers directing labour. Hence they could more readily see the merit of respecting the fishermen's strong wish to keep their own boats. There was more than one way of exploiting their labour.

Up until the later nineteenth century this presented little difficulty, because the fishery could easily be conducted from family inshore boats. Indeed the English driftermen, who had earlier used their big deep sea Iceland cod smacks for herring too, reverted to smaller boats of up to 60 feet, decked from the 1840s; and the Scots were able to continue fishing from still smaller open boats. But in the 1870s to early 1880s the herring industry entered a phase of crisis as the herring shoals began to move further out from the northern coasts. For the Scottish fishermen this brought a need for bigger, better boats. At this point they at last moved on to 55-foot decked boats. There was also the first experiment with steam drifters, the earliest at Fraserburgh, Wick and Lossiemouth in 1875–8, and then a fleet of ten built at Leith in 1881–4. They failed at drifting and had to be converted to great-line-fishing. This was partly because until the sunken 'messenger', leader or 'bush rope' was devised in the mid 1890s, drift nets too easily fouled the propeller. In addition, they met strong resistance from the fishermen themselves: 'it was a very difficult matter to get suitable crews for them.' And by this time profits from the industry had slumped. As a result, the switch to steam fishing was delayed by a critical twenty years. When it came, it was to be on the fishermen's terms.

In the meantime, for constructing these larger sailboats the fishermen sought more substantial advances from the local curers. But the curers' own expenses were rising. They too had to move to follow the herring; on the mainland concentrating on the headland ports at Wick, Fraserburgh and Peterhead, and Berwick; but also increasingly setting up brief seasonal stations in further outposts. In the 1860s they began to open stations on the Western Isles in Barra and Stornoway, and from the early 1880s again in Shetland. Many of their new stations were in remote anchorages, like Baltasound at the north of Shetland and Stronsay on the east of the Orkneys. These had neither a supply of shore labour, nor adequate landing facilities, so the curers had to build piers and huts and import a migrant labour force of coopers and women fish-gutters.

The curers thus had to lay out more and more for their returns. But the very extension of their activities brought more herring on to the market. And at the same time the replacement from the mid-century – following Scots innovations – of the old handwoven hemp nets with lighter, less bulky, machine-woven cotton nets, enabling a much larger area to be stowed, along with the bigger boats, had more than doubled catching power. In the early 1880s the market became flooded, and prices plummeted. The Scottish curers found themselves still bound to pay the fishermen well above the market level for their catch, due to the pre-season agreements, yet quite unable to get the return they had hoped on their cured herring. This system of engagement to a curer for fixed rates of payment had been dying out in the East Anglian ports twenty years before. The Scots now followed them into an open market system of sale by auction. The fishermen were left to suffer uncushioned in poor years. But it gave them a much fuller share of the winnings when times turned for the better. And unknown to the curers, the best years of all were to follow.

It was on the renewed surge of prosperity at the turn of the century that the herring industry finally took up steam power. After first attempts to power drifters had faded out, the chief advance on the boats had been steam capstans worked by very small engines, for hauling the lead rope of the nets. Steam power finally came to the boats themselves in 1897–8. The pioneer Lowestoft-built *Consolation* completed her first season in 1898. Once she had proved herself, both English and Scots were quick to follow. The first steam drifter in Scotland was brought up for a Wick crew. For the owners, the Fishery Board reported, the new boats proved at once worthwhile, some 'actually earning during the season an amount equal to the original cost of the vessels'. With such immediate success, there was no lack of shore entrepreneurs eager to follow them. But the fishermen had sufficient strength to insist on the maintenance of the traditional share system in working them, rather than the introduction of wage payment as on the trawlers.

The next few years saw the whole east coast caught up in a steam fever. By 1908, as the great herring boom reached its peak, there were 626 Scottish steam drifters, and by 1913, 884. This was more than the English ports, with 624 steam drifters by 1913. Equally striking was the concentration of boats in the chief herring ports. In Scotland Buckie, with 276 steamboats, had more than a third of the total fleet, almost double its nearest rival, Peterhead. In East Anglia, Yarmouth and Lowestoft between them had 480 drifters, four-fifths of all those in England and Wales.

This technological transformation sharpened differences both between communities and within them. It was less of a turning point for the two East Anglian ports, which were already deep-sea fishing communities. But the Scottish herring driftermen were based on inshore rather than trawl ports, and the great majority of them continued during the winter season to return to inshore white fishing from smaller boats. It was, however, easier to lay up herring smacks for the winter than costly steam drifters for which the loans still had to be paid off, and this pushed many of the new skipper-owners towards full-time herring fishing. On the other hand, the fishery in the other chief herring ports needed more hands than could be found locally. The result was the emergence of a complex pattern. First came the east-coast growth centres, and then between them smaller villages, more at risk of being left behind. Thus eastwards from Buckie the first villages were close enough to join the boom. At twenty miles Macduff, with an excellent harbour, was distant enough to maintain itself as a minor market for herring and white fish. It was the half-way villages at the centre of the chain, like Cullen and Portsoy, which were worst hit. They sank into stagnation and low pay, some of their men seeking irregular work as hands to the Buckie skippers. But the greater number of seasonal hands were recruited from much more distant parts, including the Shetlands, but most of all from the Western Isles. Here whole districts had been outpaced and undercut by the east-coast boom. It was in these moribund local economies 150 miles away that the new herring capitalism found an essential reserve of labour.

The geography of official statistics for the herring industry is in fact somewhat misleading. Skippers and crews could live in one village, work out of another harbour, and in season take on extra labour at yet a third port. Family home, base port and workplace might each be separate. This separation dates back to the shifting workplace always needed to hunt the herring. But the speed and range of the steam drifter put the final touches to an elaborate spatial pattern revolving round the migrating shoals.

The season would usually open tentatively in late May in the Western Isles and a fortnight later in Shetland, as the first herring arrived, at this stage still feeding rather than spawning. Although less numerous, the immature 'matties' were regarded as a delicacy and could fetch high prices. By mid-June the herring were also off the east coast, and the summer season moved into full swing. The main focus of activity moved from Shetland and Orkney in June–July to the north-east in July–September. During these months the herring were spawning down the whole Scottish North Sea coast. By early Septem-

ber, however, the season was over in Fraserburgh and Peterhead. So far, the drifters would have been working alongside
numerous local sailboats; but only the best were fit to continue
into the autumn voyage. The drifters too usually broke for a
week or two at this point, settling up for the summer season,
and allowing their crews an interval at home – with a chance
for the Highlandmen to take in the harvest on their crofts.

For the autumn season an extra hand was added, bringing
the crew to ten. By late September the main fishery had moved
southwards to the Northumberland and Yorkshire coasts, and
a good many Scottish drifters gave this a try next. All that
were in sufficiently good condition to ride the autumn gales
would then converge on Yarmouth and Lowestoft. The herring were now more densely congested than at any other point
in the season. The East Anglian season was open by the
beginning of October, and over by early December, when the
second major settlement of the year was made. The majority
of the Scots drifters returned home to remain laid up for the
rest of the winter, refitting during the roughest weather. The
herring shoals were much more widely scattered, but between
January and March they were spawning in the Forth, the
Minch, the Irish Sea and off Northern Ireland. The more
determined drifters followed them for a winter season. Only
in April was there a pause, almost everywhere, while preparations were made for the next summer season.

The scale of these migrations was spectacular. In 1913
altogether 1,163 Scots drifters, including 209 sailboats, made
the East Anglian voyage. Out of 12,000 Scottish women
gutters, 5,000 came south for the English season, and 3,500 of
these had set out from the Western Isles; 2,000 Highlandmen
were also taken on as crews on the east-coast boats, mostly for
the Scottish summer season only. Conversely, as more than
400 English steam drifters came north earlier in the summer,
they had taken on 5,000 extra hands in summer. Shetland, the
northernmost point in the cycle, in its record year of 1905
engaged 1,783 boats, over 900 outsiders from the south,
providing work for perhaps 20,000 men and women – as many
as the entire population of the islands. Many of these migrations could be traced back through many decades. Even
around 1820, Hugh Miller noted both Highlandmen and

English boats, from Cornwall, at the herring fishing in the north-east. Nevertheless, it was in the 1900s that these movements reached their highest intensity, to wane gradually thereafter as the industry faded. As late as 1936, when only half as many Scots drifters were going to East Anglia, 2,600 fishgirls still followed them, including 1,000 from the Western Isles.

Rewards were also distributed in an unequal pattern, ranging in 1906 from £12 for both summer and autumn seasons for the migrant women gutters and £30 for the Highland hired hands to nearly £400 for a steam drifter's skipper-owner. So the boom years were also years of widening difference of fortune among the fishermen. For the communities of drifter-owners they brought an 'unparalleled affluence'. Successful fishermen provided themselves not only with boats, but with new houses. The wartime Royal Commission of Scottish Housing was particularly impressed by the transformation of Findochty next to Buckie, with 264 of its 266 families owning their houses, where the former kitchen-and-room houses on the seashore had almost entirely given way to modern houses with water closets and storage accommodation. In Buckie itself whole new districts were reconstructed in these years with ranks of solid grey granite houses, their upper floors for net rooms with dormer windows and finials picked out in white. More modestly, some of the older village houses were smartened up with new fronts, painted a gleaming flat black, their masonry lines and exaggerated window surrounds and corner quoins sharply contrasted in white: a patently nautical redressing.

By no means all had cause to show such good cheer. On the contrary, by the last years before the First World War protest was being voiced not only from communities in decline, but also from the less privileged within the steam drifting centres too. This culminated in 1913 in an unprecedented wave of strikes and mass meetings right round the coast, which brought out into the open the diverging economic interests of skipper-owners and hired hands within the same communities. It looked for a moment as if the drifter ports might yet see the emergence of clear class divisions in the trawling industry. Findochty fishermen, meeting in March 1913 to discuss a proposal for government loans to assist boat purchase, were warned of the 'syndicates and capitalists' who loomed over them, eager 'to swallow up their industry and take away their manhood as individuals and as a class'.[7] The danger seemed real enough to many at the time. But their real problems were to be of quite another kind. For the great herring boom, and the prosperity it had brought, had only one more year to run. The outbreak of the First World War marked its end.

For forty years the fishing industry had been reshaping itself around growth and innovation. The industry had now entered an era of stagnation and contraction: three decades of global depression and war. Up to 1914 the fishing communities had been racing to overtake each other. From the First World War onwards, they would have been content enough simply to hold on. The figures indicate the starkness of the overall picture (Table 1). They also reveal how much worse hit Scotland was than England.

  From 1880 until the First World War, the Scottish fishing industry had proved as vigorous as the English. Even in those prosperous pre-war decades, it is true that increasing technical efficiency had meant there was room for slightly less men in the industry. But this was nothing to the drastic reduction between the wars, when the Scottish workforce was halved. In England too there was a marked reduction, but nevertheless it was less sharp. The basic explanation for the difference was quite simple. Between the wars, English-based steam trawling suffered much less badly than herring drifting.

TABLE 1

Fishermen and Fishing Boats

| | England and Wales | | Scotland | | Total | |
	Fishermen	Boats	Fishermen	Boats	Fishermen	Boats
1880	31,000	12,000	39,000	12,000	70,000	24,000
1890	32,000	9,000	47,000	14,000	79,000	23,000
1913	37,000	9,000	38,000	9,000	75,000	18,000
1938	29,000	6,000	17,000	5,000	43,000	11,000
1978	12,000	4,100	9,000	2,600	21,000	6,700

Steam trawling fed the home market with a cheap nutritious food. During the wars it never entirely ceased, and because food was short those boats able to continue working brought in good money, allowing their owners to re-equip. And although prices slumped in the 1920s, the very extent of the depression and working-class unemployment ensured a demand for the cheaper grades of fish. This, however, told against both Grimsby and Aberdeen, which had specialised in better-quality higher-priced white fish. By contrast Hull, which had aimed more for the cheap mass market, was able to develop larger trawlers, and send them to increasingly distant grounds. Hull also led in introducing the key innovations of radio – already installed in some pre-war German trawlers – and echo-sounders into its boats in the 1920s and 1930s, so helping its skippers to find fish as well as making their trips safer. By 1938 Hull's share of English landings, 12 per cent in 1913, had risen to 37 per cent – making it Britain's premier fishing port. It was the Arctic fishing which made Hull between the wars almost 'the only solvent fishing port in the country'. Its example was also followed by Fleetwood, especially with Unilever's decision in 1936 to base a new distant water fleet here, made up of fifteen new German-built turbine-driven trawlers. Aberdeen, whose advantage in the quality market came through rapid overland delivery of fresh fish, now suffered from its northern position, closer to the fishing grounds but further from coal and the conurbations.

In the herring industry the Scottish fishermen also found themselves at a disadvantage, due to another slight change in the migratory patterns of the herring. Up to 1910 the quantities of herring landed in Scottish ports had been one and a half times or more those landed in England each season. But for the next twenty-five years the balance swung the other way. Had the boom years continued, the Scots could have sought to recover their position through building better boats; but they were caught in a slump with a fleet which included proportionally more sailboats and second-hand steam drifters. The First World War had struck the export-based herring industry as a whole a blow from which it never fully recovered. War and revolution disrupted the entire network of international markets for the cured herring in Eastern Europe.

Subsequently it could only be patched together in parts; and no alternative markets were opened in compensation. The buoyant prices which had carried the pre-war boom were gone for good.

So great was the extent of the crisis for Scottish fishing that it led eventually to a decisive change in government policy in the 1930s, laying the basis for the post-1945 intervention which has shaped the fortunes of the whole industry up to the present. During the First World War the government took control of both the English and Scottish fleets for use as a naval auxiliary, principally in minesweeping, and put half the fishing workforce in uniform. To avoid the social embarrassment of upper-class officers of the Royal Navy mixing with uneducated fishermen, the Admiralty created a special new rank of Chief Skipper. The fishing fleets suffered such heavy war losses that some help to put the industry back on its feet was assumed necessary. In addition to a special boat-building scheme, in 1919, in view of the chaos in the foreign herring markets, the government also decided to take over – up to a certain limit – herring stocks unsold at the end of the season.

This measure was in response to strong pressure from the fishermen, and it was renewed again in 1920, but the government had never intended it as more than a stop-gap measure. Further guarantees were decisively refused. Nevertheless it was difficult for the politicians to continue to turn a deaf ear to repeated calls for help from the industry. By 1923 the Scottish Fishery Board reported a clearly deteriorating situation: 'distress was rife . . . their credit was exhausted; much of their gear was so deteriorated as to be practically useless'. The government eventually decided to introduce a temporary loans scheme for nets in 1924. But it came too late to be much used. James Duthie voiced the feeling of a meeting of 200 Cairnbulg fishermen, 'the cry today was not for nets or coal, but for bread.'

By this point, however, the interests of different groups within the herring industry were diverging. The fishermen would have been glad of any regular income, and were even talking of going over to wage payment, if only to qualify for unemployment pay. But the curers, salesmen and merchants were suspicious of any long-term government intervention which might undermine their own roles. As early as 1921 the biggest salesmen like Sir John Irvin were arguing that 'the only practical course' was to halve the drifter fleet. Eventually in 1925 they joined together to launch their own solution in the form of a private enterprise monopoly, the Herring Combine, to limit future catches and take over existing stocks, disposing of them at fixed prices.

The Combine not merely failed to rescue the industry, but exacerbated the existing tensions within it, leaving salesmen, curers and fishermen all at loggerheads. When the government, following a report instigated by Ramsay MacDonald himself (for he came from Lossiemouth), finally decided to resume active intervention with the appointment of the Sea Fish Commission in December 1933, it had to warn that there would be no assistance for the herring section until it 'first put its house into order'. In fact the Commission produced two separate reports on each branch of the industry, each resulting in the setting up of a government board. But since the report on white fish came second, the future White Fish Authority had not been able to make a significant impact before the Second World War. The Herring Industry Board, on the other hand, despite the complex difficulties of the industry, did at last bring it some measure of stability by the later 1930s.

The Board investigated new market possibilities, both at home and abroad. It looked into new processes for disposing of surplus herring, such as freezing and fish oil manufacture. It launched a home advertising campaign which significantly boosted the hitherto marginal home market. It ran a new loan scheme for nets which was used by over 2,000 fishermen. Lastly, it attempted to encourage the modernisation of the now antiquated drifter fleet. The development of new designs for oil-driven motor drifters was supported through a project at the Department of Scientific and Industrial Research. A special scheme was started, through which 130 old drifters were bought out for scrapping, and loans were made to recondition another 42. All the same this left a fleet of which half had been built before 1914, and none since 1921. Clearly only more drastic action could have brought substantial revival. But the Board found its way blocked by both lack of confidence in itself and also –

mistrust and jealousy between – even within – various
branches and sections of the trade. . . . Added to these
there are differences between adjacent ports founded often
on mere jealousy. . . . The task of the Board . . . of
bringing regulation and order into existence has been
extremely difficult and has often only been accomplished in
the face of severe protest and opposition.[8]

By the end of the Second World War, all that bitterness had
been relegated to the past through six years of common effort.
National social and political attitudes had been fundamentally
changed too. Government intervention in industry was no
longer regarded as a last resort, but as a positive good. The
result was a new policy towards fishing, developed on the
basis of the old, but of wholly new proportions in its generosity, enshrined in the loan scheme of the 1945 Inshore Fishery
Act.

The inshoremen have seized their chance. The extent of the
change in the last thirty-five years can again be most easily
demonstrated with figures. Let us this time take fish landings
(Table 2). It has to be remembered that landings in Scotland
include catches from English boats and landings in England
those from Scottish boats. Nevertheless it is clear enough that
until 1910, despite the growth of the English trawl ports,
landings in Scotland kept pace with them. But between the
wars, while England went ahead much more slowly, Scotland
slumped disastrously. The inter-war years were for Scottish
fishing the worst in a century. Since then, while English
landings have shrunk landings in Scotland have recovered, and
when allowance is made for landings by Scottish vessels in
England, the catch of the smaller Scottish fleet has now taken
the lead.

Behind this shift in fortune lie two fundamental changes.
Firstly, the unlimited exploitation of the sea's resources has
brought its own reward; and in so doing, has had to be ended.
For a thousand years or more the North Sea herring had
provided an abundant source of food for the people of Europe.
But the once-prosperous herring industry was only to flicker
again briefly after the Second World War. By the late 1940s the

TABLE 2

Tons of fish landed by British vessels in Britain

	Scotland	England and Wales	Total	Value
1890	268,000	305,000	573,000	£5,900,000
1910	435,000	655,000	1091,000	£11,000,000
1938	278,000	816,000	1094,000	£16,000,000
1945	186,000	265,000	451,000	
1960	270,000	564,000	843,000	£52,000,000
1974	477,000	477,000	954,000	£151,000,000
1978	426,000	518,000	943,000	£239,000,000
adjusted	576,000	368,000		

British driftermen were being ousted from the North Sea by German, Dutch and Danish trawlers which so scoured the Dogger Bank of immature herring that its breeding stocks were destroyed. In 1938 500 Scots drifters had still gone to Yarmouth. By 1953 they were down to a hundred, and the last came in 1967. The North Sea herring fishery was dead.

Before long other similar stories followed. When tuna, previously caught by traps or by line in the Mediterranean, was hunted out in the Atlantic by purse seiners and long-liners, the catch peaked to 150,000 fish a year and then fell away to less than 2,000 by the early 1970s. At the same time Chile, which had built up an industrial fishing of anchovies to the point when it was producing over 40 per cent of the world's fishmeal, and 15 per cent of its national workforce was dependent on the industry, witnessed the almost total collapse of the anchovy fishery through the disappearance of the fishing stocks.

Industrial nations might choose to ignore such catastrophes, but those who depended on fishing for a living could not. This produced a new alignment of interests. By the early 1970s the major fishing fleets in the world were in rank order those of Russia, Japan, Spain, the United States, Britain, Norway, France, Peru and Canada. But for most of these countries the role played by fishing in their economy was relatively small:

for Britain, for example, landings contributed less than 0.2 per cent to gross annual domestic product. The fishing nations proper were those whose fishing fleets, if considerably smaller, provided their economic mainstay. In northern Europe these were above all Iceland and newly independent Faroe. By the 1950s there were already signs of ominous falls in the catches of white fish from Arctic waters. Iceland took the first step of extending its inshore limits to four miles in 1952 and then to twelve miles in 1958, thus enabling protection of the sea's natural resources through its subsequent official conservation measures. In the 1970s Iceland again unilaterally extended its limits and a second 'cod war' ensued, with Royal Navy frigates attempting to protect British trawlers. But by then the discovery of underwater gas and oil reserves had transformed the attitudes of other coastal nations, who now also wanted to assert their own territorial rights over the sea bed. In 1975 the 200-mile inshore limit was internationally agreed. For the fishing communities of Norway, Iceland, Faroe and Newfoundland a future was assured: and the inshoremen of Scotland would have won an equal security, but for the new threat resulting from the claim of the Common Market countries, having fished out most of their own waters, to a full share of Britain's remaining resources. On that point the outcome still rests with the politicians.

For the major trawl ports the extensions of the 1970s finally and irrevocably destroyed the very basis of their economy. They transformed not only the whole North Sea but also most of the northernmost Atlantic, including all their best Arctic waters, from open ocean into a patchwork of restricted territorial waters under separate control. From the 1950s the trawl ports had been faltering, despite the building of a new diesel- or oil-powered fleet with government aid. Accounts for 1957 for an inquiry showed that already, while the inshore fleets were making an absolute profit, it only paid trawler owners to keep fishing because of the white-fish operating subsidy paid to them for every day worked at sea. And in the last ten years the trawl ports have slid rapidly towards collapse. By 1980 fewer than a hundred company boats were fishing, and both the Fleetwood and the Hull Fishing Vessel Owners' Associations had been forced to cease business. In Fleetwood the 'last' deep sea trawler ceased work in July 1982. Membership of the Hull Trawler Officers' Guild of skippers and mates has fallen in five years from 325 to 70. And at both Fleetwood and Hull rising costs and declining use of the docks now threatens their total closure as fish ports. If there is to be a future in British fishing, it will be with the inshoremen of the north.

This is not only the consequence of the new international policy of the sea. In principle the trawl ports could turn to fishing within national waters, and seize their share of the catch quotas which are being allocated. One would think too that with the advantage of their superior capital resources, they could easily take over the inshore grounds, the more so since, with the partial lifting of restrictions against small-boat trawling in some waters since 1958 there has been an inshore 'trawling revival' with a rapid growth of light trawling from the smaller ports. Light trawling is less productive than seining, but requires less skill and less labour. Surely here was a chance for the men from the company boats to push aside the inshoremen on their own grounds? Why have they failed?

The explanation lies in the second factor which has transformed the situation since 1945: the effect of the new government loans policy in equalising chances. The best equipment is now within the reach of all. So long as capital could ensure its own continued success through reinvestment in better boats and gear, rather than competing in terms of human initiative and energy, the trawl ports had the edge. But the loans policy has enabled the release of the creativity of the inshoremen: and this is a quality less easy for capital to command.

To demonstrate this we must go back briefly to the earlier years of this century. For the inshoremen had not simply been sitting, pining for the herring. Right through the steam drifter era, in one port or another, experimentation had gone on. All the Scottish herring communities also continued seasonal line-fishing for white fish. Particularly in the lesser fishing stations, a key step was the introduction from 1905 of small motor fishing boats. In the rapid motorisation which followed, Scotland parallels Norway and Sweden. Such motor boats could take part in the herring as well as the white fishery, and after the First World War their lower running costs made them competitive with steam drifters; so much so that by 1926–7 Lowestoft and Buckie had their first purpose-built motor drifters. But already by 1919 there were twice as many motor boats registered in Scotland as there were steam drifters. They had saved some of the smaller inshore communities: Burra Isle in Shetland, for example, some of the Clyde villages, and Lossiemouth on the Moray Firth.

Lossiemouth was also the outstanding pioneer of a second major innovation, seine-net fishing. Despite its similarity to trawling, seining has long been officially permitted within much of the three-mile limit. The modern method of working seine nets at sea was first developed by mid-nineteenth-century Danish fishermen. From 1918 a fleet of Danish seiners settled in Grimsby and immediately succeeded in making a living from the nearer North Sea grounds. Although some Yarmouth drifters took to winter seining in the 1920s, no other English ports imitated them. The Scots were more impressed. Buckie fishermen introduced seining to Scotland in 1920. Other Scotsmen went south to man the Danish boats in Grimsby – and a few Danes moved north too. The Scots improved on their method, with 'fly-dragging' – towing and heaving at the same time without anchoring. After 1930, Lossiemouth's seine fleet went ahead fastest through organising direct marketing in Glasgow, and grew rapidly to a hundred boats. By the outbreak of war the seiners were landing a tenth of the Scottish white catch. Thereafter they shot ahead, doubling their catch by 1945, finally by 1965 ousting not only the herring drifters but also the old white-fish line-boats. As fish have become increasingly scarce and prices higher, seine fleets from Buckie, Shetland and elsewhere, often with different specialisms in white fish, prawns or mackerel, have enjoyed sustained prosperity. Even in Grimsby today, where there is a melancholy silence in the great emptiness of the trawl dock, you can still find, in the corner where the Danes tie up, a bustle of activity.

The men from the former herring ports have gone on building their prosperity, adventuring further. Their boats, although still much smaller, now rival the big trawlers in the sophistication of their equipment. By 1939 nearly half of the Scots drifters had installed radio receivers: although they could receive metereological and market information, they were not able to transmit messages, for example in distress. Now all the inshore boats have not only both radio and vastly improved echo-sounders, but since the 1960s radar, position-finders and sonar. The position-finders enable a boat, through the convergence of three radio signals, to locate its position within a hundred yards. This gives a renewed advantage to men who get to know particular grounds well. The sonar and echo-sounders, by contrast, which can not only track the sea bottom, but also spot a shoal of fish as it moves through the sea, have enabled a much more active searching for fish. The inshoremen are no longer hunters dependent on luck and instinct.

For a small number of them, the culmination of this rapid technological advance has been the adaptation of power purse-seine netting. This was an innovation developed by Norwegian fishermen who – also backed by a strong state loans policy – have similarly leapt forward from a depressed and technologically relatively backward situation in the last thirty years. They had used the seine net for herring fishing in the enclosed fjords of the mountainous north Norwegian coast, encircling the shoals with small boats based on a mother vessel. The introduction of powered hauling blocks in the early 1960s made it possible to integrate the whole process into a single much larger boat, and with the new fish-finding equipment to venture out into the open sea. In 1965 a fleet of 150 Norwegian purse seiners suddenly appeared in Shetland waters, immediately demonstrating their immense superiority in catching power. There were difficulties in taking over the method as worked by the Norwegians, and it had to be reorganised to fit in with the simpler and more flexible egalitarianism of roles aboard the Scots boats. But since 1967 a minority of inshoremen, including some from the most isolated communities, have launched out with these still bigger new boats, whose nets enclose a water space the size of a cathedral, hunting and capturing the remaining herring shoals – and, especially in the last five years, the mackerel. While still maintaining local family-based share-ownership, they are now investing in vessels which can cost over a million pounds.

Why do the trawl ports today, moribund, seem unable to

follow their example? The answer lies in the resilience of the different social systems on which the herring and the trawl fishing were based. These social systems are not merely responses to the economy of the past, but vital forces shaping its future development. In the past, because of the elusiveness of the shoals, herring fishing was always an unstable lottery. It could not provide an easy basis for regular wages, nor, given the spectacularly high earnings possible for a successful share fisherman, could a wage-earning boat hope to attract the best men. This was why the fishing communities of the herring ports were able to maintain the traditional share system of co-venturing, despite the efforts of capitalist companies at intervals to introduce wage-earning so as to extract more profit. Trawl fishing, by contrast, could provide until recently very steady returns from fishing voyages to the same grounds, and was therefore a suitable basis for regular work patterns and regular wages. Fishing today, however, is in a confused state of transition; regulations are constantly changing, as particular grounds are closed or opened, quotas imposed to protect particular species, and so on. It has become a hunt with no fixed patterns from year to year, either of prey, or grounds, or market, or where the boat may dock for the weekend – but with high rewards for the successful. The purse seiners, because of their high cost, have to be especially mobile. One month they may be after the Atlantic herring in the Minch between the Western Isles and the mainland, the next chasing St Kilda blue whiting or North Sea sprats or Norway pout, the third after the Cornish mackerel. From Cornwall the Shetlanders will fly home to their homes and crofts fortnightly. It is a game which the share-fishermen, because their own economic interest is in such adaptability, can play best.

Part II Capital and labour

3 Trade unionism and industrial conflict

One way of looking at fishing communities is through the story of intensifying, polarised conflict between organised capital on the one hand and organised labour on the other. We begin with this approach for two reasons. The first is a belief in its importance. The labour history of the fishermen is part of the experience of the British working class as a whole. The second is a recognition of the limits to what such a perspective can tell us. For the classic capital–labour conflict in fishing is now evidently over, a phase which has passed. There is a stark lesson from its history: the self-destructiveness of this form of social organisation. But it does not point the way to the future.

It is limited as a perspective in another way too: by being almost inescapably man-centred. We shall argue from the case of Aberdeen that the labour history of fishing cannot give us its full meaning if it does not embrace women and children as well as men, home and family as well as work.

The labour history of the fishing industry has yet to be written. The very disunity of the fishermen makes it a complicated story. But as a whole it mirrors the uneven penetration of capital into the fishing industry in the contrasting stories of the trawlermen on the one hand, and in the herring communities on the other.

It is in the trawling industry, where men work for wages on company-owned boats, that trade-union activity has been most strongly concentrated for the last hundred years. Even here, however, its growth has been by no means straightforward. This partly reflects the difficulties of achieving any strong union organisation in an industry whose workforce is scattered for most of the year in small groups out at sea. Except during periods of severe recession, which are impossible times for trade-union building, there are normally only brief moments at the start of each year when most of the men are in port together, and could be mobilised for a mass rally or to threaten to withhold their labour. There are also special problems rooted in the traditional forms of work organisation on the boats themselves.

Firstly, there was the continuing legacy of the share system of payment. In the earlier merchant fishing enterprises, such as the Newfoundland fishing, the crews were paid a half share of the boat's nett earnings at the end of each voyage. This half share could be divided equally between the deckhands, but the merchants also used a system of payment known as the 'count', to urge the men on to more intensive effort, counting the catch from each 'dory' separately as it came back to the mother vessel. The 'count' was much disliked by many of the skippers, for it set the crew against each other, making co-operative tasks difficult to perform and creating bitter rivalries.

Payment on the trawlers evolved differently, but the masters' intentions to drive the workforce on by dividing them was again evident. Wage-earning had entered trawling early. It spread initially from the big Barking sail fleets to Lowestoft and Yarmouth, and thence to the Humber; and with the explosive growth of the new trawl ports from the mid-nineteenth century, it became established as the dominant system for the men. But the trawl skippers and mates and less invariably a third hand were retained on the old share system. This created an important divide between the majority of the crews and the most skilled men aboard the fishing boats, who were, as in other industries, the natural initiators of any labour movement among the fishermen. Reuben Manton, an early fishing union organiser, expressed the sharemen's continuing view when he told the Royal Commission on Labour in 1892 that formerly all the hands had been sharemen, and 'we consider that we lose caste if we work in any other way.'

Skippers and mates were paid on a different basis from the trawl crews so that they might be more effective instruments of the owners' profit-making, pace-makers over the common workforce. Although more independent, and with much better prospects for a few, they were in other senses like the foremen of a factory. In the very best years, moreover, trawl skippers could bring in tremendous earnings: later on, at the end of the First World War, for example, Hull skippers were able to take home £10,000 in a year. They still had to share the gruelling hours and bitter working conditions at sea with their crews, but the chance of such rich winnings isolated them from the men and lured them on to the extent that not a few became noted for an almost violent idiosyncrasy. Walter Wood remarked in his *North Sea Fishers and Fighters* on the 'spirit of devilment' he found among many trawl skippers, and cited the skipper who had *deliberately* rammed a rival trawler off Iceland, later pleading he was 'mad drunk at the time'.

Secondly, the division between sharemen and crew was further emphasised by the nature of authority on the boats. Once at sea, the skipper's command was absolute, whether or not he was the boat's owner and the men's employer. Nor had the men the option, like factory hands, of silent protest through absenteeism. They had to go on working at least until the end of the trip; and even then many of them were obliged to continue. A deckhand who had signed on was a servant for that term rather than a free labourer. And on top of this, especially during the peak years of expansion from the 1850s to the 1890s, a high proportion of the crews were boys bound as apprentices. Their indentures put them entirely at their master's disposal. If they absconded and were caught, they could be imprisoned. In Grimsby apprentice boys made up nearly a third of the crews of the sailing smacks in the 1870s, and imprisonments were running at 500 a year. In effect, as the leading radical politician of the time, Joseph Chamberlain, was to put it in 1881, the masters were 'reducing matters to a state of serfdom'.

The question had come out into the open through the introduction of the 1880 Payment of Wages Act, which allowed apprentices to give two days' notice of their decision to refuse to sail, and abolished criminal prosecution against them. The result was loud protest from the trawler-owners and an answering public outcry, which led to the Board of Trade inquiry into *Relations between Owners, Masters and Crews* of 1882. The employers described how since the Act there had been large-scale desertions: 'they frequently leave their smacks when passing through the dock gates to sea, or refuse to go on

board though standing on the quay side within a few feet of
their vessel.' In the past, as the manager of Hewett's 82-trawler
fleet in Yarmouth explained, 'in the event of a man refusing or
deserting I could always persuade him to go, by sending for a
policeman.' The alternative deckhands who were now being
forced on the masters were, according to Lowestoft's leading
fish salesman Benjamin Bradbeer, even worse: 'tramps and
casuals in rags and tatters. . . . They were never at sea in their
lives, they do not like the sea or the boat, and the first
opportunity they get they run away.'[1]

For most of the trawl ports the 1880 Act and the subsequent
inquiry brought the end of the apprenticeship system as a
major source of labour. But the element of 'serfdom' in the
labour contract of the deckhands was nevertheless maintained
by the masters. The Grimsby magistrates decided that an
unrepealed section in the 1854 Merchant Shipping Act, enabling them to imprison or fine crewmen for disobeying the
order of a ship's master, could also be used against men who
refused to join ship. It was this penal discipline which was
extended to other ports, and eventually, as late as the 1920s,
even to the Scottish trawlermen.

There was another respect too in which the men were not
simply wage-earners. Even before the masters began to reintroduce an element of share earnings alongside wages, certain
traditional 'perks' had continued. 'Stockerbait', rough fish
which had been not part of the intended catch for the market,
was distributed among the men. Fish livers were also treated
separately, and so were fish which men on a trawler could
catch by lines over the ship's side. Later on, as the owners
found ways of marketing these other fish too, such conventions became a source of dispute as well as supplementary
income, confusing the basic interests at stake. Owners also
claimed customary deductions for themselves, like 'pull
away'. No wonder cynical trawlermen were driven to con-
clude that 'from start to finish, the fish trade is a set of robbers.'
This was no doubt why the men, while wanting to keep their
traditional bonuses, were equally determined to retain their
basic position as wage-earners. When the owners tried to
reintroduce the share system for the Grimsby deckhands in
July 1901, they were met with a bitter fourteen-week strike,

culminating in a riot and the burning of the Trawler Owners' Federation offices. The dispute was finally settled through arbitration with a compromise, introducing a share element in pay, but keeping the main wage basis.

The Humber trawlermen had already shown earlier how far they had taken on the militancy of industrial workers. They had struck four times between 1880 and 1885 – the first time successfully but subsequently failing – against the institution of winter fleeting, which kept them far longer at sea in the worst weather. In 1884 there were also disputes over a wage reduction proposed on the sailing smacks to meet the cost of installing steam capstans, which the owners argued were put in 'to lighten the labour'. In fact, with good fishermen voting with their feet they had little choice – 'don't leave me for the sake of an engine, you may have one in my smack'; so the dispute ended in a compromise. And behind these open conflicts lay the first unionisation of the trawlermen. It was the Grimsby men who formed the first trade union among them in 1879; and its members helped Hull – where a Fisherman's Club founded in 1865 had failed – to follow suit in 1880.

Fleeting had brought the men much closer together at work; and the introduction of engineers on the steamboats from 1877 onwards brought aboard a tradition of workshop organisation. The National Amalgamated Seamen's and Firemen's Union, which organised the seamen and engineers on passenger and merchant ships, had set up special branches in the trawl ports for fishing-boat engineers by the early 1890s.

It was in the early 1890s that this initial phase of trawling trade unionism reached its peak. 'The great bulk of skippers are members,' the Hull Fishermen's Society reported in 1891. 'No union skipper is allowed to ship a non-union mate.' Like the wage-paid Grimsby cod-liners who also had their own union, they were able to win increases in 1891–2. Other separate unions had been formed for the Hull sharemen and weekly hands, claiming 800 and 200 members. In 1890, led by Reuben Manton, they combined with societies in other ports, most of which had again been initially set up by skippers and mates, to form the first nationally organised union for fishermen, the National Federation of Fishermen of Great Britain and Northern Ireland. At its brief peak of influence, coinciding

with the great surge of trade unionism nationally of the early
1890s, the Federation claimed a membership of 5,000: its main
strength on the Humber, but with a presence in East Anglia
and Aberdeen too. Its outspoken journal campaigned against
the owners as 'an INTENSELY EAGER and not remarkably
scrupulous set of capitalists'. If 'the fishing industry cannot be
carried on without WEARING MEN OUT by the time they
are only forty years of age . . . *let it go to the dogs*, sooner than a
few should FATTEN AND GLOAT on the results of the
more than work of the many.'[2]

Probably one important factor in the Federation's success,
persuading the skippers to join with the men in a common
front, was again the impact of the fleeting system. The
Grimsby owners were to scrap it in 1901. Fleeting had deprived skippers of much of their independence and initiative,
since all the boats had to follow the 'admiral'; and skippers were the backbone of this first wave of fishing unionisation.

By the later 1890s the Federation had lost its hold. In the
next forty years it was only the engineers who steadily maintained union organisation, now through separate local unions.
These were first set up when the National Seamen's and
Firemen's union collapsed following its catastrophic defeat in
the Hull dock strike of 1893. The engineers' unions gradually
amalgamated, but right up until 1975 they remained independently organised – despite the frequently bad-tempered
attempts to recapture them by the parent union, which had
soon reconstituted as the National Sailors and Firemen's
Union: or as it became known for short, the National Union
of Seamen.

In most of the trawl ports, apart from a brief gap during the
worst setbacks of the depression years from the mid-1920s to
around 1935–7, local skippers' societies were also maintained
after the disappearance of the Federation. The trawlermen,
however, went in and out of various unions. Earlier, during
the Grimsby dispute of 1901 the engineers provided the initial
leadership, but the land-based Gasworkers and General
Labourers' Union scooped up a wave of new members,
including shore workers briefly as many as 5,000. A dozen
years later, as part of the general national 'labour unrest' just

before the First World War, the fishermen seemed to be moving again. In April 1912, the Seamen's Union, in response to a request from Grimsby, agreed a reduced entrance fee 'for fishermen only, as many of these men do not average much more than 18/– per week wages'.[3] By the next year the union was claiming 2,000 local members in Grimsby, while the Gasworkers had faded to insignificance, except among the women fish-curers.

Following this success the NSFU began to intervene much more widely in the fishing industry. Its campaign was led by Captain Edward Tupper, an honorary member of its executive, an energetic and vociferous but not very tactful organiser, whose activities during the next ten years were to exacerbate the intrinsic difficulties of fishing unionisation by adding at times a bitter and destructive inter-union rivalry. Already in the autumn of 1913 he was claiming a national membership of 10,000 fishermen, and organising the East Anglian herring driftermen as well as the Humber trawlermen. Subsequently during 1913–14 the Hull and Aberdeen trawlermen pushed up their wages, and they successfully struck for increases in Dundee, Scarborough and Shields in 1914. Here again the NSFU backed them; it opened a new Shields office, and was also gaining strength in Aberdeen, where Tupper was poaching firemen from their existing local union.

The war resulted in the suspension of active unionisation along with most fishing. But its end brought an unprecedented wave of disputes. The most important were the hard-fought, complex struggles at Aberdeen and Hull in 1919, Fleetwood in 1920, Grimsby in 1922 and Aberdeen in 1923 – all ending either in compromises, or victories for the masters. Three of these we look at in detail in other chapters. But there was also a rash of strikes, on balance more successful, in the lesser trawl ports in 1918–21: Shields, Milford Haven, Boston, Anstruther, Granton, Hartlepool, Ramsgate . . . It was a moment when fishermen right round the coast seemed determined to fight for better money and better conditions: bonuses, risk money, poundage on the gross rather than the nett, time in port between trips, and so on. The high fish prices immediately after the war gave them their chance, and for a few months the owners seemed to yield. But the men were to be beaten, as much through the owners' manipulation of their divisions as through any other single factor.

One of the worst features of their divisions was the rivalry, expressed not just in poaching members but in active black-legging, between the Seamen's Union and its chief rival in the early 1920s, the Grimsby-led National Union of British Fishermen. The Grimsby Union, set up in 1917 under a retired fishing skipper, Captain Bingham, considered amalgamation with the Seamen in 1919 before deciding to go it alone as a national organisation. By the end of the year it claimed a membership of over 5,000, still concentrated on the Humber, but with active branches in Aberdeen and Fleetwood as well. By this point tensions between Bingham and Tupper had become acute. The NSFU also claimed over 5,000 members, but their main strength was in Lowestoft and several smaller east-coast ports, as well as in Aberdeen. Both unions clearly had a highly unstable membership. A year later, the Seamen's Union was now reporting a doubled membership, while Bingham's was halved. But neither could win a clear domi-nance. They sank together with the onset of depression in the fishing industry, still fighting each other. The TGWU, which swallowed the NUBF in 1922, still had a small nucleus of 500 members in its section in Hull in 1934, and also in Fleetwood. In Grimsby, and also in Aberdeen, all organisation of the deckhands had disintegrated. All that remained from Tupper's flamboyant campaigning was the bitterness of defeat.

As late as 1932, the South Wales trawlermen at Milford Haven were still up against the wall: divided and beaten along with the skippers in a long and rough strike which broke their local Deckhands Union, with a remnant joining the TGWU. When the trawling industry at last began to recover from the worst effects of the depression in the mid-1930s, the strongest ports were Hull and Fleetwood, now leaders of the long-distance Arctic fishing, and the permanent unionisation of the trawlermen thus sprang from them. In Hull the turning point was the 1935 strike over oil money. In Fleetwood it was the pioneering local amalgamation of 1936 which pointed the way to setting up a single national fishing section within the TGWU two years later. Skippers, mates and crew formed a single union here, in contrast to Hull, Grimsby and Aberdeen, where separate Officers' Guilds continued. In Aberdeen the deckhands did not have the courage to reassert themselves until after the outbreak of the Second World War, in the successful unofficial strike of 1940. By the end of the war, however, full employment had enabled the TGWU branches to consolidate their hold, and the impact of this was shown by the new unity of the trawlermen in the strike of June 1945, when the men of Grimsby, Hull, Shields and Lowestoft came out together. Nor was the illegality of their action now a sufficient threat to deter them. The same ports were out again a year later, and the Hull men in March 1947; Grimsby twice in 1961 and Hull in 1966; and in 1969–72 in succession first Aberdeen, and then Hull, Grimsby and finally Fleetwood. Again and again trawlermen were 'sufficiently discontented to risk being charged with mutiny and sent to prison'. For these men had come to believe that collective organisation and action was their best means of self-defence.

They were still far from easy to organise. The TGWU complained of the rapid turnover of fishermen members, and in the early 1960s division resurfaced with a temporary secession to the new Grimsby-led United Fishermen's Union. Nor should their victories be exaggerated, even though most post-war strikes brought some gains. Medical reports for the 1960s document the continuing toll of poor working conditions, long hours and fatigue: a fatal accident rate over twenty times that in manufacturing industry, fractures, injured backs, thousands of septic cuts – and alcoholism so severe that many boats continued to put to sea with 'so many members of their crew in a state of intoxication that their ability to survive any emergency in the first day or two of the voyage must be open to doubt'. But perhaps more significant was a shift in union aims from the 1950s onwards. Trawl hands had been registered during the war; and with this experience in mind the Aberdeen branch suggested to local owners that labour recruitment supervised by the unions might be mutually beneficial: 'if you'll set up a registration scheme, we'll weed out the bad ones.' Forced to think harder by a strike, the owners agreed: the registration scheme was introduced in 1957 – and with it, effectively a union shop. During the 1960s similar schemes followed in Grimsby and then Hull; and the major conflicts during this decade were over the Humber men's demands for a closed shop and a ship's shop steward. Linked with a forty-hour working week at sea, and more days at home between trips, these were the key demands of the 'Fishermen's Charter' of 1968. The trawler deckhands were by now third-generation wage-earners; and they had finally claimed their heritage as members of the organised working class. As a post-war Grimsby skipper put it, 'You had to be careful with crews these days. They were trade union men who were not to be kicked around like cattle. . . . And a good thing too.'[4]

In the British trawling industry – as in other north Atlantic countries too[5] – the gradual advance of trade unionism over the last hundred years reflects the organisation of work relationships along capitalist employer–worker lines, and the unions achieved their greatest strength in the post-Second World War period just as a small number of giant firms moved closer towards a monopolistic control of its finances. In the drifting industry and its inshore successors the concentration of capital never proceeded so far, and in recent decades has been reversed. This is again mirrored in its labour history.

The strongest continuity in the drifting industry is with collective organisation on a community rather than a class basis. As early as the 1830s friendly societies were being established in Scottish coastal villages like Gardenstown and Rosehearty. The Forbes Lodge of Masons in Rosehearty alone claimed 200 members in 1850. In towns all over Britain such societies played a vital role in the gradual evolution of a working class movement in the nineteenth century. But in the smaller fishing communities this was not to be so.

The herring driftermen never became wage-earners: they remained sharemen throughout. In Scotland every man aboard received an equal proportion of the labour share, except for the wage-paid enginemen and cook. At sea the skipper and men worked together and slept together, even in the steam drifters of the 1900s, in contrast to the trawlers, whose skipper by then had a separate cabin: or still more to a vessel like the Nore lightship – now moored alongside the last remaining steam drifter, the *Lydia Eva*, in St Katharine's

Dock, London – which embodies official attitudes to class and authority at sea by providing the master of its crew of six men with his own cabin, shower, toilet and personal escape hatch. It brings home the extent to which the driftermen always succeeded in resisting the intrusion of class relations in their midst.

They were, on the other hand, much more ready to see the different interests of their own community against others, and defend them. The early years of the herring industry were in fact sufficiently turbulent to require regular supervision by a gunboat of the Royal Navy from 1802 onwards. There had been conflicts between local boats and visitors in the 1790s, when an investigator of the British Fisheries Society had found that fishermen 'stole each other's catch and destroyed each other's equipment, buoys and nets'. There were again rough years in the 1850s. There were violent incidents on the Clyde as the patrols tried unsuccessfully to suppress ring netting, which was illegal from 1851 until 1867. For HMSV *Tartarus* 1852 was especially busy. From the opening fishery at Storno-way which 'under her superintendence . . . was carried out without any brawls', she was following the fleets round to the north-east coast when an incident was reported from Helmsdale:

> serious disagreements had sprung up between the hired
> men from the West Highlands and their employers. These
> men not only refused to fish themselves, but threatened to
> prevent all others from going out in the Boats, and had
> deterred several of the Boats from proceeding to the
> Fishing at a crisis when prices were enhanced by the
> shortness of supplies.

After the curers had demanded assistance to restore order, a boat's crew from the *Tartarus* was ordered into Helmsdale harbour, while she herself stood off the harbour mouth 'ready to send a further force if required for the preservation of peace'. Not surprisingly, business then went ahead; and con-gratulating herself on 'these prudent measures', the good 'ship-of-war' then headed south 'with all haste' to chase away a fleet of French boats which had invaded inshore waters off Northumberland.

There were occasionally serious fights ashore too, like the 'most serious riot' of 1859 at Wick and the 'Great Riot' on engagement night in 1874 at Fraserburgh, both drunken brawls between Highlandmen and locals only put down by calling out detachments of soldiers.[6] But in later decades – apart from some renewed conflict over the use of ring nets on the west coast – such disturbances became infrequent, and the restraining arm of the Royal Navy withdrew into the background.

It was not until the advent of the steam drifter that trade unionism made its first impact on the herring industry. Organisation began with the new wage-paid enginemen. In Scotland some of them began to join the Aberdeen trawler engineers' union from 1904 onwards. According to its secretary, the 'drivers' were not usually trained engineers, but recruited from the Aberdeen working class or from the traction engine drivers and farm servants in the countryside.[7] Their rates of pay were lower than on the trawlers. In 1907–8, 1913–14 and 1921–3 the union and its successor the Sea Fishers' Union were negotiating for the Peterhead enginemen, in the last year leading them in a successful strike against their employers: that is to say, the skippers. In Fraserburgh, however, in 1914 and 1921–2 the enginemen were organised by the NSFU – for here again Tupper was at work, building up a rival organisation. Although both unions disappear from the news after 1923, it is possible that a nucleus of drifter enginemen remained unionised through the depression years.

Several groups of ancillary shore workers were also active relatively early. The most persistently militant were the women fishworkers, of whom we shall have more to say in a later chapter. It is possible that their activity may go back earlier, for their brief strikes often went unreported by the press. Certainly there were strikes of gutters and kipperers in 1911 and 1914, and fishworkers in Aberdeen, Grimsby and Shields in 1913–14. The women received brief union backing in two of these strikes, but none led to long-term organisation. The coopers, on the other hand, were represented by the Workers' Union (and following amalgamation, the TGWU) from 1913; shipbuilding unionism crept round the coast from the bigger ports; and even the carters came out on strike in 1913, picketing street corners, unyoking horses and slashing sugar bags.

Nevertheless the real shock for the employers in 1913 was the eruption of agitation among the fishermen themselves, the hired men's movement. Its backbone was renewed protest by the seasonal Highlanders, who had now formed an organisation to voice their grievances, the Highland Fishermen's Union. From its principal base in the Isle of Lewis it had the support and active assistance of local clergy. But it set out to recruit support in all the ports. By April 1913 its manifesto could 'be seen in many shop windows in the coastlands', calling upon 'all hired fishermen to unite in an effort in support of their "just and equitable demands for a living wage"'. The union's chief demand was that hired men should be paid on the boat's gross rather than nett earnings: on the sailboats, a twelfth share, and on the steamboats, 5 per cent of the gross each. Out of this wage, they would pay for their own food on the boats. While working ashore, they asked for 1/– an hour.

Behind these requests lay two somewhat different issues. Undoubtedly the first was the impact of the steam drifter boom in widening the gap in earnings between skipper-owners, local sharemen, and hired men from the west. In 1906, an exceptionally good summer season, the hired Highlandmen on the east-coast sail and steam boats were reported as earning an average of £25 – and the few who went for the final weeks to East Anglia another £5. Malcolm Gray has estimated that in 1906 the average steam drifterman's labour share was over £90. On top of this a man with a net share would have earned a further £90, less the cost of net repairs; and the boat's owner, even after paying for interest and upkeep, yet another clear £200. With their earnings now less than one tenth of those of a steam drifter skipper-owner, it is hardly surprising that the Highlandmen – and to a less extent the hired men in the east-coast ports – felt a mounting sense of grievance.

The second problem was the confusing manner in which their payment was calculated. The hired men wanted a system which could be understood and checked. Settlement at the end of the season required an elaborate process of accounting, which was further obfuscated by arbitrary variations in custom between the ports – as to whether the cook and fireman were paid from the gross earnings of the boat, who paid for the engineman's food and so on. And the Scottish system as a whole differed from that in East Anglia, where there was no separate net share but the crews were given a larger labour share. Even the *Fishing News*, which normally favoured the east-coast owners' perspectives, conceded that settling up was 'a piece of abstruse accounting' and the hired men had 'grounds for complaint'. One major gain through the dispute was a system of publicly agreed rates, with less 'customary' variation, and especially important, 'a balance sheet to be submitted to each hired man'. This must have contributed towards trust within the community as well as outside it. Most former Buckie driftermen today remember settling up as a quite straightforward process, and recite the basic terms with the certainty of a creed: 'a third to the boat, a third to the nets, and a third to the crew'. And they were able to see all the expenses set out:

> There was everything on the sheet that'd tally right down.
> First was the salesman's commission. . . . Well, you had –
> food, the grocer, the butcher, the baker. It was all down
> there. And your oil, aye paraffin – fan I went to sea it was a
> motor boat, like-and then you had your dues – your
> harbour dues, your landing dues. It was all tallied up,
> tallied up, that was your expenses, you see. That was the
> golden line, what we called the golden line, with the
> grocer, the butcher, and the baker – he got his money! –
> supposing nobody else!

Earlier there had been much more room for argument.

In 1913 the east-coast skipper-owners were far from eager to make such concessions to the Highlandmen. But if the dispute had originally been between communities, by the end of April the north-east communities found themselves for the first time openly split along class lines. In Peterhead, where the propertyless hired men were most numerous, a branch of the Highland Union was set up under the new title of the Hired

Fishermen's Association. There were turbulent meetings in Buckie, and reports of hired men on strike, refusing to prepare for the coming season, in Hopeman, Lossiemouth and Wick. The skippers decided to keep the hired men divided, settling with their own local men first. They won considerable concessions, especially in pay for work starting and ending the season. But the tactic succeeded: the Highlandmen had little choice but to follow, and take their berths as before. The experience, nevertheless, had shaken the self-image of the north-east communities. 'With the advent of the steam drifter', the *Banffshire Advertiser* commented, 'by dint of perseverance and ability, some have risen to the status of capitalist, . . . so that now the ranks of the fishermen are divided between capital and labour.'[8]

By the opening of the 1914 season it looked as if these divisions were becoming increasingly clear. In both Buckie and Fraserburgh the drifter-owners, anticipating renewed needs to negotiate, had organised themselves in separate owners' associations. Although the leaders of the Highland Fishermen's Union were disheartened, their union had survived the winter, and were now considering amalgamation with the militant Seamen's Union. Might not the herring fishermen be polarised – like the trawlermen – between a class of owners and a class of wage-earners? And it may well have continued to move that way, but for the intervention of the First World War that autumn. For in contrast to the boom years when increasingly divergent earnings were pulling at the fabric of the communities, the drastic contraction in the period which followed the war effectively stifled class divisions between driftermen. In these years skippers, sharemen and hired hands all found themselves reunited in the common poverty from which they had but recently emerged.

Militancy in the herring communities continued after the war. As wage workers employed by the curers, women fishworkers did fight further strikes: at Peterhead and Fraserburgh in 1920; Yarmouth in the 1930s. But the dominant form which conflict now took was of communal struggle against the wider world. This turn was emphasised by the new role of the government in the industry and especially by its crucial decision to buy up unsold herring stocks at the end of

the 1919 season. This was partly made in response to the
Peterhead and Fraserburgh men who – cautiously followed by
Buckie – decided to strike in June 1919, at first against the
government, then for a minimum price from the curers. The
strike had been organised by the old local associations, open to
old grades of fishermen. Then in the early 1920s the
Fraserburgh men, with the aid of a local solicitor as secretary,
launched the Scottish Union of Fishermen. After being renamed – in order to exclude trawlermen – as the Scottish Drift
and Net Lines Fishermen's Association, it was able with a
full-time organiser to establish branches in most of the north-
east ports. Captain Tupper, who had backed the 1919 dispute,
thus found himself outflanked, with a strong following only in
Peterhead. In Yarmouth and Lowestoft the NSFU succeeded
in setting up local committees of 'all grades in the Herring
Industry' which were negotiating not only wages-cuts, but
also 'the supply of men, and for the first time the employers
grant full recognition of the Union'. But in Scotland, he had
no such success. [9]

Always run as if from above, by 1922 the Fishermen's
Association had become effectively a shareowners' organisation, ready to deal as employers with the enginemen as well as
argue with the government and the curers. Its greatest success
was in 1920 when, backed by huge meetings 'of all classes of
the community' in Peterhead, Fraserburgh and above all
Buckie, provosts in the chair, it was able to win a second
guarantee from the government. As one of the speakers at the
Peterhead mass meeting declared, 'The curers had acted
nobly. . . . In former years they depended on the fishermen to
found their businesses, and they now considered it was their
duty for this year at least to carry on without any profit so that
the workers might be employed and the industry put on a
footing.' But these splendid sentiments were not to last. By
1921, with the government adamantly refusing a third guarantee, the curers had come to accept the need for cutting back the
fleet. This time they left the fishermen to campaign on their
own. And with thousands unemployed – 2,000 men in Lowestoft alone – their threats of striking could hardly carry such
conviction. In a port like Buckie 'every day crowds of blue-
jerseyed, brown-trousered men and lads loafed about the

harbour.' Almost their only other choice was to join a trawler, and, as one old salt commented, 'As for the trawlin' at Aberdeen, I'm certain shair 'at there's nae a man'll gae tae the trawlin' unless he's sair needin' siller.' In the end their bluff was called, and the men sailed without a guarantee. The summer season was one of the worst in forty years. For the autumn, the driftermen tried to work a system of catch restriction; but neither the curers nor the English owners would co-operate, and it collapsed. The East Anglian season proved a second disaster. In despair, the men turned from their association to the religious revival which surged in its wake.

A revived Scottish Fishermen's Association was not reported until early 1924. There was a muted campaign, again unsuccessful, for government support in 1923. The fishermen's impotence was further emphasised by the decision of the curers and merchants to unite to form the Herring Combine in 1925. There were angry protests from fishermen against 'the autocrats' of the Combine and the restriction of 'individualistic effort. . . . Let free action continue'. But their only effective answer to its power could be an amalgamation of equal strength of their own. Towards the end of 1931 the Scottish Herring Producers Association was formed to bring together driftermen, boat-owners and salesmen.

The result was a re-eruption of conflict along new alignments. For the 1933 season the Herring Producers Association decided to reduce the fish salesmen's commission by cutting out the customary discount passed on to the curers. The curers refused this decision. In reply, in the Western Isles and Shetlands fishermen closed their ports and dumped their catches. More herring were dumped off Peterhead, where the fishermen decided to co-ordinate with Fraserburgh by telephone. 'While the skippers were in private conference in the saleroom, hundreds of fishermen were gathered outside anxiously discussing the position.'[10] They decided to halve the fleet, casting lots to decide who should go to sea, until a month later a compromise was eventually found.

It was at this point that government intervention in the industry was resumed with the appointment of the Sea Fish Commission at the end of 1933, leading to the setting up of the Herring Industry Board. By the later 1930s, in part due to its efforts, the industry had at last stabilised, with a considerably reduced fleet now bringing rather steadier earnings. As a result, both the women fishworkers and the hired men found themselves at last able to exert some independent pressure to improve their own position. A series of lightning strikes by herring gutters at the height of the Yarmouth season did win some advances, even if more often failing: and as before, no permanent unionisation emerged from these struggles, despite the TGWU's involvement in them:

> It was a' recht as long as you were working. But it was a long winter and you couldna pay your union. . . . You see, if folk fell ahin' the unions couldna keep up their union if you wasna putting in your money.

Among the hired men the lead came as in the past from Peterhead. Here they had for several years been asking for a switch to wage-payment and eventually, in January 1934, they were able to secure a weekly 30 shillings as an 'advance' on their share. This also allowed them to qualify for the 'broo'. The following summer similar demands for a wage guarantee were made and after strikes in Fraserburgh and Peterhead of 3,000 men in both ports, skipper-owners and salesmen agreed on a local levy system to meet the men's demands. Some skippers refused to sign, 'advancing religious reasons', but the only two who did not give way were forced to fish out of other ports. Although the levy system was not repeated, the Peterhead men were able to hang on to a minimum wage of 25 shillings, while in Fraserburgh, and in Buckie which now took up the wage system, the hired men were guaranteed 10/– a week. Although a step forward, it was pitifully small, and it is perhaps surprising that the men did not strike again. The Campbeltown ring-net herring fishermen did fight a long but unsuccessful strike, with trade union backing, against the local owners in the early summer of 1937; and there were signs of 'trouble' brewing among the 'groups at the harbour' at Peterhead, and also Fraserburgh where a deckhands committee had been formed.[11] But the herring industry's recovery had been too partial to give the hired fishermen much power. In 1938 over 40 per cent of the male workforce in Banff, Caithness,

Shetland and the Western Isles was still registered as unemployed. The local employment offices had the names of over 400 fishermen in Stornoway, 200 in Peterhead, 500 in Fraserburgh and 900 in Buckie. To strike from such an exposed position would have certainly been folly. Herring fishing up to the outbreak of war was still primarily a question of survival – as communities.

The old herring ports have now moved on to new forms of fishing, but in terms of industrial organisation and conflict the story since the Second World War has been one of continuity. On the one hand the communities have continued – with increasingly good reason – to identify the main threat to their prosperity as external. Immediately following the war, when the north-east men were led by a persuasive retired Cairnbulg skipper, 'Bobbie Borra' (Robert May), there were stoppages over officially fixed prices, net quotas, and fishermen's food rations – the 'sugar strike' and 'beef strike' of 1946–7. There were gutters' strikes in the same years, and again in 1949 and 1953; but the industry was already fading. By the 1970s the main issue had become international fishery regulations.

On the other hand, the wider spread of boat ownership since the government grant-in-aid scheme was introduced in 1945 has served to reinforce the egalitarian social attitudes of the communities. These attitudes are in evidence today not only ashore, but at work. A contemporary skipper will in fact commonly play down his authority intentionally. He takes his share of routine and often dirty tasks in harbour. At sea, instead of shutting himself up on the bridge and ordering the crew about through the loudspeaker system, he chooses to pass instructions quietly by word of mouth, sometimes indirectly, sometimes couched in the form of suggestions. In between active fishing, the bridge becomes an informal social centre with men drifting in and out, chatting and smoking – despite his own mild protests, as a non-smoker, at them 'spoiling God's good air'. And in the same spirit, when the crew are out on deck bringing in the nets with the winch, he is down among them to help as soon as there is a need for an extra hand somewhere, pulling and pushing at the net alongside them.[12] Common tasks, and a common basis of payment, bind skipper-owners and crew together; and at the same time the skipper's extra willingness to work, as well as his recognised special skill as a fisherman, helps to legitimate his higher earnings. Although by the 1970s the widening range of incomes brought by renewed prosperity led to calls for a new deckhands' union from Peterhead and Fraserburgh men, they were able to win little support.

The inshore communities today are by no means reluctant to take collective action to defend their mutual interests. When in March 1975, in protest against cheap fish imports and government failure to secure a European fisheries policy, the small boats in Grimsby – inspired by a similar French action a few weeks earlier – decided to blockade their own port, they were backed within a week by inshoremen right round the coasts. The Scots inshore fleet followed with especial drama, sailing for unknown destinations with instructions to blockade every Scottish port: 'floating flying pickets, a novel maritime addition to the techniques of industrial action'. They mounted a similar powerful demonstration in February 1981. But while William Hay, organiser of the Scots boats in 1975, was clear that 'We have to break a law to make our point', his committee took equal pains to emphasise 'that it represents independent operators who are not members of trade unions'.[13] For trade unionism is now almost unanimously rejected as an alien tradition by the inshoremen.

It follows from the contrasting patterns which we have described that both of our two case studies of capital and labour are focused on union struggles in the trawl ports between the wars: in Fleetwood and Aberdeen. Nevertheless, the story of industrial conflict in both ports is far from simple. On the one hand, clear concentration of ownership only slowly emerges; while on the other, up until the Second World War the workforce, despite an exceptional degree of exploitation, seemed incapable of any consistent solidarity. In each case the key to interpreting this confusing picture is found through looking beyond the bounds of a formal local study in industrial relations or labour history.

Tony Wailey traces back the roots of Fleetwood's slow-growing class consciousness to the inshore communities from which the nucleus of its workforce was drawn. In Marshside the network of kin relationships, the bonds of chapel and mutual aid, all but concealed the progressive penetration of its economy by a capital–labour division – until the riot of 1913. And it was in part the symbol offered by 'Old Fleetwood' which explains why the first generations of trawlermen were so slow to recognise their common class interest. Rebellion there was: but in the form of individual protest, of sabotage, of traditions like superstition turned to new purpose – until finally, on the eve of war, unionisation was at last achieved.

Aberdeen's trawling was equally built on the ruins of nearby inshore communities, and again the unionisation of the trawlermen took place only across decades of misdirected struggle and painful defeat. But this time, our chief concern is with the consequences of those defeats. They brought not only reduced wages, but the brutalisation of work, the crushing of moral values and the destruction of a way of life not only for the men, but for their families too: a debasement so severe that, in the long run, it destroyed the very workforce itself. Aberdeen's story only becomes fully comprehensible when we see that the struggle of capital and labour here was about home life as much as work; about values as much as cash. And it shows the untrammelled destructiveness of capitalism in victory with rare clarity: a scorched earth victory, burning out its own seedcorn.

Close-up: Lancashire
by Tony Wailey
4 Strike – the Fleetwood trawlers, 1920

On Friday 6 February 1920 a strike was called in the trawler
port of Fleetwood in Lancashire. It was the first of its kind in
the port: and there was not to be another for some fifty years.
The industrial turbulence which surged through Britain in the
five years following the First World War involved every major
trawl port. Each time the men went down in defeat, silenced
for decades. How can we explain the failure of trawlermen,
wage-earning workers, not just to win these particular battles,
but for so long afterwards to consolidate in unions, the slow
development of their class consciousness? The common theme
is division: the men in each port fought alone, and in every
separate struggle, deckhands, engineers, skippers and mates
were all in some way pitted against each other.

In Fleetwood, when the deckhands called the strike, the
engineers and skippers came out with them with demands of
their own. But suddenly within a week, following 'a deputa-
tion of bosuns, deckhands and cooks', the owners settled the
deckhands' claim, conceding an extra 10/– a week 'risk money'
on top of their wages and share money. There was a bitter ring
in the words of the recently formed National Union of British
Fishermen which represented them: 'If the matter were to be
settled locally and nationally, it would be better if all fishermen
were in one union.' For the settlement left the skippers and
engineers still out on strike.

The skippers and mates had two objectives. They wanted
the owners to recognise their own Masters and Mates Trawling Association; and they wanted an increased share of the
gross proceeds of the catch. In principle they were paid 10 per
cent of the net catch plus 1 per cent of the gross; but trawler-
owners would often deduct their own private orders before
the catch came to market.

When I came ashore and into the office, we used to go
down and meet them docking. The boss said to me the
first week, 'See the first twenty-five rows, Johnny, they're
for you'. 'Well', I said, 'It's taken me thirty-five years to
find out what "staff fish" meant'. The boss just winked.
'We all learn some day', he said.

On their first demand, that their 'craft guild' be recognised,
the skippers had the support of the engineers, whose Humber
Amalgamated Engineers and Firemen's Union had also help to
form the 'deckies'' NUBF. But on their more crucial second
demand for more share money, the position of the engineers
was more confusing. Since the formation of their own union
in 1898 the engineers had been against any form of share
earnings. Their Grimsby strike sheet of 1911, opposing such a
system proposed by the owners, declaimed that it 'would
create greater friction than ever between engineers and deckmen'; and they continued to object to the new system up to the
war.[1] But during the war all hands were given a 'sea bonus', a
maximum fixed rate for days at sea, in addition to wages.
After the war the engineers' attitudes seemed to change radically, and in both the Hull strike of 1919 and at Fleetwood in
1920 they actually demanded to be included in the share
system. Slowly but surely they were being caught up in its
ideology.

One of the central issues between the sections of fishermen
was the question of which worked most for their wages.
Deckhands saw themselves as doing the 'graft' on the fishing
grounds, whilst engineers sat down and drank tea below.
Trimmers and engineers pointed out that they did most of the
work whilst steaming to and fro the fishing grounds. They did
as much work – they should have as much share. Trawler-
owners were happy to have everybody on a share of the net
catch – and to see such competition and rivalry between the
men.

The Fleetwood owners kept the men fragmented in 1920 by
a combination of inducements and coercion. After settling the
claims of the deckmen and cooks they pulled their trump card.
They refused to talk with the skippers. The deckhands, having
as one newspaper put it come 'to amicable arrangements . . .

consequently resent being thrown out of work through no fault of their own'.

Between 130 and 140 trawlers lay idle by the third week. Before long it was estimated that a third of the fishermen had left to find work in other towns. After five weeks Fleetwood was virtually paralysed. The fleet was all but laid up, strung together across the deserted dock. Men walked aimlessly round the streets, whilst women sat at home worrying how long the food would last. Joint action committees to organise relief 'for the starving children' were co-ordinated by the Fleetwood Working Men's Club. It acted as the focal point for discussions, held shows to raise funds all along the Lancashire coast, and paid out relief money and food vouchers.

Mounting bitterness, resentment and frustration were exacerbated by friction in the town between union and non-union members, and between the different unions. Some skippers had joined the NUBF, and took their ships to sea with deck crews and non-union members. There was no shift towards any more united action. Instead each day, as the *West Lancashire Gazette* neatly describes the scene, 'large crowds of trawler hands assembled outside their organisations discussing their different situations.' At meetings the deckhands reconsidered, but stuck to their decision to return to work: as their secretary claimed, 'the engineers are all right, they've just been duped by the skippers.'[2] Attempts to draw in other ports got no further, for the skippers firmly opposed such a move.

The end to the strike after six bitter weeks brought out still more clearly the divisions in the workforce. The skippers celebrated 'a bloodless victory . . . With arbitration there would be no necessity to strike'. But the fishermen and their families would not easily forget the weeks for which their families had gone hungry. As the men came down to listen to the speeches at the dock gates, the differences came over loud and clear:

First came Mr Earle, Secretary of the Deckhands Union. The men kept at a distance from the speaker. Earle asked the people to come closer as he wanted to tell them a few home truths. He said 'some of the other unions were out to break the deckies' union', but he could tell them they wouldn't accomplish this.

Someone shouted out 'Blackleg'. Earle directed them to a place, the engineers' offices, where they were experts on blacklegging. The men continued to keep aloof and some cried 'keep away from him', with the result that Mr Earle had to give up.

Engineers were well to the forefront of these meetings. When 'J. S. Fry of the engineers stated that "the owners, I near said masters" – to which the crowd shouted back "no, no" – had agreed to get all the men through the union', he was cheered. Captain Hall the skippers' leader presented their continuing view that, 'while the men were fighting for their rights, they realised that their interests were that of the owners – and they would seek to maintain that.'[3]

The trawler owners' position was well summed up at the speech made to their annual dinner, during this 'unfortunate . . . time of turbulence', by their President. They used to be called 'the fishing fraternity', he said, but now

they spoke of themselves as the fishing industry (hear, hear). Capitalists were coming in and were going to take a prominent place in the industry. . . . So far as Fleetwood was concerned, they welcomed them, and as an association were prepared to place all their resources at their disposal. He congratulated all upon the good feeling that existed between ports. . . . If they united, they would be strong and it would be to their mutual pleasure and advantage.

It is indeed the view of one leading economic historian that the industrialisation of fishing came fifty years behind that of manufacturing. But such praise of capitalism came in stark contrast to the calls from a minority within the workface for collectivisation and nationalisation of the industry. In between lay the middle ground, a vast thicket of contradictory ideas rooted in the peculiar nature of the industry: the cultural terrain on which the owners were most secure.[4]

The arbitration award was announced two months after the ending of the strike. Trimmers were given an extra 14/– a week; engineers a share of '2d in the pound on nett earnings', but.no wage increase; skippers and mates nothing. Through their concessions the owners now had their whole workforce involved in the share system. From now on, disputes over 'stocker money', 'pull away', and the fiddling of the settling sheet, would affect all sections. Internecine division and corruption became accepted as inherent to fishing, even dangerous to question. As the 1935 Sea Fish Commission noted, deductions from the gross takings were 'not clearly specified', and accounts rendered in such varied forms that they 'cannot easily be checked; and the right of access to an owner's accounts and books . . . are rendered nugatory by the apprehension which undoubtedly exists . . . that the exercise of such rights would jeopardise a man's employment.'[5]

Thus through a combination of control over information and the attitudes which the share system encouraged, the owners maintained their dominance over the men's consciousness. But if their success stemmed immediately from the direct post-war economic circumstances, its roots went back to a century of experience in the inshore communities. It is that path which we now need to retrace.

5 Community: life in the inshore village of Marshside

God bless the painters when the leaves begin to fall
God bless the shankers wi' the winters sudden squall
God bless the shillers who only skin the willens
God bless the village full of crying children.

First settled on land reclaimed from the sea in the eighteenth century, Marshside was situated on the southern flank of the Ribble estuary and some four miles from the Lancashire resort of Southport, and forty miles from Fleetwood. Marshside is now no more than a suburb of that town, but at one time it held itself in high esteem as a flourishing fishing village. Shanking for shrimps around the flat muddy shelves of the estuary was the major source of earning for the village and formed the basis of its economy. Our concern here is with the life of the village from the middle years of the last century down to its decay at the eve of the First World War: with the features of the local economy which helped to form the basis of a community, and to give the village a firm sense of itself. Religion and family also played an essential part in constructing this way of life. Yet in the last years before the war this bonding of the village was scissored as economic issues cut through it, and its decline attributed to the new, and now bitter, divisions between the shankers and the men who bought the shrimps off them, the badgers. What underlay this sudden, unprecedented eruption of conflict?

The railways were the harbingers of change. The first one came from Liverpool to Southport in 1850. A great boost to the village followed as Southport grew tenfold in the next fifty years, presenting a buoyant luxury market for shrimps on its doorstep. Before long Marshside shrimps were no longer being merely sold 'rough' to shops in the town, but carefully shelled, cooked in a dressing of butter, mayonnaise and cayenne, and sent off to wider markets in thousands of little enamel pots imported into Marshside from the Potteries. By the late 1870s, a number of roles had been created within the community. The men who caught the shrimps were the shankers. Those that shelled them, the old, the injured and the children, were the shillers. Lastly, those who received the catch, who cooked and potted and sent them to market were the badgers. From that time onwards Marshside was to grow through exporting shrimps to all parts of the country, but always under the shadow of the town:

> That's when you could reckon on it . . . the time I suppose when it all got started . . . that's what me dad always said an m'granny. . . . M'granny sold fish up in Banks and she said the same they all did. . . . The bit I've read says as much. . . . It started up here wi' the railways.

As the shrimping industry expanded, every section of the community was drawn in. The maintenance and repair of boats, nets, baskets and carts formed only a part of it. The women had to help not only with 'shilling' the shrimps, but to look after the fires and prepare boiling pots ready for dipping them, and to help their man down with the catch after he'd come 'sweatin' and latherin' like an old horse' back across the dunes, the shrimps packed into his 'leep' and strapped behind him. After the shrimps were dipped, it was shilling time: 'Me dad used to have his tea and me mother an' us lot would get pickin' an then he'd join us later. . . . then if it weren't too late we'd take them round t' the badger'. Only when his shrimps had been 'shilled' and taken to the badgers – 'We'd sometimes have a sack dumped on the porch at eleven at night and then we'd shill em' – could the shanker think about relaxing until the dawn took him out again.

From the start fishing was a family concern. Sons followed their fathers and relatives shared boats. Pluck Wright's father shared one with her two uncles while Harry Penn's old man went for a long time with his brother. Pee Will Rimmer's household also had a long tradition of boat sharing and Dick Wright served his time as a 'putter' before he could get in on one of the boats. In 1863, four years after the longest pier in the

world had been built at Southport, twenty-nine boats were
anchored there in the deeper water, an indication of the way
the town was to help the fleet in its early days.

> Me grandad 'ad one o' those early boats an' by the time he
> packed it in he had four o' them, then me dad and uncle
> and all our lot – his brothers – used to run them and take
> our share but the old man, he was the one that did best.
> They were his boats, see; we only took a share.[1]

There were four shares to each boat, one share for each net.
One man would take a share apiece and 'dealt his own net'.
The net was his own property; but the badgers came increasingly to own more boats as their businesses built up.
Even after he got married, John Ball continued to work for his
grandad. In this hereditary system, the sons of those who
possessed boats would only become owners on the deaths of
their forebears. Others 'bought themselves into shares' if they
had been able to save or borrow, or – later – had joined in the
'Fishermen's Provident'.

How did the badgers come to set themselves up in business?
In the 1841 census there were nine fish sellers. Then years later
the number had risen sharply to twenty-three. At this stage,
nearly all were women. It was they who undertook the long
journeys, taking their 'rough' shrimps to market in baskets
and barrels, or by cart to the inland towns of Lancashire. But
with the growth of Southport with its luxury trade, soon the
shrimps were being prepared for bourgeois consumption.
With a market close at home, women found themselves settled
with another role, as shillers. They ceased to be fish sellers.
After about 1870 most of the buying and selling was done by
about twenty men.

These new fish sellers divided between badgers and shrimp
dealers. The dealers were 'small men' who generally caught
their shrimps themselves and hawked their small catch around
Southport's pubs and fairground. At the height of the summer
season perhaps upwards of thirty operated from the village.
Their market was strictly local. But the badgers 'in the true
sense of the word', of whom there were never more than
half-a-dozen, expanded their trade to all parts of the country.

Slowly they began to buy up more and more of the catch; new equipment – stoves, weighing machines, ice barrels – moved into their sheds; and daily trains brought them thousands of small enamel jars from the Potteries.

The 1891 Southport directory lists the main badgers of Marshside, the full-time employers whose businesses centred on the shrimp trade: William Watkinson, Albert Wright, Fred Wright, John Wright, Robert Blundell, Robert Houldsworth and John Ball. Of these main badgers, the three Wrights and John Ball were local villagers. What is more, their families had been amongst the first to settle on the marshland, first as shepherds and later as fishermen, families whose fortunes had prospered over the years and were able to take full benefit of the new markets. Albert Wright and his family moved into a bigger house in 1861 with more land behind it to develop his badger shed.[2] By the First World War his firm employed nearly fifty villagers. The other badgers had come to the village after 1870 and in the case of the Watkinsons and the Houldsworths, had started up sheds almost immediately. All were Primitive Methodists, which helped the newcomers to integrate themselves within the life of the village. Another advantage, which helped to extend their power, was explained by Harry Penn Wright:

> Only the little fellers see could take so many shrimp, they didn't need for what 'ud be a great deal for fitchin' them about the pubs, they'd put a restriction on you . . . 'Well, lad, how many heve thee? Ah cun take six pints off thee an no more . . .'
>
> But the big uns the Houldsworths and the Wrights . . . they'd take as many shrimps as you like an'more.

The 'big uns', the badgers, could take all they could buy to meet their extended market. But in the end their own efforts to maintain supplies turned against them. They began buying in imported shrimps from Holland. From their very power, slowly but surely a gulf of animosity opened between them and the other Marshside families.

The fishermen or shankers would fish in the Ribble estuary and down the Mersey as far as Formby Point. Two men fished together in 'Nobbies', originally 36-foot boats but extended to 42 feet after the Sea Fishing Act of 1886. The shankers' life was not only perilous in the stormy winters, but dogged with innumerable other deprivations. They had no oilskins, just coats buttressed together with patches of red lead and easily soaked through. After tying up at Southport pier head after a day's work, they had a three-mile walk home with the shrimp baskets on their backs. Their hands often bled from constant handling of the rough shrimps.

In summer and late winter, 'when there weren't any about', the men would trawl for fish. When there was a little bit of everything and not much of anything, in winter, 'we'd take both trawl and shrimp nets with us, and sometimes come back with nothing – no nets, no fish, nothing . . . We had some terrible winters then.' The best shrimping months were the 'back end' from September to November, when the shrimps usually fed at night: and the fishing was done then too:

> fine thinkin' nights when the moon were up and you'd think you were all alone an' you'd look around and you'd see the fleet stretched out beside you and them just lying quiet on the water . . .
>
> Going home in the morning and them callin', 'Aye aye, Pee Will, has thee done anything?' . . . You'd never tell . . . Not telling each other where the fishing was.

Harry Penn's old man bought his boat *Kathleen* for £80 in 1886: the equivalent of nearly two years' full earnings, 'for if you could get a pound a week fifty weeks a year, you'd think you were doing good'. He bought it with the help of the 'Fishermen's Provident'. Later, as the channels silted up, horses and carts were also used, especially in the warmer weather when the shrimps were in the shallows. Around the turn of the century, 'you could get a horse for a fiver, no more than a tenner, but a boat would cost you ten times that. . . . There weren't many that had a cart an' a boat. . . . Why there were no choice – you'd go for the boat.'

The shrimp shellers also formed a distinct social group in the village. A good shiller could shell a quart of picked shrimps in a hour, riddling the carcass from nearly 400 rough ones. They

were paid about a third of what the fisherman got from the
badger: up to the time of the 1913 strike, 5d a quart. In almost
every Marshside cottage the image lingers of a group of
villagers huddled around a table, their heads sunk into their
shoulders and faces intent only on the great mass of shells,
whilst the fire in the grate lights up the shadows. Children too
were expected to take their part, although there was little
money for them:

> You'd shill before you went to school and you'd shill when
> you came home, an' if you were five minutes late your
> mother would want to know. . . . There was a job for you
> then, see. It'd be three or four in the mornin'
> sometimes. . . . We didn't have too much time for
> playin'. . . .
> After they were done we . . . took them up to the
> badgers. That was our job as well, an' we collected the
> shrimp bill an' the money off him each week an' brought it
> home an' put it on the table.[3]

Like many other Marshsiders, Pluck Wright's father would
mend his nets in the winter; for with regard to both time and
money, the seasons greatly influenced their lives. If £1 a week
was 'doing good' for Harry Penn, John Ball could remind him
'that we'd had three and even four pounds some weeks'. It all
depended on the autumn 'back end', after the shrimps had
bred. Knowing the sparseness of the winter months ahead, the
men would always try to put something by from these weeks.
For Pluck Wright's family £20 was good luck, but John Ball
had sometimes put as much as £90 by. If the weather continued
lenient, the men would go for fish, especially if a shoal of plaice
were running; and this often led to friction between shanker
and badger. They took two nets instead of the single shrimp
net, so the catch was divided two shares to the men and one to
the boat in contrast to a half share each when going for
shrimps. The men would go for the better share-out 'and the
badger could go whistle for his shrimps'.

During the hard months, the men eked out a living, seeking
out various kinds of temporary casual work in a way which
was typical of the casual labouring villages at this time. Some

would rent tourist cab horses from the town and cart for the
farmers to Liverpool or Ormskirk markets. Carts were also
used for 'wrecking' or salvaging off the shoreline, whilst bird
catching was done regularly by groups of 'net men' – sheppie
pie made from starlings was a regular winter dish and linnets
had an actual cash value:

> We'd go tuttling for them buggers . . . me and mucky
> Tummy wi' whistles made from cartridge cases . . . Ah'd
> tuttle an' Tummy'd snare thum as they came down. . . .
> Th'hens we'd let go . . . an' sell the cocks to Bluddy John
> . . . E'd sell thum in Preston Market . . . tanner a time.

Taking all these bits and pieces of secondary earnings, it
becomes difficult to judge an inshoremen's earnings. Leone
Levi gave the annual average for fishermen of all sorts in 1885
as £22, but inshoremen were harder to pin down. There was
much common sharing too: 'if you had some spuds, you'd
say, "Come over an' I'll give you some", an' maybe he'd give
you something else'. Pluck Wright's people lived next to a
man with hens: 'he'd give you eggs and you give him something that you had back.' Alongside this exchange of goods, all
three grocers in the village gave credit, especially during the
winter:

> The Co-op'd allow you five bob a week but only for so
> long . . . You had to pay back the best you could,
> sometimes 6d, sometimes a shilling a month . . . waitin'
> for the good months.
>   One time things were so that they wouldn't give any
> more . . . we were all on the Poor Law . . . There were
> three winters (1908–11) when everyone were on it . . . The
> Salvation Army came up with soup kitchens.[4]

In these bad times often the only money coming into many
village homes was that earned by the women who shilled for
the badgers. In 1907 they were earning around 8/– a week; and
those wages had become a necessity.
  The dunes surrounding the village were full of willens, and
the women would go out scouring for them and cut and braid

them for baskets. Although there was one full-time basket-maker in the community in 1891, he sent his wares mainly to the town, and in general each family was responsible for its own needs. In winter, as the baskets were woven and the sails mended and the boat hulls tarred and pitched, the shankers would congregate together on the patch behind the cobbler's shop to braid and mend their nets, or on cold or wet days sitting inside the long workshop. There were so many arguments and debates here that the room became known as the 'Shankers' Parliament'. It was here that many a communal movement was first mooted.

Probably the most important benefit scheme begun in the village was the Fishermen's Provident Association, started and run by the fishermen themselves, through which they clubbed together to buy and insure their own boats. Started in 1877, it came mid-way through the forty years that saw the great growth in the number of fishing boats at the pier head. It had some sixty boats on its books at its height. Subscription charges were 2/6d a quarter, and shares in the Association 5/– each. Groups of men were nominated to travel to all the boatyards of the estuary, looking to see if there were any second-hand bargain craft, and to buy them when there was a demand from the members. This explains how in March 1887, when the badgers were paying £100 for a shrimp boat, it could be resolved that 'Sam Wright be allowed to have the Enigma for £35 and that he pay £5 down and £5 per annum.'

The Fishermen's Provident helped numerous villagers. Like everything at Marshside, it must be seen in the light of Southport's great expansion: but it also indicates how the village was seeking to maintain its own interests and identity in the shadow of that great growth. To survive economically they had to specialise, organise – just as they had in their fishing. They could only depend on themselves, and they knew it. In just the same way through their own welfare system in the Tontine Club and the Rechabite Society they sought to avoid the misery of abject poverty. Both were actively supported, as their record books confirm. Shares in the Rechabite cost 4d a quarter, and each share paid out half-a-crown panel money. Most villagers held three shares, paying a penny a week to a collector. Sickness benefit of 7/6d a week would be paid for the first six months – it would then be halved. After a year it would be halved again, but after that it would go on indefinitely, providing a form of pension for the old and the injured. There were also burial shares costing 5¼d a quarter, and worth £5.

With its dependence on a single economy, it was not surprising that the community had such a 'sense' of itself. These associations grew out of that closely inter-related system. Through their 'Fishermen's Provident' the village was able to ensure that boat ownership was not confined to some few rich families, nor to the badgers. During hard times the shankers knew that they had only themselves and their families to rely on. An extract from the Association's minutes reads: 'money has been paid out towards the complete wreckage of a boat, and that John Jacks Rimmer be nominated to collect the amount off all the membership in the village'.[5] For Marshsiders, mutual organisation had grown out from the extended family to become interwoven with the fabric of community in all the everyday comings and goings of the village.

In 1841 there had been one main family in Marshside, the Wrights, who altogether occupied over thirty households. The Rimmers, the Balls, the Johnston and Sutton families also had strongholds in the village. Together with the Wrights, their names made up 90 per cent of the population. And as late as 1914, these same family names still accounted for half the village population. As in many other fishing villages this paucity of surnames led to the use of nicknames, either from some past deed, or taken to indicate ancestry. Bobs Pluggin Tom's boy was walking down Shellfield Road when a stranger asked him if he knew where Robert Wright lived. The boy shook his head. His uncle came out from a house nearby and the boy asked him if he knew about Robert Wright. 'Why, it's the father you stupid bugger!' The boy only knew his father by what everyone called him, and that was Bobs Pluggin Tom.

For these children of the village, the centre of their existence was William Wignall's sail loft and the sweet shop with brown shutters on the corner of Shellfield Road. Up to 1876 this thoroughfare had been known as Dangerts Loam, and like many other groups of cottages it reflected all the village's great family names and nicknames. The 1851 census showed that most of the village lived in huddles of cottages rather than streets proper, with names like 'Wrights Houses', 'Johnston Houses', 'Cotty's Brow', 'Old Ralph's Place' and 'Fine Jane's Lane'. The past and the present were worn in the same old clothes.

As with the boats, there was also a hereditary system of cottage sharing. Many cottages had extensions built onto them to accommodate newly marrieds, or until the couple could find another place. Pluck Wright's brother lived with his wife in their cottage until an uncle found them another place in Shellfield Road. Harry Penn's father was promised an old cottage by the cobbler on condition that he renovated it. The rent was to be 3/– a week, but the cobbler got a better offer from one of his relations. Owdy Penn got angry, especially as he needed somewhere to live. 'Te bluddy chapel roof'll fall on thy head', he said to him; and relations between the two were never good afterwards.

The influence of Primitive Methodism was strong in the village. It was one of the roots of the community's independence and self-sufficiency. Nearly all its organisations, from the Fishermen's Provident to the Rechabites and the prize choir, were stems that branched from the Chapel's main trunk. 'The Prims' had come early to Marshside: the first services were held in 1820, in a barn belonging to Thomas Wright. A chapel was built fifty years later with funds raised by the villagers themselves. With its hymns, its music, its story-telling and its ranters, it produced a communal atmosphere and a religion that was 'preached not at but by the poor themselves'.[6]

Meanwhile Southport was still growing – from 5,000 in 1830 to 50,000 by 1870. It left Marshside in increasing isolation. By the 1870s Southport's expansion eastwards had absorbed the neighbouring fishing community of Little London. Here the men had been 'proper fishermen', inshore trawling in spring and summer, fishing out of Cardigan Bay in winter, regarding the Marshsiders as 'messers'. But Southport emasculated them. Little London boats first took the tourists 'quality sailing'. In winter there was work with the Corporation, and at the gasworks, built close to the heart of their community in 1878. When the fairground opened on the foreshore, many of its stallholders were Little London fishermen. As it integrated itself with the town, Marshsiders expressed an increasing sense of difference in their phrase towards Little Londoners: 'leave it t'thum down there.' And Marshside's jealous protection of its own independence brought in return comments such as 'they was all related an' had names like Jebs Pete Toms Willy. Who has names like that if they're not all mixed in together?'[7]

Changes were taking place within the village, however. It was no accident that of the eighty-eight new families living in the village by 1902, only eight were employed as fishermen. The rest were mainly associated with the building trade, and reflected the growth in employment away from the village. Of seventeen children baptised in the chapel in 1907, only three had fishermen as fathers, although twelve had the old family names of Wright, Rimmer and Johnston. Nor was the Fishermen's Provident faring any better, for there was only one new boat insured between 1893 and 1903. On the eve of the First World War an old fisherman was to comment, 'there were ninety boats here twenty years ago – now there are only fifty and the reason men are leaving them is that they can't get a living.'[8]

One serious problem which affected everyone in the village was the silting up of the main channels. The building of draining walls all along the Ribble estuary, and land reclamation from the sea, had proceeded so fast during the late nineteenth century that by 1888 a quarter of the 58 square miles of the estuary had been completely reclaimed. Marshside was in fact caught between two ports, both needing to expand to cater for industrial shipping. Preston on the Ribble to the north had won parliamentary consent to constructing large draining walls to control the river and provide a quick shipway to the sea. The Ribble, once a tortuous, winding river, was cast straight as a die by the end of the century, cutting off the smaller estuary channels on which Marshside depended. And to the south was Liverpool, whose dredgers dumped millions of tons of sand between 1890 and 1920 into the last remaining waterway, the south channel. As one expert noted, 'if only a portion of this was carried by winds into the fishermen's channel, it would account for the great depreciation and filling in of its watershed.' These developments accelerated Marshside's decline; but they must be seen in the context of wider economic changes.

Southport Corporation's attitude to the fishermen was stated plainly by one of its councillors: 'The fishing industry is not now the asset it once was to the town, I am sorry to have to say this.' Supplies of fish could be brought in from Morecambe, Fleetwood or the Dutch ports, and be preserved and stored in the badgers' cold rooms until ready to be despatched. As the town mushroomed in growth, the Southport directory of 1900 recorded that 'fishing, once the main employer, now comes well behind the Corporation and building trades.' Similar tales were told elsewhere in the fishing villages of Lancashire. At a conference in Morecambe, many voices were raised about the danger to the trade. One fisherman, declaring that 'musselling was far more important than the trippers', said he did not want to see his industry die. In the 'good' times before 1900, 'fishermen were not carrying a hod or mixing mortar or sweeping the streets.'[9] All over the country inshore communities were under similar pressure; and most of all where heavy investment was encouraging the growth of tourism and a building boom.

At the same time improved communications and the expanding shrimp market indirectly accelerated the decline of Marshside's fishing. 'So long as Southport remained small and the outlying districts alone knew of the plectoral delicacy, the positions of the potters and the fishermen was one of harmony.' But with the combined effect of growing markets and diminishing local fishing grounds, the badgers were importing more and more shrimps from Holland. By 1913 there were between seven and eight hundredweights arriving daily into the village. Increasingly isolated from its own means of subsistence, Marshside was more and more dependent on external factors for its own local way of life. The weights that held the balance were slowly tilted towards decline. Perhaps it was symbolic that the shankers should look inward to their own community, and vent their rage on those nearest to home.

It took until 1913 for the storm to break. The past winter had been disastrous for the men. The badgers had broken the Fishermen's Amalgamation by paying higher prices for shrimps taken by non-members of the organisation. Worse still, that spring had seen the council's refusal to support the cutting of a new channel: 'They talked about us gettin' a dredger and us doing the work ourselves, but nothin' did come of that . . . It were no bluddy use.'[10] As the imported shrimps flowed in, the men stood idle and suffered.

The minutes of their Fishermen's Association give some indication of how they felt. 'The badgers only studied their own interests. . . . The badgers were out making money at the expense of the fishermen.' Albert Rimmer warned that:

> They didn't want to use violence, but when it came to such a state of affairs that their wives and children were crying out for bread and butter and the fathers were willing and able to work but couldn't, then the men with justice must protect themselves. . . . The badgers had made their money out of the fishermen and now they were trying to clem them out.

The last straw came when a couple of the badgers suddenly dropped the price they paid the men, from 1/4d to 1/2d a shilled quart of shrimps. It was no good blacking these badgers: they merely imported more shrimps. But when some of them threatened to smash any form of shankers' organisation and blacklist troublemakers, the men decided they had had enough. One fine morning in May the village erupted.

Contemporaries who had forgotten the economic differences within the village were astonished by the violence directed against mutual neighbours and kin, who were joined by the bonds of the same quiescent religion and prayed in the same chapel. The men smashed open caskets of imported shrimps and destroyed them. They cut the telephone wires so that the police could not be called. Owdy Wright had petrol stored in his front room; and but for their arrest during the day's fighting, he and his mates would have burnt the badgers' sheds. It was not only the men who rebelled that day – all the village was up – shillers, and putters, as well as shankers: for 'as their way of life in the better days had been shared, so their sufferings were those of the whole community.'

Those days in late May 1913 were more than scattered outbursts against the drop in prices enforced by the badgers. The records of the Fishermen's Association testify that the people could see their way of life was dying. A spokesman for the local Conservatives came down to offer them courage:

> The public was for them, the law was for them, and if any amendment to the existing law was requisite, they would get it. . . . Theirs was a moral cause, and no moral cause did fail eventually, either in a nation, community, or individual.

The Marshsiders tried to form a National Inshore Union of Fishermen to strengthen their position. These were the years of the great national pre-war 'labour unrest'. But their union did not make much headway. The men were still wondering how to form it when the Great War came upon them, and instead of their names being enrolled in strong numbers, many were found engraved on chapel walls and village greens the length and breadth of England.

Marshside was not alone in its decline. Its experience, in some form, was shared by most of the inshore villages right down the west coast of England and Wales, from Morecambe to Cardigan Bay. Matheson's comment on Welsh fishing in 1929 could have been equally applied to Lancashire:

> In the 1880s our fishing was still conducted to a great extent by small privately-owned boats sailing from almost every little harbour. Soon the industry was to be altered without recognition with the growth of steam trawlers and the large ports.[11]

The first steam trawler came to Cardiff in 1888. Only five years would separate the time when Milford Haven, Swansea, then Fleetwood, would acquire them. Here lay the catharsis of change.

The riot of 1913 in Marshside was that community's response to its sense of losing control over its own way of life. It was in that respect a very different conflict from the strike of unionised wage-earners in Fleetwood, the largest port on the west coast, in 1920. But Marshside provides a connection as well as a contrast. For Fleetwood developed at the expense of the villages; and the new port grew from the old, not just materially, but also in its spirit. Within its very heart, the vestiges of the old were to be a vital feature, playing a critical part in shaping the consciousness of the trawlermen.

6 The old ethic and the new – inshore village within a trawler port

The rise of Fleetwood to become the chief centre of the region's fishing industry dates from the 1890s. At that date, with good town markets close at hand, hundreds of small boats were working out of villages similar to Marshside. But the growth of steam trawlers rapidly transformed this situation. As late as 1906 Fleetwood's catch was still only three times that of the small fleet from Liverpool; but by 1913, its landings were more than ten times the total for the whole of the rest of the Lancashire coast. Fleetwood had only 32 trawlers operating in 1903, but more than 100 on the eve of war, with a workforce swollen from 200 to more than 1,000 men. In 1904 its trawlers made 600 trips to the fishing grounds, in 1914 over 4,000.

Alongside this growth came developments with the ownership of vessels and technology. The Fleetwood Fishing Trawler Owners Association was formed in 1909. A year later it set up an ice company. In 1911, with capital from both the owners and the railway companies – the Lancashire and Yorkshire and the Great Western – the old timber pond was filled in and a new fish dock was completed at a cost of £2 million. By the first year of the war a new market had replaced the old one. Previously the fish had to be carted across the railway lines and past the coal bunkers to be sold. Because of the way in which trawlers took coal from the steel grabbers, when the wind was blowing, or in summertime, the fish would often be coated in black dust. With the market came three new cantilever cranes able to reach right down into the bunkers. Clouds of flying dust blowing down the quayside became a thing of the past. By the early 1920s Fleetwood was taking nearly half a million tons of coal a year, and investment had grown to five million pounds.[1]

These changes did not take place in a vacuum, however.

The new and the old were constantly intermingled and in many ways coalesced. A fleet of up to seventy smacks with three- to five-men crews continued to exist through the first decade of the new century, although with each year their numbers declined. In the 1870s such smacks could be bought from a boatbuilder for £100 deposit, paid off in quarters with no insurance required. Although they could be away fishing for a week at a time, they seemed part of the inshore culture. Many inshore fishermen sailed with them to continue earning in winter – or to save money for small boats of their own. This form of saving and subsistence had important ramifications for the future.

It is important to remember too that in 1903, whilst there were only 288 men working on the steam trawlers, there were ten times that number working from inshore boats and smacks in Fleetwood and the surrounding fishing villages of North Lancashire. As we have seen from Marshside, if women, the elderly and children were all involved, this figure could again be multiplied fivefold. As late as 1928 figures show that of the total men fishing in England and Wales, more than 50 per cent were inshore men with over 20 per cent combining inshore and trawling activities side by side. This was after the watershed of the war when, as one observer commented, 'many of the inshore villages were left in a languishing condition', and it was 'estimated that the total number of inshore fishermen had declined by about 7,600 men – 40 per cent – between 1913 and 1928'.[2]

It must also be emphasised that although Fleetwood had become a major centralised fishing port by the end of the war, ownership of boats was still largely diversified amongst many small firms. As late as 1927 there were as many as sixty owners out of a fleet of 178 boats. With the decline of inshore fisheries elsewhere, it meant that men were often found on trawlers with a long history of inshore fishing behind them, so that although the distribution of capital resources had become increasingly unequal, this had not brought an automatic change of attitudes on the part of the fishermen. The 1920s were a decade in which an intensification of capital concentration was taking place throughout the fishing industry. But this new controlling force, which the owners themselves had in some form recognised, was hidden in a mask of ideology maintained by the 'small boat' mentality of the men whose life experience had been formed in the inshore villages. And it was the owners' intention to ensure that this consciousness characteristic of the self-employed was carried over into large-scale trawling.

The owners were fortunate that in Fleetwood there existed a ready-made example of the older modes of production on their harbour steps: an inshore fishing community known as Fleetwood, but which we shall call here Old Fleetwood. In understanding the problems raised by the strike of 1920, the hinge proves to be Old Fleetwood. This community served as a transitional base which kept the small-boat ideology intact.

The little inshore boats tied up along Jubilee Quay were a constant reminder to those who came home shattered from middle-water fishing. Marra Wilson bought a new one for £120 in 1919, but there were many more 'just make-shift jobs' that could be had for less than £60; and for those that had been brought up in and around the Lancashire fishing villages, this was a powerful enticement to just go trawling for a certain amount of time and then get out. The longer they stayed, the stronger the dream became. Robbie Wilson fished the middle waters for six years between 1923 and 1929 before coming inshore back to his family.[3]

Old Fleetwood acted as a symbol, a reminder of the past, to those who now laboured in a totally different economic environment. There was always the chance of owning one's boat. What was more, inshore fishing at Old Fleetwood was turning into something of a success story. Far from wanting to stay in trawling and to help organise its workforce, many men saw work there as a purely transient phase in their lives. Such attitudes posed problems for any attempt to build a strongly organised labour force.

A co-operative had been formed in 1914 among the inshore men. Like the similar attempts made at Marshside and in many other Lancashire fishing villages, it was set up in opposition to the local badgers. In Fleetwood there had been just

> a couple of badgers. . . . And they'd tell the men how
> much fish they could get. They had their favourite boys

and then favourites grew smaller and smaller till the others couldn't stick it no more. They had a meeting an' decided to do it themselves.

As at Marshside, the badgers tried to break them by offering higher prices.

> We weren't making much y'know. These badgers Jonston and Hudson, they offered us half a crown a dozen if we'd take them back. An' three of them went and left us. . . . After we'd been going a year or two they'd have nearly cried to come back to the prawn house. . .

The 'prawn house', as the new marketing co-operative was known, received a boost in the management of its affairs when 'each of the two government enquiries into the inshore fishing industry, conducted in war-time, found that the best means of preserving and reviving this industry was to form a collection of societies on the lines of the existing Agricultural Organisa-tion Society.' The Fisheries Organisation Association came into being late in 1915, and the official name in Fleetwood was now the Wyre Fishermen's Co-operative. In this way formal recognition was given to a collection of small masters:

> Aye, it were all the inshore men that started it, then Morecambe made one the next year. A couple of Lytham men came t'see me an' they were swearin' all over. We had women pickin' in the back an' I said t'keep it low. They said how they was being treated and Pat said why don't y'get y'heads together an' do as we've done. They did too, at least in Morecambe.

The co-op was responsible for marketing and distributing the men's catch. It paid the boat-owner the market price for his fish (minus a percentage for the upkeep of the place and the manager's wages) and then the boat-owners would in turn pay their second man. Payment was by results. There were three shares to each boat, the two men and the boat all taking a share apiece. In winter, when the boats could not get out, the co-op would pay out the dividends on the year, but again, only to the boat-owners. 'We used to get a bit of bonus at year end in prawn house . . . well, it kept us going them few months. . . . We'd have the profits amongst the boats then y'know'.[4] The dividend was paid out to each owner according to how much he had caught throughout the year.

It was striking to find such a system of payment by results flourishing within the different environment of trawling. But for the trawl-owners, anxious to perpetuate the traditional fishermen's small-owner philosophy, Old Fleetwood provided a constant reference point. Because it portrayed all the elements of a traditional local 'fishing fraternity', the influence of the inshore community was totally disproportionate to its size.

Nowhere was this more clearly seen than in the arrangement of Fleetwood's housing. Most of the inshoremen lived in a tight collection of streets – Arthur Street, Lower Lune Street, Pharos Street, Aughton Street, Custom House Lane – in the oldest and most northern part of the town known as the Mount:

> I remember Manty Wright coming out t'look at sky in his
> old long johns. It didn't bother him, innocent see . . .
> stood in the street in his long johns looking at the sky . . .
> He knew where he lived . . . Friday night was pay night
> and I could walk around to all the fishermen and see all of
> them an' be back in the prawn house in half an hour.

This town-centre housing of the inshore community was in stark contrast to the difficulties that faced trawlermen who wanted to move into the town and settle there. Indeed, the absence of such opportunities made it difficult for there to be any strong community area based on trawlermen themselves. It also partially explains the historical ascendancy of those who had lived there longest. The idyll of their way of life was regarded as a feature, an illustration of the sturdy individualism that was still seen as the dominant characteristic and ideal of the town. Trawlermen's housing did not get off the ground until the 1930s when council housing estates were built on the western perimeter of the town. Until then, lack of accommodation always gave a transient nature to the comings and goings of the trawling workforce.

Even the skippers' leader, Captain Hall, had complained in 1920 that 'he himself could not get away from the club and there were hundreds like himself. . . . What was the use of bringing fishermen into the town if they could not get anywhere to live?' In the late 1920s it was still reported that 'thousands stayed in lodging' in the town. The first council scheme was not considered until 1926, and took until the 1930s to complete. At one time the local paper became so concerned that it carried out a survey of the amount of money leaving the town in the form of allotments to fishermen's wives. By 1928 more than a fifth of the trawlermen were sending money away to families – 40 per cent of them elsewhere in Lancashire; and these were only the married men. Many single young men just had their landladies pick up their weekly money, or let it mount up at the company office. They would then go home with the pay-off and give a certain amount 'in bulk' to their parents. Fleetwood trawlermen had been drawn in 'from all over'. An example is the 28 men shipwrecked on two trawlers off the Outer Hebrides in 1928. Only 9 came from Fleetwood itself: 3 were from Ireland, 1 from Grimsby and 1 from Lowestoft, and the rest from other Lancashire towns and villages.[5] Fleetwood, like other trawler ports, attracted and recruited many of its men from its own shire. But by the same token, many of those who fished from the port did not make it their home.

Without a family-based trawling community, and with little time ashore together, Fleetwood's trawlermen were notably poor in communal institutions. There were no brass bands, no prize choirs – these had been left behind in the old villages. But what was to fill this gap? A new attitude to fishing responding to the new economic conditions thrown up by trawling? Not immediately: for there were too many contradictions inherent in the industry.

If we look back on the broad historical pattern up to this point in the 1920s, we can see that as the family work unit and dependence on the extended family network so evident in Marshside declined, a similar pattern was re-established in Fleetwood but with one very important difference. In the nineteenth century, emigration to urban centres was a new and unknown venture for dispossessed village workers. Similarly, fishermen who left villages like Marshside to come to Fleetwood were setting up their industry in a completely new and untouched environment. Fleetwood had not existed until the 1840s when it was colonised by the lord of the manor of Marshside, Sir Peter Hesketh Fleetwood. Since its basic industry was fishing, and it was as such a self-employed community from the outset, it had to create its own forms of social welfare. Old Fleetwood, with its firmly inter-related basis in housing and employment, was well placed to recreate this traditional solidarity. But it had to do so within a new economic environment.

The two most vital illustrations of the inshoremen's economic constraints were the original need to form the co-operative to market their catch, and some years later – in the early 1920s – the purchase of a fish shop. Normally, when winters were bad, the men would have had no fish to sell and would have had to live off their savings. Even with a co-operative, no marketing could take place if there was no fish. The purchase of the fish shop meant that the manager of the co-op – he ran both jobs – could now go down onto the fish trawling dock and buy as much fish as he wanted for the shop. In the words of one man, 'it were that shop that saved us.' Records from the co-op diary for Easter 1927 give some indication: 'Only two of our boats prawning . . . big demand. Fish dear, bought a box of spraggs £3, bought six stone of Carrswood . . . fish shop took seventeen pounds'.[6]

The inshoremen, despite owning their boats, had thus become dependent on the large-scale production alongside them.[7] And Old Fleetwood became integrated into the trawling economy in other ways. The wives of inshoremen worked alongside those of trawlermen in the fish-curing houses and salting houses of the town. Forty women worked in the co-operative itself; three hundred were employed by Gourocks rope works and net-making factory. There was a growing variety of jobs in shops and other service work. In their leisure, too, the women were being drawn into a wider world. For Mrs Pluck Wright of Marshside in her youth 't'go out of village down to Southport were a real red letter day'.

When the Fishermen's Co-operative in 1927 noted, 'girls on holiday all gone off to Morecambe', they indicate that by then there was a much more independent attitude on the part of women, breaking out of the old family networks.

Combined with this came a noticeable decline in a religious activity – and once again work roles were a principal influence behind the change. Many of the inshore fleet would be working on a Sunday, something unheard of in villages like Marshside or the Cardigan Bay communities. Men who had been deep-sea trawling and now ran their own boats could say that 'Sunday were just another day if you'd been trawling, and fishing were no different.' It was probably this that older fishermen meant when they spoke of trawling as 'corrupting fishing'. Dick Wright remembered how 'at one time chapel were full of fishermen but then there were a change, a big change'. He was one of the few who now attended service. What had been known as the fishermen's chapel, the Primitive Methodists on West Street, was turned into a cinema some years after the war. And on one good Sunday in October 1927, the co-operative diary records that 'ten of our girls were on the dock picking prawns, big success, weather very fine.' To have inshore fishermen and women working on Sundays would never have been tolerated in the older villages. In Marshside, before the war, a man named Angry Peter was not spoken to for months on end after 'he'd tried his hand on the Sabbath'.[8]

If there were influences from the wider society acting on its own family and cultural patterns, the present reshaping the past, nevertheless the essential point is that Old Fleetwood provided a living link in the transition from petty entrepreneurship to large-scale capitalisation. Through its example the attitudes of the past were continually re-invoked in the present, and the inshore philosophy thrust upon the new industrial conditions. It is these conflicting strands of thought which point the way to an explanation of the ambiguities of the 1920 strike. The realities of life experience can lag behind those of economics. 'Although inshore fishermen formed more than a third of the total number of fishermen in England and Wales in 1928, their landings of wet fish in that year were under 2½% of total landings.' In Fleetwood itself a fifth of the men still combined trawling and inshore work in the early

1930s. And the influence of the image, the collective life experience of an inshore village in the midst of a great trawler port, attaching the outmoded philosophy of the past to the relations of the present, provides the kind of paradox, indeed, which Karl Marx himself surely had in mind when he wrote that:

> History is nothing but the succession of separate generations, each of which exploits the materials, the capital funds, the productive forces handed down to it by all preceding generations, and thus, on the one hand, continues the traditional activity in completely changed circumstances and, on the other, modifies the old circumstances with a completely changed activity.[9]

7 The aftermath of defeat: the paradox of rebellion and organisation

Throughout the first two decades of the century the employers had been able to make use of the conflicting strands in fishing to their own advantage. This situation was not to change until the later 1930s. In that respect at least, the strike of 1920 marked no sharp break with the past. Indeed it left the trawler unions so divided that the masters had little difficulty in pressing home their advantage. For the acceptance of the 'share principle' in fishing was to have dramatic results when the government decided on decontrol of the industry in February 1921. A new and revised scale of wages was to take place from 1 April 1921. This scale of wages fully reflected the weak position which the fishermen now held in the industry.

Skippers might be told that 'they were now on their own', but it was in word only: as a result of the revised scale of wages, skippers and mates in the three largest English ports now had 'trip money payments abolished'. Their share money was to be kept fixed at $1\frac{3}{8}$ and 1 share of the 14 shares in the boats and 'skippers and mates [were] to be supplemented by £100 and £25 annually provided that such bonuses can be paid out of profits after meeting all charges and expenses and allowing ten per cent to owners and provided also that they have stayed in vessel twelve months and have not transferred to another one without the owner's permission.' For the owners to be able to get agreement to such a statement in writing in itself indicated the scale of their victory. The skippers were caught in the mid-way territory between own-ers and men; their vacillations reflected this, undercutting any effective form of organisation.

The deckhands fared no better. A regular sea bonus of 6/– a day, that had been in operation since 1919, was scrapped. In its place came an extra penny in the pound share money. The same was given to engineers – though chief engineers also lost

8/– from their basic. But it is in the case of the trimmers and deckie-trimmers that we can best see the true weight of the changes. A trimmer's money had been 69/– a week plus a sea bonus of 3/– a day. This combined wage of 90/– a week was cut by more than half to 42/–: but 'poundage of a penny in the pound was granted'.[1]

All down the west coast similar tales were told. Milford Haven trimmers' wages fell from 90/– a week to 70/–, and the men had to work a 12-hour shift instead of an 8-hour one. They too began to receive a share of the catch. In comparison with other groups of workers, fishermen were being crucified. Railwaymen's wages were down from 68/– to 56/–, dockers from 16/– to around 12/– a shift, and the miners were losing 2/– a day on their shifts: but this was nothing to 42/– and 48/– a week lost by the Fleetwood deckmen and trimmers. The miners, dockers and railwaymen, moreover, fought these cutbacks. There was no such opposition from the trawlermen.

If Old Fleetwood stood for the maintenance of traditional values ashore, on board the trawlers it was the skippers who took this role. They were the ideological lieutenants of the owners – in a Hull skipper's phrase, 'We hate the system, loathe it, abhor it, yet feel there is no other way.' They, as much as anybody, were caught between the old family modes, being 'one's own man', while at the same time having their autonomy stripped away from them by the increasing build-up of companies and capital relations. Their situation was complicated by the fact that all skippers had started as deckies and could remember well the period spent in the foc'sle. Consequently between mates, skippers and deckhands there was a shared experience of roles that hampered any united opposition to trawler-owners. Certainly skippers would assert their authority in no uncertain terms:

> The skipper didn't do much when the fish was brought in
> and being gutted. It depended on the fish; sometimes we
> wouldn't sleep for a week. We never had much time with
> one pig. We were going home one time so we fixed and
> tidied the nets and stowed them away to give us a bit of
> time extra in port. When the skipper saw this he turned

about and headed back out to sea. 'Shoot the nets' he called out. When they came back up again they were all ripped and fouled up. 'You'll do it in my time now,' the skipper shouted. Oh, he was a swine, a real pig.

Another – who had again, subsequently become a skipper himself – stated that:

> If a cowboy came in wi' a good crew, he'd as much like fall in the same. The skipper could make it good or bad. If we had us complaints, we'd make sure skipper heard it. If he was a good man – ours was – he'd take note. If he didn't . . . there wasn't much you could do.

In comparison with these skippers' views of earlier ones they had sailed under, the deckhands' image of them was not so very different:

> Sometimes we'd dock and land on Saturday. The skipper would go with his brothers to the football. We'd have to wait about until he got back, then he'd call us up to his cabin to pay us. Just to show us who was boss. Other times we'd finish up at two in the afternoon and have to be out on the six o'clock morning tide. You had to do it – there were plenty to take your place in those days. Used to be long queues along the dock wall. Pierhead jumpers waiting for a chance.

This man stayed with the same skipper for six years, and reckoned him to be a good fishing man. One important inheritance from the past was respect for 'good fishing skippers'. This had its influence on the standing of a family too. One deckhand gave his definition of what made a good skipper:

> Hard men; knew where the fish were successful. Ones'd come from the families, go on their dad's boat. Learn right through that way. Good catches, aye it takes skill. They got computers these days but it still takes t'know the grounds. You have t'know where to look, an' what to do

with the gear . . . like I say, most of them came through family. You'd have a few come through by themselves but they weren't so many.

One ex-skipper mentioned a Fleetwood saying that: 'the only skippers that stayed that way were if you were in two families' pay.' Another said it was a disgrace to the family if the son didn't make skipper after his father, and so every opportunity was given him. Often they were pushed. This ex-skipper wanted originally to be a doctor, but his father was a part-owner of a boat in Aberdeen and needed his son's help if they were to build up a 'fleet'. He was a skipper by the time he was twenty-one. Many skippers were the first to admit that when young they had sailed under bastards, and were every bit as vituperative as the deckhands in their condemnation of them. But once skippers, they no longer belonged to the deck. They had other interests of their own.[2]

A further factor in complicating the situation was the number of small family firms in Fleetwood; and when we add old inshore Fleetwood – where a makeshift Lancashire Nobby could still cost less than £50 – it becomes easier to see how traditional attitudes could be maintained. With the exception of Aberdeen, Fleetwood in the 1920s had the highest proportion of small firms among its owners of all the major trawl ports. Boat-owners with nine or less boats made up more than half of the total fleet, in contrast to 40 per cent in Grimsby and as little as 25 per cent in Hull. Nearly a third was in the hands of owners with five or fewer boats, three times the proportion in Hull and twice that of Grimsby. The explanation for the large number of small firms lay in Fleetwood's dependence, at this stage, on the near and middle-water grounds. Fishing from Iceland was comparatively rare in the 1920s. Linked with it was reliance on an old fleet. Even as late as 1934, 90 per cent of the fleet ranged between fifteen and twenty-five years old, with only twelve new boats built throughout the 1920s. As a mere 6 per cent of the fleet, this was in stark contrast to the new boats of Grimsby and Hull.

The many small firms and old boats not only made conditions bad at sea, but reinforced the tradition of 'family firms'. They provided a link back to the earlier mode of family fishing; and more importantly, made it easier to 'black' any trouble-makers. Networks linked the trawler firms, the families who supplied many of the skippers, and also the subsidiary shore enterprises. The role of the fish merchants may provide an illustration.

In 1913 there were as many fish merchants in Fleetwood as in Hull, but they handled only half the catch of the east-coast port; and many of them were at the same time owners of a boat or two. The Fleetwood Merchants' Association had only been formed at the end of the First World War. Kelsall comments that Fleetwood's concentration 'on the "prime fish trade" helps to explain the existence of so many small merchants'. By the same token, 'the interests of the trawling section are not only confined to fish. Several of the Fleetwood trawler owners are also fish merchants. Having a stake in merchanting, they claim, reduces monopolistic tendencies.' This 'smallness', this interlocked network which still gave the impression of a family-run industry, made it easy to nip in the bud any attempt at organising the boats:

> union was a bad name, keep bringing it up and you were out of a ship. If you spoke too much about them then you were a Communist and there weren't many of them that held jobs. . . . The owners used to say that the only good fisherman is a hungry fisherman.

Another dockhand remarked:

> There were no strikes when we were trawling, though plenty of squabbles like. There were a skipper who tied a bloke to the mast for not turning to . . . he got into a lot o' trouble about that. The unions were starting up but I was never in one.

Another point of influence was through the ships' husbands, who were responsible for getting the trawlers to sea, and at the same time acted as 'checkers' on the men. This again inhibited any open signs of rebellion, for the husband could make sure that trouble-makers or organisers could be without a ship for long periods. Up until the Second World War, the men still

used to sign on in the company offices and much has been
made of the bribes, fiddles and extortion resorted to on the
part of the husbands. They were also responsible for liaisons
with the oil and liver companies, to see how much the men had
earned. This often led to abuses in the settling sheets; but any
questioning could again lead to being 'blacked'.

> They were all in it together – the owners, oil companies,
> chandlers an' the like. There was only one thing they
> didn't control an' that were the coal and they would have
> that if they could. We knew what we had but often enough
> they sell us short. . . . You'd just have to whistle and
> walk away.

The same point about the men's fear of losing their jobs is
made by the Sea Fish Commission's 1936 report. Even today,
according to a contemporary report on labour indiscipline in
the trawling industry, one of the major causes of the 'sense of
them and us' between fishermen and owners is attributed to
'the men's contact with the ships' husband. A servant of the
owners with a willingness . . . to resort to dubious practices –
threats and fiddles – not always stamped upon by the owners,
to achieve their aims.'[3]

After their collective defeats of the early 1920s, what form of
rebellion remained to the fishermen? To answer this question,
we need to penetrate behind the romantic views of the industry which could deceive even as percipient an author as
J. B. Priestley:

> I had a talk with one of the trawler owners who told me,
> among other things, that the trawler crews were still a race
> apart, perhaps the last of the wild men in this tamed island
> of ours, fellows capable of working day and night without
> food and sleep. . . .
>   They were also capable of going on the booze with equal
> energy and enthusiasm. They are intensely loyal to their
> skippers, he told me, but do not give a damn for anybody
> or anything else.

This romantic impression obscured the hard facts of control by the owners. If, on the surface, fishermen appeared loyal, it must be seen in the context of recognition of that overall power. It meant that any action taken against the owners or indirectly against the skippers had to be subversive: a form of seafaring Luddism.

The Fleetwood owners were constantly bemoaning the 'cowboys' who held up ships for refusing to sail for no apparent reason. 'Some think it clever to rebel against the bosses when they've no cause to,' their President declared in 1920. According to the newspapers, it was because of drink that men missed their ships. It was not always the drink, however:

> I've been there when we were knocked and needed a blow and they still wanted us out again in less than a day. We'd say well we'd decide someone to stay away for sailing right on the last minute, see, and kick up hell if they stuck a 'jumper' on. We'd miss the tide and get a few hours and then pay matey's fine. That was the way it worked.

Superstition was also used as a way of gaining time ashore. Skippers told me there were tales of men refusing to sail if a crewman came down to the quayside whistling when the wind was in the east. Others would not sail on a Friday. The *Fleetwood Chronicle* mentions a fisherman who refused to sail at Christmas because no oranges or nuts had been put aboard. Three of his fellow crewmen also walked off. And other acts, like throwing nets overboard, fouling winches or engine gear, were common occurrences too: furtively spoken about in the pubs, though hardly discussed in newspaper reports.

All these were delaying tactics calculated to keep the ship in port and gain the men more time. There was moreover a class basis to many such subversive acts. Between 1925 and 1930 the local newspaper reports on average of seventy cases a year being brought to court against men who had held up ships. In many the superintendent's comments were of this kind:

> A deckhand in the trawler 'Claudia' was at Fleetwood police court on Saturday sent to prison for 28 days for

failing to join his ship. Another deckhand, Alfred Kissock, charged with the same offence, was fined 40/– and one guinea advocate's fees. He chose to go to prison. Supt. Sherman, in reading their previous convictions, said they work in company like many of their fellows.

This 'company', the 'cowboys', have figured throughout the history of trawling right up to the present. Their role as class-conscious rebels has never been sufficiently recognised. Because of the weight of power against them, their militancy had often to be disguised in forms which were acceptable, like drink or superstition. This was especially so in the 1920s, when their unions had been fragmented, ships had been laid up, and there were thousands of men looking for jobs. In the year of the General Strike, because of the shortage of coal, almost two-thirds of the fleet was idle: yet 'the trawler owners had their best year since the war' despite 'the labour difficulties'. When Jeremy Tunstall observed of the quiescence of the Hull fishermen, 'their fatalism is tinged with silence', he ignored the extent to which trawlermen knew the full weight of the forces aligned against them, and how effectively these forces were used both economically and ideologically to thwart any coherent opposition. Fishermen who rebelled in these years had little alternative to taking individual and anarchistic action. The thousands of tons of ships' tackle that was found when the fish dock was cleared in the 1960s were a testimony to this fact – and by a further twist of fate, the remnants of the now decimated inshore fleet are now engaged in salvaging the iron of these men's rebellion.[4]

Although in 1939 twenty-one separate companies still owned Fleetwood's 112 trawlers, by this date ownership was less diversified than this suggests. By the mid-1930s there had been a number of mergers which allowed Marrs, the Boston Deep Sea Fishing Company and the Ross Group to emerge as the largest owners in the port, whilst the Lever Combine had also moved into the industry with its fleet and processing plants. Closer analysis of the 1939 figures shows that five companies now controlled 80 per cent of the fleet. And because the bigger firms tended to have the larger and more modern trawlers, their relative importance was still greater than this.

Nevertheless, there was still a considerable degree of small-scale production continuing alongside of the new large-scale enterprise; and this served to camouflage the impact of change. The local newspapers never tired of publishing stories of skippers who had bought their way into boats and become their own men, whilst their feature romance stories sang the parallel theme of the poor deckhand who rose to marry the director's daughter. 'A feature of the year was in the added increase in the number of skippers who have bought their own boats; two men start afresh whilst four others have added to their fleets,' commented the *Fleetwood Chronicle* in 1935. Such items occupied more newspaper space than news of the latest merger.

It was this see-saw advance, the combination of small-scale ownership with the intricate cross-concentration of major interests, which had so effectively served to hold back the development of any straightforward class consciousness in the trawling workforce in earlier decades. Hence it is no accident that with the new concentration of capital, the 1930s also saw a move towards the strengthening of the fishermen's organisations: but again in ways which were often strained and contradictory.

The Transport and General Workers Union had absorbed the NUBF, the deckhands' union, in the strike of 1920 and in the late 1920s and early 1930s many more deckhands began to join this body. But there was still much friction with the engineers and it was not until 1935 that a definite move was made towards reconciliation, in part as a consequence of the strike of that year in Hull.

In Fleetwood the TGWU were also organising the men on the dock. The dockers had suffered a serious defeat in 1926 when the president of the owners' FFTOA, which was also responsible for dock labour, had declared that 'in future men will be engaged as required, irrespective of whether they are union or not'. Since then the dockers had been rebuilding their strength, despite friction with the official union leaders, for example in 1931 over decasualisation of port labour, or in 1935 when the men called for strike action and the union officials announced that 'there would be no strike as the men have the interests of the port at heart'. In particular, the union leadership did not share the growing feeling among the men that more militant action was needed, and that it must include not only the dockers but also the fishermen.

In March 1936 two dockers, who had signed on trawlers as cooks, were accused by union officials of advocating unofficial action on both dock and ship. In their calls for mass organisation, it was alleged that 'Brothers Oldfield and Bangley collected subscriptions for the dockers' "Searchlight" movement and that they upheld certain statements made about union officials.' These militants were disciplined, but they were kept within the union; and membership continued to· increase, especially amongst deckhands. Eventually, after many lengthy meetings, the deckhands, cooks and bosuns of Fleetwood became the first major port in the country to announce that they had carried a vote to amalgamate with engineers. This was in July 1936; and that 'Brother A. E. Arnold proposed and Brother S. Martin seconded that the Fleetwood Committee approve the proposed amalgamation scheme to go forward for the approval of the general body,' and for the management committee to 'meet E. Bevin, General Secretary, regarding the terms for the prospect of one fishing unit inside the Transport and General Workers Union.'

Two years later in 1938, when the amalgamation of engineers and deckhands was completed, the minutes of the new organisation read 'that a month's notice be sent to the owners stating that on and after the 1st of October, no union members will work or sail with non-union men'. And concerning divisions of labour, 'that under no circumstances would the deckhands agree to the suggestion of the FFTOA that mates be exempt from being members of the union.'⁵ This was a far cry from the days of 1920 when engineers, deckhands and mates had been at each other's throats. The depression years and unemployment, combined with the trawler-owners' attacks on a divided workforce, seemed at last to have forced the men to come together into a single organisation. If 1920 had been a time of sectional strife, then by the eve of the Second World War a consolidation pact had been built up amongst the fishermen on clearer class lines. This change in spirit must be seen against the background of increased capital concentration and also government intervention in the industry which was undercutting its old ideological framework. But there was no smooth transition from independent inshore fishing to wage-earning trawling. There were as many unifying threads as contradictions. Even today, Fleetwood men still think of small boats, or will talk in pubs of 'ways of stopping the bastard' without ever going near a union office. The paradox of rebellion and organisation remains an essential element for any analysis of the fishing industry.

It has been a part of our purpose here to understand 'the consent given by the masses of the population to the general direction imposed on social life by the dominant social group.'[6] How have fishermen, for all their deprivations, so rarely stood against the powers which have succeeded in transforming a family industry into the present-day monopoly of great firms? If we started this work expecting a clearcut development of attitudes in response to new economic forms, a class consciousness answering capital concentration, the uneven and contradictory course of real events has not allowed of any such straightforward explanation. The truth lies in a much more complex interweaving of economy, community and consciousness.

Close-up: Aberdeen
8 The nemesis of steam capitalism

Aberdeen's grey face glints as it turns. From the south, it is still the final industrial city, its serried tenements marks of poverty, last outpost on the line; but for 'the Northmen' of the Moray Firth and beyond, Aberdeen is the first southern metropolis, comfortable and cunning. From landward it is staid enough, cathedral, college and neat-faced shopping city to the bothy-ballad countryside; but the sea has always given it a rough underface. Today at the waterfront, the old grimy steam trawlers, 'Smokey Joes', have given way to the brightly prosperous yellow and grey North Sea oil supply boats; and at the airport 'the rig crews roam in and around the bar drinking like human blotting paper while their helicopters crouch outside waiting their next cursing load,' their wives left behind to suffer the 'intermittent husband syndrome' which the deep-sea fishermen's families once knew so well. Aberdeen has entered a new era in which the fish market will no longer be its economic hub.[1] But it has a past too telling to be wisely forgotten.

Late nineteenth-century Aberdeen was a company boom town too. Its trawling industry was a new creation, based on the market, transport, capital and labour resources which a city could provide.[2] Aberdeen in 1880, with a population of over 100,000, was the northernmost first-class railhead in Britain, and the nearest major city to the fishing grounds of the northern North Sea. But up to this point, although its harbour was used by visiting boats, the city itself had only a handful of local inshore sailboats worked by men from Footdee and Torry, two hamlets facing each other across the mouth of the harbour and the River Dee to the sea. The first Aberdeen steam trawlers, introduced in 1882–3 by local merchants and most notably the fish salesman and curer Thomas Walker, provoked the Footdee line-fishermen to bitter protest, calling on the city provost to ban the innovation.

Perhaps partly in response to Footdee's hostility, the chief trawlermen's quarter developed in Torry. The original small cluster of cottages here was soon linked to the city by a new road bridge across the Dee and by streets of tall stone tenements climbing steeply up the hillside from the river bank. Huddling along the river's edge and under the railway viaduct arches into the city followed a series of small fish-filleting and smoke-houses, providing work for women from the incoming families. Aberdeen had a hundred trawlers by 1900, 218 by 1913. After the war the trawl fleet went on growing, more slowly, to reach 255 in 1938. And besides the trawlers, attracted by the new facilities which they stimulated, Aberdeen grew as a line-fishing port too, both for traditional sailboats, and for a more specialised great-line fishing which developed from steam boats in the North Sea and also Arctic waters. Aberdeen had a fleet of 68 steam liners in 1903, and by the 1920s, with the addition of seasonal drifter-liners from Peterhead, of over 120; but it then shrank rapidly, so that only 26 regulars were still at work in 1938. The small inshore sailboats rose and fell more quickly, peaking to over 130 in the 1890s, and falling steadily to less than 20 in the 1930s; but by this time there was also a fleet of 30 small motor boats making a living in the shadow of the trawlers. Altogether the workforce directly engaged in the city's fishing industry was 9,000 in 1905 and 12,000 in 1930 – and of the city's entire population a quarter must have been dependent on fishing.

It was the trawling boom which made Aberdeen in the thirty years from 1881 the fastest growing city in Scotland. The local shipbuilding industry, inconveniently far from either coal or iron, had been moribund. But it at once seized the chance of revival. Altogether 267 trawlers were to be built in the port in the twenty years from 1883, at first chiefly commissioned locally, but by the 1920s also for French, Belgian and South African trawler-owners. Similarly, the need for fish boxes and barrels stimulated an import trade in Scandinavian timber. Ice was also originally imported from Norway, but by 1891 three local ice factories had been set up. Yet other enterprises grew to supply the steamboats with coal.

And at the heart of the whole development was a radical new system for handling the fish landed.

In the past fishermen had either worked by arrangement for particular curers, or sold their fish direct to fishmongers, or sent their families to hawk it around the city. But as soon as regular trawling was established, daily auction sales were introduced, which offered both a quicker sale and more competitive prices. And the fish salesmen, who were paid a percentage commission, benefited most directly of all from the rapidly increasing landings. They became a key interest group in the city, partly because they remained relatively few. In 1900, while the number of Aberdeen fish-curers had risen to more than a hundred, there were only fifteen firms of sales-men.

The first outcome of their influence was the construction of a municipally owned fish market in 1889. Later extended round all three sides of the Albert Quay, it provided a third of a mile of direct loading off the boats and onto the railway wagons. It was the largest fish market in Britain and probably the best: as the chairman of the new White Fish Commission put it after a tour of the ports in 1938, 'Aberdeen Market is, in my opinion, the best constructed and cleanest port market in the United Kingdom, in contrast with Grimsby, a great port of which the market consists of wooden pontoons which absorb the slime of fish and can never be kept really clean.' He was equally impressed that the fish landed was 'of very high quality'. In the early stages of the trawler boom, fish-curers dealing in smoked haddock and cod for local consumption had provided the basis of the market. But with less steaming time in returning from the fishing grounds than Hull or Grimsby, notably quick clean handling facilities, and a daily fish train to London from the 1880s, Aberdeen soon became known as the prime port for fresh high-quality white fish throughout Britain: and in the inter-war years, as motor lorries began to overtake the fish trains, it also established its dominance in long-distance fish trucking.

Nevertheless a reputation for quality also brought inhibitions. Aberdeen still had the highest percentage of fish caught by line of any major port in 1938. More seriously, its fleet was too influenced by the better prices fetched by high-quality fish to risk the steaming time needed to reach the prolific Arctic grounds which made Hull's fortunes. Aberdeen trawlers had already been looking for fresh grounds outside the North Sea by the early 1890s. The Fishery Board reported the 'new venture' of trawling off the Faroes in 1892, and by 1894 'frequent visits' to the Western Isles, Shetland, Faroe and Iceland. But despite the prospecting of the White Sea in 1908, and the 'fresh spirit of enterprise' shown by boats going to Greenland and to the Barents Sea – a round voyage of 3,700 miles – in 1928–9, the basic pattern changed very little. The average number of days spent at sea had even fallen to less than five by 1928; and in 1932 over 80 per cent of the catch was from the North Sea and west coast, 10 per cent from Faroe, 4 per cent from Iceland and a mere 3 per cent from further waters.

Although the argument for near-water fishing had originally been economic, by this stage it scarcely seemed convincing. As early as 1907–9 Aberdeen trawling went through a bad patch, with up to 40 boats laid up in the summer months, and two companies bankrupt. Between the wars there were many considerably worse years. In 1922, for example, it was reported that scarcely any boat-owners covered their expenses, 'most lost heavily', and 86 trawlers were laid up for the summer. The accounts of Richard Irvin and Sons, originally a Tyneside firm but Aberdeen's second largest firm of owners between the wars, show that from 1930 until 1939 their trawlers made a loss in nine out of ten years. Yet while local trawlers were laid up, Aberdeen's fish-filleters and curers were complaining that they needed more cheap fish. The gap was therefore met by landings from German and other foreign boats, which supplied as much as half the local market by 1930. Why were the local owners missing this opportunity? It is hardly surprising that the leaders of Aberdeen's fish industry faced increasing criticism. The *Fishing News* was already in 1926 attacking their lack of 'enterprise' and failure to keep an 'up-to-date' fleet. By 1934 a whole series of articles was run under the title, 'Whither Aberdeen? Other Ports are Forging Ahead'. A year later a correspondent declared: 'Aberdeen is still engaged trying to make a living on the standards attained in the years of the early 1900s. Just thirty years behind the times and really proud of it.'

It was an exaggeration, of course. Nevertheless, one reason why the local trawlers were being kept to the safer nearer waters was undoubtedly failure to maintain a modern fleet. By the mid-1930s four-fifths of the local boats were over twenty years old. Some innovations had certainly been introduced. By 1938 all had echo-sounders, and half had radios and direction-finders as well. But this could not obscure the fact that for lack of new boats, the whole fleet was on the edge of obsolescence. And sometimes even small steps forward met with remarkable resistance. The Fishery Board officers complained that they had been pressing the owners to supply boxes to the boats, so that fish could be boxed at sea and arrive in fresher condition. 'They have previously been recommended to adopt this method but they are very slow to accept any improvement.' Only after 1933 when a fleet of Swedish seiners began landing in Aberdeen and taking the best prices did the local owners, after first trying to push them out by organising a boycott of ice supplies, reluctantly follow their example. Meanwhile the curers had been equally reluctant to install any labour-saving machinery or refrigeration, and still used wooden troughs and tables instead of porcelain or stainless steel. 'Fish merchants will walk if they cannot go top speed.' Even at the fish market itself the White Fish Commission's visitors found that commercial attitudes did not match the excellence of the facilities, for prices were kept artificially low by local rings: 'it is pretty obvious if you just watch the sales and see the fish knocked down to one man and half a dozen men putting their checks on the boxes.'[3] If the trawl boom had been launched in a spirit of competitiveness and innovation, the Aberdeen fish trade had by now become a notorious example of entrepreneurial self-protection, lethargy and inaction.

How had this change come about? Part of the explanation lies in the structure of ownership in the port and the changing character of the owners. Most of the first generation had started from a relatively small basis and many must have shared the Protestant devotion to hard work and thrift which was typical of provincial Victorian small businessmen. There must have been exceptional energy in a man like Robert Brown, born in the 1850s in Fife, sent to sea as an apprentice, who set himself up as a curer, had two trawlers by 1890 and became director-manager of the key Bon-Accord Ice Company; or in his contemporary Richard Irvin, fish salesman from North Shields, who created one of Aberdeen's largest fishing enterprises, leaving a fortune of a quarter of a million, known into old age as an 'ardent Presbyterian'. Examples of a similar spirit can certainly be found among the smaller boat-owners – some of them skipper-owners – of a later generation. There was John Leiper, for example, a sail fisherman who had moved in from Cove, and by the 1920s was working two trawlers of his own. A teetotaller, and sixty years a Sunday School superintendent at Torry United Free Church, he 'could go into the pulpit and take a service better than a Minister. He studied the Bible at sea, when you're on the watch.' He is best remembered for his trawler the *Shalome*, with its Old Testament name and Bible-reading deckhands.

Leadership of the industry had, however, by this date passed to a different class of owner: to men of wealth like Sir Andrew Lewis or Sir John Irvin, whose knighthoods indicated their membership of the national business élite, with its less rigorous, if broader social and moral values. Irvin, for example, held in many respects to his father's values. He was an elder of his local kirk where the boys' club was 'a work close to his heart', founder and president of the Aberdeen Steam Fishermen's Provident Society which provided sick pay and widows' pensions – through subscriptions from the men: 'a great Christian gentleman'. But there was a great gulf between him and the men on whom his wealth depended. He never went out trawling himself. His heart was rather in the pursuits of another social world: in golf and billiards, 'his home, and hand-made furniture, and his garden.' He was 'an abstemious man, but when he did entertain he was generous with the wine.' With his handsome three-floored granite house, his chauffeur and coach house, Irvin 'was a big shot: he had a big house in Queen's Road, that was the élite people there, the purple belt – it was all the leaders of Aberdeen, oh yes.'[4]

In fact the structure of trawler ownership in Aberdeen was far from simple. Quite a few boats were shared between a group of owners. There was also a very small number of skipper-owners – five have been identified for 1913. But most boats were owned by landsmen, at first as individuals, but soon many as companies, so that by 1910 there were 163 company-owned boats – half the local fleet. After this the proportion remained stable. Many companies were very small, with perhaps just two boats. And as a whole, small owners survived to a remarkable extent. Thus in 1939 still only 28 per cent of Aberdeen's fleet was owned by firms with ten or more boats, little more than the 24 per cent of 1910. While Aberdeen had lost the advantage of individual commitment found in a skipper-owned fleet, it had not gained the fully decisive power through concentration of capital resources which could be brought by company ownership.

On the contrary, it appeared to have become entangled in a highly confusing web of interests. The original owners had been principally fish salesmen. Very often they continued to earn more through selling as agents to a large number of boats, in some of which they took shares, than as direct boat-owners. With company ownership the source of capital shifted from the fishing industry to the local middle classes as a whole. Not only had the great majority of shareholders no connection with fishing, but as an examination of new companies of the 1900s has shown, even half of the powerful group of directors holding seats on more than one company board had no prior fishing interest. Trawler ownership was thus spread through the general business community, rather than forming a distinct group. But at the same time it became tied through interlocking directorships to ancillary interests in fish-curing, ship-building, and above all, with ice and coal supplies. By the end of the First World War the Board of Trade companies register shows that Aberdeen trawling companies were almost invariably 'at least partially controlled by men whose profits might come not so much from trawling itself as from the activities associated with trawling.' The larger the trawling company, the more extensive its spread of interests was likely to be. For example, Andrew Walker of Walker Steam Trawl Fishing Company, fish salesmen and trawler-owners operating a fleet of twenty to thirty boats, was reported at his death in 1926 to have also been 'actively concerned in the firm's subsidiaries, North Eastern Ice Company, the paint firm Isaac Spencer and Company, and the United Kingdom Tug and

Trawler Insurance and Indemnity Association Ltd'. At the same time Richard Irvin and Sons, in addition to a fleet of over thirty boats and extensive interests in the herring industry, had two subsidiary companies, Ships Stores and Repairing Company, and Clyne Mitchell and Company, and smaller investments in fourteen other fish processing, coal, ice, salt, shipbuilding, engineering, motor and welding enterprises. It was therefore quite possible for profits to be made through subsidiaries, even when the trawlers themselves were kept working at a loss. Irvins, for example, while making a loss from their trawlers, were nevertheless able to show a profit from their fish selling in each of the five years 1935–9.

It was this interlocking structure of ownership, in which the primary interests of the trawlers became confused with those of subsidiaries, which according to the *Third Statistical Account* militated against a progressive policy: 'It is difficult to find any other explanation for the inaction of the thirties.' And certainly this was the common view of the fishermen themselves, bitter against the exorbitant prices charged by inefficient supply firms, expressed in the proverbial comment: 'It all comes out of the cod end.' 'Everybody was after the trawlermen! From the grocer to the trawler-owner hisself! Every little thing they used to try and pare off them. . . .'[5] Aberdeen trawling, in short, if born of the thrust of individual capitalists, was now languishing in a net of mutually protective gentlemen.

Meanwhile, as if a mirror image, the character of the trawling workforce had changed in precisely the opposite direction. The men who worked the trawlers became separated from those who owned their boats by a rapidly widening social gulf – indeed, a sharper case of social polarisation would be hard to imagine. There must at the start have been a good deal in common between the owners and the first trawlermen, who were chiefly drawn from the small boat-owning, religious-minded families of the nearby inshore villages. The trawling workforce grew very fast, building up to 600 by the early 1890s, 1,000 by 1900, 2,000 in 1910 and over 3,000 in 1930. There was no basis to provide for such rapid growth in the city's existing fishing hamlets of Footdee and Torry. The first source for labour was therefore the sailboat fishermen of the neighbouring creeks to the north and south. Aberdeen could offer them better prices if they kept at work in their own boats, and regular wages on the trawlers if they decided to give them up. Sucked in by the city, one by one the fishing stations for thirty miles in each direction collapsed – some gradually family by family, others, like Oldcastle twenty miles to the north, from mass migrations. By the depression years of the 1920s, the trawl port's pull was felt still further round the coast in the Moray Firth, substantial numbers of 'herring scalers' – as the Aberdonians dubbed them – moving in from Buckie, Cullen and elsewhere to seek a better living.

Certainly many were forced into these moves – 'it was poverty drove them out'; but there was often ambition in them too. The trawlers initially offered an improvement in working conditions. They were still fishing quite close to the city, but in safer, larger, more convenient boats than the inshore yawls. Steam power, the *Fishing News* suggested in 1913, should be regarded as one of the 'humanising agents' influencing North Sea fishing: 'it minimises the precariousness of the life, and shortens the periods of absence from home.' The steamboats also offered good wages. The 1913 agreement between owners and men gave the deckhands 5/– a day at sea and a bonus of just over 1 per cent on the ship's net earnings; engineers a higher daily rate of up to 8/4d without a bonus; and skipper and mate no daily wages, but around 10 per cent and 8 per cent each of the ship's takings after wages and running expenses had been deducted. In a good year a trawler deckhand was therefore earning as well as a lower paid artisan, such as a skilled building worker.

A top skipper could do very much better than this. Figures are hard to come by for this period, but certainly during the exceptionally prosperous First World War years which followed there were tales of skippers presenting their wives with diamonds and furs, pianos and motor cars, while during the shortlived post-war boom English trawl skippers were reported to be taking home £10,000 a year. Even if such winnings were an outside chance, the lure of the trawlers for an ambitious fisherman is hardly surprising. In quite a few skippers the hunt for the jackpot could induce a spirit of sheer recklessness, in daring to set to sea in the worse possible weather, or in poaching in illegal inshore waters under the guns of the Fishery Board's patrol boat. When fired on, as one skipper put it in 1921, 'you will run like blazes until overtaken, one feels the old war time glow, one realises that life is worth living.'

It is also clear that skippers were quicker to respond to changing economic opportunities. Fleetwood had three times as many skippers as boats for them in 1936, when for want of ordinary deckhands ships' husbands were forced to 'scour the public-houses, clubs and town in search of crews'. Similarly Aberdeen was able to recruit trawl skippers from a much wider area than its deckhands. Some of the earliest skippers came from East Anglia. Torry, 'well up into the thirties, was a proper English colony', and there was 'still frequent interchange' of skippers and mates with the English ports of Shields, Grimsby and Hull.[6] Equally important, there seems little doubt that in their personal and family lives a much larger proportion of skippers than ordinary trawlermen were able to assert individual attitudes which set them apart from the common standards of the city.

There was much less to draw the ordinary trawlerman – or to hold him, once he had lost hope of becoming a skipper himself. Many of the migrants from the fishing villages must have passed quite quickly into other kinds of city work. Because of the relative scarcity of deckhands, the firemen and two engineers on the trawlers – who made a third of a total crew which was then only nine including the skipper – were almost invariably brought in from the general population of the city and surrounding countryside. Even so the trawlers suffered from recurrent shortages of labour. In 1899 the Orient Steam Fishing Company was finding difficulties, because of the full employment brought by the Boer War, in picking up surplus labour even in the congested crofting districts of the west coast. In 1913–14 boats were held up in port through scarcity of hands, and there were complaints that 'wasters' were being attracted into Aberdeen trawling to make up the crews. In 1918–19 when labour supply was again short, there were suggestions from the Fishery Board that school education, and a more attractive share system, might be used to attract more young men into trawling. Because of the drastic unemployment of the years which followed, no action was in fact necessary until the economic recovery of the 1930s. There were moves in 1936 to establish a training school for young trawlermen. But the industry's difficulties have not been solved. After the Second World War the trawler-owners turned to demobilised Polish soldiers as a stop-gap remedy, and a vocational training scheme was set up. Subsequently, pressed by union strike action, a joint registration scheme was introduced in 1957 to raise the level of the workforce. But these concessions came much too late. Crewing remained 'an acute problem' up to the last years of profitable trawling. During the 1969 wage strike Robert Muir, spokesman for the owners, described the fleet as 'too large for available man-power': its size would have to be cut. And even in the late 1970s, with an active fleet down to less than eighty boats, the trawler training schemes could not be supplied from the city's own fishing community, but had to be filled up with boys recruited from declining industrial cities such as Glasgow and Dundee.

The increasing difficulty experienced by the owners in maintaining even a shrinking workforce springs from several causes. The first was the course of wages. Between the wars the daily pay of deckhands reached its peak in 1919–21 at 11/6d a day, with engineers earning up to 18/– a day. It was then re-duced to 9/6d and 14/– respectively, and except for a further temporary reduction from 1932 until 1935, remained at the same level until the Second World War. Deckhands continued to receive a small bonus on the boat's earnings and also the traditional perquisite of stockerbait. In 1921, when they were also still receiving a war bonus in risk money, and a good conduct bonus, it was estimated that they were making an average of £4 15s weekly, but by 1929 this had fallen to £3 10s. This was in itself a reasonable wage for the period, but it meant that in real terms trawlermen's incomes had dropped slightly in comparison with the general increase in working-class earnings since 1913. The relative positions of skippers – the men most committed to the industry, whose sons were norm-ally its most likely recruits – had by contrast fallen back quite decisively. In 1929, a relatively good year, they were estimated to be earning around £7 10s a week, and in 1932, a poor one, no more than £5. And such averages conceal many worse trips. John Fitzpatrick's father had been drawn to Aberdeen from Scarborough by the prospect of a better living as a company trawl-boat skipper; but he remembers as a child in the 1920s,

> seein' my father goin' awa' 14, 13, aye, 15 days doon to Faroe in the wintertime, he'd come in and I'd hear him say to my mother, 'There'll be nae pay this week, this trip.'
> 'Nae pay, nae again', she used to say.
> And I seen my father gan oot sayin' to my mother, 'You'd better gie us a pound anywa' to pay ma grub', and mother had to gae'im a pound to pay, for his grub – and he'd 'ave bin away about 17, 18 days and na'er a penny left.[7]

This was a pitiful reward by comparison with the glittering inducements of 1910–20. And on top of this, skippers found themselves in an increasingly vulnerable position at the hands of company managements which, with poorer returns, were now seeking to lay up unprofitable boats. Earlier, the trawl-owners had helped to single out skippers from the crews, separating them at sea in their own cabins, giving them a different basis of payment, and higher incomes, which allowed them to set up their own organisations and social life ashore. 'We've got a union of our own, a guild, which is the upper class,' remarked one skipper. And, 'taking it all over, it wasn't a practice for the skipper drinking with his crew', a trawlerman reflected, 'You'll find the skippers are quite on their own.' On their own, they were easier to manipulate, to set against each other – and against their crews. The companies worked together to keep skippers in place:

> A skipper in Aberdeen could not leave a boat regardless, he wasn't makin' anything, and he'd like a shift . . . If he did leave, he didn't get a job anywhere else. . . . If he left, he had to 'walk about' – he didn't get a job . . . until eventually they'd say, 'Ah well, he's walked around long enough now, we'll give him another one'.

Skippers were expected to take the full blast of managerial resentment:

> They'd take you into the manager's private room and you'd get a telling off, and if you deserved it you got it, believe me. . . . You went down you got a roasting, you know – what we called 'the sweating room'.

If a skipper had too much of his own point of view, he risked finding himself blacklisted:

> He just picked up a phone and said, 'All right, don't employ him as a skipper'. That was it – as easy as that. They wouldn't accept you as a skipper. The word was passed around.

And above all, there was the constant pressure to squeeze more and more effort from skippers and crews to scrape takings from the falling markets, pitching every boat against all the others:

> You're great friends ashore, but, unless you're really great pals, you never pass information. If you're on fish you make clear of your pal in a roundabout way, you don't broadcast it until you get your share and you're away home – then you'll let him know. The competition's really fierce and there's an awfu' pressure on skippers . . .

Against the boats at the back of the race there was the constant threat that,

> they'd sack the skipper. The competition was fierce. They were quite right, because an owner canna have a ship at sea that doesn't make a profit. He puts his ship into the sea to make a profit.

Some might accept the logic of such an economic system, but it left other trawl skippers perplexed, embittered in their isolation. Some saw the secret of success as '90 per cent good luck'.

Others cultivated an authoritarian ruthlessness, taking out their anxieties on their crews:

> if you'd been a skipper you have to be like Joe Stalin, that was my idea, trust nobody but yourself.[8]

This tension, deliberately heightened by company policy, further worsened work conditions which were in any case deteriorating. The boats themselves were ageing, and they were rarely maintained with the care which the inshore skipper-owners gave to their own boats. Trawlers were at best washed in harbour, rather than scrubbed. By the 1930s, with the rising standards of sanitation and ventilation in new boats elsewhere, Aberdeen deckhands were complaining that the local fleet was obsolescent, 'primitive, and fifty years behind the times' – 'just scrap heaps'. Immediately after the Second World War the *Third Statistical Account* described the boats as generally over-crowded, smelly, cramped and ill-equipped and often kept 'in a disgraceful condition', rat-infested and insanitary.[9] And although those steam trawlers have now been scrapped, it is still a shock to see the oil-driven trawlers which have succeeded them, moored in an ill-kempt row along the Albert Quay. Their paintwork even freshly renewed is at best a sloppy patchwork slapped on without care; and for the most part they look more like a set of dented, rusting sea-going dustbins.

At the same time, while the original trawlers had fished quite close to Aberdeen, now they were out working in more exposed waters, and some were facing the bitter cold of the far north. Trawlermen still had to work on the open deck, jolting and bucking with the sea, no more than a low rail protecting them, and machinery and winches unguarded; but they were now working quite often in darkness, sometimes on an ice-covered deck. The original gains in safety brought by steam trawling were as a result sharply reduced. The death rate remained at a very high level, and there was a still heavier toll in accidents and chronic illness. Even among trawlermen fit enough to remain at work, the White Fish Commission reported 'much sickness among the crews, stomach and rheumatic troubles being especially common'. Men injured at work had to wait several days before any medical attention was available. It was not even possible, after working in freezing wet conditions, to dry out properly. George Glasgow showed me his hands, with three fingers missing:

> My hands all went. . . . When we was at sea you used to get an awful lot of broken wires aboard the ship and they went into your hand. . . . We used to go down to the engine room and put our hand in hot water and with a razor blade we used to open them up ourselves – . . . infected. Long spells on the deck got in and hauling the trawls, you see, the hands just – if you went down to Iceland in the cold weather, it didn't need to be Iceland . . . with the wind off the land. . . .
>
> I went up to the doctor, 'Well', he says, 'We'll have to see about this', and it was two they took off the first time . . . And then the other went like it . . . Aye, a doctor told me since I was up here, 'It's like this Glasgow', he says to me, 'your bones is done'.

The work was not just dangerous, but for exceptionally long hours – which, by comparison with any other occupation, seemed less and less justifiable. The sixty- or seventy-hour week of Victorian industrial workers' had fallen to fifty hours or less. But on the trawlers, although deckhands could rest on the way to the fishing grounds, once there they would have little sleep. A union report of 1931 stated that on some boats the crews worked thirty hours without a break. This was perhaps exceptional, but there is little doubt that many skippers and crews were exhausted by the pace of work, and this was one reason for the surprisingly numerous accidents to trawlers on their way to or from the fishing, running aground off the Buchan coast, or even at Aberdeen's harbour entrance.

The problem of exhaustion was closely linked to that of drink aboard. The Aberdeen trawler *Ulster* was wrecked in January 1925, with the loss of five lives; the mate had fallen asleep at the wheel. The evening before sailing he had spent with the crew in the Grampian bar. When he took over from the skipper he 'had a good drink in, and he thought it best to give the vessel plenty of sea-room'. The cook, with whom he had been quarrelling in the bar earlier, 'could not say that the mate was teetotal, but he was quite normal' before sailing. Certainly it was 'quite normal' for crews to set sail half drunk. Some men ashore would regularly start the day with 'your first drink in the morning, that's "your morning" you know, a glass of whisky and a bottle of beer'; and if a boat was preparing to sail in the afternoon,

> the crew aboard like you see, they get there and they say, 'All right then, we sail at five o'clock' – 'Five o'clock?!' and, 'The pubs don't open yet! Not so likely! We're having a drink first' – well that finished up at eleven o'clock ye see.

While on the Moray Firth boats a drunken fisherman would probably be left behind, a responsible Aberdeen trawl skipper had to take a different attitude:

> I'll be in charge of them and I'll look after them. . . . If there was four or five of them coming down drunk, you see, when I was skipper I'd say – . . . 'I'm not going just now, we'll go later when you're all sober again.' But if only one man came down drunk I'd say, 'Come on, get on board, get away to your bed'. And I would be in charge.

Once at sea, drinking aboard was unheard of among most of the inshore and herring drifter crews. But with the trawlermen it was a normal practice. On further-water boats, duty-free drink – the 'bond' – was a perquisite added to wages. Some skippers issued rounds of whisky to encourage the men at work on the Arctic grounds, but others allowed the 'bond' to be opened on the way north and consumed in a mass drinking spree. 'You get a right skipper to dish it oot, he dish it oot right, but of course there's some that overdid it.' The crew could add beer and whisky of their own. William Mitchell, who started as a trawler engineer in 1918, remembers how trips would start with,

> a sing-song aboard the boat, everybody did, had a good bucket in. You see if they came aboard with drink you didn't say anything to 'em. I always came aboard with

whisky. . . . They were a jolly crowd. . . . The men just
sit down and get drunk and the skipper can't do anything
with them. . . . It's their money, it's their drink and
they've got to get on with it.

On at least one occasion he was lucky not to be wrecked like
the *Ulster*. He was steaming the *Ocean Princess*, under a skipper
originally from Cairnbulg, up the north-east coast,

gang along t'the fishing grounds. So, 'Fancy that', I says,
'This boat's only going round in circles.' So even his
second was drunk. And fireman. 'Ah', I says, 'I don't care
for that'. I got up – gave her a good – fired the boiler and
gave her about half an hour. I warned the bridge, said
'That's nae guid is't?' for a good bit, and let them – 'Stop
her'. It didn't stop them. Well I – . . . (I'm) up a ta'in the
boat . . . till they all came to themselves.

He was in charge of the boat until the following morning. 'I
was only one that was sober. Oh yes, I got the proper skipper's
treatment. That was the finish. But it was happy days then.'[10]

The blur of alcohol was a protective device for the trawlermen. It was encouraged by the trawler-owners through the
supply of the 'bond', by the acceptance of drink by English
skippers who brought their own work conventions north, and
by the general prevalence of heavy drinking in the city of
Aberdeen. To teetotal religious fishermen from herring ports
like Buckie, no wonder work on the trawlers came as a shock.
But it is equally striking how few of the migrants who stayed
on were able to maintain their earlier attitudes. We found that
among Aberdeen deckhands and engineers nine out of ten
were drinkers, and among skippers six out of seven. And
while the normal effects of drinking were no doubt congenial
enough, it could also bring into the open some of the acute
tension inevitable among a cooped-up over-worked group of
men. When the *Ann Melville* was about to sail in January 1926,
for example, the cook arrived drunk, announcing that he was
not 'going to sea (and) didn't care a damn for the owner, the
skipper or the police'. He punched the skipper, shouted – 'If I
had a knife, I would put it in your heart' – and made for the

cutlery drawer; and was only foiled by the mate and the skipper's brother who at that moment seized him to protect the skipper. In another incident in September 1927 the skipper of the *Ben Barvas* was attacked by a trawlhand, who arrived with a friend, both drunk, and asked the skipper to engage his friend as a deckhand. 'On being refused his request, he struck the ship's master . . . kicked him . . . knocking him down . . . and pushed his fingers into his eyes.'

It does not take many strokes to make a picture. On our own first visit to Aberdeen to talk to trawlermen, we immediately met a retired skipper whose own son had been murdered aboard a trawler two years earlier as skipper by one of his crew. A few hours later, at breakfast in the Fishermen's Mission, a group of younger trawlhands at the next table were talking of a shipmate whose funeral they had attended the previous afternoon: his body had been dredged from the dock a fortnight after falling into the water at night on his way aboard, dead drunk.

Originally the Aberdeen trawlhand had cut an attractive, if slightly flashy, figure, as a strong young man with money jingling in his pocket. According to a booklet of around 1900:

> He affects the wearing of a 'bowler' hat, jauntily perched on his head, and the heels of his boots are higher than those of the footgear of the ordinary 'landlubber'. He is partial to a good cigar, and usually sports a heavy finger ring.
>
> There are few mysogynists in this particular walk of life, and the inamorata of the trawlermen presents a brave show with her sealskins and gaudily coloured hat.

But in the more recent past, as the Aberdeen *Evening Express* has put it, 'their image has been a fairly poor one. Reports of rowdiness, drunkenness, irresponsible behaviour have clouded their reputations.' In fact brutality on the Hull and Grimsby trawlers, especially towards apprentices before the First World War, was more savage and frequent than any violence reported on Aberdeen boats. Nevertheless, it required only the occasional reporting of such shocking incidents to create a highly unfavourable local picture; and according to the *Third Statistical Account*, 'local newspapers contain frequent reports of trawl-hands refusing to sail, deserting, getting drunk, stealing from vessels, and committing other actionable offences.' A young Torry trawlerman in the 1930s on the look-out for a girl to court would hardly boast his job when he walked the monkey parade on Union Street, knowing that people thought of fishermen as 'a heap of rubbish'; nor was he likely to want his own son to follow an occupation he himself thought was 'nae fit for a dog'. The compulsion of tradition – strongly reinforced by the lack of other local opportunities – could still win recruits; but they went as men chosen for condemnation by fate. A trawler mate from Foot-dee, for example, swore that none of his children would ever go fishing: 'he wouldn't take a dog to sea'. But in 1935, when he died, he had hardly been a week in the grave when his son took the old man's seaboots and gear, and joined a boat. He did it for the wages – 'for the siller' – almost as a betrayal: 'he did it for himself'.[11]

It is little wonder that the trawl-owners found increasing difficulty in securing men for such a demanding yet derided occupation. Yet it was essentially the system which they themselves had created which lay at the root of their difficulties. And they continued to pursue policies which damaged the trawlermen's reputation still further, by branding them as law-breakers: as thieves at work, and as deserters.

On the inshore boats and the herring drifters, because payment is directly based on a share of the boats' nett earnings, theft of gear or of catch is effectively unknown. But the trawlhands' bonus was too small to give them a similar commitment to the venture, so that they were tempted to seek shares in other forms. It seems unlikely that thefts from boats could have matched those from the docks and city factories. Successful prosecutions were not common. Nevertheless the trawl-owners gave maximum publicity to their fears that their crews were gangs of thieves. In October 1924, and again in February 1927, formal notices were issued to crews by the Aberdeen Steam Fishing Vessel Owners' Association, declaring that 'members of crews of vessels going south for coal have been selling gear, old rope, firebars, etc., from the ships to dealers in the towns', and warning that they would 'prosecute the delinquents with the utmost rigour of the law'. In March

1927 the Association told the Fishery Board that it was 'having numerous complaints of heavy gear bills more especially from owners of boats operating in Faroe waters'. With an ageing fleet, heavy gear bills were to be expected in the North Atlantic, especially in winter. But the owners had 'a strong suspicion that gear is being sold from local boats to Faroe fishermen or others'. Despite their contacts with the Faroese police, it remained an unsubstantiated suspicion. Nevertheless, it helped the owners to shift the blame for the industry's economic problems on to their men.

A similar effect was achieved by branding the crews as fish thieves. It was a traditional practice in the fishing ports for men to take home fresh fish for their families at the end of a trip, and some fish was also always given to the boys from poor families who asked for it at the quay, and would then hawk the fish round the town. The Aberdeen owners disapproved of such charity, and tried to stamp it out. In 1922 they were pressing the city council to introduce special bye-laws to suppress the giving away of 'illegitimate "fries"' at the fish market. The crews were regarded as having a right to haddocks for 'fries', and the skippers and mates could give away more fish. They would do this especially when prices were very low: occasionally a skipper-owner would even empty his fish boxes on the floor, and invite bystanders to help themselves. But generally 'those outside the crew who received "fries" were friends of the skipper. They were usually unemployed fishermen . . . (who) come down for a "fry" so that they may give their children a decent meal once a day.' The number of these gifts appears to have been trivial – on average a mere four per boat. But the owners continued to campaign loudly against the abuse, prosecuting trawlermen when they could, and asserting that 'hundreds of fish are stolen from the Fish Market every year'. Perhaps so; but it seems unlikely that fishermen were the main culprits. 'They was all lifting', commented a market porter. 'Some of that fish whispered off! Colossal!' It was certainly noticed how reluctant the merchants were to prosecute.[12] And they too, as we have seen, had their own illegal devices for lining their pockets through operating rings at the auctions. But the trawl-owners took no effective steps against this. The trawlermen were an easier target.

The conversion of traditional charity into a crime was part
of a basic conflict of values between owners and men, the
supplanting of an older communal generosity by the harsher
ethics of capitalism. This conflict was also waged on a still
more elementary level: the trawlerman's right to a home and
family life. It was as a consequence of his struggle for this right
that he became categorised as a criminal deserter.

It is hard to imagine an occupation less conducive to ordinary
family life than trawling. Trawlhands spent most of their days
in a rough male world, entirely separated from women and
children, dependent for their primary consolation on drink;
and at the end of each trip they were cast ashore for a few hours
in their homes, if not intoxicated, certainly utterly exhausted.
It is no wonder that their tempers were often short, and
violence broke out ashore as well as on the boats. There were
again gruesome reports to be read in the local press. In August
1914, for example, a young trawlerman, originally from
Grimsby, was in court for ' sensational affair'. His sweetheart
had decided to break with him after two years because of his
'drunken habits'. Utterly jealous – 'he would not allow her
to look at or speak to other men without making a row' – he
stabbed her. Two other cases in June and September 1920
involved married trawlermen. The first 'was in the habit of
drinking, and lay in bed all day. Some of the neighbours give
the wife money to keep body and soul together'. He beat her
systematically: 'when a row began', he would lock the house
doors, so there could be no witnesses. The second husband
was sent to prison for assaulting his wife and son while drunk.
Claiming that his wife had attacked him with a poker, he
knocked them both down, kicking his boy on the floor,
shouting 'Die there'. He had nine previous convictions for
assault and ten for breaches of the peace. It seems all too likely
that such reported incidents represented only the visible edge
of widespread domestic violence. The life story interviews
bear this out. As we have seen, nearly all the men were
drinkers. Of those informants brought up in Aberdeen rather
than migrating in later, four out of eleven had fathers portrayed as very heavy drinkers, violent to their wives or
children, keeping them under thumb with threatened or ex-

ecuted 'punchings'. If a boy disobeyed such a father, 'You were murdered.' And if not in such an extreme form, the physical punishment of children was normal in almost every family. An angry trawlerman could hit hard. One man believed his mother had 'died of a broken heart'; while a daughter summed up another father, 'He was bottled.' The best that a wife could hope of such a husband was that before going to the bar, he would bring in his earnings from the trip; and that when he eventually reached home drunk, it would simply be to sleep it off. Any considered concern with the care of his children, or the family budget, let alone help with the household tasks, would be out of the question: 'They down tools then.'

There can be no doubt that the whole work system served to reinforce the belief that the home ought to be the wife's sole burden and responsibility. It was in recognition of this that by the Second World War most firms had introduced a weekly allowance paid directly to fishermen's wives in advance of settlement at the end of each trip. And conversely, the struggle against such influences at work can be sensed also in the minority of men who held, with an intensity itself significant, to markedly different standards in family life.

It is noticeable that some of these men had switched relatively late in life from line-fishing, with their wives and daughters helping in their work; and they were also more likely to be religious than was usual among Aberdeen fishermen. It was men of this kind who worked the twenty or so 'Sunday boats', back home each week for the Saturday evening 'Gospel hauling' service. But although some trawlermen, especially of the older generation, put in an occasional church appearance, most were indifferent to religion. Footdee and Torry had been affected by earlier revivals, and Torry had a strong congregation of Close Brethren in the 1900s. But it was led by prosperous small business families who saw the fishermen's quarter as a mission target, later despairingly abandoned. Trawlermen certainly believed in the supernatural: they were strongly superstitious right into the 1930s. But many looked on the churches with open hostility, as clubs of the well-to-do. 'They were always the biggest hypocrites, the religious men'; Aberdeen abounds with churches, but 'What do they do?' 'If there's a better world above, why are we working down here?'[13]

One man of particularly strong religious conviction, a trawler engineman and cook from a country background who was a Salvationist, was clearly regarded as exceptional for his attitude to home life. He would 'cook, bake, wash, anything you like.' Marriage to him was 'a partnership'. At weekends he and his wife were known as inseparable:

> If you saw me out, my wife was always with me and we was always arm in arm. It was just our style – always arm in arm, and always in step.

Eventually he decided to give up working at sea, because 'my wife was at home and stuck with a young family and . . . I'd be able to help.' Less drastically, an Episcopalian who had moved in from Stonehaven also maintained distinctive standards of his own. He was a trawler mate, with a sharp sense of his own dignity as a skilled man. He made his children eat separately, after the adults. But he clearly valued his hours at home. He too refused to cut into them by mixing socially with his shipmates ashore – or by punishing his children for misdeeds while he was away. And he liked to help in the house – 'when he was in from the sea he always made the tea, at tea time . . . He had so little time, that he was always with the family.'

His son, who became a skipper and also married in 1939, inherited similar attitudes: 'We'd just a short time ashore, am I going to go away to a club drinking with somebody else and leave my wife and family? No, we're a family, we were family people. I just couldna – never thought of doing it.' He took special pride in helping with his infant son. 'When I came home, I looked after that child – all night. If that child woke up . . . I was there to give him his bottle . . . Not the wife.' It is revealing of the basic situation that even such a man saw the basic responsibility for home and children as the wife's. 'She's got to bring up the children, pay all the bills, look after the house, while we're at sea, we canna do it.' But equally striking is how his ambition was focused on his home. 'You wanted to make money for your family, and to get a better life.' He had been brought up in a Torry tenement, but as a skipper he could move into the city suburbs. 'That was my incentive. To push on.'

Skippers had indeed a more realistic chance of maintaining a family life in this way. Some certainly were hard drinking men in the style of their crews. But among our seven life stories, only one was of this type. Of the rest at least four could claim, as one dubbed himself, to be 'a great family man'. Another not only cleaned the house while at home, but was also a keen cook. They were characteristically moderate drinkers, rather than teetotal. They were not normally actively religious, although more of them had a church connection than among the crews, and none was openly hostile towards religion. But it is a man of deep religious commitment who has left perhaps the strongest evidence of the concern which a fisherman could feel, against such odds, for his family life. Andrew Craig had been born south of Aberdeen in the inshore village of Portlethen and moved into Torry to work on the great-line steamboats. In 1910, just before he was thirty, he became a skipper and married. He belonged to the Open Brethren and he was a teetotaller. When ashore, he would spend his time visiting his family and kin; on Sundays attending church in his blue serge suit and bowler hat, and for tea afterwards to his mother's. But for the long periods when the great-line boats were away, he could only send postcards home to his wife and children. Dozens of these cards have been kept in a family album, recounting the weather and catches from Faroe, Shetland, Ireland, Fleetwood or Yarmouth; formal enough perhaps, except for the odd phrase which asks after the house, or an injury to one of them, or tells how he misses them. He writes to his son, 'I feel strange for want of your loud voice to break the monotony'; or again, ends another card, 'It seems a long time since I was at home may get a chance home soon Love to all at Home.'[14]

It was not the policy of the trawling companies to feel concern for such emotional needs. On the contrary, they saw their interest, when fishing was prosperous, as requiring the least possible hours in port, so that their boats could be working as continuously as possible. The result was a head-on clash between owners and men, fought out in a struggle which reached its climax immediately after the First World War.

One of the direct consequences of the rise of a wage-earning labour force in trawling, in Scotland as in England, was the introduction of trade unionism into the fishing industry. The Scottish north-east as a whole was never a strongly unionised region, nor have the fishermen ever played a leading part in Aberdeen's city labour movement. The first labour councillors were elected in 1884, and there were lively socialist branches active in the 1890s. By the mid-1920s over a quarter of the local workforce was unionised, most notably in shipbuilding and engineering.

Among the trawlermen the first sign of organisation was in 1891, when they formed a small branch of the Humber-based National Federation of Fishermen. According to the union's journal *The Fisherman* it was beset with problems: employers who wanted to 'flood the place with men' in order to bring down wages, disappointed fishermen 'lured here by false promises', Tynesiders who stuck to their own paddle-steamers' union, and other '*Rotten Hearted* fellows (who) left our ranks and actually say they do not care how their fellow workers are paid so long as they themselves are paid well.' Within a few more months it had petered out.

The first permanent union in the industry was therefore the Aberdeen Steam Vessels Enginemen and Firemen's Union formed by the trawl engineers in 1899. Within a few months it had a membership of 200, and it proved stable. In 1904 its secretary became Joseph Duncan. Duncan was very soon using it as a base for a much wider policy. By 1912, when he also became first secretary of the Scottish Farm Servants Union – and so began to organise the rural hinterland from which so many of the trawler engineers were recruited – his office on the quayside had become a recognised centre to which the coopers, dockers and also local building workers turned for help in reconstructing their unions.

At this point the local fishing industry was hit by the great wave of national labour unrest which preceded the outbreak of the First World War. The first to come out were the women fishworkers, who struck for a wage increase on 14 April 1913. The dispute began in two firms, from which a hundred women formed a procession, marching through the streets 'shouting and gesticulating, and singing "Rule Britannia"'. They secured the support of Duncan, who within three days had successfully negotiated them an increase. It seems likely that some of these women had also joined the Scottish Fish-worker's Friendly Society, formed in 1912 and registered in February 1913, primarily for the herring girls of the other north-east ports, but with its 'central office' under Bella Jobson in Aberdeen. Within a year it had reached the remark-able figure of four thousand members.

By the autumn the trawlermen had successfully followed their womenfolk's example, again aided by Duncan. A threat of a strike, backed by his union, proved sufficient for him to negotiate a wage increase in November for both engineers and deckhands. This was not the first time that the trawlhands had acted with success collectively, for they had threatened to strike in 1903, and won after their case was referred to arbitration. But to move from such occasional action to a permanent trade union organisation proved much more dif-ficult. It was estimated that only 5 per cent of the deckhands belonged to any union in September 1913. The position was further complicated by the development of rival attempts to organise the trawlhands by Captain Tupper of the National Union of Seamen, who came up to Aberdeen in July 1914 with characteristic 'bluster, bombast and braggadocio'. While his statements cannot be taken literally, the local men must have found some new attraction in 'firebrands of the Captain Tupper type' for him to be able to claim a local membership of nearly 2,000 trawlermen a fortnight later. Nor did this end the complexities. In 1910–11 an Aberdeen branch of the Hull Trawl Fishermen's Protective Society was representing skip-pers prosecuted for illegal trawling off the Shetlands. And in June 1914 the skippers formed their own trade union and benefit society, the Aberdeen Fishermen's Society, to be absorbed by the NSFU in 1916. It had a hall and a co-operative trading department, and it was initially backed by 300 skippers.[15]

In contrast to trade union organisation nationally which grew with four years of full employment, the war weakened all the fishing unions; and in the years which followed, they were still undermined by inter-union rivalries. The trawler enginemen's union continued, renamed after 1922 the Sea Fishers Union. The coopers were absorbed by the Workers' Union but broken by defeat in a four-month strike in 1922. Militancy among the fishworkers evaporated after August 1919, when a hundred women came out on strike for a wage guarantee but were persuaded to return by officials of the Workers' Union Fishworkers Branch, of which nothing further is heard. The skippers were reported to still be mostly with Tupper's NSFU, until May 1921, when they formed their own Skippers and Second Hands Guild – the key organisation in the industrial disputes of 1922–3. It then seems to have disintegrated, and a new Skippers and Mates Association was only formed in 1937.

The position with the deckhands was still more confusing. Tupper was probably behind the trawlermen's protests against foreign crews in Aberdeen in May 1919. Later in the year, however, the new rival NUBF set up its own Aberdeen branch, despite heated objections from Tupper's supporters, with their national leader Captain Bingham acting as its secretary. The trawler-owners seized this moment to send both unions reeling with the September 1919 lockout – of which more in a moment; and although they survived, neither could establish a clear hold. By January 1921, when they had between them less than half of the workforce, the owners easily immobilised them and imposed a 10 per cent wage-cut by negotiating with them separately. Bingham used the dismay in the wake of this failure to form a new Aberdeen Trawl Fishermen's Union in May 1921, but this never established itself, and with the secession of the skippers and mates both unions faded. In 1923 and again in 1932 the trawlhands' case had to be put through the Sea Fishers Union, which explicitly opened its ranks to cooks and deckhands in 1924. But the trawlermen did not strike again on a wage issue for twenty years after September 1919, and their next action, the successful strike of January 1940, was unofficial. In the meantime there was little they could do to protect themselves, even faced with what looked like an unjust settling sheet. There might be an argument that 'the wages were nae right, or a complaint about the grub bills . . . but then, what could you do? If ye'd any complaints then, well – you was told to "roll'em up, roll them up in the gear on yer bed" and that was it . . . you was finished.'

Part of the difficulty in organising trawlermen in trade unions was due to their dispersal at work over widely distanced fishing grounds. 'The only time, in fact, when concerted action can be taken is the first week in January, since most skippers try to make port for the New Year celebrations.' Another obstacle was less tangible, but perhaps more fundamental. The trawlermen who fought out the industrial struggles of 1919–23 were probably still mostly first-generation wage-earners, whose fathers had worked their own boats. They had not shared the historical experience which had deeply implanted class consciousness on the Victorian industrial working classes. The trawlermen were the first of their families to face the full impact of industrial capitalism. They were driven to fight by the remorselessness of the new system by which they found themselves captured, and willing to use the weapons of the strike and the trade union which it had generated, but they did so more in the defence of older inherited values than in the cause of new ones. They fought with an essential ambivalence, which bears moving echoes of the death struggle of the Pennine handloom weavers against the textile factory.

The clearest evidence of this ambivalence is the strike of 1923. It was undoubtedly the most bitter battle of these years. But it was not between masters and men. Nor was it over wages. So paradoxical was the situation that even after a series of violent clashes between strikers and the police, the leading owners were prepared to say that 'the men had behaved as gentlemen throughout the strike', while the government felt itself powerless to intervene because this was 'not an ordinary industrial dispute'.[16]

The issue at stake was the right of German trawlers to land their fish in Aberdeen. Resentment against foreign landings had been for many years inflamed by the fact that in order to respect international freedom of the sea, the government did not prevent foreign trawlers from fishing in some inshore waters which had been closed to British trawlers. The foreign boats at work in the Moray Firth were a particular grievance.

In the early 1900s a fleet of thirty English-owned boats was fishing in the Firth, using Norwegian registration as a flag of convenience. In 1909 this practice was stopped by further legislation which prohibited foreign trawlers from landing fish caught in inshore waters. This restriction appeared to set a precedent. In terms of quantity the most important foreign landings came from the far northern waters where very few Aberdeen boats ventured, and local fish processing became partly dependent on this supply of cheaper fish. The First World War gave local boats a temporary monopoly – and also fuelled their dislike of foreigners – but before long the outsiders began to seek their place in the market again. Clearly only two effective responses were open to the trawl-owners. A nationally-organised boycott of foreign landings in all the fishing ports might have been sufficient to force legal restriction by the government. Alternatively, the Aberdeen owners could have used their capital resources to provide the kind of new boats needed to compete effectively in the further waters.

Instead they played a puzzling, even devious, game. They were hoping for subsidies from the government, both for equipment and running expenses. They also wanted to cut costs by keeping wages as low as possible. Both purposes were served by using the trawlermen as their foot-soldiers. While the owners issued dignified protests and appeals to the government, the men could be incited to bring about a crisis. If the trawlermen won, the owners could profit from better prices, while if they were defeated, they would be too weak to demand wage increases.

The setting of the trap can be seen early in 1922. As German landings in Aberdeen began to increase, the owners called conferences against fish 'dumping by foreigners' and issued protest statements. The *Fishing News* ran lead articles with headings such as 'Ourselves First: British Markets for British Fish', and commented, with suggestive surprise, that although considerable crowds of fisherman watched the German landings, 'no hostility was shown to the crews' and 'no attempt was made to prevent the catch being landed'. The Skippers Guild was, however, already backing the call for a local ban on German landings, and before long threatening more drastic action. In January 1923 matters came to a head when 'with the sympathy of the local trawlowners' they decided to strike. At first it seemed that this had enabled the Trawler Owners Association to force the fish salesmen to accept a ban, but any agreement crumbled when Peterhead publicly welcomed the German trawlers as 'an open port'. The trawlermen stopped work on 24 February; pickets were organised, and one by one as the boats returned, the entire fleet was laid up.

The men argued during the initial negotiations that the best solution would be to equip a fleet of forty Aberdeen boats for Icelandic fishing, so that dependence on German supplies would be removed. But the owners do not seem to have responded to this. Tension was meanwhile mounting. Skipper Nutters, the only local man still sailing, had to be escorted home through a booing crowd of 2,000 on 12 March, and the next day the police had to prevent the crowds from dumping his fish in the dock. 'Attention was next directed to the Iceland sales, where Lord Provost Meff (Meff Brothers, fish salesmen) was busy disposing of the catches of a few German boats. Considerable horseplay followed, a few boxes of fish were seized and tipped into the dock, and Mr Meff booed and jeered at.' When Meff reappeared the following day, a ring of police protected him from a crowd of 1,500 strikers, 'and amid the jeers and shouts of the mob, the fish were disposed of'. Later on there was 'an angry demonstration' outside Meff Brothers, and a German flag was hoisted on to a car radiator. Dislike of Meff was clearly especially intense, because he headed a city council which was attempting to conciliate in the strike, and at the same time took an unequivocal stand for one side in the dispute. He was said to have even gone round the city lodging houses threatening unemployed men that their doles would be stopped if they did not go as fish-porters to unload the German boats. And pressure may well have been needed to get men to work as porters, when they had to be given police protection, and in some instances were even stealing past the pickets disguised 'by wearing the best of their clothes, bringing their wives along, and, in a few cases, pushing perambulators'. As skipper George Clarke protested to the Fishery Board, 'Now Sir we are taking this very hard. To think we should beat these brutes and now to see them come and laugh at us and take our living away. . . . The men are getting very angry . . . ashamed of the Country they fought for. And all this strife and poverty just to oblige a few fortune hunters.'[17]

By this stage the argument had shifted. The men no longer had any hope of economic betterment: as Sir John Irvin put it to a great benefit concert held at the Music Hall at the end of April, they would be content in 'obtaining a bare livelihood'. They were now fighting with their backs to their wall for a threatened way of life, against both enemies without and traitors within; a battle in which local and national patriotism had become thoroughly confused. At the same meeting there was 'extraordinary enthusiasm' as another owner uttered the battle-cry – 'Aberdeen must be quit by the Germans'. It was in this cause that the struggle moved towards violence culminating in late March and early April. The first serious incident was on 27 March when crowds at the quay boarded a German ship, 'took possession' and smashed the wheelhouse windows and broke the stearing gear. Three days later the local blackleg trawler *Fly* was boarded 'in the darkness of the night' by 'a party of men, armed with crowbars'. They 'wrought extensive damage' to the winches and engine pumps, smashed the compass to pieces, wrecked the other wheelhouse fittings, and emptied the boilers of water, though leaving the fires burning, so that the entire boat was nearly blown up. Eventually in the first week of April there were 'wild scenes' in the fish market itself. On 2 April 3,000 fishermen made a mass entry, threw off the mooring ropes of four German boats, and pelted their crews with fish and ice until they had steamed to a safe distance. When one boat tried to land at another quay, they followed it, but were blocked off by the police, who caught the crowd in a semi-circle and then charged them. Meanwhile crowds of up to 500 were blocking the bridges into Torry, and surrounding fish-porters returning home from work. After two had been knocked down by trawl skippers, the police decided to intervene here too and disperse them with baton charges. They were met with 'a shower of stones, pieces of coal, and several bottles', supported by more missiles thrown from over-looking windows; and many others 'ran into the lobbies of the dwelling-houses in order to escape the advancing police, and after the officers had passed, they came out and stoned them from the rear.' But perhaps the scene which most cogently expressed the strength of local feeling was on 3 April. The police were now guarding the market in the aftermath of their savage baton charge of the previous day. Both Torry and Footdee rose as communities. As the strikers marched the streets 'their ranks were swamped by recruits in answer to calls of "Up Fittie" and "Down with the Huns".' Men and women came out with sacks, old fishing creels and baskets, filling them with stones, gathering pebbles from the beach, and assembling at the twin piers on opposing sides of the harbour entrance. The channel here was only a hundred yards wide, and they took their stand to keep the Germans at bay. Before the police eventually arrived to disperse them, five boats chose to run the gauntlet of the crowds, and 'the sound of breaking glass and the smashing of woodwork showed the damage that had been done'.[18]

The strike finally ended in mid-May when the trawler-owners decided to accept a limited quota of foreign landings. But almost half the skippers were by now unwilling to accept any compromise, and although they went back to work, they refused to sign the agreement. The fish merchants were then able to discard it as invalid. The strike had essentially become non-negotiable for the fishermen through its rapid trans-formation from an economic issue into a struggle for the community of interest of fishermen – including owners and employers – against the outside world, and against the para-sitic merchants who both acted for them and betrayed them. And if it had any tangible outcome, it was to complete the effective destruction of trade unionism as a power in the port for two decades.

That destruction had begun with the defeat of 1919 on another issue which was again primarily a matter of values rather than economics. Capitalist steam fishing operated in a way which was, as we have seen, highly destructive of family life, and only a small minority of trawlermen were probably able to withstand its impact. It was no accident that in Yar-mouth, Hull and Grimsby the trawling workforce was built up to a large extent from bound apprentices who had frequent-ly been workhouse orphans, and thus had no family life to lose. Even so the great majority of them never served out their time, despite the fact that those who absconded were regularly imprisoned. In England deckhands who had signed on and then refused to sail could be similarly disciplined. The use of this whip made trawling the only ordinary civil occupation in Britain in which being late for work was an imprisonable crime. In Scotland, however, the 1854 Merchant Shipping Act did not apply. Nor was there any such coercive discipline traditional in the fishing industry, on which the new trawl-owners might have drawn to cow their workforce and win public support. For a considerable period they had to be content to hold their employees with the wages they could offer. At the end of each trip, usually less than a week, it was open to the men to rejoin or leave the ship as they wished: it was customary 'simply for the skipper to ask his men if they wished as individuals, to sail with him for the succeeding one'. Consequently it was quite possible for a man to choose to take more time ashore at home at the expense of his own pay. For the owners this meant either a constant changing of crews, or a less quick turn-round of ships than they wished.

They first tried to deal with the problem by making the payment of back wages dependent on punctuality in 1904, but this move failed. They then turned towards breaking, and branding, their workforce along English lines. In 1914 the *Fishing News* was publishing correspondence on 'Disobedience in Aberdeen'. There was an urgent need to 'put a stop to the wholesale delaying of trawlers by members of the crew'. Laws were needed as 'in all other large trawler ports where a man stops a ship he is punished by fine or imprisonment. That is the reason why so many wasters come to Aberdeen.'

The matter was delayed by the war. It came to a head in the autumn of 1919. The industry was at this point booming and the trawl-owners conceded an increase in wages at the end of August. But the men were demanding in addition a full 24 hours clear after landing had ceased and they were allowed home at the end of a trip. The owners claimed that they were suffering too much from 'the malingering ashore of members of crews' who decided independently to stay at home. The difficulty was chiefly caused, according to a union official, 'by the boys who have been serving'. This appears quite probable from the tone of the protest meetings which the men were holding in support of their claim: 'We are entitled to more after what we have been doing in the trenches and mine-sweeping. These slavery days are past.' But the heart of the matter was spoken by a trawler cook: 'The fishermen's principal griev-ance . . . was that they had no home life . . . practically no time to spend with his wife and children.'[19]

The trawl-owners decided to force the issue when it became clear that the men's organisation was threatened by the emerg-ence of inter-union bickering. At the beginning of September they suddenly declared a lock-out and laid up each boat as it returned. The *Fishing News* conceded that the men had a reasonable case for more time at home, and as the dispute went on report that 'public sympathy is undoubtedly growing on behalf of the men'. But the employers, while prepared to advance very slightly the financial settlement they were offer-ing to the skippers and the engineers, remained determined not to concede the trawlermen's principal claim for a clear day between trips. Nor could the men's disunited unions force their point. When after eleven weeks a settlement with the owners was reached, all they could achieve was the concession that on the very small proportion of trips which exceeded ten days, the men could have one day ashore without pay. The extent of the defeat is underlined not merely by the subsequent collapse of the men's unions, but also by the ease with which the owners were able to abolish even this small concession. In March 1922 the unions waived the 'lie-day' without a protest.

The masters had also paved the way for the change they really wanted. There was again no protest from the unions or the men when legislation was introduced to extend judicial coercion to Scotland. Indeed the *Fishing News* claimed when the Merchant Shipping (Scottish Fishing Boats) Bill was under discussion in July 1920 that 'trawler owners and the better classes of trawl fishermen are now anxious that the bill should become law.' It provided not only for the punishment of 'deserters' by the magistrates, but also signing on by the fishermen, who had to give notice before leaving employ-ment. It seems probably that at least Captain Bingham – who had worked with a similar system in Grimsby – believed that signing on might provide a better basis for trade unionisation, but he proved mistaken. When the Act came into operation in the autumn of 1920 it simply presented the employers with a hammer with which to finally crush the independence and self-respect of their workforce. With the slogan, 'Hitting the Sluggards', the *Fishing News* anticipated the end of 'the "deserter" nuisance'. In the spring of 1921, while the employers were bargaining the 'lie-day' against a drastic wage-cut, the first fishermen were being arrested and convicted. And the pace quickened. In January 1922 nine men were convicted in a single session. The prosecutor thought their behaviour a 'remarkable circumstance, in these times of unemployment. . . . The men had decent and remunerative work. . . . It was difficult to understand how they thought so little of their work, even from their own point of view and selfish interests.' No doubt difficult indeed, for one who could spend every night in his own home. But as subsequent cases were to show, Scottish trawlermen had not merely lost the right to spend an evening with their wives and children, or with friends, but they could be fined or imprisoned for accepting an invitation to a marriage, being ill, attending the death of a brother, or arranging the funeral of a brother's wife. Yet the *Fishing News* continued to believe strongly in the merits of the law. When a Hull magistrate complained in 1935 that to be obliged to sentence for not joining ship, which he could not himself regard as a criminal offence, was an 'unhappy' branch of his work, he was roundly attacked by the paper: 'malingerers are not to be allowed to penalise the vessel.' The *Fishing News* found much more sympathy for the Fleetwood magistrate who asked, 'Should defaulting fishermen be flogged?' It disagreed, because this was 'hardly likely to heighten the esteem of fishermen'. But it would be a definite improvement if the magistrates would give stiffer penalties. 'Let the magistrates put into force the powers they already possess.' They should send more trawlermen to prison.

It was a degrading law, through which the owners set their own seal on the demoralisation of the trawling workforce; a fitting symbol of their labour policies. 'The trawling industry's really finished,' one of their successors told us.[20] But it should not be forgotten how it was finished. Neither the new sea limits, nor North Sea oil, explain why the trawl-owners have failed to compete in the new conditions which face them today. For the root of their problem is a long-standing one: their inability to hold an adequate workforce. And the cause of it lies in how they worked the trawlers: in a form of exploitation which took in skilled family fishermen, made them into paid labourers, assaulted their moral values, drove them towards drink. What place is there in the harsh system which they imposed, for fostering the co-operative adaptability – let alone imaginativeness – which is needed to succeed in fishing now? The industry they created is indeed almost finished: and one can but gasp at the ruthless logic of a steam capitalism which had such power to suck men into its system, transform their work from a way of life into a form of bondage, break their family lives, degrade entire communities – and, ultimately, bring about its own destruction.

Part III The economy and the family

9 The penetration of capital and the family boat

Fifty, perhaps even thirty, years ago the future of British fishing seemed to lie with the great trawl ports. The decimated inshore communities could have been dismissed as anachronisms whose days were numbered. It had not happened that way. It could well be argued that today, those which survive anticipate one future choice of direction for the developed economies of the world. But why have some survived to flourish, while so many have perished? What explains their economic vitality? The answer could be relevant to the future not just of fishing, but of our own social economy as a whole. To seek it we must look more closely at the complex mutual interactions between family, the moral order and the economy. Let us begin with economic power: with the control of working capital.

The survival of family boats and share ownership, of co-venturing and petty enterprise, even in a technologically sophisticated, high-investment industry, looks at first sight like a 'survival' in a rather obscure occupation which has somehow escaped the full rigours of capitalist rationalisation. But in fact it certainly cannot be simply due to the late penetration of capital into fishing. Since the middle ages the North Sea herring fishery and the deep sea ventures to Iceland and Newfoundland had depended on merchant capital to build and fit out ships and to market catch. In fact up until the second half of the nineteenth century all the larger fishing vessels were worked for merchant-entrepreneurs ashore. This was true both of the more substantial East Anglian sailing drifters before the herring boom decades, and of the growing fleets of North sea trawling smacks.

In this sense the introduction of capitalist steam trawling built upon a long-standing tradition of shore-ownership for deep-sea fishing vessels. But in two other ways steam trawling did mark a sharp break. Firstly, the steam trawlers brought such a steep rise in cost that they were clearly far beyond the financial reach of even the most successful inshore skipper. A Yorkshire family coble in the 1880s could be bought and equipped for under £30. To build and fit out a steam trawler cost around £3,000; and by 1914 it had more than doubled. This escalation in costs immediately gave overwhelming advantages to shore-owners with capital, and in itself would suffice to account for the dominance of company-owned boats in the new steam trawl fleets. But secondly, because a new workforce had to be created for trawling, the shore-owners replaced the old share system of paying crews with a regular wage. The regularity of the catches and cash takings of the early steam trawlers moreover made it easy to offer good wages compared with earnings from a share in a sailing smack – and at the same time assure a handsome profit to the company from each trip. But through this change the old ladder which gave a real chance to the most successful fishermen of eventually becoming owners themselves was effectively knocked down. Even though skippers were kept on the share system, and some elements of it later reintroduced into the crew's wages, its function had become symbolic. The gap between the companies and the fishermen was widening too fast – and the companies kept all the key cards in their own hands.

Steam trawling thus developed a system of economic and social relationships which was close to the patterns of ownership and control in British industry more generally. In most ports there were from the start one or two companies with substantial fleets, linked up with other firms active in fish sales, marine engineering, boat-building, and coal and ice supply. There was also room for large numbers of small companies both in boat-owning and in shore enterprise. Gradually, however, the interpenetration between spheres of activity and also between the different ports increased. Since 1945 this process has rapidly accelerated with the development of great international companies in the food industry. The result has been a swift concentration through the takeover of local companies, which is not always obvious because many of them continue to be worked under their old names. By 1966 it was estimated that three firms controlled 44 per cent of the entire trawling fleet. The smallest of them was Boston Deep Fisheries, with thirteen fishing companies as well as subsidiary interests in food distribution and marine engineering. The others were two giants: Associated Fisheries and the Ross Group. The first controlled seven trawling companies and their subsidiaries, three cold storage firms, three catering firms, and ten other various food and engineering concerns; the second owned twelve trawling companies and a whole series of other enterprises in food processing and distribution, road transport, broiler raising, catering, cold storage, and oil refining. And in December 1965 only a reference to the Monopolies Commission foiled a £15 million takeover bid by Ross for Associated Fisheries.[1]

Given national economic trends, such tendencies are hardly unexpected. What does require special explanation is the degree to which the remaining sections of the fishing industry have held off similar developments of concentrated capitalist boat-ownership, despite an increasingly active interest of the giant food firms in their spheres too. Nor should this phenomenon be seen as the mere holding at bay of a fate to which they must one day succumb. The past shows many times in the last hundred years when similar gloomy prophecies were made and seemed equally credible. The family boat and share-ownership are part of a system which the inshore communities have had to recreate generation after generation in changing economic circumstances. And at no time in the past has it been more pervasive or stronger than it is today.

It was certainly much less widespread in the original full-time fishing settlements as they evolved in the eighteenth century. In north-east Scotland the landowners in many cases built the people boats along with their homes, taking a half share of the fishermen's catch in return. Nor did the crofter-fishermen of the outer islands at this stage own the boats which they worked. Landlord or merchant-owned boats, worked on a half-share system, were still usual in Shetland until after the 1880s, and in Lewis until well into the twentieth century. The family boat, in short, is a relatively modern 'tradition'. It is in fact a consequence of the rising market economy rather than an older system maintained in the face of it. The reason for this is clear enough. To construct seaworthy fishing vessels requires specialised skills and particular materials, such as suitable timber. A roughly weatherproof house can be thrown up almost anywhere from the materials in the ground itself by the collective effort of a group of men: but the same is not true of a sea fishing boat. In the outer islands there was no local timber available for boat construction; and even where materials were cheaper, boat-building craftsmen had to be involved. Boats therefore demanded cash outlay. For the earliest fishing communities, winning a living at the poverty line, that meant they were a luxury beyond their means.

In both East Anglia and the Scottish north-east it was the nineteenth-century herring boom which led to the firm establishment of boat ownership by the fishermen. It appears that the relatively larger East Anglian drifters went over to the share system in the 1860s. But the north-east Scots herring fishermen had already secured ownership of their boats and gear by the 1820s. Instead of working for landlords, they engaged themselves seasonally to curers, fishing for prearranged prices, provided certain quantities were reached. Settlement was at the end of each season. Meanwhile the curer might advance money to the fishermen to equip their boats. After an unsuccessful season a fisherman would be in debt to the curer, and after a run of bad seasons could lose his boat to him. But while this happened in individual cases, the rising prosperity of the industry meant that it was not the general pattern.

The position of the curers, the key figures in this early stage of fishermen ownership, helps to explain the lack of any tendency towards concentration of drifter ownership. It was extremely easy to set up as a curer. In Scotland there were probably some 400 curing firms by the 1830s down the whole east coast, clustering in the main landing centres. Over the years some concentration occurred, but not much. In Fraserburgh, for example, there were sixty curers in 1830 and still over forty in 1880. Although three larger, longstanding firms took a quarter of local production, half was by small new firms. Indeed a typical firm lasted less than five years. A curer needed little fixed capital: a cooperage, barrel and salt store, a 'farlin' (trough) and an open space – which could be hired – for the gutters to work; and sufficient work for just one full-time cooper making barrels through the year, and a dozen fishgirls and labourers for the season. Apart from an initial bounty paid on engagement, settlements with the fishermen were not made until the cash from sales early in the season was already in hand. It was a risky business, but because it required only small resources to start, 'there developed a strong social tradition in the fishing towns of people of varying background and occupation engaging in curing as a speculation'. Their most common origin was from among working coopers.

The biggest resources in the industry were required by the merchants who bought the cured herring from the curers. They had to make their profit from buying their stock cheaply during the fishing season, and reselling over a period of up to a year. No doubt the merchants made the biggest takings from the industry, and had they chosen to participate more directly in its running their impact would have been very powerful. They were one source of capital for curers, who would receive loans on condition they sold their product at previously agreed prices. But the merchants did not push further than this for two reasons. Firstly, as outsiders, and by the mid-century mostly Germans, they would have found it difficult to exercise control over local businesses and boats. Secondly, while they needed a sufficient catch, it would not have helped them to have become directly involved in maximising production, as this simply brought down prices. The curers always feared a glut; while as speculative brokers, the merchants could be sure of their profit. Thus through encouraging small-scale local enterprise, they cushioned themselves against the setbacks in the industry. In bad years there would be bankruptcies among the curers, lost boats and thin faces among the fishermen, but – out of sight – the merchants were safe enough.

In the 1870s to early 1880s the herring industry did indeed enter a phase of crisis, which hit both curers and fishermen. The development of the fishery, especially once the shoals began to move offshore, demanded increasing investment by the curers. They now had to set up curing yards in remote landing stations and bring up migrant labour to work them. For the fishermen, to pursue the herring fishery offshore now required a larger and more expensive boat; and there were also the new cotton nets to buy. Hence they needed more advances from the curers. But these very efforts brought more and more catch on to the market, with the result that prices collapsed. In a falling market, the Scottish curers found it impossible to continue with engagements at fixed prices; and despite the fishermen's protests, they broke with customary engagement and replaced it with an open market system.

This crisis was resolved through a restructuring around a new financial system. In the first place, additional capital resources were tapped. Up to this point, after the earlier phase of settlement, local landowners had only contributed to development through harbour construction. But from the 1870s the local banks, most notably the North of Scotland Bank, also began to back the industry actively, at first through advances to the curers, and later through direct loans to the fishermen, thus bringing to the fishing the indirect support of the accumulated wealth of the region. It could have implied radical change in the industry, but the banks, perhaps because their policy was to win custom through general goodwill in the community, made little attempt to impose their own standards of business efficiency. Few curers kept adequate accounts and many even left it to the banks to sell for them. The bankers were 'very free in their policy' and 'seem to have exercised little care about the business quality of the borrowers'.

For fishermen, borrowing was never so easy. With the rising cost of boats, they could only hope to maintain ownership 'at the cost of prodigious efforts of personal saving'. But at just this moment they gained both in independence and ability to save from two directions. The first was a change within the communities, which was probably accelerated by the economic distress – the spread of the temperance movement with its ethic of thrift. Money which once would have been spent on the bottle was now put aside for new gear. Without this new self-discipline, it is difficult to imagine how the fishermen could have achieved their astonishing level of saving and capital investment in the steam-drifter era to come.

The second change followed from the end of the engagement system. Beginning in Peterhead in the late 1880s and reaching most areas within five years – Shetland by 1894 – the curers abandoned pre-fixed payments and public auctions were introduced in newly constructed fish markets. The new system meant the fishermen were worse off in bad seasons, but equally it gave them a much fuller share of the profits in a good year – and as it happened, a series of bumper seasons was to follow as the industry picked up again in the mid-1890s.

Disengagement left the fishermen without an easy source of loans, but the curers were succeeded in this role by the new fish salesmen. These potential new masters undoubtedly presented another threat to the fishermen's independence. Often drawn from the biggest curing enterprises, the salesmen were a much smaller group, very powerful in their localities: in Fraserburgh, for example, nearly half the summer catch was handled by three firms. But it was perhaps more important that the fishermen were now backed by men whose incomes depended on commissions, normally 5 per cent, on sales from the boats which they represented. Unlike the curers, they therefore had a direct interest in the success of the fishermen.

The renewed herring boom led on to the successful pioneering of the first steam drifters just before 1900. Here was another sudden jump in costs. A new sailing drifter could still be built for £600 in the 1900s, but a steam drifter cost over £2,000. Nor was it certain which way the salesmen or the major curing firms would react. Some were not averse to wage-earning boats in principle, and prepared to hedge their bets. James Mitchell and Sons of Fraserburgh and Lerwick had invested £674 in a trawling company in 1898 in order to spread their interests. There were many others eager to back steam-drifting companies once the first boats had proved successful. More 'capitalists' had announced plans to follow and 'several limited liability companies' had been formed to raise money, the Fishery Board for Scotland reported for 1899, while in Peterhead a Steam Herring Fishing Company had been established with plans to build its own fleet. For the fishermen it was now 'practically impossible to obtain the most improved means of capture without co-operation with capitalists', as the Board put it. Here indeed was a threat to the old order of family ownership.[2]

It survived partly because of the special character of the

herring industry. Richard Scase and Robert Goffee in a recent study of small business and self-employment in the modern economy have shown how it flourishes in trades demanding intensive labour input – ranging from old industries like printing or textiles and footwear, to new technologically innovative specialisms like electronics or plastics; and particularly those which serve markets whose needs fluctuate.[3] The herring fishery clearly fits this general pattern. It was a labour-intensive specialised trade with marked seasonal fluctuations in activity (although in this case it was nature which shaped the market). The sharply varying pace of work at sea between intense labour and idleness again favoured a system of self-motivated labour. And in contrast with the regular takings from trawling, the elusive migratory shoals brought highly varied, uncertain earnings, even for steam drifters. This made it dangerous for any company without a considerable number of boats to commit itself to regular wage-payments for crews over a season. Lastly, while trawling capitalism was built afresh, the capitalism of drifter-owners was operating within the existing framework of an international mercantile industry whose customs were now well established, and would be strongly defended by the herring fishermen themselves.

The fishermen, moreover, had their own bargaining advantage. Steam power certainly relieved them 'of much of the arduous labour inseparable from the navigation of sailing boats', as well as bringing them back quicker to market and home. But so long as a respectable living could still be made from sailboats, good crews would refuse to join the steam drifters unless fair terms were offered. Given the uncertainty of *any* boat's success in a particular season, to guaranteed high wages a steam drifter-owner would have had to risk making a substantial loss. Nor could local owners like salesmen and curers have imposed a radically new system like wage-payment without risking the goodwill which was essential to their existing businesses. It was not long since the 'enterprising capitalists' who started the trawling industry in the north-east had had 'to risk the fusillade of stones when passing too near the villages when landing fish' and suffer the indignity of 'their effigies being burned in various villages'. The first Scottish owners and crew thus made the key decision that, rather than introducing wages, they would adapt the old share system. Instead of splitting nett earnings after running costs, this sum was now divided in three: one third to the boat, one third to the owners of nets, and one third to labour. Apart from the cook, only the engineroom men were paid wages, generally from the boat's gross earnings. With some local variations, this was to remain the system throughout the life of the steam herring industry: an economic basis which gave the fishermen a chance of a full share in its profits. And as the astonishing steam-drifter-building campaign demonstrated, the drifter-men seized it.

Nevertheless, partly because of the widening divisions of economic fortune which steam drifting brought within the herring ports, considerable anxiety continued to be expressed. By 1911 the Scottish Fishery Board could confidently maintain that the drifters were still owned and – even on a mortgage – 'managed by the fishermen, and none of the other partners has a say in their control'. But many fishermen, nevertheless sensed themselves as coming more and more into the power of 'syndicates and capitalists'. And still more foreboding was the view of the north-eastern socialist and fishermen's union organiser Joseph Duncan:

> The grip of the capitalist is already firm on the industry and will tighten with time. The fishermen will follow the way of the landward worker into the position of propertyless wage workers. . . . Capitalism has no sentiment about villages and no attachment to any place. Its concern is with profits, and it is only a question of time before the centralisation is more complete and the depopulation of the herring fishing villages as mournful as that of the villages of the white fish.
>
> The fishermen are following in the wake of the weavers, the shoemakers. . . . The fishermen will know for the first time what it means to seek a master. . .[4]

What was the truth? Had the driftermen achieved the impossible, and won a steam fleet of their own? Or had such a massive investment transformed the power structure of the industry? How had the switch to steam been financed?

The European merchants who still had the largest capital resources in the herring business had withdrawn from any direct local investment by this time. The foreign export buyers had become shadowy figures: 'important-looking men with big gold watch-chains', 'diamond rings, cigars, plenty of – whoosh', glimpsed during the season at the north-east ports and Yarmouth. Capital was now provided through a combination between the local banks, fish salesmen and other 'landowners' who took a direct share in boats, and the resources which the fishing families could raise themselves. The bargain might take some unravelling. A Macduff fisherman, William Falconer, explained to the North Sea fishing inquiry:

> We raise a drifter in this way: – say there are three fishermen, which is the usual thing in Macduff, we can raise £600 either in cash or by bond on properties, the bank lends one-third, and your vessel costs £2,400; with the bank's third and our money that amounts to £1,400. Then we approach some capitalist, who is willing to take an equal share along with us, £600, and that makes £2,000. Then you approach a fish salesman, and he lends you, through the bank, £400, and you give him your business to do . . .

Thus the three fishermen start with under £200 each. To raise what they need, they give a half-share in their boat to the landsman, as well as probably mortgaging their homes, and starting off £1,200 in debt. In such a way men with very limited means could clearly begin. But at the same time they remained highly vulnerable.

Undoubtedly a key factor was the continuing support of the local banks, especially the North of Scotland Bank. Its general policy was to lend up to a third of a steamboat's cost, depending, as John Reiach its Fraserburgh agent put it, on 'first of all, the character and style of the men who ask for the advance.' Local reputation rather than wealth was also the essential qualification with other lenders. In Peterhead, for example, Robert Stephen secured his drifter with the aid of five landowners – coal merchant, blacksmith, baker, sailmaker and carpenter – and he had been 'dealing with everyone of these men except the carpenter since I was a boy'. In the same spirit, they were forbearing when individual fishermen ran into difficulties. Reiach's claim that he had 'never known of a bank insisting on a sale, but I have known of a capitalist insisting on a sale', was not contradicted. Opinion did differ over the advisability of involving the assistance of a landowner other than a fish salesman. While this certainly left the fishermen in full control of all their operations, the drawback was that another landowner would have less hesitation in selling out in bad times: 'he expects a good percentage for his money, and if he is getting nothing he likes a change.'[5]

With the fish salesmen the primary motive for investment was different. They made advances, or took a share in the boats, in order to secure their role as salesmen, and win goodwill for their ancillary activities as ship's suppliers: 'We are naturally looking for business coming from it.' Normally a salesman who provided loans for a boat acted as its agent and manager, not only selling its catch but keeping its accounts and paying its supply bills. Reiach maintained that discontented fishermen would easily dismiss their salesman 'and be readily taken up by others' because of local competition. But many fishermen clearly felt themselves under some pressure: 'bound', as the Fraserburgh fishermen's association secretary put it, to take all their supplies from the shore-owner, who sometimes even told them when and where to fish: 'They are not able to control the finances of their boats and they are tied.'

The realities of the situation were probably most clearly revealed in the policies of the leading salesmen. Over time the biggest firms, with the resources to operate at all the main herring stations to cover a drifter's operations through the season, steadily strengthened their hold by buying out local businesses. After the First World War their dominance was confirmed by the depressed state of the herring industry, which made it very difficult for new rivals to establish themselves. Fishermen could not be attracted to new firms by offers of fresh loans: their problem was mounting debt. After a good season, bills were settled at once, 'but if it has been a bad one they must wait.' Above all, the fisherman would try to protect his savings in the bank: 'Na, na, a'm no' gaun tae tak' my guid money oot o' the bank tae pay you; ye'll juist hae tae wait for it . . . .' Hence after a very bad season the first victims were the new local tradesmen and curers who had earlier provided the seedbed of competition: two Buckie curers, for example, who failed to survive the winter of 1923–4, Simon Flett and Joseph Mair, collapsed with debts of £8,000 and £12,000. A big firm could easily ride two or three times this loss in a year, and afford to hold on to stocks until the market recovered.

Their power and potential influence became still stronger after 1925 when the curers, exporters and continental merchants joined forces in the British Herring Trade Association. The Herring Combine was intended to stabilise the industry at a reduced level, through limiting catches and disposing of them at fixed prices. The only curers to resist were some in Shetland. With their resources 'practically exhausted', as the Fishery Board reported in 1926, the fishermen would have been hard put to resist an attempt by the big salesmen to take direct control of the industry. 'The entire community is at the moment living in an elaborate cycle of credit.' A later inquiry in the 1930s by the Sea Fish Commission reported that of 430 boats investigated, very few were clear of debt, 357 owed the salesmen alone an average of nearly £600 each, and many were 'also heavily indebted in other directions'. At this point, with only 28 firms of herring salesmen still operating in the whole of Scotland, and the three largest disposing of 40 per cent of the catch landed, it would have required little more push to reach for monopoly.[6] The salesmen desisted, because they did not believe this would serve their interests.

A striking confirmation of this is provided by the evolving policy of Richard Irvin and Sons. This firm was primarily interested in trawlers, which it operated out of Aberdeen on normal company lines. In 1910 it took over Provost Leask's business in Peterhead, and began acting as salesmen and agents for a fleet of 26 drifters in which he had minority shares. Two years later the directors were told that these share drifters had paid a better return on capital than the wage-earning trawler fleet over the previous five years. They were also advised to back a new coal business set up by a group of Peterhead fishermen: 'they were all what we term independent fishermen and we do the fish selling for the greater part of them so we must be careful not to offend them.' Subsequently Irvins took over other sales businesses in Fraserburgh and Buckie, went into curing, and in 1913 built their first drifter. In 1920 they bought a fleet of a dozen wholly owned drifters and for a while some of these were run alongside their share fleet. But these company-owned drifters failed to pay, and in 1931 the firm decided the remaining eight were 'to be worked in future under the Scottish system under which fishermen have an interest in their vessels'. Meanwhile, despite successive years of working at a loss – continuously, for example, between 1931 and 1934 – they showed scrupulous care in sustaining individual ownership in their share-boat fleet. The local reports to head office from the ports show a close watching of boats in difficulty, from disputes between owners or from mounting debts, but the local agent always looked for a solution which kept the boat working independently. Irvins were full owners of 6 out of their 61 drifter share boats in 1925; and by 1939, when the fleet had grown to 70, they still had full control of only 6.[7]

The big salesman's view was most vividly expressed, to the pre-war North Sea fishing inquiry, by William Meff. Already six years city treasurer in Aberdeen, he was head of Meff Brothers, as well as being also chairman of the Bon-Accord Ice Company, a director of the Aberdeen Coal Company, and involved in the Grimsby Coal, Salt and Tanning Company. His firm acted as agents for a hundred drifters, and they had helped in financing over seventy of these. He left no doubt as to who was master when a boat was in trouble. That very year he had taken over two boats. There had been 'one down in Cockenzie. I had to take the boat from a crew there'. The other had been more recent: a fisherman whom he had helped to joint ownership along with another fisherman of a steam drifter costing £2,600. 'I built a drifter for him.' Earlier in the season, 'the man was not doing as I should have liked, and I called him into Aberdeen and spoke to him several times, but could not convince him that he was doing so bad.' The fishermen might be legal owners; but when he chose, Meff called the tune. 'I called that man a fortnight ago, and I told him this could not go on, and I said to him, "I believe I can sell that ship for £2,000", and I made him and his partner sell.' As a result, all that they had saved had gone: 'they have lost the lot.'

Meff would use his power against an individual in whom he had lost confidence. But he had no intention of creating a drifter fleet under his own direct ownership. On the contrary, he believed that the earlier drifter experiments in the 1880s had been 'a complete failure' just because 'the men were not financially interested in them'. When steam drifters were worked by wage-paid crews 'it was nothing to have a fleet of nets ruined at one time.' Meff's policy was to expand his business by finding men whom he could set up as drifter-owners: 'I have always looked out for successful fishermen.'

The survival of boat-ownership among the fishermen thus rested as much on the will of the salesmen as on the niceties of legal ownership. Nevertheless the formal position is also revealing. According to the North Sea fishing inquiry, in 1911 only about one seventh of the fleet was wholly owned by landsmen. Most such boats were registered in Aberdeen and Peterhead, and in Peterhead only 40 per cent of the steam fishermen held even net shares, so that over half were propertyless hired hands. But in the other ports the great majority of owners were fishermen, and at least half the boats, although generally mortgaged, wholly owned by fishermen. In Buckie over 700 fishermen owned shares in steamboats and 1650 – almost all the local driftermen – held net shares. The shipping registers confirm this picture.

The evidence thus fully supports two fundamental points. Firstly, a group of individual fishermen, starting from re-sources scarcely equal to those of the average skilled industrial worker, had made themselves share-owners of steam enter-prise. Secondly, they had achieved this not only with the encouragement of other business interests in the industry, but equally through collective self-help, pooling their savings and working together as families. As George West, the Macduff fisherman, put it: 'It is like this throughout the Moray Firth, that one relative helps the other.'[8]

From the 1930s onwards the detailed story is less easy to follow, because comparable sources are not yet available. But in any case, if the fishermen were able to survive the depress-ion years, their subsequent success requires less explanation.

Since 1945 they have had the backing of the state loans available under the Inshore Fishing Industry Act. The support available has varied somewhat, particularly in the scale of the outright grant which has been attached to loans under the Act: at first 30 per cent of the cost of the boat, but later rising to over 50 per cent. A minimum down-payment of at least 15 per cent has always been necessary, but this could be raised either by selling off an existing boat, or through a loan from a local merchant or a bank loan guaranteed by a salesman. Since 1968 additional help in securing the initial deposit has been available through a scheme for fishermen living in their area sponsored by the Highlands and Islands Development Board, and this also extends to the purchase of second-hand boats. As a whole the policy undoubtedly represents a very substantial government backing to fisherman-ownership.

It is true that by comparison with policies in some other maritime countries it remains relatively modest. In Norway the State Fisheries Bank was set up as early as 1921 to make loans to the 'simple ordinary fisherman', although without sufficient funds to make a really significant impact until after 1948. Following this, under the 1956 Concession Law fishermen were effectively guaranteed control of boat-ownership, for all newly registered fishing boats, unless replacing an existing boat, had either to be owned by working fishermen (of at least three years' standing), their relatives, or companies controlled by fishermen. The Norwegian state has also secured its fishermen a dominance in the shore market, for the 1938 Raw Fish Act gave approved fishermen's sale organisations – in effect, their co-operatives – 'the sole right to the first-hand sale of all fish', with the result that by the mid-1960s these fishermen's organisations were handling 98 per cent of all landings in Norway. The Irish government has more recently introduced a similar scheme, and marketing is also handled by co-operative organisations in Newfoundland and in Japan, the foremost fishing nation on the Pacific. In Britain, the state has provided no such framework and fishermen's co-operatives have only a minimal place in the market. Here governments have continued to support local boat-ownership while ignoring the increasing penetration of fish marketing, processing and distribution by giant capitalist combines.

Yet even so, through a period of rising prices the British state grant and loan schemes have undoubtedly provided a sufficient financial foundation for the family enterprise of working fishermen. This is despite the fact that in the last twenty years most of the locally based salesmen's firms have been taken over by the big combines. The penetration of centralised capital has halted at that point: partly intentionally, partly because of setbacks when they tried to go further. One salesman managing boats for a firm now controlled by a big national explained how it had been 'a learning experience' for management when they first moved in. They had found it necessary to drop the remote employer–employee style of the trawling world and talk to skippers as equals, learning to use first names with them. Some branches of the old firm where the new managers failed to recognise the social attitudes of the inshore ports effectively collapsed – 'there'll be only a shell left . . . We're in a very delicate kind of business – we have to avoid offending our customers, or the skippers'll go somewhere else.' For the same reason, although the present firm uses its influence as far as it can, it cannot determine the pattern of boat-building and acquisition in its fleet. 'The initiative comes from the skippers. . . . They come to us for advice – and they reject it out of hand!' When a good skipper has a doubtful plan, 'We put every obstacle in his way as tactfully as possible'; but if he is sufficiently determined, rather than lose him 'it'll go through.' For today, the possession of capital is no longer the crucial deciding factor; while the salesmen and companies still remain dependent on the skill and adaptability of the best fishermen.

It may be that recession in the fishing industry will bring renewed threats to fishermen-ownership, and probably to the viability of many inshore communities as a whole. But for the past thirty years a more immediate danger has been the impact of prosperity. The steam drifter boom strained the unity of the fishing communities. The rise in profits since 1945 has been still more startling for the new generation of go-ahead fishermen. At the same time the social separateness of the fishing communities has been invaded by the forces of the mass media led by television. The wives of prosperous young fishermen can afford not to go out to work, and to furnish their sitting rooms with luxurious wall-to-wall pile carpets and giant black three-piece suites. But they still have to suffer the loneliness of their men being away at sea. Why not seek similar earnings for much shorter hours ashore? For the most successful fishermen, it would have seemed in principle possible to buy more new boats, and transform themselves into shore capitalists within the industry, so that the communities became increasingly split between owners and hands – with the latter having little to lose from turning to an ordinary wage-earning job.

It would be rash to suggest that there have been no tendencies at all in this direction. They are there. But it is still more remarkable how far they have been held in check. In a very thorough recent investigation of Burra Isle in Shetland – where commercial fishing goes back at least three centuries – R. F. Byron has concluded that, so far from a tendency towards the concentration of ownership in recent years, the trend has been in the reverse direction, so that 'the total number of shares dispersed through the community has been increased steadily.' Nobody holds a share in more than one boat. Nor are shares normally passed down through inheritance. The Burra fishermen believe that it is wrong 'to be an owner without also being a worker'. Hence the attempts of fish factory firms to buy their way into the local fleet have been firmly resisted: nobody will sell them a share in a first class boat. Nor will an exceptionally successful fisherman invest his profits in a second boat to be worked by others. Such a clear picture would not emerge from a similar study of every north-east port, and it partly reflects the strength of Shetland individualism and egalitarianism. It is interesting that similar refusals to co-operate with 'attempts of land-based entrepreneurs to take control over production' have also been reported from Scandinavia. But it is also important to notice that however long-standing such basic social attitudes may be, present local conventions regarding boat-ownership are a modern development. Family ownership of boats was not traditional in Shetland, and has become customary only within living memory.

The explanation, it is clear, lies once again in the changing interaction between the financial structures of the fishing

industry and the consciousness of the inshore fishing communities. And in this consciousness, while local social attitudes may vary in detail on many points, there are certain
shared fundamentals. Firstly, what is most admired among
them, and brings most prestige, is not wealth or formal social
position, but *skill*. What counts is not so much owning a boat,
as working it successfully. The boat is seen less as a piece of
property than a precious tool, a productive instrument. It is in
any case rightly recognised that while a working boat can
bring excellent returns, even in use it is a quickly wasting asset,
and not a secure investment. This is why fishermen have long
preferred to put their long-term savings elsewhere, most
commonly in the bank. And secondly, because fishing must
depend on co-operative teamwork at sea, there is a strong
disapproval within the inshore communities of forms of behaviour which could generate social friction and division: such
as arrogance or anger, domineering or displays of wealth. This
again operates as a continual social pressure today against any
marked trend towards concentration of boat-ownership. It
serves to make the successful fishermen socially a very different being from other entrepreneurs who may in fact command considerably smaller financial resources than he does.
A recent Norwegian study observes that 'the successful
businessman aims at keeping or creating social distance between himself and his clientele, and achieves success by not
being involved in a local neighbour-kinship network. The big
herring man, however, has quite the opposite aim for his social
activity, as the really stable and therefore efficient net crews are
bound together by a tight neighbour-kinship network.'[9] Economic and social relationships, in short, are inseparably locked
together. And this, as we shall see, makes all the more important the inshoremen's demonstration, through the era of
steam capitalism into the advanced technology of today, that
conventional capitalist inequality does not offer the only viable
path to prosperity.

10 Women in the fishing

Fishing is commonly thought of as a man's trade. In fact it is an occupation peculiarly dependent on the work of women. There is, first of all, the direct productive contribution of women's labour, on which the fishing industry has always relied, as have the economies of so many other kinds of industrial and agricultural communities throughout history. Secondly, there are the special responsibilities which women must carry because of the absence of men away at sea. Lastly, there is also the role which has been principally theirs in all human societies, of creating the next generation, both in a physical and moral sense: of bearing and raising children.

While it is the men in most communities who alone catch the fish, they have normally relied on women both in preparing for the fishery and still more for disposing of the catch afterwards. Peter Frank has described the critical contribution of female labour to the nineteenth-century north Yorkshire inshore communities. The women and girls of Staithes, Runswick and Robin Hood's Bay had to search out 'flithers' for bait from the rocks, some walking up to twenty miles to find sufficient supply; clean and bait the men's lines in their living rooms; help them launch their cobles; and once the catch was home, split and dry some for preservation, or sell it fresh at the Whitby quayside stalls or in regular rounds through the town, the Eskdale farms or the Cleveland ironstone mining villages. It would have been similar in line-fishing communities the whole length of the English and Scottish North Sea coast:

> We'd a' to work j's'like slaves, necht and day. We'd to rise through the necht, with the tide, and ging to the mussels and pick up our mussels out of the cal' water and take them up to shiel them. And the limpets. To bait the lines . . .
>
> You reekit the fish . . . put them on spits, through the

logs, and you reekit them. . . . It took about three hours to
reek a fish, and then, fen the sawdust gae down, the reek
got awa', they were left there till morning. And then you
get awa' and selled them . . . I selled the fish wi' a creel on
my back . . . Roun' the toon and roun' the country . . .[1]

The women's labour in mending drift nets, gutting and
kippering, and again in selling fresh fish locally, was equally
vital to the herring fishery. But as a large-scale export industry, the bulk of the work in fish preparation and distribution in
this case took place outside the home from a much earlier
stage. As a result ashore – in contrast to patterns at sea –
wage-earning militancy became more characteristic of the
herring industry than the white fishery. The women herring
workers, the 'quines' of the trade, were straightforward employed workers, never entangled in share-earning; so that
their consciousness was able to develop more directly, and
find expression separately from their men, and so, at certain
times, to speak for their communities when the men were
silent.

There were three main groups among them, and although
all were low-paid, some were more seasonally and irregularly
employed than others. Firstly there were the networkers, who
were locally based. In Scotland they remained largely employed on a family basis, and unaffected by unionisation, but
in East Anglia, where net shops were more generally commercially organised, the Workers' Union was representing the
Yarmouth 'beatsters' in 1925. Secondly, also locally based,
were the women attached to smokehouses: kipperers, and also
white-fish filleters. In the kipper-houses, tall buildings with
revolving flues rather like oasthouses, the herring were split
(from the 1930s by machine), gutted, dipped in brine and
colouring, hung on racks of 'tenters', and then moved into the
smoke-chambers, where fires were lit on the floor from
sawdust and shavings. Since inshore white fishing was at its
peak in the winter interval between herring seasons, the
smokehouses could provide work of one kind or the other
with some regularity through the year. It was indoor work,
and older women especially generally preferred it. The fact
that a good filleter was not easily replaced also gave them a

certain security. More recently filleters have been formally trained; and even between the wars:

> you dinna go in right straight as a filleter. They say that the fish trade's nae a trade, but it is. You start wi' the bottom – headin', washin', picklin', tyin' smokies, goin' into the kelns, learnin' to pack – everythin'. They say the fish trade's not a trade but it is.

Like the networkers, the women in the smokehouses were not generally unionised, but during general periods of unrest they certainly showed a willingness to strike. In fact the strike wave which was to sweep through the fishing industry in 1913–14 was heralded by the Aberdeen women fishworkers who struck for increased wages in April 1913, parading the streets 'singing and shouting lustily'. Their success was followed by that of the Grimsby fish-curers in September, and the Peterhead and Fraserburgh kipperers in June 1914. The North Shields women also came out but met with stronger resistance, and despite backing from the locally strong National Amalgamated Union of Labour their strike was still unsettled at the outbreak of war.[2] The smokehouse women were also active in the turbulent period immediately after the war. The Peterhead kipperers struck in July 1920, again followed by Fraserburgh; but after a few days had to return to work on their old terms. There was a last strike by the Grimsby fishworkers in 1924. After this they appear to have remained quiescent until the later 1930s, when there were signs of a renewed attempt to unionise the Aberdeen women.

The third group were, however, much the most consistently active. These were the 'gutting quines', the seasonal herring gutters. Some worked only locally, but many, especially the younger women, followed the seasonal migrations. They worked in crews of three, two gutters and one packer. The herring were gutted, salted, graded, and then packed in barrels between layers of salt. After settling, the next day, the barrel was topped up with more fish, and again after ten days. Each crew was responsible for the whole sequence. The work was in yards, generally with little or no cover. 'The packer usually did all the financial transactions. She it was who decided which curer they would work for, and she it was who generally kept a tally of barrels so that the crew's money would be correct at the end of the season.' The curers paid them piecework by the barrel, plus an extra hourly rate for upfilling. Those working away from home received a weekly wage of 10/– to 17/6d too. Also early each year the curers engaged women for the season, paying them 'arles':

> you'd to sign a paper, and you got arles. . . . Ye were arlesed, ye see, ye was fixed. Fen ye took up your arles, ye was fixed. Ye couldna ging to another body to work. . . . Well if we get awa' and workit to another body, ye was ta'en to court.

This retaining fee was normally 10/– or £1 between the wars, but local women who had no weekly wage might be paid higher arles: in the 1930s it was £3 to £6. At this date there was at least for a brief period a 'strong and representative' section of the TGWU negotiating their annual terms, and at least for insurance purposes they had been organised earlier on too. The Scottish Fishworkers Friendly Society had a membership of 4,000 herring workers in 1914.

They were not only willing to attempt organisation, but also much readier to strike than the other women workers. These strikes were often jocular occasions. In 1911 it is said that a strike 'was started by someone putting a red rag on a broom, and going round all the yards managing to encourage everyone to come out.' In June 1914 an unsuccessful one-day strike of Peterhead herring gutters was led by 'young girls . . . egged on by one or two married women who cared more for the fun of the thing.' There was again a rash of strikes in the 1930s. Before the autumn season in 1931 there were mass meetings of women fishworkers in Peterhead and Stornoway protesting against a reduction of the weekly wage offered by the curers. After they had reached Yarmouth 'a lightning strike among the Scottish fisher girls paralysed business', and the union was able to negotiate a compromise. In 1935 there was an early summer strike at Castlebay in the Western Isles, and in the autumn of 1936 a much more serious dispute in

Yarmouth, led by Maria Gatt of Rosehearty. It was rough for a while, with mounted police on the streets, but Elsie Farquhar of Buckie remembers that they all rather enjoyed it – and got their wage increase. There was another stoppage in East Anglia again in 1936, this time backed by the Scots fishermen, against taking fish caught by English boats on Sundays, and 'curers had no alternative but to concede the point'. Two years later in the autumn season of 1938 they failed to reimpose this restriction, or win a wage increase, from a one-day strike.[3] And after the Second World War there were again strikes in 1946, 1949 and 1953 – the first winning not only higher pay from the curers, but a more generous coal allowance from the government.

What was the reason for this recurrent, and at times light-hearted militancy? The solidarity of the women was no doubt heightened by their work conditions. The curers paid the travel costs of the women working away from home – unlike the seasonally hired Highlandmen, who had to find their own way to the east coast ports. For journeys to the south, special trains were organised, but women who went to work on the islands had to go by overcrowded boats, many lying for long hours on the deck, others crowded below 'with what I would call cruelty to animals', as a Lossiemouth man told his MP in 1914. Those who had to continue beyond Lerwick were literally conveyed in cattle boats, 'a most miserable experience'. Once arrived, they had to work for very long hours at great speed – 'with almost military precision', as a factory inspector commented. In the early 1900s the hours were unregulated. Work started at six in the morning and went on until dusk if need be. In 1913 the factory inspectors negotiated an agreement with the curers for an alternating ten- and thirteen-hour day, but it is doubtful if it was observed. During their long hours standing at the 'farlins' the women's chief protection was their special work clothing: high leather boots, oilskin overall skirts, home-knitted woollen scarves, and cotton rags which were wrapped round their fingers for protection. Despite this they suffered so continually from 'deep and painful ulcers' from the brine that local churches in many ports ran mission stations with lady 'dressers'. Even in the late autumn they were expected to continue working in the open 'exposed to rain, sleet, and wind', standing into the night ankledeep in 'quagmires of mud, sand, and fish refuse'. After 1918 the Inspectorate tried to insist on first-aid stations, rest rooms, canteens and lavatories reasonably close to the yards, but the industry's depression made this impossible to enforce. At Yarmouth and Lowestoft the women were accommodated in seaside lodgings, often sleeping three to a bed and six to a room. Those away for the Scottish summer season had only makeshift housing: wooden huts in rows, commonly six to a cubicle lined with bunks and with a stove in the middle. Sanitation was primitive and inspectors reported that 'kidney complaints' were frequent among the women. Nevertheless, their morale was said to be high, the huts 'clean and well kept', homes indeed where the girls would receive 'their friends, and make merry, as they like to do, on Saturday evenings, either singing hymns or by very vigorous dancing'.

For the gutting season was an important part of the girls' social life: indeed, it was when many of them met their future husbands. This was one way in which their work tied in with the fishing families. And another link further heightened their willingness to fight for higher wages. Their earnings were a family extra. Those in severe need could and did travel elsewhere for permanent work. They were simply seasonal, employed wage-earners. Unlike the fishermen, they had no shares in the herring trade. They thus had less to lose than the men: and, as many of them remember immediately now, they were full of spirit – 'We were young then.' At the height of the season, too, they could make a sharp impact with a sudden, brief strike. George Slater the Aberdeen curer warned in 1931 against forcing an issue with the women over Sunday fishing in East Anglia: 'You are treading on dangerous ground. Once give the women the upper hand and they will dictate to you all right.' But just because they could paralyse the season, the women would rarely press too hard for fear of bringing its total collapse. Their strikes were, in short, not just wage demands for themselves, but symbolic protests against the poverty of the fishing families as a whole. They were in a sense the unspoken voice of the men in the depression years. 'The curers just keepit ye doon and doon, until ye grew that you'd to fecht for yourself.' As Maria Gatt put it: 'We knew we were exploited but what could we do? We knew the whole system depended on us, so what could we do?'[4]

Shore work in the fishing industry is certainly less demanding and time-consuming today than it was in the past. But despite the shift from family living-room or open yard to factory production, and from door-to-door hawking to self-service from the supermarket freezer, it is still women who provide most of the workforce in contemporary fish processing and distribution. The same patterns also emerge from studies of other countries: in Malaysia, Scandinavia or Newfoundland, women again appear as net-makers, fish-sellers and gutters, their contribution to the local fishing economy markedly similar and equally indispensable.

In most fishing societies the division of labour between the sexes seems in one respect quite sharp: work ashore may be left to the women, or shared, but work at sea is reserved for the men. This feeling is so strong that in many places women will not be allowed on a boat which is setting out to fish, and in the past fishermen might take it as a bad omen, and perhaps even turn back home, if they met with particular women on their way to the harbour. Sea work was men's work; and for women to have any place in it would be a pollution. Behind such superstitions lay a basic principle – also shared by most agricultural societies – that women, because of their responsibility for children, should not work too far from home. But this applied with much more force to those who were already mothers than to young unmarried women; and in any case the principle was rarely explicit. As a result, in response to economic pressures fishing communities have sometimes developed divisions of labour demanding regular large-scale migrations by seasonal women fishworkers far from home, like the annual round of the Scottish herring girls. And similarly, although less commonly, women can sometimes also be found at work on the boats and catching fish.

Sometimes this has arisen when work which is allocated by custom to women is partly conducted aboard the ships. This explains the presence of women gutters and filleters on contemporary Russian fish factory ships. A similar instance from the past is provided by the Labrador 'floater' cod fishery, which was operated from the late eighteenth to the mid-twentieth centuries from the Newfoundland outports on a seasonal basis. Fishermen would move northwards for the brief summer weeks, setting cod traps and working from their small 'dories', either based on a larger schooner, or on a cluster of huts ashore. They took up girls and young women with them, both as fishworkers and as cooks, who would work aboard the boats as well as in the huts. These Newfoundland outport women were often already notably handy with a gun from going out to hunt for winter food; so in the cod season some would also take their chance for a little 'jiggering' for fish themselves. Another context, again ambivalently between sea and shore, in which women directly helped the men in catching fish was in the earlier method of seine-net fishing in north Norway, when the beach was still used as a base from which the shoals of fish could be encircled, and 'men, women and children' would join in 'the land haul', taking their proportion of the catch which was landed.

There are also, however, some communities in which women quite openly fish from the boats too; for example in southern Brittany, or north-west Spain. In the early nineteenth century women fishermen were reported in the sheltered inner fjords of the Norwegian coast. Here some also became skippers of cargo boats; and occasionally life-boat heroines, like Grace Darling in Northumberland. But perhaps the most remarkable instance is to be found in the Baltic coastal communities of Sweden. The social division of labour here derives from an amphibious combination of farming in the sheltered inshore waters, at first with traps and later from boats, which persisted from the middle ages up to the twentieth century. As a result, sea-fishing rights became owned, and allocated by rotation, by the farmers of each settlement. As a medieval law put it: 'He who owns land, owns water.' It was a society of peasants, women as well as men, living 'with one boot on the farming land and one in the fishing boat'. Women had not only to market fish and mend nets, but to go out on the small inshore boats to fish for bait. Where there were cows grazing on small islets, they also had to handle boats regularly to see to the milking. Generally it was the younger, unmarried women who undertook such work, and in most districts they were not on the water at night; but there

1 Frank Meadow Sutcliffe captured the essence of the Whitby inshore fishing
community in this photograph taken in the late 1890s. The two men sit on their broad
coble, beached in Whitby harbour. Beside them stands a fisherwoman, Bella Black,
whose work at home baiting the lines and mending gear is as vital as the fishing at sea.
She has brought down newly baited lines and a bladder float, and is ready to take
away their used lines and overalls which she holds.

2 A group of Norfolk longshoremen from Sheringham in sea-boots and souwesters
beside their boat. The oars are in position for pushing it up the beach—with a ride for
the visitors' child on a seaside holiday.

3 Marshside shrimp boats tied up at Southport pier, *c.* 1900. These two-man 'Nobbies' could fish the shallow Ribble and Mersey estuaries. After landing, the men would walk three miles home to Marshside with the shrimp baskets on their backs.

6　George Reid (1836–1922) and his wife Jane Priest (1838–1915) baiting haddock lines at Portsoy, *c.* 1890. George Reid had been a seaman on Baltic merchant ships before buying a small inshore boat, the *Flower,* with two other men. Jane Priest, who came from Sandend, east of Portsoy, and characteristically known by her maiden as well as her married name, was responsible for dividing the catch into three shares at the harbour. She would then take home her own share in her creel, salt and smoke the fish, and sell it. Besides their own seven children she also brought up her granddaughter, Peggy Mair, who writes 'she had plenty customers and we always had plenty for ourselves.'

opposite

4　(centre) The Yardie, Buckie, the oldest part of the town, keeps some of the atmosphere of the earlier inshore communities strung round the north-east coast. Lines were baited in the street or the living room. Later the original thatch roofs gave way to slate, and dormer windows were added to provide well-lit attics for mending herring drift nets.

5　(bottom) Baiting lines at Buckie before the steam-drifter era. In the basket is grass to put between the hooks, to prevent them from tangling.

10 Men on deck, women and children on the beach, as the Fleetwood steam trawler *Imelda,* owned by Marr's and skippered by L. G. Jinks, sets out for the fishing grounds in 1924. The trawling companies allowed their men the right to one day at home between trips, and if they failed to rejoin ship the could be fined or imprisoned. 'The fishermen's principal grievance', an Aberdeen trawler cook said of the 1919 lock-out, 'was that they had no home life'.

opposite

7 (Above left) and 8 (above right) Skipper Wharton of the smack *Unity* at sea, and with his wife at home in Lowestoft: an unusual pair of photographs from an album of *c.* 1900 at the Fishermen's Mission. The Mission's own smacks brought medical aid, tobacco and mission services to the men and boys—frequently pauper apprentices—at sea.

9 (below) Another photograph from the same album shows the danger of trawling operations: even after the advent of steam fishing, the catch was transferred by open rowboats from the trawler to the fast steam cutter which took it ahead to market, leaving the men to work on at sea. In 1894 alone 494 fishermen were killed at work.

11 While herring was gutted ashore, trawlermen had to gut their catch out at sea: Grimsby men working in rough weather, *c.* 1960. In the previous five years there had still been 200 fishermen killed at sea—three times the death rate for coal miners.

opposite
12 (top) Aberdeen trawlermen at work in 1962. There were no fixed hours, but an 80-hour week was common. Exhaustion, and duty free drink, lay behind the frequent groundings of trawlers on their way to or from the fishing grounds.

13 (bottom) Aberdeen steam trawler *Carency* aground at Staxigoe, near Wick, 29 June 1957, with lifeboat alongside.

14 (above) and 15 (below) The transformation of the Buckie district herring fleet from sail to steam. Two photographs of Portknockie harbour, the first taken in 1890 (a memorial stone is being laid), the second *c.* 1908. The new steam drifters cost over £2000, three times a sailboat, but the Moray Firth herring fishing communities made this technological leap while maintaining their family share-ownership system and refusing to work company boats as wage-earners.

16 William Geddes first sailed is his father's zulu, seen here painted two years earlier at the East Anglican fishing in 1906. In the background is Yarmouth pier. Also in the crew were two of his uncles.

17 Skipper Jim Pirie, known as 'Thaicker', of the Buckie steam drifter *Berrie Braes*.

18 The crew of one of the earliest Buckie steam drifters, the *Star of the Sea*.

19 Joch and Lass Bruce of Portessie, Buckie, at home in retirement. Joch first went to sea as a cook on his father's Zulu in 1922, and was fifty years a share fisherman on steam and motor drifters. Lass worked as a herring girl and as a servant.

20 William Stewart of Buckie started as a cook in 1919 and worked as a drifter fisherman and fireman, and an Aberdeen trawler deckhand and engineer, before returning to Buckie for the seine-net fishing. He finished up as a share fisherman and cook on the *Transcend,* seen here landing catch in 1964.

21 Grimsby girls at work in a net factory, *c.* 1910. In the herring driftermen's families net-mending was a home task for wives and daughters.

22 Coopers at Lowestoft, *c.* 1920, with their herring barrels. The need for thousands of barrels at each station ensured these skilled men regular work through the year, and some of them would set up independently as curers.

23 The Buckie hunger demonstration of June 1920: with 300 drifters in harbour and all shops shut, 10,000 men, women and children marched to a mass meeting demanding a government subsidy for the herring industry. The banners carried reminders of the war: 'Starvation our reward for services rendered'; 'Fishermen fought for a guarantee for Belgium; they now want a guarantee for themselves.' A week later the government gave its guarantee.

24 Two Buckie herring girls, Nellie Reaich—later to marry William Stewart—and her friend Ann Cowie. They stand outside their house, new-built from the prosperity of the steam drifters, in leather thigh boots with their fingers bandaged for protection.

25 (opposite, top) Herring girls gutting on the harbour front at Stornoway, Lewis, with barrels behind, c. 1910. In 1913 altogether 12,000 Scottish women gutters followed the migrant herring, 3,500 setting out in June from the Western Isles, and 5,000 coming south for the autumn season in East Anglia.

26 (above) The herring sail fleet in Castlebay, Barra, *c.* 1885. Most of these drifters
had come from Scottish east-coast ports. By the 1900s the drifter fleet also included a
few first-class local sailboats, as well as the Zulus and steam drifters from the east
coast, and 400 steam drifters who came north from East Anglia for the Scottish
season. In the foreground are black houses, one roofed with an upturned boat, the
others more typically with thatch weighed down by stones, leaving the outer upper
edge of the massive walls exposed to rain: longer rafters were a luxury in the treeless
Western Isles. Across the bay can be seen the low, fertile island of Vatersay, then a
sheep farm. In the 1900s land raiders led by landless fishermen-cottars from the
Castlebay foreshore seized Vatersay and set up the crofting township where their
descendants still live today. The photograph is by James Valentine.

29 Shetland men, women and boys landing from rowboats and sailboats: one woman carrying lines, another a bladder float. The boat shape with raked stern balancing the prow can be traced back to the Vikings. Shetland fishermen would row the larger rowboats, the sixereens, three men on each side, fifty miles into the open Atlantic to the edge of the continental shelf for the open haaf fishing. 'Return from the fishing', taken by George Washington Wilson, *c.* 1885.

opposite
27 (top) Coll on Lewis was also a sheep farm until after the First World War when, following land raids, it was divided into a crofting township. The crofts of land raiders and other families at Coll in 1977.

28 Mission service at sea, *c.* 1900.

Contrasts in contemporary fishing:
30 (above left) Shetland boats in Lerwick harbour, 1970;

31 (above, right) little but the motor marks an advance as eight men help to haul a two-man salmon boat from the open Atlantic at Bauline, Newfoundland, 1980.

32 (below) the *Zephyr* from Whalsay shooting as a vast mackerel shoal turns into Lock Eriboll close to Cape Wrath, 1980: when the crew pick up their head rope their net will have enclosed the volume of a cathedral.

33 (bottom) an abandoned Grimsby trawler rusts in Aberdeen fish dock.

were others whose women also participated in the tough and dangerous herring fishing further off-shore, working and sleeping with the driftermen in their small open boats.[5]

Women then, have almost everywhere made a central contribution to fishing economies through their roles in fish processing and distribution, and in preparing for the fishery; and in some few districts have actively participated in the fishing itself. Both need emphasising, just because the conventional image of fishing as a male occupation grossly undervalues the real – and potential – part played by women in the industry. The exceptions also bring out the importance of local variations between fishing communities. And this again applies to the more special position in which the women of these communities can find themselves, as a result of the absence of men which the fishing economy imposes.

The fishing economy has a double impact on the character of the family, forcing it in two directions away from the conventional ideal of modern family life, with its focus on home-centred togetherness sharply separated from the impersonal harshness of the world of work. By taking men away from home regularly, often for weeks on end, fishing makes such a conventional ideal very difficult, if not impossible, to realise. On the one hand, the women are left with most of the responsibility for the children, the home and its finances. On the other the men learn self-sufficiency, including often basic domestic skills, in the exclusively male society of the ship. They can easily fall into a distanced relationship in which the men, when ashore, prefer the company of their mates to the family, and treat their wives simply as 'providers of sexual and cooking services', as Tunstall wrote of the Hull trawlermen. One East Anglian who worked with them, Jack Rose of Lowestoft, remembers how 'On the big trawlers the blokes used t'call their wives up . . . Some of 'em used t'abuse it. Yeah, some o' these here stalky skippers did, yuh know! That'd be, "We'll be in so-and-so, ow darlin'. Git yuh knickers orf!"'

Clearly the isolated responsibility of the women was most extreme when the men's work imposed long seasons away, like the deep-sea trawling on the Icelandic or Newfoundland banks. But family relationships seem to be most seriously affected when working conditions were not only especially bitter and far distant from home, but the men sense the degree of their own exploitation by merchants or employers. Such experience may harden them, and drive them towards compensating self-indulgence and assertions of their own male authority when they come home. The picture of exploitation at work reverberating in family alienation which we have seen from Aberdeen could be paralleled by stories from the old Breton and Norman deep-sea fishing ports like Fécamp and Paimpol, or Lorient today; or from the northernmost region of Norway, where the deep-sea trawling is dominated by the company port of Hammerfest, and domestic violence is reported as a social problem to a degree quite exceptional in Norway. There is a similar historic legacy too, behind the attitudes of modern Newfoundland fishermen who expect a woman to fetch 'a drink for her husband from the water barrel or food at his demand'.[6]

Conversely the impact of harsh work experience may be modified by earlier family traditions. There is evidence, not only from Aberdeen, but also from Hull and Grimsby, that a minority of men maintained different attitudes, especially among those grades who most often came from former inshoremen's families. Among East Anglian trawlermen and driftermen of the 1900s there was certainly a very striking sharing of domestic tasks while ashore. It would be misleading, therefore, to suggest the nature of the men's work *determined* a particular kind of family relationship. A different cultural inheritance could contribute to shaping another outcome.

For paradoxically, while being pulled into separate emotional worlds, both husband and wife also acquire overlapping skills, a shared competence for domestic tasks and responsibilities, which make a married 'partnership' a real possibility. This is one basis for the striking domestication of men, their contribution to child-care, cleaning and cooking, which can be found among fishing families in East Anglia or in Shetland. There is also, commonly, a second, economic, dimension to this potential 'partnership'. For the fishing family, like the families of peasants and small farmers, or small business people and shopkeepers, may be held together by more than the ties of emotion. Where family boat-ownership continues, the family constitutes not merely a home, but also the basis for an economic venture; and even though the shift of the women's work from the home to the factory reduces their direct participation, while they are still processing local catch they are still caught up in a common enterprise. All this gives women the possibility of achieving, within the fishing family, a degree of independence and power which is unusual.

In the Scottish north-east line-fishing communities the traditional dependence of fishermen on their wives was so widely recognised that the family has been recurrently described as a form of 'matriarchy'. As Sir Walter Scott put it in 1816, 'the government is gynecocracy'. Their responsibility for both preparation for the fishery and sale of the catch gave women a clear practical basis for power. 'Them that sell the goods guide the purse – them that guide the purse rule the house.' And there are indications of a similar tendency, more or less accentuated, from many maritime societies. A study of *Takashima, a Japanese Fishing Community*, noted how the need for fishermen's wives to take economic decisions while their men were at sea gave them 'more freedom of speech and action than wives in farming communities'. Raymond Firth found 'one of the notable features' in a Malay fishing community was 'the freedom of the women, especially in economic matters'. In addition to fish-selling they launched into other independent trading and craft enterprises of their own. They were often net and boat-owners, and could well have 'the deciding voice' when a question of sale arose; while in buying new equipment they were 'equally important as advisers and often leaders in matters of investment'. The Fanti women of coastal Ghana are again independent small entrepreneurs; and in the Pacific, it was among the lake-dwelling New Guinea Tchambuli, where the women fished and farmed and wove and sold mosquito bags while the men attended to their elaborate religious rituals, that Margaret Mead could report that women had 'the real position of power in the society'.

Similar instances can also be found in Europe. In coastal regions of Scandinavia where merchant seafaring or long fishing seasons left the women to run the small family farms on their own, this could sometimes lead to recognised economic power through owning land or boats. On the island of Laesö, between Denmark and Sweden, where the men were seafarers, farms were in fact normally inherited from mother and daughter. On Laesö women were said to have become unconcerned about conventional housework; and they would drive the cart, even if there was a man in it. In the Swedish shipyard town of Landskrona it was the Borstahusen inshoremen's wives who owned and ran the three largest fish shops; and fishermen here had the reputation of being stupid by comparison with women. In Iceland women have even rubbed in their social power by the one-day general strike of 1975 – against men. Elsewhere, in Galicia in north-west Spain women are reputed to dominate the local community, not only inheriting both land and boats, but fishing themselves too. And even as close as west Wales there are coastal villages where it is said that 'women were naturally accepted as equals', taught navigation, and ready if need be to pilot their husbands' ships from the China Seas 'round the Horn and safely back to the East India Dock.'[7]

It would be wrong, however, to see such patterns as peculiar to maritime communities. Wherever men work away from home, the power of women is likely to be emphasised. It can equally be observed in the families of Quebec or northern Sweden, where the men work away logging in the woods, or central France where the women of Creuse or Limousin run their small farms while their men take seasonal industrial or building jobs – or still more strongly in the West Indies, where overseas migration has been a basic feature of island social and economic life at least since the 1830s.

Neither the mere absence of men, nor a vital economic role, on the other hand, necessarily bring women increased independence or respect. A recent study of *The Real World of the Small Business Owner* emphasises how frequently women are 'the real financial decision-makers' in such firms, acting as secretary and accountant as well as undertaking most domestic responsibilities singlehanded. But 'for their pains women will get little personal recognition or reward. Real money will rarely be paid to them.' With the man running a business from the family home, it is easy to see the woman's difficulty in

winning recognised independence or a formal economic stake
in the business. But the absence of men at the fishery does not
guarantee this either. *The Raft Fishermen* of Coqueiral in
Brazil, despite relying for most of the year on their wives'
independent earnings in the straw industry, will rarely take
their advice when buying new equipment nor give them a
share of its ownership. Similarly the Newfoundland inshoremen of *Cat Harbour*, who rely on their women as fishworkers,
commonly 'avoid their wives' after work, except to return
home to be served food. Here women rarely own any property at all. It would be against local custom for either boats,
cod traps, or even houses to be left to them. Lacking any
recognised standing, they have become regarded as essential
by the men in a sense which is simply derogatory and demean-
ing:

> A man without a wife is like a man without a good boat or
> a good horse and a woman is, in the division of shares of a
> voyage, considered an item of her husband's capital, just as
> a cod trap or an engine.[8]

In understanding these marked differences, one important
clue must lie precisely in just such local customs of control
over property. Such instances in which women are both
propertyless and without social recognition can be set against
their shares in boat-ownership and stronger social position in
Malaya, Scandinavia or Galicia. Elsewhere women may be
rarely boat-owners, but hold a compensating power through
owning the land they work while the men are away at sea. In
Shetland, for example, in the early twentieth century nearly a
third of the farms were held by women; and the proportion
seems to have risen still higher in some of the most active
fishing districts. On Out Skerries the crofts are almost exclusively passed down from women to women, just as on Laesö.
Another instance is provided by the south Breton island of
Houat, where although legal titles may be shared, the formal
administration of property in land is left entirely to women.
They work the land and run the agricultural co-operative.
Ashore, indeed, 'l'homme est simplement tolerée', confined
to enclaves like the jetty and the café; and his social reputation

at the mercy of the women's gossip network. The women's power here goes back at least to the early nineteenth century, when Bachelot de La Pylaie remarked on how they held the authority in family matters, and people would defer to their views even when contrary to those of the formal 'Chef de ménage'. This strict separation of male and female spheres of work and power was reflected in the customary lack of any close informal contact between young men and women, and the formal moral order symbolised by the seating apart of men and women in the church.[9]

The convergence of all these factors is certainly not a matter of chance, but it is more difficult to decide which leads to which. At Houat economic and social attitudes have created special local property customs; but the reverse can also happen. A study has been made of marriage and inheritance between 1890 and 1940 in two hamlets a mile apart in the same north Norwegian fjord, tied together by a network of kin through intermarriage. Although in both hamlets equal division between children should have been followed, in practice this was only true of one of them. In Laknes the right to use a certain number of salmon nets depended strictly on the share of beach owned by each household, and families took great care to avoid splitting the beach rights, leaving them only to sons who would work together, and pressing their daughters to find husbands in other villages. But Strandslett, where land was abundant, operated the full generosity of the traditional inheritance of the region: all children, legitimate and illegitimate, male and female, receiving their complete share. The power and responsibility of women, in short, is shaped by a complex interaction of economy, social attitudes, law, religious doctrine and family need – within which the formal law, local convention and actual practice of inheritance are simply one significant and revealing element.

Through inheritance, however, we have also stumbled on the varying social situation of children in fishing communities: and so to the third role of women within them – as bearers of their future. We have left this role to the last for a double reason. The first is that childbearing and childrearing is a special task for women in fishing communities principally because of the extreme degree to which they lack men's support in it. Their work means that all fishermen must be to a greater or lesser degree absentee fathers. They are more present in inshore communities, where boys will begin quite early to work with their fathers ashore or in short journeys on boats. But even here much of the socialisation of boys into male roles was customarily through their contact with older retired men, grandfathers and uncles rather than fathers. Nor can there be any doubt that everywhere the basic responsibility rested with the women. A measure of the burden which they had to bear alone can be provided in simple but stark statistics taken from the East Anglian oral history evidence. The death rate of brothers and sisters of informants from different branches of fishing can be compared, to show how far the greater or lesser absence of a father could affect a child's chances of survival. The figures show that in the families of the driftermen and trawlermen, whose fathers were away for the longest periods, it was more than *double* that in the inshoremen's homes.

The second reason is fundamental to our argument: and we therefore develop it more fully in the rest of this book. For if the task of creating the next generation is a universal one, there are great differences in the manner in which it can be carried out. And it is just these differences which provide one key reason why some fishing communities survive, while others have perished. In raising children, women not only carry and give birth to them, and nurture these through infancy, but at the same time they shape their earliest attitudes. They create the new generation socially as well as physically. They hand down to children their 'mother tongue' and stand beside them as they first try to understand their place in the world. Certainly social attitudes and individual personality evolve and develop through later years too; but the foundations are laid at this earliest stage. And such a part in creating and shaping future generations must give women a crucial role in social change. For the genesis of social change is through the mutual interaction of economy and social consciousness: and if the moral order, social attitudes, religious doctrine or ideology, have any critical influence on the economy, its prime mediators must thus be women and children.

Close-up: East Anglia
by Trevor Lummis
11 Luck: longshoremen, smacksmen and driftermen

We have shown, from two directions, some of the links between the economy and the family in fishing. In each case it has become clear that the particular form they take must be understood in relation to cultural attitudes. It is therefore to the ideology of fishing communities that we turn in our next two chapters. We see the relationship of ideology to economic and social structure as again mutual. Thus in this chapter we illustrate how the changing economy can reshape beliefs; and in the next, how attitudes can influence the economic future.

Fishermen are rightly famous both for superstition and for religious enthusiasm. But there can be many different sources for the strength of such 'traditions' among them. We have seen how in the aftermath of defeat superstition was seized on by Fleetwood trawlermen as a device for securing more time ashore. One can imagine too a twinkle in the eye of the fisherman from Portsoy, a decaying Moray Firth port, who would refuse to set out on a Friday, saying: 'A craw wouldna start tae build its nest on a Friday.'[1] To speak of superstition not as a historic hangover, an economic handicap, but as an instrument of modern industrial workers, even a covert form of class consciousness, is indeed to turn the conventional picture of traditional attitudes on its head. Yet the case can be made with the Fleetwood trawlermen; and we shall find another – but different – paradox in considering the beliefs of East Anglian fishermen. For it is a major theme of our book to challenge the notion of straightforward 'progress', or 'decline', from a 'traditional' past to a 'modern' present.

This is particularly relevant to any discussion of fishermen's attitudes to the supernatural, where the significance of local variety is too easily lost in blurred general stereotyping. There *is*, indeed, a common world of ideas among fishermen. It would be easy to show right round the coasts of Britain the common existence of attitudes such as fear in passing ministers of religion or particular women on the way to join ship, or taboos against mentioning pigs on board, or whistling at sea. But this would be to construct a world of symbols detached from the precise contexts, the day-to-day needs, in which superstition is always locally rooted: a world of symbols denied their social meaning.

The scattered communities strung round our coasts have been bonded by seasonal movements, intermarriage, and permanent migration; and in the same fashion they have regularly exchanged ideas and innovations, whether in consumer goods, or fishing techniques, or religion. But some have taken a much deeper root in one part than another. Thus Protestant sects, although they had some following in all regions, had a much greater hold in the Scottish north than in East Anglia, where the stronger presence of a somewhat dry, but well-endowed, established church helped to keep them at bay – and maybe also to give more shelter for the survival of superstition among fishermen.

Certainly it could not be argued that it reflected the backwardness of the local fishing economy. Today most of the East Anglian fishing stations seem deserted or decaying. The herring has gone, and only a few motor trawlers still work from Lowestoft. The occasional inshore boats elsewhere, some even now needing to be dragged up the shingle beaches to safety, look like idiosyncratic remnants of rural backwardness. But on the eve of the First World War East Anglian fishing was still an industry of distinct national significance. Its three counties held a quarter of all the fishermen of England and Wales. In terms of landings Yarmouth was the second port in the country after Grimsby, and in terms of men Lowestoft, with over 5,000 regular fishermen, again second only to Grimsby. The backbone of the East Anglian fleet was the 570 steam drifters registered at the two ports in 1912, and the 239 sailing drifters working out of Lowestoft. The figures for both boats and men represent a 20 per cent increase over those of 1903. We are looking, in short, at a dynamic local industry which, along with the Humber ports, was at the forefront of English fishing.

It provides a particularly interesting context for investigating superstition, for it combined both technologically advanced and traditional equipment and methods of working. It can be divided into three sectors, which we shall consider in turn: the fishing of the inshoremen, the smacksmen and the driftermen.

Technically, and also commercially, the most 'traditional', least-changed sector was inshore fishing, or 'longshoring'. Typically working from small villages scattered along the coast and river estuaries, with comparatively poor or expensive communications with the large markets, longshoremen remained much nearer to the 'traditional' ideal of the self-contained fishing community providing for its immediate hinterland. There were many exceptions to this picture, particularly in Essex where the numerous rivers afforded safe anchorages for large boats, in spite of a lack of harbours, and conditions for a specialised shellfish trade where the bulk of the catch would be sent to distant markets. But in general, their capital investment was low; and so was their level of personal risk – and their financial rewards and expectations. On the sea coasts of Norfolk and Suffolk, the boats were undecked vessels under 20 feet in length, a limit imposed by the need to be able to 'beach' the boats on the open shore and to drag them above the high-water mark. Lack of harbours and local geographical conditions thus placed practical constraints on the development of this sort of fishing. This also helps to account for the 'traditionalism' of these fishermen. An engine considerably increased the weight of a beach boat, and took away space from carrying fish. With its running expenses it was an investment of marginal value for inshore fishermen supplying local markets.

While the essence of inshore fishing was its variety, we can take the work from the middle of the region – Thorpeness, Suffolk – as an illustration. From January into March there was little fishing, because weather was bad and during the cold the fish moved away into deeper water away from the coast. Owners would spend their time overhauling their gear and boat. Their 'mates' would be unemployed, looking for odd jobs ashore to find another bob or two. The year's fishing would start with trying for lobsters 'after the first few sunny days', with hoop nets. Once it was clear that the lobsters were moving, lobster pots would be put down and fishing begun in earnest. By this time crabs would be in season too. About the middle of May trawling for plaice and soles would begin; shrimps would come in during the summer season, or a mixture of the two, according to the fisherman's commercial judgment. The herring season would come in October and then sprats in November and December. For all these activities there would be a two-man crew, except for sprat fishing when the boats carried three men.

The takings were divided by shares – generally one for each man and one for the boat, plus, with the larger sprat-boats, one for the nets. Earnings were low – a little above those of a farm worker, for a hard and demanding life.

> Oh they were long days they were, long days. Been
> fishing all night, then got to walk to Leiston, that's three
> miles, six miles there and back – or Aldeburgh's two mile
> to take your fish – there wasn't much sport about that.[2]

The local market could only take so much fish: the rest was simply thrown away. This did not encourage additional effort, or allow a gulf to develop between owners and men. Inshore work did not bring any expectation of big earnings. The longshoreman had his independence, his chance of good seasons and modest comfort, but that was all; and an adverse season would mean hardship and poverty.

Perhaps more than the fishermen in the other two sectors, the inshoreman was master of his own economic effort, within the constraints of the market and location. He owned his own boat and gear and chose when to work himself. He was fishing local grounds, close to the safety of the shore, which he knew both from his own experience and knowledge handed down in the family. If the fish were there, he had the skill to find them and catch them; if they did not arrive, there was nothing he could do. His only pressure was to provide what he and his family felt to be a reasonable standard of living, and part of his contentment came from using farm labourers as a measure for his own 'prosperity'.

Verbatim accounts of superstition can convey the 'quality' of their commitment better than any abstract analysis. We shall therefore provide typical examples from interviews with men from each sector. Those with inshoremen provided only brief accounts, such as this from Thorpeness:

> *Did the fishermen have any superstitions or customs at all?*
> Well, some of 'em didn't like a parson to go aboard, or if they met a parson they would think it unlucky. Yes, that's what some of 'em reckoned. But there's nothing in it is there? Some of 'em wouldn't sail on a Friday. Not to start afresh – we'll say we had been after crabs and lobsters, we'd bought all our pots ashore, we're going to start trawling after shrimps, wouldn't start on Friday some used to reckon. There was nothing in it. No.

This man started fishing with his grandfather after leaving school in 1902. Thorpeness was then a very small isolated fishing village. Superstition was clearly not widespread or important; and he knew of it, rather than believing in it. An account from nearby Aldeburgh confirms this general outlook:

> *Were there any superstitions connected with the fishing at that time?*
> No, not with the fishing, only thing was we never started to fish on a Friday.
> *That would be like a change of season would it?*
> No. Perhaps like now, you'd be fishing, and perhaps you'd have a blow for five or six days, and if you stood ashore for four or five days and that came fine on a Friday, you wouldn't go.

Further conversation revealed that Aldeburgh men would not go to sea if pigs were mentioned, and they did not like parsons. But like many local inshoremen, this man had also been fishing on the Lowestoft trawling smacks and may have absorbed some superstitions there. This low level of superstition seems similar around the coast, with even less in the remote Essex marshland villages. Mersea and Tollesbury interviews gave not whistling, and not placing a hatch upside down, as the only customary taboos. The latter is also mentioned in accounts from Harwich and Leigh-on-Sea. But nobody ever mentioned refusing to fish if any taboo was broken, suggesting that commitment to them was not very high. On the other hand, from both Harwich and Leigh – neither of which was either remote or even rural – we also find a belief in the malevolent effects of certain individuals. A Leigh inshoreman remembered:

> Well in my younger days superstition was a hatch turned upside down, if anyone turned it up with the bearers across – bad luck. I don't believe in that. The old fishermen were – not my generation – my father and all them, they was very superstitious.
> *Can you remember any others that they had?*
> Yes. There was Poll Brock, she had a cast in her eye, and they always used to say she was bad luck. They'd go out there and not have a very good catch, and they'd say, 'I knew I wasn't going to do any good' – But there was nothing else on the boat they were superstitious over. It was just the hatches upside down.[3]

This suggests that the extent of superstition at sea was distinct from the general level of belief in the 'supernatural' in the shore community – a point to which we shall return. But when these village inshoremen talk about work superstitions, one has the impression that they *know about* rather than *believe in* them. *Not one of the purely inshore fishermen told a story about work superstition.* This contrasts sharply with the smacksmen and still more with the driftermen, whose accounts are extensive.

The smacksmen were the East Anglian sailboat trawlermen. Their industry had developed on a large scale from the 1860s when Hewetts of Barking (London) moved their fleet to Gorleston (Yarmouth), and until the firm collapsed in 1900 Yarmouth was a slightly larger centre than Lowestoft. After that trawling was largely confined to Lowestoft. As a substantial industry it was remarkable for continuing with a traditional technology. Partly because of the high local cost of coal, steam trawling did not develop in East Anglia, and the large smacks, of up to seventy tons, had to continue to work the less efficient beam trawl. Their crews of five were paid wages of 10/– to £1 weekly, with skipper and mate on shares. Despite very low profit margins and a rising bankruptcy rate, the smacksmen were able to survive into the inter-war years by supplying the highly commercial London market with quality fish. They worked the southern North Sea grounds, which because they had been somewhat overfished hardly merited the attention of vessels steaming down from the Humber, 'bringing in an annual harvest of 12,000 tons of turbot, brill and soles; those working for the *gourmets*, while trawlers and drifters work for the people.' But work for the luxury trade in their 'graceful sailing vessels' was far from comfortable. Smacksmen had to fish the North Sea throughout the year, risking the winter weather in sailboats, with each trip away lasting about a week. Despite their 'traditional' gear, they were enmeshed in the modern commercial world.

Superstitions among the smacksmen primarily concerned wind and weather and safety at sea: that is to say matters of death and danger. They shared the widespread beliefs that parsons, pigs and rabbits were unlucky, and extended them to include ferrets and rabbits – indeed as one man said, 'any animal'. And despite the philanthropic work of the Mission to Deep Sea Fishermen, which from 1885 operated trawlers fishing in the same waters as the smacks and supplied them with medical help, tobacco and knitted comforts, and would take crews aboard for divine service in calm weather, the smacksmen never overcame their prejudice against parsons, expressing feeling against them more frequently than inshoremen, even if less strongly than driftermen.

A more remarkable aspect of smacksmen's practices was their widespread use of blasphemy to raise a wind. A sailing trawler needed quite a fresh breeze to work effectively, as well as to land its catch in prime condition. A calm could ruin a whole week's catch. One skipper remembers how his skipper,

> if that was a calm, he used to climb up the rigging, up the mast head with a chopper – said he'd chop the Lord's head off if he didn't give him some wind. And when you were

hauling in the mornings if there weren't enough fish to his
liking, he used to scoop 'em overboard, he'd say, 'There
you are you Old Bugger,' he say, 'you can have them for
your breakfast.'

And yet with all his, what do you call it – badness? I used
to laugh to myself when I used to stand on deck and look
down the skylight and look at him, he sat there, and get
the Bible out, and get his glasses on, read the Bible. Cor'
he was a wicked old sod. Called the Lord all the names you
could think of.

Here as in most cases the ritual was invoked by the skipper.
Another approach was to 'buy' the wind. Several interviews
give accounts of personal experience of the effectiveness of
this. The ex-trawlerman's evidence which follows also illustrates how selective fishermen were in their beliefs. We had
been talking about the driftermen who would place a coin in
the end float of the net to 'buy the herring':

Were there other things like that?
No, wouldn't make any difference, they used to do it just
to buy the herring, but that didn't make no difference. But
I will tell you what did. When they've been laying in a
calm – over with a bob and buy a shilling's worth of wind.
And they knew it. Yes. If you bought a shilling's worth of
wind it's ninety percent you were going to get a gale of
wind.[4]

Drifting, the third section of the East Anglian fishing industry,
was its most modern and progressive branch in the 1900s.
Yarmouth had been a major herring port since the middle
ages, but the industry was now being transformed through the
advent of steam fishing. A steam drifter cost up to £3,500 in
the 1900s, compared to up to £1,000 for a trawl smack or £75
for a beach boat. Nevertheless many of these modern new
drifters, unlike the trawlers, were owned and operated by their
skippers. Such men were in fact the most prosperous members
of the East Anglian fishing community at this time. Owners,
skippers and crew were all remunerated on a share basis. And
the need to find regular employment for this increased capital-

isation drove the driftermen right round the British Isles in pursuit of the migratory shoals of herring and mackerel.

Yet despite being clearly the most modern, prosperous and dynamic sector of the local fishing industry, the driftermen were undoubtedly also the most superstitious. They constantly reiterated the importance of 'luck' in the herring fishing industry. They held far more superstitions than the other fishermen, and they held them with greater conviction. Two longish extracts can best convey something of the quality of the difference, and of just how much more bound-up in actual remembered activity were the superstitions of the driftermen. This first one is from a Norfolk drifterman who sailed from Yarmouth:

Of course superstition did weight tremendously heavy along of practically every boat, and every one of the crew, in the fishing industry. For instance if one skipper saw a black cat, that was a bad omen, or another one saw something else, that was a bad omen, while for others it was luck. There were two – very lucky skippers. And one of them I was with, he would not allow a pack of cards aboard his ship. The other one – to go to sea without a pack of cards aboard his ship he might as well have left his nets ashore. That – that's perfectly true. ·
So there wasn't any sort of agreement on what was lucky and what wasn't?
No. Now to go back again to personal experience. I was along of one of the tip-top skippers. He was a man then could always demand what ship he liked, you see. Every firm was eager to employ him. 'Cos he always carried such an amount of luck. Well, all right. We got sent home. We were round in the Minch, Hebrides. So we duly arrived, and I was mate then . . . (Next morning) the ship's husband stood on the quay, he said, 'You aren't going to have the *Toiler* Herbert, you're going in the *Lassie*.' Well the *Lassie* had a very, very bad reputation. Nobody had earned any money in her – for years. And all our own hearts dropped. But it was the end of the season then you see, all the others were ready, and crewed up. That was either that or walk about, so we went aboard. We got her

ready for sea. Now I want to tell you the perfectly true
story because there'd be no sense in saying otherwise. We
went to sea. Everybody round about us could get good
shots of herring. We got nothing. One week we earned
twenty-five pound. We went the next week. Same again.
Surprising how people are alongside there, easy within
talking distance, can get a boat load, and you in the middle
got nothing. Incredible, but perfectly true. We went three
weeks like that. Well in that three weeks these men that
I've been telling you about on the wharf – they're also
ex-fishermen and rank with superstition. They kept
saying to me – as I landed what few herring we did get,
say, 'There's something unlucky aboard of her. There's
something wrong with her. If you do see anything or do
find anything throw it overboard afore you get out to sea.'
Well I used to laugh at 'em. I was superstitious you know,
myself, but I used to laugh at 'em, say, that's the luck –
can't believe in such stuff as that. That's just our luck. Well
now – the true story is this – I hunted up and down, in and
out, I couldn't see anything wrong. But eventually I
opened a little side door on the engine casing, and I did see
something there that was wrong, and I – my place was
forward leaving the harbour – but I found this and I
thought to myself, oh that's going overboard before I get
out. I wiggled my way aft, nobody see me, nobody see
what I did, I throwed it over the side, honest truth, we
went to sea that night, we filled her full of herring, we
come in and landed, we went out again, we filled her full
of herring again, we come back again. We did so that three
nights in succession, like that, and of course when you got
these big shots that was necessary to call these people in to
lend you a hand to clean nets, and busy cleaning our nets
and getting the herring out the conversation was,
'Somebody's done something, somebody's done
something. Altered her luck, altered the luck.' And I
amongst them you see, 'Don't talk so silly there's no luck.'
And none of the crew knew. Well it was remarkable.
Remarkable. But we went then from the lower ship to the
tip top ship before the season ended. And was almost half
the season over before we started. Then again . . .

What was it you threw over then? What was the unlucky thing?
Oh, that was what we call a scutcher, it's a wooden –
scoop, that – that you have to unload your herring. They
don't cut 'em you see. Held about – a stone of herring –
each scoop you see, and it was upside down. Strange thing
about this superstition, if you shot you see, and you'd got
four baskets in the kip you'd get four baskets in the herring
nets in the morning. Very very unlucky to put them there.
You see. And it – and it often happened so, you see, and all
these sort of things. Never put anything upside down.
This thing was upside down. Over it go you see.

Such a wealth of detail from personal experience rarely occurs
in smacksmen's accounts and never in those of inshoremen.
The story illustrates two aspects of luck, the all-pervasive
concern of the driftermen. The first is the bad luck imparted by
an implement for handling fish left upside down. It could have
been a fish basket, but in this case was a scutcher, hidden away
so that nobody had been able to correct the fault. The second
aspect is the luck carried by an individual skipper.

This is constantly referred to by driftermen. Our next
extract, from a Norfolk drifterman, shows the same intense
personal involvement, but this time with the luck of a particular man:

What about superstitions, were fishermen very superstitious?
Some of 'em were. Yes.
What sort of things?
Well, I remember one being down to Lerwick along of
Wee Green, in the *Ocean Searcher*, I had been with him two
or three year before. He's a queer man. And he went to the
Yarmouth Stores to pay up for what we'd had there you
see. Ropes if you wanted or anything. And that poured of
rain, and he gives him a black oily coat. Well – we went to
sea two or three nights, we never got a – never see a fish.
He said, 'That's that damned oiler. That's what them
buggers give that to me for', he said. He got hold of that
and chucked it over-board. And we steamed off about
twenty miles – he shot and he got a hundred and twenty
cran, filled the old girl right up. 'There you are,' he said,

'damned oiler, that's what done it, anything like that.' And
I've seen him go home, and he'd have on a nearly new suit
next day, 'til you were getting herring, if you were getting
a lot of herring he'd come and change. And I've seen him –
you'd be starting to haul before he turned out, and I've
seen him jump down the hold all in among the herring
right up to his waist, nothing only a suit on. Brand new
suit. And he would go down the cabin and change and he'd
come and chuck it overboard.
He'd chuck his suit overboard?
Yes. Yes, got a good shot, he reckoned that was our luck.
All them sort of things. Queer man. Good as gold he was,
best skipper I ever sailed with. Give you anything. . . .
Do you think there was anything in his superstitions or not then?
No, I don't think that. I didn't pay no regard to it.
*I know Scotch fisherman didn't like anyone mentioning rabbits
and things.*
Oh no. No. This old Wee Green, he didn't like you to talk
about pigs. If you were down the cabin, 'That's enough –
that's enough of that,' he said. And yet he'd have half a pig
when you went down to Lerwick in the salt. So he had
some salt pork going down there. He'd take half a pig in
the salt.[5]

These accounts from the three sections of the East Anglian
fishing industry may be taken as typical. They show a distinct
continuum in the level of superstition, whether judged by
memories of what others did, or personal practice. We find
ourselves with the surprising conclusion that superstition was
most extensive in the most modern commercial fishery, and at
its lowest level in the most traditional sector. Why?

Two recent attempts have been made to explain fishermen's
superstitions in North America within an anthropological
framework. Both start from Malinowski's theory of magic:
that it should be understood as a response to uncontrollable
economic risks and personal uncertainties. John Poggie and
Carl Gersuny compared textile workers and fishermen in one
New England community, and concluded that the greater
superstition of fishermen was due to their higher level of
personal risk. But clearly there may have been other differ-

ences, including economic ones, between the two groups.
Patrick Mullen proposed economic certainty rather than personal risk as the major determinant on the basis of a far more
cogent comparison between Texan 'sea fishermen' and 'bay
fishermen': 'the economic factor has not been stressed in
discussions of the anxiety-ritual theory, but I feel it is of great
importance in establishing the context of anxiety.' We agree;
but before turning to the East Anglian evidence on this point, a
further potential problem needs to be considered.

Malinowski has been criticised for failing, through his
concentration on economic factors, to take account of major
features of magical practice within the community such as
maleficent magic and witchcraft. Fortunately in the East
Anglian case it is possible to compare attitudes in different
fishing stations along the coast. This suggests that there was
little difference in levels of either superstitious or religious
beliefs. East Anglian fishermen were on the whole not notably
religious, seldom attending church or chapel after adulthood.
On the other hand informants from throughout the region
volunteered accounts of witches, ghosts and other supernatural occurrences from personal experience – while ashore: yet
these informants were not usually the most superstitious at
sea. The villages of the inshoremen, notably less superstitious
about work, tended to retain a rather higher level of magical
belief than the larger towns like Yarmouth and Lowestoft
where the more superstitious deep-sea fishermen lived. Thus a
Mersea man remembered how, when we first went to sea
locally,

> No, I don't think they were superstitious. Oh yes, if you
> were in a Lowestoft smack you daren't talk about a pig or
> mention pork.
> *But you didn't bother around here?*
> No, we didn't bother with that, no.
>   Yet I had a man with me reckoned his Aunt Kate was a
> witch. He'd get the red hot poker and go right through the
> boat properly, 'Come out you old bugger! Come out you
> old bugger!' – that's if you had been out a couple of times
> and didn't get anything you see. 'Old Kate has got it
> again', he'd say. Yes, and they reckoned that old seaman

was a bit of a witch, they said you'd got to keep on the
right side of him.

It seems more likely that a belief in witches came from the
community rather than the occupation itself. Conversely there
was a remarkably low involvement by the shore community
in magic rituals connected with the sea. Almost the only
superstition which seems to have been observed was for
women not to wash linen on the day their man started a
voyage, for fear of 'washing him away'. Some people had
heard that fish's bones should not be burnt, or that a boiled
egg's shell should be broken to stop a witch putting to sea in it,
but did not observe such taboos or take them seriously. This
again supports the view that occupational rather than social
factors account for fishermen's work superstitions.

The East Anglian evidence also contradicts an interpretation
of superstition as primarily a response to personal risk. Certainly inshoremen, the least superstitious, were also less at
risk. But we can also divide the 'deep sea' category between
drifting and trawling, each of which had a different level of
economic reward and also of danger. Most driftermen worked
a season from May until December so that they were ashore
during the roughest winter months; and when working, since
they had to land their catch daily, it was easier for them to stay
in port when the worst weather threatened. The smacksmen,
on the other hand, worked the whole year at sea, at risk for a
week at a time, and without mechanical power to help them
escape or ride out gales. From accidents to local fishermen –
whether working from the port or away – reported in the
Lowestoft Journal we have constructed mortality figures for the
years 1894–1913, which give death rates from accidents ranging from 1.04 per thousand in inshore fishing, and 2.08 in
drifting, to a horrifying 7.69 in trawling. If personal risk
determined superstition, the trawlermen would have been the
most superstitious by a large margin: but our evidence shows
the contrary.

The concept of 'economic anxiety', on the other hand, fits
much better. Certainly inshoremen seem to have had the least
economic anxieties. Their ventures were small-scale, and
often depended mainly on sheer effort and application, like

'fishing' for cockles which were raked up by hand, or hand-dredging for oysters. In this inshore work differed from both trawling and drifting.

Trawling with sail calls for an exceptional level of skilled ship handling; a carefully acquired knowledge of the precise contours of the sea bed in order to locate the fish; and meticulous navigation to avoid fouling the ship's gear in a sea liberally strewn with wrecks. 'A man must be uncommon stupid if he don't know the different sorts o' bottom', a smacksman, in this case from Grimsby, explained in the 1880s:

> The North Sea is all banks an' flats an' pits. . . . About east'ard of the tail end o' the Dawger we find light-coloured sand with small white shells, some of 'em so small as yer can hardly see 'em to be shells at all; a bit further east is what we calls the 'coffee soil', close again that comes red sand. Now, all that's a mighty fine spot for haddocks. . . . There's soft mud, an'a awful bad smell along of it; then there's shingle, an' big rocks, as breaks yer nets all to shivers. . . . There's nothin' in the world can be easier, when you've once learned yer lesson, than to pick yer way about in the North Sea just with nothin' else to guide yer than the depth o' water an' the natur'o' the bottom.[6]

It was with the aid of such local knowledge and skills, often handed down from father to son, that the Lowestoft smacksmen continued to pick their way around their chosen grounds into the twentieth century. It is thus not surprising that smacksmen, while always acknowledging some element of 'luck', would frequently ascribe good fortune to 'skill'. Only the skipper and mate of a smack were on share. The crew's wage was fixed and did not depend on the success of the trip. There were no wild variations in earnings. Trawling was a steady form of employment, with certain returns but little expectation of making large sums of money. The smacksmen's principal anxiety was to be successful enough to satisfy the owner, and so avoid being discharged.

The driftermen, by contrast, worked in a situation in which, whatever their skills, earning in the end depended on a collective gamble. The general whereabouts of the herring shoals were well known and hundreds of drifters would shoot their nets alongside each other, drifting with the movements of the tide until they hauled their nets in the early morning. There was nothing a particular crew could do to improve their catch: they simply had to wait for the herring to swim into the nets, and boats fishing close to each other could suffer extremes of fortune. 'Luck' was therefore all-important. And with all the crew 'co-venturers', paid wholly on a share of the earnings, it brought very different outcomes.

The share system of itself accounted for one striking aspect of social relations within the drifting community. There was no wage bargaining to draw out the class consciousness of the Lowestoft and Yarmouth driftermen. When the owners put in more capital, the men also earned more. Since boat-owners were usually former skippers, there was little sense of class difference between them and the fishermen. The owners, as one Kessingland fisherman put it, 'weren't uppish or ought like, they were just – they were just people. . . . They would pick you up and give you a lift home. . . . They mixed with you.' Skippers and men all started as boy cooks on the boats, continued to work side by side, and even the most successful kept to a simple working-class style of life.

The system of payment meant that each member of the crew depended on the outcome of the season's 'venture'. Men might work the five months of the Scottish season and 'pay off' without a penny, simply because they had not caught enough fish to pay their expenses, let alone a return in their share of the labour. On the other hand, just because their earnings were directly linked to the net *product* rather than to net *profit*, they stood to win in a good year an income far beyond the expectations of most working people. It was quite possible to earn, between May and December, £180 – more than double the earnings of an East Anglian craftsman in a whole year, and four times that of a farm labourer. Even more strikingly, a high proportion of these takings might be won within a few nights in an entire season. Sometimes a member of the crew might decide to take a night off, arranging for a substitute to take his place with the appropriate portion of the share as his reward. Now and again, as in this instance from the 1920s, the outcome would be spectacular:

> One of our deckhands was courting, he hadn't seen his sweetheart not for ten weeks and he wanted another night with her. So he approached one of these people on the quay and asked how much he wanted to go off for a night. He said, 'Well they're earning nothing on the North Sea, but I don't like to take your money – I'll go on what we get'. Well we went to sea. We shot. And three boats alongside each other all got a bumper catch. It took us fourteen hours to haul, we started at midnight and we got finished at half past two, then we had to clean our nets. Take them across to Ymuiden and then come back again. So when we came back again to harbour – we made £762 out of that one night's catch and we'd grossed £750 for the ten weeks in Scotland. So now, this spare hand took £25 for his one night's work – well it ran into two days – you see. He took £25, it was more than Albert – who had this night ashore – got for his whole twelve weeks in Scotland. And of course you could multiply those cases. They weren't isolated cases by no means.[7]

The driftermen's earnings, in short, were both uncertain, and potentially astonishingly high. Inevitably the whole crew shared the anxiety as to the economic success of the voyage. To make matters worse, moreover, the most money was made by a high catch when others were doing less well: a heavy catch in times of glut was almost worthless. Successive improvements in catching power, and then the greater range and speed of the new steam drifters in converging on the best markets, had further intensified this problem. The advantage of a 'crack' crew came only *after* they had caught the fish, in their speed in hauling their nets and making for port, and endurance in continuing to work at high pressure if their 'luck was in' with a succession of high catches.

Here then we come to the heart of the matter. The technological revolution and capital intensification in drifting had at the same time reduced personal danger, and intensified the risks in the economic outcome. It was the screwing up of the

pitch of collective anxiety which provided such fertile ground
for superstitions which, although general among fishermen,
were most widely practised here. It is especially significant
that only the driftermen employed magic ritual to increase
their catch. They alone would place silver in the fishing gear to
'buy the herring', or call on the Lord to favour their nets as
they were cast.

We have spoken so far of the work context of superstition in
each sector as a whole. But as Mullen remarks, 'Each individual is affected to a different degree by the beliefs of his
culture. . . . Since individuals differ in their ability to withstand tension, the ones who have the greatest need will
internalise magic beliefs to the greatest extent.' The psycho-
logical dimension which he implies here must have its importance. But individuals differ in their roles as well as
their personalities. In the East Anglian fishing, a good many
men moved between branches of the industry. Through this
we can see how the behaviour of the same individual could
vary in different work contexts. One drifterman, for example,
would work his own inshore boat from January to May,
during the break in the drifting season:

Did you do anything (on the drifters)?
Ah, we used to chuck a penny overboard to buy 'em. Cast
the nets in the name of the Lord always. Always, when
you used to shoot, and you always shot the nets the side
the Lord shot his. What he told the disciples, you always
shoot your nets the same side. Yes. And that's one thing I
will say about a fisherman. 'In the name of the Lord, pray
God he send what he think fit.'
You'd say that every time?
Every time we used to shoot our – well, not everybody but
– we used to. I was talking about the drifters now. Not the
longshore.
The longshore wouldn't say that?
No. Just chuck 'em over.

Further conversation made it clear that while the ritual was
in his experience always observed on the steam drifters, he

never saw it with the inshoremen, even when they were after the same fish with the same gear. Yet he himself appeared convinced of the efficacy of magic. He gave the only account of magic at work to come from a fisherman who had worked inshore. His dog had caught a rabbit and laid it against his boat, just as they were about to set off fishing. He wanted to return home and lose a day, but his mate urged him to ignore the omen. They sailed, only to lose two trawls over ground they fished regularly and *knew* to be free of any obstructions. Clearly he believed in magic. Yet his practice of a particular ritual depended on whether he was working inshore or drifting.

The focus of superstition upon skippers can be explained in a similar way. It was not just that they belonged to an older generation. It was on the skipper that responsibility, and therefore economic anxiety, bore heaviest. Driftermen much more often describe successful skippers as 'lucky' than as 'skilled', and owners shared this attitude too: indeed one skipper was thought so *lucky* that 'every firm was eager to employ him'. Aboard ship, it was the skipper who maintained observation of superstitious practice and expressed the fiercest resentment if a taboo was broken:

I've been told that a lot of fishermen didn't like it if you mentioned rabbits at sea?
Oh dear, blast no. They don't. The oldest ones. The younger ones now, like my age, we didn't pay no regard to it. I was along of a skipper – in a drifter – he was a mild sort of bloke and we was fishing out of North Shields. I come on the deck this here morning, he was in the wheelhouse looking out of the window, and we weren't getting many herring see. And we knew he didn't like that. And we were singing – and then there would be one shout out, 'Pigs! rabbits! ferrets!' Cor blast, he slammed the wheelhouse door and he ran aft out of the way. We laughed. Yes, oh he was dead against any mention of anything like that.

This man was born in 1888; but others twenty years younger tell similar stories. Another crewman remembers being laid up

in Lerwick. 'We weren't getting much herring.' While the
skipper was ashore, the other men dared him to draw a pig.

> I say, 'Yes, give me a pencil', and I drew this great big pig.
> And then I painted it. When he (skipper) came aboard, he
> got into the wheelhouse – 'Who drew that on there?' he say
> – 'Keep that mooring fast – I am not going to sea.' He said,
> 'If I knew who did that I would give him a good hiding.'

Crews generally showed a greater willingness than skippers
to mock at ritual. Two men remembered how as the skipper
called them to cast 'in the name of the Lord', one of the crew
might shout the name of a local parson or prostitute. But both
also mentioned that they were not getting much fish; which
must have undermined the authority of their skippers.

Skippers were not only anxious to observe traditional
rituals: some went on to invent their own practices, rather like
gamblers' fetishes – special good luck rituals of their own.
One man, for example, who became a skipper and owner in
the 1920s, refused to ascribe his life-long success to skill or
ability:

> *Why do you think that some men were so successful?*
> Well that's what we call the luck of the sea. They would
> know: they had some other instinct. Not long experience,
> I don't mean that. . . .
>   Perhaps a dozen of you would all shoot down alongside
> each other. One of those would get a big shot, two or three
> a reasonable shot, and a couple would get very little. . . . I
> can't explain it. But it must be some instinct they have
> because it went on so much. And I think life's like that . . .

He went on to compare a particular crewman who 'was always
winning' at cards, raffles or sweepstakes, with skippers who
always enjoyed a prosperous season.[8]

Unlike a trawler skipper, who rarely owned his boat, and
whose range of economic expectations were low, but normally fulfilled, the drifter skipper stood a chance of winning a
'fortune'. But once his savings were invested in such a venture,
his whole material well-being depended on his own con-

tinuing success. Although there was little he could do to influence the size of catch, his decision also determined the income of every member of the crew. With such isolated responsibility without rational skills to command the outcome, no wonder the drifter skipper was the most superstitious of all East Anglian fishermen. Here was the secret of a paradox, of a world in which attitudes seemed to reflect economic structure in a reverse mirror, in which captains of a modern industry were driven back to seek refuge in the images and delusions of 'traditional' superstition.

12 The Protestant ethic, the family and the economy

Fishermen are as renowned for their religious enthusiasm as for their susceptibility to superstition – and rightly so. For you can find churches, chapels and mission halls as widely scattered round the coasts as taboos. This is so on both sides of the Atlantic. In one of the outports of Newfoundland, the most prominent building will be either a gleaming white wooden temple or a carpenter's gothic church. In one outport the descendants of Irish fishermen-farmers, who until twenty years ago grew potatoes on lazy-beds in the old way, still crowd the road outside their Catholic church with people and cars on a Sunday morning; elsewhere the Anglicans, Methodists, or Salvation Army will have the hold – or in recent years, especially on the economically hard-hit northern shore, the Pentecostals. In a similar way Scandinavian fishing communities from the mid-nineteenth century began to set up their own churches. In Sweden they formed independent Methodist and Baptist and later Pentecostal congregations; in western Norway the evangelicals of the coastal 'prayer house belt' stayed within the established Lutheran church, but elsewhere turned to the Pentecostals and Laestadians; while the Faroese became Methodists, Salvationists and Plymouth Brethren. In Britain the established church kept its dominance in the earliest fishing towns which had churches and clergy before the Reformation, but elsewhere – and especially in Scotland – the Scandinavian pattern was repeated.

The Scottish fishing settlements had mostly originated from the late seventeenth century onwards, so that they were not originally provided for by the Church of Scotland. Some of them were altogether neglected. This again left space for the growth of a variety of independent religious forms, whose influence still remains strong today. Many Scots fishermen continue to refuse to fish on Sundays as a matter of strict faith, just as it was at one time for the entire Scottish inshore and drifting fleets. As recently as the 1950s they celebrated the introduction of inter-ship radios by creating their own form of religious broadcasting: for as one strong-voiced Fraserburgh skipper, William Whyte, remembers, when they were driven by rough weather to take shelter off the west coast, he would lead the combined crews in radio hymn-singing.

Such enthusiasm was not unique to the Scots. There are fishermen's choirs from Filey in Yorkshire as well as the Moray Firth. In Staithes the influence of chapel even reached the pubs, in Sunday evening gatherings for hymn-singing and more recently from a juke-box with 'numerous recordings of popular religious themes'. In Cornwall it was Primitive Methodist fishermen who led the riot of May 1896 against Sunday fishing by the East Anglian driftermen at the spring mackerel fishing. In East Anglia too, there were exceptions to the general air of relative indifference, like the Salvationist stronghold of Sheringham among the smaller ports, or in Lowestoft itself the Bethel and St George's Road mission hall. This had its own band, and as Ned Mullender of Pakefield recalls,

> We didn't have no minister; anybody could git up. I remember goin' there one time an' there was an old skipper called Nick Fisher who got up. He was a gret ol' man with a beard an' I can remember him sayin', 'Here we are together, brothers an' sisters, arter a long, dreary, ol' West'ard woyage': 'woyage', he said – not voyage! . . .
>
> They used t'vary the services. One time there'd be Brother So-and-So git up there an' give a few words. Another time someone else. Like that. My uncle Jimmy, he used t'git up there an' say a few words. You used t'git all the ol' Sankey an' Moody hymns as well. . . . Yes, I can remember that right well. You'd have 'Lead Kindly Light' an all them sort. 'Keep the lower light burning', that was in the book as well.

More generally Norfolk and Suffolk fishermen would crowd the old parish churches for annual 'Harvest of the Seas' thanksgiving services after the home fishing, when lifebelts would be hung from the parson's pulpit and drifter pennants stretched from wall to wall above the altar.

It was from East Anglia in fact, that the last great evangelical revival began. It broke in Yarmouth; at the close of the disastrous autumn herring season of 1921. Led by the 27-year-old fisherman Dave Gardiner and the cooper Joch Troup, from the start 'it was very emotional. . . . They were fainting . . . flinging their hats in the air and burning pipes.' Within days it had spread northwards to Scotland, as the boats returned home: empty of the melodeons, gramophones, clothes and sweets which families had been eagerly expecting, the crews instead out of pocket and in debt – bringing comfort to the spirit alone. Here it momentarily gripped whole communities. In Inverallochy, the *Fraserburgh Herald* reported, the village shop and club had closed as the people awaited the imminent second coming of the Messiah. Children, instead of skipping, were kneeling in circles in the road praying. By the harbour two hundred fishermen stood listening to Bible stories 'and after each parable had been explained they knelt down together on the shore and engaged in silent prayer, wringing their hands and swaying their bodies to and fro'. And at night a great bonfire stood against the sky, an offering to the heavens of the worldly goods

that stood between the converts and grace. A huge pile containing such things as cigarettes and pipes, playing cards, draught boards, ludo, tiddle-de-winks, snakes and ladders, dancing pumps, etc, etc, was fired, and fanned by a high wind, was speedily devoured while their former owners knelt around the conflagration in the ring and sang and prayed.

For many 'the excitement' was soon to wane; but there are others for whom those days still seemed a turning point sixty years later. As one put it of the Yarmouth Baptist preacher through whose words he was converted,

I'll never forget, he preached on the potter and the clay . . . and I never heard his like. . . . He brought God into your life someway – I just can't explain . . .

For fishermen and their families, unusually vulnerable to the blows of fate both from the ups and downs of an unpredictable economy, and also from accident and death in the face of the elements, religion could offer comfort, meaning and purpose in life, and hope for the future. They turned to evangelical Protestantism, however, not because some ubiquitous inner characteristic predisposed them to emotional hymn-singing, but more from the longstanding failure of the established churches to recognise their needs. Church and Kirk, even if nowhere near a fishing settlement, expected its people to come to them; but the sects were prepared to go out to find the people. That was one reason for their success. The other was the chosen moment. It was no accident that the great revival of 1921 came with the shock and despair of economic crisis. The earlier revivals, whose uneven impact partly accounts for the sharp regional differences in Scottish religious patterns, can be seen in a similar light. The highland revivalism of the 1830s gripped a crofting population bewildered and demoralised by mass eviction and clearances from their land and homes. The industrial lowlands were hit by an explosive revival during the severe economic depressions of the 1840s. Neither of these two campaigns had much impact on the Scottish north-east coast whose economy was then flourishing. The third wave of conversion, the 1859 movement, came from America, by way of Northern Ireland – where the economic difficulties of the old linen districts again partly explain its lasting impact. It was taken to the Scottish fishing towns by the three-month mission of a curer-cooper, James Turner, whose business had failed. And the deepening crisis of the herring industry from the late 1870s coincides with when the Open and Closed Brethren, the Church of Christ and the Salvationists won their first permanent footholds in the ports: nuclei from which, when depression returned in the 1920s, they struck out to establish a formidable presence round the whole north-east coast.

In these bleak times, when economic failure added its special bitterness to a long-standing sense of social rejection by the wider society, Christianity could provide more than immediate consolation. It could also offer a whole new moral vision in which the conventional judgments of the social world were

stood on end, and a new future became possible. Had not the
first apostles also been fishermen of whom in their own time it
was said that 'they were unlearned and ignorant men'? The
sense of transformed destiny rings through the hymn which
James Slater, a young drifterman 'saved by grace' at a Salvation Army open-air meeting on the shorehead at Portsoy in
1923, wrote later, setting his lines to the tune 'Harbour Head'
by the Buckie fisherman Simon Flett:

> That distant port! is Glory there,
> Its joy and bliss we all may share;
> Trusting the Saviour till at last,
> We shall the anchor safely cast.
>
> There is a Pilot! Christ the Lord,
> There is a Chart! His faithful word;
> And Light divine; so clear so bright
> Shines through the gloom of sin's dark night.
>
> Heed then His voice, while yet you may,
> Trust in the Lord, trust Him today;
> So shall we gain that blissful shore,
> Safe home at last, safe evermore.[1]

Nor was it just a question of new hope for the after-life for
most of them. The building of a better world about them was
to begin now. And how they set about this could have a
fundamental impact on the future of entire communities.

Religion may be an outcome of economic change. But it can be
a cause of it too. At the simplest level one could demonstrate
this by citing the impact of a particular doctrine. Conscien-
tious objection was adopted by the fishermen of many north-
east ports along with their conversion to the Brethren sects.
This was in the depression years; but subsequently in the
Second World War, when their boats were among the few
which fished almost continuously, it was this pacifist faith
which gave them their special chance of economic success.
Temperance provides another clear example. And more
generally, the connection between economic attitudes and
Protestantism, argued by Max Weber in his classic *The Prot-*

estant Ethic and the Spirit of Capitalism, has influenced historians and sociologists for decades.

Unfortunately all too often the subtlety of Weber's original argument has been forgotten. This has led, for example, to somewhat unproductive attempts to quantify the relationship between religious belief and economic success. Weber did not argue that Protestantism caused economic achievement. Much more plausibly, he believed that economic change required the presence of, at the same time, both opportunity provided by a particular economic and social context, and also attitudes which encouraged people to take their chance. Protestant or not, without opportunity there could be no economic achievement. Furthermore, the role of Protestantism, and especially in his view Calvinism, was indirect: in encouraging the growth of a 'rationalistic' culture in which economic decisions were based on the calculated pursuit of profit, and which fostered an ethic of hard work and personal thrift. Weber's views on rationalism and traditionalism will not concern us here: they are singularly unhelpful when applied to the cultures we are considering. In fact they seem to us to be based on unspoken assumptions of cultural superiority, not dissimilar from those of 'modernisation' theory, which make them inherently defective. On the other hand Weber's concept of the indirect role of certain forms of Protestantism in shaping secular economic attitudes still seems a very perceptive approach.

In Britain the influence of *The Protestant Ethic and the Spirit of Capitalism* has led, in reverse, to suggestions by historians that one major cause for the long-term decline in the British economy after 1870 may have been a lack of 'industrial spirit'. Even after industrialisation the old aristocratic values of culture continued to prevail over those of trade and industry. So far from the latter ousting the former, entrepreneurial families gradually ceased bringing up their children with the old Puritan values, of hard work, and self-discipline in seeking their own salvation. Instead, as manufacturers became assimilated into the upper classes, their children would be sent to fee-paying public schools where they learnt to govern, rather than to work; and to spend their resources on the conspicuous luxuries of society life – drinking, entertaining, keeping a large house with servants, even on gambling and women – rather than in profitable investment in the manufacturing enterprise which had won them their social position. If it could be proved, such an explanation of economic decline would clearly be of immense contemporary political as well as historical significance.

Unfortunately the argument has so far rested largely on speculation. We have as yet no history of the entrepreneurial family in Britain. Nor do we know much, either from historians or from social scientists, about the changing relationships between family, economy and moral attitudes. Clearly in exploring such issues we need to see specific religious doctrines, and also the more diffuse general social influences of the churches, as simply elements within a wider moral order of family and community. Certainly it is easier to document doctrines preached from the pulpit and published in books of sermons than to trace changes in general attitudes. Yet these latter are what counted. We need to pick out the changing character of the local values which were shared between neighbours and workmates, passed down to each new generation – which could never be just a matter of Sunday services.

The economic rewards of the Protestant ethic were certainly not a new discovery of Max Weber. They had long been part of our own folklore. Certainly Hilda Shedd, starting her teacher training at Cambridge in 1908, was unlikely to know of his original German articles, when she was given an autograph book for her birthday, in which M.J.S. inscribed as the first entry:

> You can climb to the top of the loftiest hill,
>> If you work.
> You can make of yourself whatsoever you will,
>> If you work.
> A faith you must have, rooted deep in your soul,
> A purpose unshaken, a firm self-control,
> Strive on, without ceasing; you'll reach to the goal,
>> If you work.

We do not know what Hilda Shedd made of it. But the lines would have been well understood in the Scottish north-east, for their stern clarity encapsulates three crucial strands in the social ethic of Protestantism: the call to work; the necessity for self-control; and the chance to create a future of one's own.

These strands may each be given different shades of meaning. Nor should they be seen as in any sense exclusively Protestant. The call to work in particular can be found in all sorts of human societies; and in any fishing community depending on a hard-won subsistence from the sea, work is likely to be assumed as a basic social duty, whether or not it is given a religious significance. Indeed it seems more probable that work is likely to become a cult when it is less essential, as with the Calvinist merchants of the seventeenth century or the rising middle classes of Victorian Britain.

Work certainly did become an obsessive concern with the Victorian middle classes. One can see this again and again, whether one looks at the trainee elementary schoolmistress, or the Poor Law official imposing the labour test in the workhouse, or the Anglican preacher attacking beggars and scroungers after traditional charity, or the whining Nonconformist foreman of Robert Tressall's *Ragged Trousered Philanthropists*. And the greatest minds wrestled equally with work. The labour theory of value was a central doctrine of the classical economists, turned upside down by Robert Owen and Karl Marx to lay the moral foundations of a socialist society, and inside out by John Ruskin and William Morris to provide its most fundamental fulfilment. It is clear too that Victorian skilled men did find a deep pride in their manual skills and the products of their labour. Ruskin himself could not have expressed that feeling more eloquently than a north Welsh blacksmith, born in the 1890s and taught his trade by his father:

> As soon as I got strong enough I used to beat the iron. Hit the iron. Hammer the iron. And watch. . . . I think I learnt about music from my hammer, I would listen to the different notes and rhythms it produced. This was the work I love. . . .
>
> And whenever I get the call from this world, there's many more things left behind me here. I haven't got a wife and children regrettably, but there are a lot of things here,

that show I've been here, and that are going to stay. The fact is if . . . you've made things, you've done something.

Fishermen cannot claim the craftsman's satisfaction in making things, but they do share an undeniable pride in skill at work. Indeed, it is on a skipper's skill in finding fish that his authority at sea and prestige in the community ashore rests. The roots of this fundamental social attitude are almost certainly independent of Protestantism. But it fitted in well with its values.

For highly successful skipper-owners, hard work could offer a moral justification for wealth, provided that they put their profit quietly into the bank, or towards a better boat, rather than spending it in social display. In this their conduct matched that of the Calvinist merchants on whose 'inner wordly asceticism' Weber based his arguments: men who saw themselves as 'called' to do the work of God, their economic success a sign of God's blessing upon them, and their abstinence from enjoying the wealth they had created a further token of their moral virtue. But it is the egalitarian ethic of fishing communities rather than religious doctrine which provides the most powerful restraint against display of wealth: an attitude found in many communities of widely differing religious perspective. And similarly, if the Biblical quotation, 'In the sweat of thy face shall thou eat bread', which seventeenth-century pastors would cite in their exhortations still echoes behind the phrase of the Buckie fisherman today, 'You must work before you eat, with us', it is nevertheless again more likely that Protestantism was reinforcing an existing morality, rather than creating a new one.[2]

The case is different when we turn to self-control. A much more direct contribution was made by Protestantism to the fishing economy in terms of the temperance movement. Scots herring fishermen had not always been non-drinkers. When Hugh Miller went out with the Cromarty men in 1819, the nets were no sooner shot than 'the skipper's bottle was next produced, and a dram of whisky sent round in a tin measure'. At this time whisky was also drunk to seal a bargain. And Fraserburgh, Wick and Peterhead curers up to the mid-century would agree on engagement to supply a crew with a gallon and a half of whisky for every week at sea.

It is not easy to plot the spread of temperance among fishing communities exactly, but the turning point seems to have been around 1880. A history of Eyemouth written by its Congregational minister reports that the village was in a very rough and drunken state until 1873, worse than nearby farming villages, but from then onwards teetotalism gained a foothold, and 'by degrees the wedge of total abstinence made a cleavage in the community'. It looks too as if it was the younger generation of the 1880s who led the north-east communities into temperance. Peterhead's old fishermen in the 1920s still spoke of a past in which fisherfolk were 'careless, godless, and addicted to drink', but the younger men were 'proud of the fact that they have never known the taste of spirits'. As a result of this transformation, 'money that used to be spent at the publican's, and go to fill his pockets, has been laid aside to the fishermen's credit, and houses, boats and other gear have been bought with the money that used to be wasted on drink.' The men's conversion was no doubt in part a response to the hard times of the 1880s; but abstinence was also to be the foundation of their future prosperity. It provided a critical new impulse towards thrift. There would be no drinking aboard the Scots steam-drifter fleet.

Total abstinence from alcohol was a peculiarly Protestant form of morality, and even among Protestants the absolute taboo was a nineteenth-century innovation. The Victorians also preached the virtues of sexual 'thrift', arguing in some cases explicitly for its economic benefits in reducing the number of children a family had to support. It is of course Catholics rather than Protestants who in this sphere have been most sympathetic to absolute prohibitions. But sexual 'puritanism', if not specifically Protestant, was undoubtedly strongly reinforced from the pulpit, and through the church courts which continued active in Scotland into the nineteenth century. And they were backed by a national law of bastardy which insisted on discrimination against children born out of wedlock.

This official intolerance had one fortunate consequence for the historian, in the production of regular statistics of marriage and of extra-marital fertility. From these it is clear that at least from the 1860s into the 1930s very late marriage was characteristic of the whole of northern Scotland. Throughout this period mean age at marriage ranged from 29 to 32 for men, and from 26 to 28 for women. It was highest of all in the north-west. But figures for illegitimacy reveal a very different picture, for the rates were very low for the far north and north-west, especially the outer isles, but by contrast notoriously high for the north-east. In Banffshire, which includes Buckie, between 1858 and 1886 over 16 per cent of all births were illegitimate. But while in the outer isles the fishing and farming populations were inextricably mixed, this was not true of the north-east, and once the county figures are broken down it becomes evident that there were noticeably lower illegitimacy rates in the coastal parishes. More detailed occupational calculations prove that even in this region fishermen and fishermen's daughters were comparatively rarely responsible for illegitimate pregnancies, or even for premarital conceptions subsequently concealed through a quick marriage. Perhaps most interesting of all, there seems to be very little connection between this sexual self-control and religion. It does not appear to have mattered greatly in practice that illegitimate children were relatively tolerated in Shetland, while in Lewis the power of the Free Kirk ensured that they were an irredeemable social disgrace: for although Lewis had the lowest illegitimacy ratio in Scotland, Shetland was second to it. Nor is there any sign of higher illegitimacy ratios in those remote islands or socially marginal newer coastal settlements which had been left unprovided for by the parochial system.

The paradox is driven home by the fact that during the 1880s, just at the moment when the hold of religion was becoming stronger among the fishermen of the north-east, the figures show a small but distinct rise in illegitimacy associated with them. The reasons were that their sexual self-control, and the signs of change, were bound up with the nature of the family economy. Marriage among fishermen had to provide a working economic partnership. This made for caution in choosing partners: fishermen, it was reported from Buckie in 1858 'do not marry at an earlier age'. But by the 1880s, the

longer seasons away from home in the drifting were under-
mining the old basis of marriage. At the same time the crisis in
the industry meant that there were more likely to be intended
matches broken off through a young fisherman's difficulties in
making a start. Contemporary observers shrewdly pointed
their finger at 'the demoralising effect the Yarmouth fishing is
having on the male fishing population'.[3]

If sexual self-control has to be understood in terms of a
wider social morality rooted in the economy, this must be all
the more true of the last, and for us perhaps the most crucial
strand in the Protestant ethic: the chance to create a future of
one's own. On this Weber – who like most men of his class and
generation, had little chance to see the significance of child-
rearing – took too limited a view. There can be many kinds of
future: in this life, or in the next; tied to the destiny of a
common social group, or discovered as an independent individual. Whether a community emphasises one or the other
will deeply influence the way in which its children are brought
up, and through this the creativity, the willingness to change
and to innovate, of subsequent generations.

It might be thought that the logic of the Protestant ethic
would press almost invariably towards the development of
independent conscience. But in *The Protestant Temperament*, a
study of the patterns of child-rearing and religious belief in the
colonial elite of early America, Philip Greven reveals an
extraordinary range of attitude. At one extreme there were
authoritarian families, often of Puritan ministers, who believed that children should above all be taught self-denial,
regular habits, and submission of their wills to the authority of
parents and God. They saw salvation as a gift of God: it could
not be independently won by free will and good works. In
training their children, some emphasised reasoning, others
chastisement. But their aim was always to inculcate both 'love
and fear': 'a humble, broken-hearted love', fit instrument of
the divine will. At the opposite pole were those well-to-do
merchants and plantation owners who cultivated a sense of
self-worth and self-respect through unchecked and intense
love for their 'much indulged' children. Among such parents it
was a common saying that 'To curb their children is to spoil

their genius.' And in between were many varieties of 'moderate' opinion.

We shall find echoes of just these differences in our Scottish
fishing communities. But if we want to link them with
economic development – which was not Greven's interest –
we face the difficulty of lacking a wider framework within
which to form our interpretations. In the first place there is an
acute lack of evidence from which the history of the family can
be constructed before the mid-nineteenth century, except for
the upper classes. This problem applies particularly to the
history of childhood. It means that most of the broad canvases
with which historians have tried to sketch out the evolution of
'the modern family' or of parent–child relationships are mar-
red by misleading and sweeping generalisation on the basis of
scant evidence. They tend too to treat the story as one of
cumulative progress from the barbarity of antiquity to the
sensitivities of the present. Yet when we do find ourselves on
firm ground, the scene is surprisingly different from how we
might have envisaged it: there can be no doubt, for example,
of the real strength of parental love among the peasants and
shepherds of the Pyrenean mountain hamlet of *Montaillou*,
whose daily life Le Roy Ladurie has reconstructed for us
through the testimonies recorded by a mediaeval inquisitor.

Secondly, most contemporary social science has worked
within the assumption that family patterns are a consequence
of social and economic structures. There is, for example,
comparative work by anthropologists which suggest – in line
with our own argument – that primitive hunting and fishing
societies, in contrast to those with settled agriculture, place a
higher emphasis on bringing up their children to be independent 'achievers' rather than obedient and reliable. Similarly,
American sociological research has reported that parents with
a small business background are more likely to encourage
independence in their children than those employed in large
bureaucracies. But these are studies of consequences rather
than causes. They do not consider how these economic structures were created in the first place; nor do they show the fate
of children brought up differently in the same social context.
Where interesting suggestions have been made on these issues,
like David McClelland's historical comparisons in *The Achiev-*

ing Society, or Basil Bernstein's in the sociology of education, they have rarely been backed by convincing research. This neglect itself reflects a surprisingly general lack of interest by social scientists in the mutual interaction of family and economy.[4]

It is fortunate that for the last hundred years the evidence for constructing a more reliable account of changing family patterns is there for us to gather – by collecting life histories from living memory. This was what we did for our own earlier book *The Edwardians*, for which we used not only documentary sources but also a special oral history survey of over four hundred interviews, designed to represent the population of Britain as a whole in the first decade of this century. These life histories made it possible for the first time to map out the differing family relationships within Britain at the turn of the century. Let us briefly summarise one aspect of them.

We found that there were marked variations, not only between social classes, but also between regions. For many we were also able to see an explanation in the economic situation of the family. We shall take the case of the use of corporal punishment by parents of children as an example. Contrary to the conventional wisdom – which is supported by a good deal of recent family history and sociology – it turned out that physical discipline was not a universal day-to-day instrument of child control in the families of our grandparents. On the contrary, in most families the authority of parents was so little challenged by children that there were few occasions when their parents might have wished to punish them in this way. The shop manager who 'only ever hit my youngest lad once' may be taken as representative. 'The only time was', the boy had knocked some bread on the floor and wouldn't pick it up. 'And I made him pick it up because I knew I had to be master.' One can also find many households in the working class in which the father commanded undisputed obedience without recourse to any force: 'He never hit us . . . Well, he'd no need to hit us . . . He didn't tell us twice.' This was especially characteristic of skilled workers' families, but was also common among the unskilled and farm labourers' families in the south.

In the regions which had industrialised earliest, the Midlands and north, we found by contrast a much more frequent use not only of slapping, but also of harsher forms of chastisement. We suspected that one cause of this might have been the social strains caused by the industrial revolution, and the harsh discipline of a factory workforce often recruited at first from pauper children: the stresses and brutality suffered by earlier generations vented on their own children, and setting up patterns which had continued even when the conditions of factory life had modified.

It was at any rate certain that relative poverty, in itself, did not result in a stricter upbringing. Probably the freest, even though they were not the least punished children of the 1900s, were those of the very poorest, 'roughest' city families. Here it seemed clear enough that the basis for their independence was economic. Their parents, underpaid and often out of work, were unable to provide for their basic needs beyond infancy as well as the children could themselves. And there was no space in their homes for family life: often no furniture, no regular meals. Such children therefore 'fetched ourself up' on the street, begging or stealing clothes and food, and picking up casual earnings. Long before they left school they could be free of financial dependence of their parents. One South London coal-heaver's son, the youngest of thirteen children dispersed between relatives and truant schools, described how, while his parents moved between pub, workhouse and prison, he was out selling papers or firewood, pushing a barrow vending hearthstone and vinegar, peddling envelopes in pubs: 'That's how we used to get hold of money. No, we never used to get anything out of our parents. They never had enough for their beer.' Here we have an independence and freedom in childhood which reflects the difficulty of keeping a home together for those at the bottom of a very unequal society: the powerlessness of parents.

At the opposite end to the social scale, however, another kind of relatively unrestricted childhood could be perceived, this time based on an abundance of resources. As one critic put it in 1905, in the most 'advanced' homes of the well-to-do, 'punishment is taboo. Long moral lectures . . . with an occasional intimation that the lecturer has been deeply grieved and

hurt, are . . . to take the place of old-fashioned punish-
ments. . . . The vagaries of some seven-year old lady . . . will
occupy the entire time and attention of one medical specialist,
one ethical lecturer, two parents, and a nurse . . .'[5] Here was
the vanguard of the 'progressive' child-rearing of the mid-
twentieth century. Clearly such parents, besides possessing
ample means, must have been unusually open to new ideas and
influences.

It might be easily assumed that 'enlightened' views of this
kind have spread in a straightforward way down the social
scale from the more educated and better-off classes to the rest
of the population. But our interviews also showed that the
historical process could not have been so simple: for we found
the most generally 'progressive' parents in early twentieth-
century Britain as a whole were those of a particularly 'primitive' region, the Shetlands. It was in searching for an explanation for this remarkable regional variation that we began the
research which led to the writing of this book. Despite such
questions, however, we were left in little doubt of the role
played by the changing social economy in moulding the
family. But what of the reverse relation?

A useful parallel here can be drawn from the history of the
family in Sweden, which has the advantage of oral source
material from earlier collectors going back to the mid-
nineteenth century. Here it has been shown that two contrasting family types developed in the south of the country. One
was the family of the prosperous farming peasantry, formal
and controlled: they secured their continuing economic
strength through careful marriage and careful husbandry of
their resources. The other was the landless family, which had
to use a different strategy, rearing its children to early self-
sufficiency. This was a response to economic difficulty; but
also, through sending out migrants and developing new economies in marginal areas, in itself contributing to economic
change.[6] This contrast between the closed, conservative family of the farmers and the open, innovatory independence of
the labourers may be a very significant clue; for it fits strikingly with the findings of two of our own more recent research
projects, the one on the Scottish fishermen, and the other on
the upper- and middle-class family in the early twentieth

century. And it leads us back to the role of the Protestant ethic in both economic growth and decline.

Our life histories showed there had been important differences between the child-rearing practices of the upper classes and the industrial leaders of the same years.[7] Upper-class 'society' before the First World War functioned both as a means for regulating entry into the class – either through marriage or money – and for supporting the political needs of landowners. Society was managed by upper-class women; it was their business to ensure that sympathetic newcomers were influenced through encouragement, while those too radical to be tamed were frozen out. Upper-class childhood was essentially a training for running either 'society', or some part of the Empire – whether a country estate, a regiment or a colony. A direct role in industry or finance was still not regarded as a desirable ambition. Upper-class children were well provided for, and at home they were rarely physically punished, but their upbringing was certainly not 'progressive' in the modern sense: it was rather a system of emotional hardening and withdrawal of love designed to produce adults with sufficient self-control to assume the duties, values and customs of upper-class society. From infancy, upper-class children were brought up separately from their parents, sleeping and eating in another part of the house, cared for by a servant. Most children only saw their mothers regularly for an hour a day after tea, and fathers were still less available. And by the age of ten boys – and some girls – would be sent away for a tough boarding-school education. The gulf between parents was such that a nurse was a much more common confidant: parents were viewed with awe, rather than intimacy. Childhood was a fitting preparation for an adulthood in which feeling was regarded as essentially undesirable. As Mrs C. E. Humphry wrote in 1902, 'The Englishman trains himself from boyhood to a stern self-repression. He will show no feeling if he can help it.'[8]

Entrepreneurial children were handled in a very different spirit. In some respects this was quite consciously: they would be given mechanical toys, cars and electric railways, rather than rocking horses, and later trained in science and technology as well as classics. But there was an equally notable contrast in the underlying atmosphere, which is less easy to characterise. This is because the essential thread which seems to link the families of active industrialists in an element of deviance, even eccentricity, which prevented them from absorption into the attitudes of upper-class society: protecting them from its scorn for money-making through business or 'trade', and admiration for conspicuous social display and leisure.

Major innovative entrepreneurs were themselves usually men of phenomenal energy with a demonstrative zest for life, which burst out in a variety of directions: food, travel, clothes, games, even open-handedness with money. In their personal lives they were dominating, hot-tempered and frequently autocratic, but emotionally unusually demonstrative. Some of them found home life insufficiently congenial to give it much time. But a much more striking tendency is towards a family intimacy and closeness, in sharp contrast to the normal upper-class pattern. Sometimes this takes a religious form, a sectarian family piety; but there are other equally interesting instances of a more 'modern' kind of intimacy, more explosively expressive, tolerating argument and even swearing in company. There are also a minority of cases in which extremely deprived childhoods – for example, in an orphanage – also led to successful entrepreneurial careers. But above all, for a variety of reasons – some as adherents of a minority religious group, some as migrants, some as members of a local urban business social circle – these familes rejected the traditional status values of upper-class society, and instead judged themselves by their own standards: they shared a high regard for individual worth and achievement. Conversely, some move towards 'gentrification' was noticeable in the life stories of those entrepreneurs who experienced at least a phase of severe economic decline or bankruptcy.

Even such manufacturing families, however, suffered a recurrent problem through the natural cycle of succession. Founder-entrepreneurs in particular when old tend to remain autocratic, while they become less in touch and sometimes much more conservative. If they remain in control, and fail to allow room for their heirs to make a creative contribution in their turn, the family firm becomes vulnerable to crisis. But this could be mitigated when the family structure and hierarchy was sufficiently open and informal to accept argument and disagreement. Here again religion could play a crucial role in shaping attitudes. The willingness of the venerable George Cadbury, for example, who was born in 1839 and lived until 1922, to be overruled by his sons as junior directors in the family business was a direct reflection of the Cadbury family's Quaker egalitarian individualism.

It looks, in short, as if one key factor in sustaining entrepreneurial initiative is the social encouragement of individuality. Some entrepreneurial families could be said to fit Basil Bernstein's characterisation of 'person-orientated families' in which 'the child learns to *make* his role rather than this being formally assigned to him', and communication is open, in contrast to 'positional families' where 'the area of decision-making is invested in the member's formal status', argument is discouraged, and commands more often backed up by blows. But our own research suggests that the ways in which individuality can be fostered are too diverse to be so simply captured. They range from positive forms of encouragement such as a 'progressive' emotional expressiveness, or a religious conviction of personal salvation, to an essentially negative protection from the general values of higher society due to social isolation or disadvantage.

These findings coincide closely with our interpretation of fishing communites, and their struggle for survival in a changing community. For where family boat-ownership has survived, these communities are in a sense entire societies of individual petty entrepreneurs, of co-venturers whose occupational continuance has depended on a recurrent adaptability to changes in fish stocks, technology and the market. They thus require a moral order which encourages not only solidarity – to maintain a workforce – but also adaptability. That double need is nicely put in the local saying of the go-ahead modern Swedish fishermen of Fiskebäck outside Göteborg: 'We must pull the youth with us.' In fishing early retirement is justified not only by the nature of the work, but also to give the young men a chance, in their twenties, to become innovating skippers.

A recent economic study of the highly successful Norwegian purse seiners has pointed out how their example directly contradicts the assumption common in the literature that 'egalitarianism makes innovations impossible or that innovators often become alienated from the people, or indeed are "aliens"; that is, from a different ethnic group or social stratum'. For while these facts may be correctly observed, the wrong explanation is being drawn from them. Like the Shetland or the Buckie fisherman, 'the Norwegian herring fisherman seems to have solved this problem of producing entrepreneurs from his own ranks (skippers and net bosses) while at the same time, maintaining an egalitarian pattern of interaction and values.' Their attitudes to their children are also closely comparable. The fact is that the conventional wisdom stands the truth on its head. It is not the egalitarianism of the wider society which has stifled creativity, and forced innovators into social isolation, but its demand for the social conformity and quiescence necessary to maintain *in*equality. The importance of the fishing communities is that they show the viability of an alternative way: for it is only such socially isolated groups which have been able to sustain up to the present the truer form of egalitarianism which fosters real social independence and individuality.

Fishing communities have been helped in sustaining their distinctive, egalitarian values by a social separation sometimes due to low status – as an enclave within the port – and sometimes to sheer physical isolation. Very often, as with Nonconformist manufacturing families, this has been further reinforced through the moral autonomy which they have gained from religious separatism. The Free Kirk of Lewis has this in common with the Brethren of the north-east. But perhaps most important of all is the degree to which they are able to encourage individualism – and with it even eccentricity. The case studies which follow show how closely, in the family boat-owning communities which have succeeded best, this is linked to local economic adaptability. For the few successful entrepreneurs, there must always be many more who try their hand.

In such encouragement formal religious belief certainly can be an important element. Two contrasts are especially essential. The first is between the teaching of hope by some churches, and of submission to fate by others. The second is between the influences of multiple sects competing locally for individual members, and the more inclusive dominance of churches like the established Auld Kirk, and also the Free Kirk of Lewis, which believed their 'mission was the conversion not of individuals but of the whole social order'. But differences are not explicable in such terms alone – especially of religious doctrine. In Weber's own words, 'it is not the ethical *doctrine* of a religion, but that form of ethical conduct upon which *premiums* are placed that matters.' On the vital doctrinal issue of predestination, the ability of men and women to make their own choice to be saved, to make new lives for themselves, a doctrine especially emphasised by Weber, the formal distinctions between Lewis, Shetland and the north-east were slight. Much more important was what was emphasised, and how this religious perspective tied in with the moral and social attitudes of family and community: the egalitarianism within the family, and rearing of children to independence with little physical punishment, which characterises Shetland and also parts of Scandinavia; how in Buckie prosperity was seen to depend on moral worth, and there was a pervasive belief in effort and competitiveness, inculcated from childhood; while Lewis children were taught submission to God, obedience to their elders, and conformity with their peers.[9]

The relationships between family, moral order and economy are in short mutual and inseparable. The economic system, technology and resources create a framework within which men and women must win a living; and because they must eat to live, its constraints are fundamental. But the economy is made by society. And two essential parts of its making are through the moral order of the community, and within the family. Hence its historical evolution cannot be adequately traced or interpreted by the male-generated abstractions of self-contained economic theory in isolation. The unpaid labour of women within the household is not merely an essential part of the existing structure at any time, but also, through the bearing and rearing of children, the foundation of the social economy of the future. Those children will shape that future.

Part IV Community and individuality

Close-up: The Moray Firth
13 The moral order of free enterprise: Buckie

North of Aberdeen the mountains recede a little from the coast, and a hump of green farmland, Buchan, juts into the North Sea. Peterhead and Fraserburgh are astride its furthest projection. The land then retracts sharply before the open bite of the Moray Firth, fifty miles across at its extremities, and slicing half-way through northern Scotland. The farmland meets the sea along most of its southern shore in lowish cliffs and rock, providing at best small coves and beaches for the string of tight fishing villages which crowd beside them. The Firth was their home ground. At the mid-point in the string is Buckie. Today with its commercial high street, morning quayside bustle, ranks of neat two-storey terraces of white-edged grey stone, and groups of older, cloth-capped men sitting on benches or standing at street corners, it has very much the air of a veteran industrial town. There is no tourist office in Buckie.

The town goes back in origin at least to the seventeenth century, and some of its later fishing families like the Murrays, Cowies, Coulls and Jappies were already present by this date. But it was no more than a minor, and judging by photographs, rather impoverished village until the mid-nineteenth century, living like its neighbours from the inshore white fishing and the seasonal herring shoals in the Moray Firth. Their white fish catch was 'salted in pots on the beach, and dried on the rocks'. The close single-storey rows in the town's oldest quarter, the Yardie below the cliffs, still convey something of its earlier character. In the 1790s Easter and Nether Buckie, owned by Lord Gordon and Mr Dunbar respectively, had between them only 700 people and a mere fifteen large line boats, all belonging to the two proprietors. Nor were the men of Buckie then noted for their industry. Dunbar used to go 'down to the shore

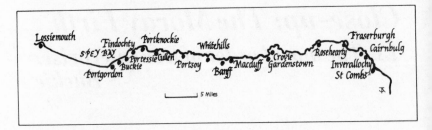

in the morning with a stick in his hand and drove the fishermen to sea': and he punished those who refused to obey by putting them in iron manacles or 'joogs'.

Yet by the 1890s the Fishery Board could report that Buckie had developed 'by leaps and bounds in the last thirty years'. The new registration district formed for its section of the coast counted well over 3,000 fishermen and 700 boats in the two decades up to the First World War. But more remarkable still was the nature of this concentration. Buckie in 1913 claimed a third of the entire Scottish steam herring fleet. It had become in a dozen years the foremost steam drifter home port in Scotland, second only to Lowestoft in the whole of Britain. And its fishermen had succeeded in achieving this transformation from sail to steam, with the help of capital advanced by local salesmen and bankers, while preserving the family boat ownership which they had established by the early nineteenth century. How had they pulled off this extraordinary slap in the face to the advancing combines of capitalist steam fishing?

The first factor which had turned the original small settlement into a pole of attraction for the adjoining coast was harbour construction. Buckie had no harbour at all until 1843, when a communal effort was spurred by the town's dynamic first Free Kirk minister, Robert Shanks. He paid for most of the materials, 'often "gaffered" the men himself, and it was no unusual sight for him to be seen with a pick or shovel in his hand. Each boat's crew contributed so much towards the undertaking.' This wooden harbour was soon swept away by the sea. It was eventually replaced by another on the same site, built by the Cluny Estate in 1880. But by the 1890s this much improved harbour was already crowded, so that Buckpool and Portessie within the town, and the adjoining villages of

Portknockie and Findochty which were being drawn into Buckie's orbit, were attempting rival improvements. Soon after 1900, however, the Buckie town council succeeded in purchasing its harbour from the former landowners. Major extensions followed, notably in 1912 – at the cost of £180,000, partly raised from a dividend of 7½ per cent which the fishermen promised on their boat's earnings, and again in 1931.

This willingness to act as a community in order to provide basic facilities has remained important as from the First World War onwards the town has faced the challenge of survival rather than growth. By 1939 the Buckie district's fleet had shrunk drastically to just 224 boats, half of them ageing steam drifters and the remainder sail or motor boats, in all capable of providing work for scarcely a thousand fishermen. In an attempt to diversify as the herring continued to fail, a town friendly society was set up by subscription in 1931, the Buckie Development Association, to equip thirty boats for haddock line-fishing. Not much came of this; but official backing for innovation was again conveyed by the provost's presiding over a special lunch in 1933 to launch a new type of diesel-powered drifter. And ultimately the same spirit rescued Buckie from the fate of a 'problem town' when the herring industry shrank to final extinction after the Second World War. It was the council which planned the cold-storage and ice-factory facilities needed, and went on in 1955 to reopen the fish market, having secured the fishermen's agreement to land there for a three-month trial, to win renewed prosperity as the leading white-fish port of the Moray Firth. More recently, in 1973 a group of Buckie skippers formed the Fishermen's Mutual Association. Now the biggest fishermen's co-operative in Scotland, its role in maintaining the town's economy includes not only acting as salesmen and chandlers for some forty boats, but also running a net factory, taking over a ship-building yard, and encouraging the building of new boats.

Thus local initiative has provided one important basis for Buckie's continuing success. But while in the provision of facilities, this has been as a community, the equally vital experimentation with fishing grounds and techniques has been the separate, individual work of the crews of fishermen. Their adaptability and mobility has been essential to the town's economic survival. It may indeed be that at one point a relative natural disadvantage pushed them in this direction. For on Buckie's local section of the Moray Firth coast the inshore white fishing declined earlier than elsewhere, and the Fishery Board reported it as almost abandoned by 1903. Anson could find here in 1932 only 'a few old men still earning a scanty income with hand-lines'. The Buckie fishermen thus became especially dependent on the herring; and as their prey moved further offshore, they had to be prepared to follow it.[1]

Buckie's nearest rivals, Peterhead and Fraserburgh, were by contrast both more cautious in their espousal of the steam drifter. One disincentive was that in both towns just before 1900 local companies had tried to set up steam trawling without success. In Fraserburgh, where the combination of herring with white fishing remained viable, an alternative future was already seen in developing petrol motors for smaller boats. And both Fraserburgh and Peterhead were still close enough to the herring shoals for their sailboats to earn well, and also to remain major landing and processing centres. Here, as in Lerwick in Shetland, the wealth won by salesmen and curers is witnessed by the substantial granite houses with servants' attics which rose in the towns' most select streets. Buckie could not wait for the trade to come its way: it had to go out and find fish.

Its fishermen were thus continuously exploring and experimenting. In 1911, for example, the Fishery Board reports them pursuing the 'newer method' of cod nets, first tried in the Moray Firth in 1906. In 1913 a new type of convertible drifter-trawler reached the town. In 1920 it was the Buckie men who introduced the Danish seine net to Scotland, and during the 1920s the town was the chief home port for large seiners, landing in Aberdeen, only after 1930 eclipsed by Lossiemouth which had found a better outlet in Glasgow. They also experimented early with motor boats, with a dozen in 1913 and as many as 130 in 1920. In the lean depression years many Buckie men tried their hand at trawling too. Even today out of the fleet of 150 boats registered and based in Buckie, now mostly seiners but including some small trawlers, only one-third works out of its home port at the Moray Firth scampi and white-fishing. Of the remainder one or two will work as far away as Cornwall, but most are split between Aberdeen or Peterhead and the west coast of Scotland, brought into harbour there for skippers and crews to bus home for weekends in Buckie and its adjoining coastal villages.

Buckie's wholehearted espousal of the steam drifter was nevertheless its supreme moment. The first steam drifters to succeed were Lowestoft-built in 1899. But very significantly, in 1896–7 the Fishery Board had reported that an 'industrious and enterprising' group in Buckie had launched a first-class steam liner, the *Star of Hope*, in an attempt to emulate the growing steam fleet in Aberdeen. Because of lack of experience with this type of fishing it did not pay, and had to go over to trawling. It was nevertheless a key move: the first Scottish steamboat to be commissioned and owned by 'a crew of *bona fide* fishermen' themselves. It signalled the reassertion of traditional ownership under steam power. Two years later, immediately they had proved viable, within months Buckie crews were seeking steam drifters. Three were being built for the town in 1900 – including the first in a local yard – and six more the next year. In 1903 its steamboats made net earnings of from £1,200 to £2,000 each. In the ensuing fever 24 new steam drifters were bought within a year. There was, as the Fishery Board put it in 1906, 'a spirit of emulation' among the fishermen in their competitive 'desire to possess a steam drifter of larger dimensions and greater speed than those of any other in the neighbourhood'. By 1908, as the great boom peaked, with a new steam drifter now costing £3,000, Buckie had 208; in 1913 276, leading Peterhead, its nearest Scottish rival, by almost double.

It was in these triumphant years that much of the town's present ordered fabric of stone terraces was built. Buckie had become the pulse of a trade in perpetual motion. It was the home base of a community dominated by skipper-owners, whose boats circulated the British Isles from the far north-west in early summer to East Anglia at the end of autumn, largely crewed by local share-fishermen, driven by wage-paid enginemen, pulling in extra seasonal crewmen as 'hired men', on a labour share only, from the distant western and northern isles, and followed by thousands of women fishworkers drawn both from those parts and from among their own wives and daughters. What kind of society had made, and was made by, this economy?

Buckie was a single-industry town, whose whole social life was closely tied to the cycle of fishing. For the men, this is hardly surprising, but it was equally strikingly the case for the women. Let us therefore turn first to them: to the thousands of 'gutting quines' who followed the movement of the herring shoals from port to port. Among them each year would be a substantial contingent from Buckie. We have already seen something of their tough working conditions and spirited wage disputes. But going gutting was not just a job.

It had become a basic part of the family life cycle. Whole families followed the herring together, transferring their children from school to school. Because the drifters landed daily, the women could see much more of their men than would have been otherwise possible. 'We came down here not only to earn money, but to be with our men', a reporter was told in 1938. 'As it is, most of the men are not at home very much'. Many of the more prosperous skippers' wives did not trouble to take on work, but simply made the seasonal move as a holiday.

Girls therefore expected to follow the herring too. After leaving school at 14 they would usually work the first year or two in their home port, waiting to make their first journey away from home until 16 or 17 – the very age when they were likely to begin courting. This annual mass migration of young women provided a rare opportunity for unsupervised matchmaking. It is recalled with a sparkle in the eye. Although the hours there were longest, Lerwick was probably the liveliest station, the greatest fun. 'We didn't need to go near the Shetland girls because our own girls was there!' At the end of the week, while the girls shopped and cooked, the young men would often help clean out their huts, and afterwards take out a fiddle and dance into the night. There were no landladies to tell them to go home. For some, this could be quite a revelation. Mrs Christian Marshall first went to Shetland in 1913, to the huts at Baltasound:

There was no ceiling – there was only the rafter beams, you could go over all the rooms if you went up in the top.. . . . I was only sixteen year old. . . . And of course, the melodians was going – that's the first melodian I had ever seen in my life – it was a Swede that had it and there was a cement patch outside and we used to go out and dance – that's where I learnt to dance! We used to go out and dance, they sat and played their things, and then Andrae – the provost, Sottie's Andrae – he used to say, 'Come on now girls, bedtime!' and we was just like sheepies doin' what we was telled, pushed up the stair to our bed. . . .

So when we were supposed to be in our beds, you know what we were were doin'? We were seein' who's comin' in next door, we climbed up – we'd had a chair – we'd only the one chair in the place – wi' this chair we'd a turn about till we could see what was goin' on in the next hut – and they were nae in their beds until it was rising time! We went into the next . . . and we looked over – did nae occupy their time with men at all! . . . But the Wick women – oh! what a time they had! Ach, ah' the men was aboot! Ach, with the foreign boat and al'things. What a time they had. We finished our education, eh?! Ach, it's true – what we didna ken, we learnt then!

Yarmouth landladies usually expected girls home by ten at night, and frowned on visitors. With its beach, cinemas, music halls, pubs and on Sunday churches, the town offered more organised entertainment. On Saturday nights large crowds of Scottish fishermen would stand about in the streets too, especially at 'Scots corner' close to the White Lion pub, and the newspapers sometimes reported rowdy brawls with the police here. Some normally upright figures may have let their hair down in Yarmouth: one fisherman convicted was married with two children 'belonging to a respectable Buckie family', confessing to his offence as 'a teetotaller's lapse'. But Yarmouth generally had more of a family air than Lerwick, for it was at the end of the East Anglian season that presents of all kinds were brought home – Yarmouth rock for the children, novelties and furniture in which many local shops kept special lines for the fishermen, paintings of their boats, clothes for the family, even motor cars slung onto the boats. It was a time for weddings too, some of them begotten in the weeks beforehand.

This close interweaving of family and occupational patterns can also be seen with the networkers. Although nets were now machine-made, they were still owned by the sharemen and the mending remained a family responsibility. There was a great deal to do, since a drifter would carry a dozen or more drift nets owned by each shareman; and they needed to be changed for the autumn season as well as completely overhauled in the winter. In Buckie the work was usually carried out in the upper storey net lofts. A more prosperous family would hire help: Murray Lockie's family took on four outside women. There were also a few small commercial net shops, where women worked for wages repairing nets. In general, however, the family had to look after its own, with perhaps a little free help from a neighbour or a girl who might be paid a penny. Both men and women were involved, but there was a marked division of work, with the women cleaning the nets and mending the smaller holes, while the men saw to the corners, the weights, the strings, and the net shape as a whole: 'the women mended and the men repaired'. Boys and girls were both expected to prepare needles. Murray Lockie had to get fifty needles ready after he came home from school. But it was the women who most often stayed up until midnight or after at the mending.[2]

A Buckie fisherman thus needed a wife who was a skilled worker in his own industry. It is not surprising that with scarcely one exception, all whom we spoke to had chosen wives from other fishing families, even if from another port. There was a north-east saying, 'No man can be a fisher and want a wife.' A wife was an economic necessity. In early nineteenth-century Buckie a wifeless fisherman had to hire a servant and pay her in fish. That was in the days of inshore white fishing, when women would help drag boats down the beach and carry their men aboard through the water so they could set off dry, as well as baiting their lines and selling their catch. In the past, with their shawls, striped skirts and creels on their backs, women fish-hawkers were a familiar sight in the lanes behind the coast, often passing on news and picking up a meal as they sold their goods or bartered them for farm eggs or honey.[3]

'The wife occupies a far more important position in the family than in other situations,' wrote the Rev. A. Anderson of Whitehills in 1845. 'She adopts a tone, and is allowed an influence which in another condition of life would appear little consistent with either feminine propriety or domestic order. . . . She still usually claims the disposal of the entire proceeds of the white fishery . . . as her exclusive prerogative.' We can presume that the earlier pattern of marriage in Buckie would have been similar. But Anderson noted how the rise of the herring fishery had 'in some degree lessened her pretensions', for it rested less on her exertions. There was, however, again a role for the wife in selling catch locally. In Fraserburgh as late as the 1880s skippers' wives would often take 'the lion's share of the work' in hauling the baskets of catch from the boat to the pier. Most men continued to consult their wives before making a substantial investment in fishing equipment; and in many, household and fishing finances continued to be inextricably mixed – 'mother was the Chancellor of the Exchequer and everything went from her hand into her purse, everything came out into this boat.' In some ways the long seasons before the boats settled up increased women's financial responsibility. In the depression years families had to live from advances secured on 'tick' from local tradesmen; and with debt to pay off, it was essential that when the man came home with his earnings he 'laid it onto table. He got his tobacco, maybe a shilling or twa for his purse'.

Some men inevitably resented this control. There were stories of the Peterhead fisherman whose wife 'held a tight hand on the domestic purse, and that "Bow" had money to spend only when he asked for it for some specific purpose' – which did not run to a newspaper; or of the Buckie man blown 'sky high' by his wife for secretly deducting money for a drink – 'With you cheating me like that you won't get any pocket money.' For a century there had been complaints that on the north-east coast 'the women enslave the men to their will, and keep them chained under petticoat government.' Even in the 1950s the *Third Statistical Account* was to describe the women not only as family 'Chancellor of the Exchequer', but on critical decisions as 'the masters. . . . They had the authority in the house. . . . It seems to have been a matriarchal society . . .'[4]

There was a catch here: the observation might equally be turned on its head. Might it not be a sign of men's mastery that they could abandon the burden of all this domestic responsibility to their wives? It seems most likely that in the earlier period marriage among the inshoremen had normally been both an economic and a moral partnership. The men were rarely away from home for long. Hugh Miller wrote how in the 1820s, 'when the children of mechanics are at school, those of the fisherman are either employed in baiting hooks, or in digging for the sand worm. When they become a little older the boys accompany their fathers to sea.' An old Buckie fisherman, reminiscing of a childhood in the mid-nineteenth century, remarked how 'parental control was a good deal more relaxed during his father's absence'. It could be that with this went a sharing of other domestic tasks. One could perhaps see some relics of a former flexibility of roles in the willingness of the young fishermen to help clean out the gutting girls' huts, and conversely during the preparations for the summer season, when for once the women would go on to the boats to help give them a spring clean. But even if there had formerly been such flexibility within a 'partnership' form of marriage, it is clear that the pressure of the developing steam herring industry was towards another type of family structure. For by the early twentieth century Buckie steam drifter households were more generally characterised by a very marked role division.

Those same forces which had brought steam capitalism to triumph had left their clear impact on the pattern of family life. There was first of all the simple effect of working at a distance. As early as the 1850s there were complaints from some middle-class observers of the 'lack of parental control' and generally 'demoralising effect' on the fishing families of Buckie, 'owing to the father's long-continued absence at Lewis and other fishings'. The effect was similar right round the coast. 'We had to bring up the families because the men were never at home,' commented Mrs Gilbert Buchan of Inverallochy. 'You never saw them for weeks.' And the consequence was a shift in responsibility for discipline, just as with the trawling families. 'The bairns were more afraid of their mothers than of their fathers,' said her neighbour Jessie Annie Masson. 'Their fathers were inclined to spoil them when they came home.'[5]

But the disintegration was not pushed further, as in the trawling industry, through the impact of drink and domestic violence. The second force in the driftermen's families was religion: a religion of restraint. Their economic success had only been possible through the abstinence of teetotalism and thrift. Their whole way of life was founded upon self-control. For the ordinary man, if not for the religiously inspired, this self-control depended on clear rules of conduct, and therefore strongly reinforced any tendencies towards a rigid allocation of roles within the family. Maybe away from home, just where other breaches of the moral code most often occurred, and individual passion broke through with its emotional fire, men might get down on their knees and scrub for women. But at home such feeling could less easily be expressed. The image of a respectable man was more severe.

The third force was class. We have seen earlier how the drifter-boom brought sharp new divisions of fortune into the fishing communities. With them came inevitably some of the symbols of respectability, of class, which were common throughout Britain at this time. One was dress. In the 1920s a Peterhead drifter skipper was a 'big man' who 'wears his bowler hat when entering or leaving harbour, or about town. . . . Some of the most advanced have even been seen going to sea with a collar and tie.' Such follies do not appear to have been usual in Buckie. But another indication of social standing at this time in the wider society was the employment of domestic servants. This could not only relieve parents of cleaning, cooking and child-care, but make such tasks seem beneath the dignity of the respectable employer. This attitude does seem to have left its mark in Buckie. Its women were still accustomed to starting adult life as low-paid employees, but their men's expectations had been lifted. Buckie was the town of skipper-owners *par excellence*. During this period most boats carried a boy, who was treated like a servant by the rest of the crew. 'The *loon* . . . was at everybody's *beck and call*. From the skipper to the deckie all had occasion to call on his services, it could be lighting the skipper's pipe when he was at the wheel, or running a message when in port. He was expected to *fetch and carry* as was required and that promptly.' And how far some of them had also come to expect to be served at home is shown by the appeal for help which William Smith of Buckie made in 1934 to the Secretary of State for Scotland. 'I have six children eldest sixteen and not working, their mother has been dead three years past, I have a servant employed.' He was a drifter skipper, but his boat had sunk. 'Now I am out, can't meet my debt . . . Since then I have no money and can't find work.' But what he seems to have felt most of all was his lost ability to secure the support of domestic service, unpaid or paid. For if he went fishing he had to leave four children at home, the eldest aged twelve, 'without mother or servant'.[6]

The heightened divisions between the sexes in many Buckie families is conveyed by Bella Jappy, a steam-drifter deck-hand's daughter born in 1914. Asked whether boys helped with housework, she said:

> Oh no! I think not! The men and the boys were very much the Lords of Creation in the fisher – well I know in our house. My father would never take a drink of water to himself! He just sat in his chair and he says, 'Ye bin (go) for a drink o' water to me' – you see? They did nothing – I never ken if my man how he went on, but our boys did nothing in the house. Nothing at all. The girls had to clean their shoes and brush their clothes and all that sort of thing. The boys did nothing. And to think of washing their shoes. . . . Oh no, it was terrible to think that they would have to do anything like that.

Women also had to hand-knit many clothes at home, and sew other garments. Girls were taught sewing at school. Washing was another lengthy process, since clothes were first washed, then bleached, and finally rewashed – a more elaborate sequence than was normal in working-class households in Britain at this time. In Buckie housework too was exceptionally time-consuming and demanding, when compared with the simpler standards which were still usual among less prosperous inshore fishermen elsewhere. The set days for scrubbing and polishing their newly constructed houses hinted of an urban form of competitiveness between neighbours. Homes, with their treasures brought back from Yarmouth, must also serve as showpieces. In all the work which ensued, the sharp role division between husband and wife had its counterpart in that between son and daughter. Joch Bruce, a skipper's son, explained how,

> You never went courting on Friday, no, never with a young lass. That was called black-leading night . . . It was all large grates, and there were dressed-up grates with ovens and that, grates with big round plates and that, well that was black-leaded and polished. And the kettles were polished, the cast iron kettles, they were polished – they were scraped every day in fact. Oh aye. . . . That was why we never got them out on Friday! They were all cleaning on Friday!

Such male abstinence from housework could have been found in most Buckie homes at this time. Our interviews suggest that three-quarters of the men never played a part – except possibly in emergency – in cooking or cleaning at home, either as boys or later as husbands, even though almost without exception they had learnt to cook and clean aboard ship.

It was not only the physical chores which fell to the women but the responsibility for child-care too. They were again socialised to this early. Mrs Stewart, a skipper's daughter, felt as a child that girls had no chance to enjoy pranks like boys: 'when I was young I was always nursing babies'. These were other families' babies, not just their own. For a father to take an active part in the upbringing of children was seen by some people as an 'interference' in what was the mother's job; and of the fathers for whom we have information, certainly four-fifths seem to have been happy to observe such a convention. Discipline was almost invariably left to the mother. Children were brought up quite gently, but firmly. They were expected to be truthful, and respect and obey their elders, neighbours as well as immediate family. They were not encouraged to join in adult conversation. In a good many families they ate apart, as was quite common in the respectable artisan or lower-middle-class family of that time elsewhere; and they were rarely allowed to stay up late to join in adult social occasions. In general, none of this required much punishment. In perhaps a third of the homes no physical discipline was remembered, while in the others there was just an occasional slap from the mother. None used canes, nor was there in any case the violent 'thumpings' of some of the Aberdeen trawlermen's homes. Quite commonly old people said, 'My father never lifted a hand to me.'

In many families the mothers also took more of an interest than fathers in their children's progress at school and sub-sequent choice of career. Willie Stewart's father, for example, had been a skipper when he was a boy, but his mother did not want her sons to follow the fishing. She got one brother a job as a bank clerk, another became a seaman, and he was himself apprenticed as a carpenter. 'It was my mother who was the instigator of all this, not my father. My father said if we went to sea that was all right. But she said she wanted something better than that.' Of course had such dissociation been too common, the fishing economy would have withered for lack of recruits. More often quite a tight bond between fathers and sons did develop. As a boy grew older he would begin, in the old way, to work with his father, helping to mend the nets and joining him out fishing, usually at first in a little line-boat. After leaving school he would work locally for a year or two, and then join a drifter as a cook at the age of sixteen, very commonly on his father's boat. Some felt that the combination of parental and work discipline could be too much. As Joch Bruce put it, 'Every father was hard on his sons – breaking them in for the sea you know – and you were far better to go with strangers. . . . You learned more in a way – there was nobody *drilling* you on as you would say.' Ashore too a boy mending nets was very much under his father's control. Joch Bruce remembered coming downstairs after mending all day, wondering if his father would let him go out that evening, or decide to go on with work again into the night. Murray Lockie too recalled how when working as a cook under his father 'even on the boat father would tell me that "little boys should be seen and not heard"'. Yet on the other hand once this stage of training had passed, work discipline on the boat could result in an equally sharp reversal between generations. A skipper's authority at sea was accepted without question. It was not uncommon for quite a young fisherman to be given his chance to prove himself as a drifter skipper. Murray Lockie became a skipper at 21, and six of the eight men working under him were relatives, including his own father – and others old enough to be his grandfather. Yet his father 'never interfered'.

In Murray Lockie's family the women did the housework, and outside girls were simply taken on to help with the net-mending. But it was quite common for the families of more prosperous skippers to employ servants. Although earlier a few may have employed regular living-in servants, by the early twentieth century they were daily helps and their employment tended to vary with the seasons. Between the fishings there was a lot of extra washing and mending of clothes, boot-scrubbing and changing of chaff mattresses for the boats, and many gutting girls were glad of some earnings during this break. Significantly, such domestic service was a very different social experience from that with the Buckie middle-class townsfolk. An employer was not called 'Madam' or 'Mrs'; ordinary first names or tee-names (family nick-names) were used. Everyone ate at the same table. 'They treated us well, the fisherpeople we worked for. We were just one of them.' As an alternative to such daily work, girls could go into full-time service living-in either in the town, or further afield. Such a choice undoubtedly depended very directly on their immediate economic situation. The local fishery officers noted how in 1921 'many women workers who have failed to secure employment with herring curing firms have gone, temporarily at least, into domestic service.' But it was an indication of how closely domestic work had become linked with social standing that while the daughters of successful skippers would take work as gutters, they were not prepared to become servants. When Bella Jappy was asked, 'What kind of people had servants?' she said, 'Well, the better-off people . . . Better-off folk had servants, while the like of us – we went out to service between the fishings.'[7] It was through domestic service that the women of the poorer fishing families most directly experienced the growing impact of class distinction within their own community.

For servants, class was real enough. Those few who found themselves work as maids in the country houses of the land-owners behind the coast might have been able to glimpse some of the refinements of class perspectives at the upper level too. Just south of Fraserburgh, for example, 'in the midst of a wooded demesne, contrasting with the bare country around', was Philorth, seat of Lord Saltoun. The family estate extended to 11,000 acres. 'Fraserburgh is the family borough, we founded it and kept it going you see.' The establishment at Philorth comprised a whole hierarchy of servants, from the housekeeper and butler, governess and footmen, down to the nursemaids, stillroom maid and scullerymaid. Lord Saltoun thought the locals 'very intelligent people, very quick'. But the family knew very clearly where to draw the line in social mixing:

> *Would they have entertained the doctor, and the local solicitor, would they have invited such people to their home?*
> I remember the local doctor was a very good doctor. He came to shoot – at a shooting party, and had lunch, and I remember he started off entertaining the company with a spirited defence of Judas Escariot, which embarrassed my mother very much indeed, and in the end – in the end, Lord Borley who was sitting next to me said, 'Well after all', he thought, 'he was a pretty shabby fellow.' Does that answer your question?

But what did class mean for most Buckie fishermen and women? How far did they share in the class consciousness which had become so strongly developed in the urban indus-trial working class elsewhere in Britain? Certainly they gener-ally held a view of Buckie society as a hierarchy. At the top they would place the professionals, to whom the fishermen would lift their cap – the ministers, and perhaps the teachers; then the commercial middle class, the bankers and trades-people; next the skilled craftsmen, like boat-builders or masons; then the fishermen themselves; and lastly, casual labourers, such as navvies and dustmen. One notices, however, how the hierarchy stops with the professionals. The landowners are out of sight: even though much of Buckie was split between the Cluny Estate and the Gordon Estate, and Gordon Castle itself, seat of the Duke of Richmond and heart of a 70,000-acre estate, a mere seven miles from the town. Buckie fisherfolk seemed singularly oblivious of this nearby presence. It is also striking that no special role is given to the fish merchant. In *Caller Herring*, written by a local playwright W. R. Melvin in 1913 and set in the older part of Fraserburgh, the fish merchant is portrayed as 'a hertless monster' who has practically the whole neighbourhood 'dependent on me for everything – money and all. I hold them in the hollow of my hand, dictate my own terms, and flourish like a bay tree.'[8] This would not have been the common view in Buckie.

Nor, in contrast to most manual workers, did Buckie fishermen go on to see an especially fundamental divide, and a conflict of interests, between the working classes and the employing classes. They most certainly did not have a 'proletarian' class consciousness. Instead they held a very distinctive perception of social class, which sprang from the nature of the fishing economy. Buckie fishing families were not just workers. As boat share-owners they were also co-venturers and petty capitalists. In their own lives, the distinction between employer and employed remained obscure.

It is true that at one point it looked as if the social impact of the dynamic growth of Buckie's steam capitalism would force a new class perception on the community. In 1913, the year in which the Highlandmen led the hired men in a concerted attempt to unionise, the town was struck by a rare wave of sectional militancy. For there was by now 'a class of men even in the Buckie district who have fallen out.' Buckie had the highest concentration of steamboat-owners, and almost all local driftermen held net shares; but there was still a minority of local hired men working for a labour share only. The Highlandmen's campaign was answered by turbulent meetings and strike threats from hired men meeting in Portknockie, Portgordon and the Buckie Fishermen's Hall – the last setting up an independent trade union and negotiating committee.

The Buckie skippers quickly responded by forming their own exclusive association which proceeded to negotiate. Settlement did not prove easy, and was not reached until after 400 hired men had come out on strike. It was Buckie's first experience of such internal class conflict. Previously 'a sort of family feeling' would have made such a dispute inconceivable. 'Twenty years ago', as the hired men's chairman, William Reiach reflected, 'the fishermen were all as one, but now it was a case of capital against labour.'[59]

The steam-drifter boom clearly carried with it the seeds of a profound change in the community's social structure. It was avoided partly because, by 1913, the boom had passed its peak, partly because Buckie itself continued to be so dominated by share-owners that the hired men were in a much weaker position than in Fraserburgh and Peterhead and partly because the inter-war depression of the herring industry hit all sections of the Buckie fishing community so acutely. The register of unemployed was not intended to include share fishermen, who were ineligible for the 'broo'. Nevertheless there were 600 Buckie fishermen registered as unemployed in 1921. Seventeen years later, in 1938, there were 900. In such a situation the old values of a community of poverty reasserted themselves. Lying behind this, however, was the constant pressure of the share system itself.

The share system undercut class attitudes in two ways, for it fostered both individualism, and an interdependence across the normal boundaries of class. A fisherman depended on his individual reputation to get the loans he needed to buy a boat and its gear, and keep it supplied and maintained. Individual reputation was a matter of common knowledge. As James Murray the Buckie fish salesman told the North Sea fishing inquiry, 'A man asking for a drifter in a district like Buckie, if he is well known and deserving it, he gets it and he would get it today.' Bankers could easily enough check opinion at the harbour. They knew a good fisherman by the look of him, by the appearance of his boat and his crew. When the boats were away, the Buckie newspaper would publish news of daily catches in other ports with the top Buckie boats listed, and local offices posted full lists in their windows, just as today on the fishquay in Buckie harbour, tallies of daily landings are chalked up on a board like a competition score sheet. As George Murray put it, 'We knew them all.'[10]

Interdependence, on the other hand, was encouraged by the elaborate local web of credit. The fishermen relied on bankers and tradesmen for loans and on the salesmen also as accountants and financial managers. The officers who kept the Buckie shipping registers from 1907 would seem to have ignored most of the mortgages held against boat-owners. But they show that a landowner was part-owner of one boat in three, although very rarely a whole owner. There was, moreover, remarkably little concentration of landownership. A variety of lawyers, doctors, merchants, boat-builders, salesmen, drapers, bakers and engineers participated, but each in one or two boats only. Boat-ownership continued to function as a local form of small saving for townspeople right through the inter-war years. And the local house-builders and boat-builders, the ship's chandlers, net-makers and grocers, all depended on the prosperity of the fishing for their own livelihood. Most of these tradesmen lived mixed up with the fishermen in the same streets, and many were former fishermen, retired because of accidents or age.

Similarly, the share system strengthened family interdependence. Many skippers wanted to spread the risks of their undertaking by encouraging others to take shares in their boat: it was a form of insurance. The registers show that there were up to six, but more usually two or three share-owners for each boat. The skipper – or in perhaps one in five cases a close relative – would be one; and it looks from the surnames as if two or more members of the same family had joined as owners of more than half the boats. They occasionally include women – wives as well as widows. And because of the extent of intermarriage, nearly everyone in the fishing community was related to a skipper, while every skipper had relatives who were deckhands. Among the fathers and sons we interviewed either one or the other had been at one time a skipper in four-fifths of cases; and with the rest, either an uncle or a brother was a skipper, or at the very least a share-owner in a boat. And again, skippers and deckhands of the same family tended to live close together. Quite commonly, as a family grew, the house might be divided up, with the net loft converted for a married son and daughter and the parents living below, or another house might be bought or built across the street.

It seems thus to be almost literally true, as Buckie people remember, that in those days there was 'a boat attached to every house'. But the real importance of this memory does not rest on its literal truth. It represents an interpretation of local society. Except in rare, brief moments of crisis, the men and women of Buckie saw themselves as belonging not to conflicting classes or sections, but to boats and families. The key to the absence of conventional class consciousness, and the principle through which the community was to be understood, was the possession of a family boat. The original fishermen had often been small farmers and crofters driven from the land, a peasantry – to use the word in a technical rather than pejorative sense – forced out onto the sea. As their forefathers lived from their holdings, they now had to live from their boats; and the family attachment, which had once been to the land, was transferred to the boat. In this special sense, the first fishermen thus recreated their social world as if they were a 'sea peasantry'. And something of their vision still held even when their descendants had become small capitalist entrepreneurs in the era of steam fishing. The boat was not just an investment or a tool, it was a matter of family pride. Why else was such a concern taken with the details of its appearance, the mahogany of the cabin, the metalwork, the carved name on the bow, the delicate paintwork? 'So spick-and-span are some of the Moray Firth drifters . . . that they would stand comparison with many a private yacht,' wrote Anson in the depressed 1930s. 'Their drifters!' he exclaimed of the Portessie boats in Buckie harbour, 'painting, graining or polished brasswork! And how astonishingly clean and cosy are their cabins!' Even today, whereas an Aberdeen trawler will be lucky to get a bucket swilling, a Buckie or a Fraserburgh boat gleams with fresh paint, and the inside is brushed with the care of a home. Boats, as the registers again show, changed hands only at fairly long intervals. Most remained under the same names for at least ten years, and even when there were changes they were more often to eliminate a landowner's share, or record a death and succession within the same family. And in the naming of boats too, a parallel can be seen with the importance which many small farmers feel in keeping the family name on the land. Very often a boat's name is continued when an old boat is replaced by a new one. The actual choices of names vary: some suggest virtues, some are fanciful. And many Moray Firth fishermen name their boats after women in their own families, or their children. James Mair, an old Buckie fisherman, observed 'the growing practice of fishermen calling their boats by their own names' in 1913. 'It would be more like the thing', he suggested sarcastically, 'if they would call their boats "Mortgage".' But he struck at the heart of the matter too, with a quotation from the forty-ninth psalm: 'Their inward thought is that their houses shall continue for ever and their dwelling places to all generations: they call their lands after their own names.'[11]

The strength of this family attachment to particular boats, each working in competition with others in the local fleet, has made it difficult for Buckie fishermen to see much value in organising themselves together for mutual economic interests. But in times of crisis, they can certainly rally impressively. The Buckie demonstration of July 1920 to demand a government subsidy for the herring industry was reported as the greatest meeting ever held on the Moray Firth 'for peaceful purposes'. With 300 drifters in harbour and all shops shut, an immense procession of more than 10,000 people marched out from the town to Portessie, its banners carrying reminders of the war: 'Starvation our reward for services rendered'; 'Fishermen fought for a guarantee for Belgium; they now want a guarantee for themselves.' At the harbour a smaller meeting decided to take 'drastic action' to stop 'blacklegs', sending Buckie boats up to Lerwick to 'get them to stop'. A week later the government had given its guarantee. And there were again mass meetings, which succeeded in winning a weekly minimum advance on earnings of 10/– from the salesmen, demanding a wage guarantee from the new Herring Board in the spring of 1936.

Outside such moments of united communal response, however, Buckie fishermen are reluctant attenders of meetings. Local fishermen's associations have tended to be short-lived, or survive only nominally. The town has its local business society and also a highly successful boat insurance society; but the very recent success of its fishermen's co-operative marks a sharp break with earlier disinterest and failures. Two earlier fishermen's co-operatives for selling catch and supplying boats, the Findochty and the Buckie and District Fishermen's Co-operative Societies, were both formed in the summer of 1920. The first dissolved a year later, the second in 1926. Similarly no local trade union among fishermen has lasted more than a few weeks, local strikes have been very rare, and Buckie men and women have not played any prominent part in the strikes at other herring ports. Their characteristic attitude towards trade unions is indeed much more commonly one of decided hostility. They may regard unions as having a place on the trawlers, but certainly not on the share-boats. There were union members in the Buckie boatyards, where many of the workers came from fishing families, but even here the presence of trade unionism was nominal. 'If you spoke about anything to the boss when I was a lad, if the boss said anything and you answered him back, "Out!" You were out the gate,' Willie Stewart remembered. 'They had a union there but oh you were forsaken up here.' Commitment to trade unionism, or to co-operatives, required a recognition of sectional economic interests, as workers or producers, which conflicted with the Buckie fishermen's basic understanding of their own community.

The fishing families saw themselves instead as a class of their own, united, and wrongly undervalued. Between themselves, Buckie men and women used Christian names and tee-names; a skipper was not even dignified as 'mister'. There was no raising of caps. Fishermen's children all played together, skippers' children along with the rest, and all barefoot in summer too. As a deckhand's daughter put it, 'we were one class together'. But the farm labourers' children or raggedly-clothed navvies' families she avoided: they were said to smell. At school however, it was the fishermen's offspring who were made to feel inferior, even the skippers' sons. George Murray recalled how the schoolmaster, 'When I told him I was going to the fishing, he said "You're a fool".' Peterhead fishermen were even expected to walk on a different side of the main street from the townsfolk. Willie Stewart summed up the common feeling: 'Fisherfolk were very ill treated – well they were nae ill treated, but they were little thought of by the townspeople.'[12]

Paradoxically the most prosperous drifter skippers helped to confirm this under-estimation. Many encouraged their children to move out of the fishing economy altogether, into the professions. A very few families owned two steam drifters, but they did not go on from this to try to build up fleets like the trawl-owners. Nor did they take on the middle-class style of life which their resources might – at least in boom decades – have allowed. At the most, they built themselves a larger stone house, up on the hill brow. Today they would buy an expensive car too. But they were always held back in two ways. Firstly, they did not wish by taking on new airs to offend the men with whom they still worked, on whose effort and goodwill they relied at sea, and whom they had often known since childhood. Secondly, they always knew that the prosperity of the fishing might again collapse as suddenly as it had in the past. Similarly today many retired skippers carry the memory of the humiliation of the 1930s when, 'out of their starvation looking us in the face', they were forced to work as wage-earning trawlermen, even as casual labourers, at harbour-building, or in the fields at harvest. Murray Lockie, one of Buckie's most respected skippers, recalled:

> I worked in the harbour, when they were making the harbour, the new basin in the harbour, with a pick and a shovel. . . . I had a pick and a shovel – and boy oh boy it was terrible, you know? – The idea, the idea of being a navvy! Ye ken? And then the wife and them passing and you were at your pick and shovel. It was very, very degrading . . .

And once the fishing did fail, the boats lost their value almost as rapidly, and a life's investment might become almost worthless. It was this vulnerability, combined with the fact that at the fishing itself they remained workers along with their crews, which gave even those skippers who kept going a pejorative view of their own calling. As George Garden put it, 'Fishing's a hard life.'

No doubt the common threat of poverty helped to sustain common sociability ashore. Better-off families would help others, but in a secret way which avoided any social humiliation. For Zetta Doran, a child of the depression years –

> It showed you a sort of communal spirit which was there then. . . . There was a butcher in Buckie and my mum says that every Friday, there was a parcel of meat behind the door. Nothing was said – but it was left there. And there was a woman had her little croft at the end of the street, you know? And there were little pails of milk appeared now and again.

But normally, when fisherfolk would call they went straight in: 'strangers knock, friends come in.' It was an open-door community; and as today, food was always offered to a visitor – 'the table was always laid for anyone who came in.'[13] Apart from casual calling, at weekends there were commonly larger gatherings in the homes when there might be hymn-singing or melodion-playing.

The sense of community was also reinforced through the marking of deaths and marriages. After a death, the body would lie in the home, and neighbours came in to sit through watchnights, again with hymn-singing. The funeral itself would be a street service held outside the house, with the coffin placed on two chairs in front of the door. Weddings were also open occasions, with no formal invitations. Houses would be flagged and boats in harbour decorated – with pots, kettles and forks for a cook. The neighbouring women would join together in boiling dumplings, for the feast and dance in the Fishermen's Hall. The fishermen would go to these occasions in their standard weekday uniform of jerseys. 'The fisherfolk was in that day, was a' penny-fitting. . . . It was just a'body was in the same fitting. And a'body kent t'other. And a'body gae togither': so the ideal may be summed up.

It was an identity so intensely localised, so tied to a particular neighbourhood of fishing streets, that Buckie fishermen came nearest to seeing their world in class terms when they described its division into local territories. For George Murray the key boundary was the railway line – almost in American style:

> All this men far' here down to the Seatown – down to the Yardie, as they call it, that's away down at the water edge – they're all fishermen, every one of them. The houses are all fisherhouses there. Till ye go up over the bridge, and then you're in among – what we call 'the granders'. The granders. The grand people, the grand folk . . . – the townspeople. Aye, there's the fisherfolk and the towns- folk, you see. Aye, that was the division – and the train line was the – over this side was the fisherfolk and then on the other side of the train line was the townsfolk. . . . We used to have a lot of fights you know, in the time of snow, with the townsboys and the fisherboys, aye, up over the bridge there.

These fights between fisherboys and granders are widely remembered, and provided one of the few ways in which latent class hostility could be expressed.

There were territorial fights too between the fisherboys and farmboys from the country hinterland, along with mutually exchanged abuse, 'country yokels' shouting 'dirty fishers' or answering the tag 'country swine' with their own chant:

> Fishing dowdies bait the line
> Catch a codie give to the swine.

In this case rivalry reflected more the lack of contact between the workforces of the two local economies. Fishermen here very rarely worked on the farms; only a few of the poorest took on potato lifting, or corn stooking and thrashing when out of work. Some rented potato plots from farmers, but this again was exceptional. Generally the fishing families showed remarkably little interest in gardening or keeping hens or animals for themselves. On the boats almost the only men recruited from the countryside were the engineers and fire- men, and these were regarded as a separate group, wage- earners rather than sharemen, known as the 'down below men' or 'the black squad'. Intermarriage between country families and Buckie fishing families was very rare indeed, and the only case among our interviews was not from the town, but the declining fishing village of Portsoy. Between the fishing communities themselves, on the other hand, there was much intermarriage. Nine-tenths of those we interviewed in Buckie had found their wives either from other neighbour-hoods of the town, or from further along the coast. Many met as we have seen during the seasonal migrations, but other matches – as well as rivalries, leading to fights between the boys – sprang from promenading at weekends along the brae. They could easily spot those from other communities by their accent, and there was again a set of nicknames: the boys from Findochty were taunted as self-righteous (the 'justers') and from Buckie itself as 'big-headed'.

Perhaps most revealing of all, however, were the fights up and down the brae, for these reflected an economic division among the fishermen themselves. It was the more prosperous skippers who moved up the brae, and Buckie people knew this. But they insisted that the division should be seen in terms of individual success, within families. Lass Bruce was asked:

> *Was one bit of the town more respectable or posher than another?*
> Well, there wasn't more respectable, but, well, you're
> close to it now. We're down the hill, and up the hill was
> always supposed to be more posh than down the hill – but,
> the houses, the ones down there, there was always the
> same class of people . . . The younger men built bigger
> and better homes, you see, maybe they were more
> successful.
> *So the people who stayed would have probably been slightly
> less well off?*
> No, they were just as – it was just the sons and daughters
> married and then they built their own house on the top. In
> fact some of them in the older houses were better off than
> the people in the posher ones.[14]

The very individualism, in short, which created divisions among the fishermen by raising some above others, also serves to deflect any threat to the sense of common identity to which all wish to hold. It is this combination of belief in both

community and individualism which lies at the heart of Buckie's social consciousness.

For the belief in individualism is equally pervasive. Skippers
who had got their own chance in the years before government
loans were regretful that others had been denied their opportunity. 'Some of that men that was going deckhands in the
boat, I believe they were more fitted to be skipper tha'them
who was i' the wheelhouse. But they never got the chance,'
said Murray Lockie. 'Then, if ye hadna the money ye never
got the chance. If your father hadn't a boat you never got a
chance.' George Murray, also a drifter skipper, similarly
observed, 'We had fathers you see, had boats before us, and it
was a fine chance for us'. But the chance had to be seized; and
that did depend on character. At the other end of the scale of
fortune the poorer fishermen who remained deckhands all
their lives tended to regard chance as luck, but they too
believed in individual effort. '*We* got the hard times of the
fishing,' reflected Willie Stewart: but, 'You've got to work.'
Similarly, Bella Flett saw the misfortune of poverty as partly
due to character: 'there's a certain class of folk that no matter
what they get, they'll always be the ragamuffins. They could
be earning the same money as the folk next door, and yet . . .
some folk don't seem able to cope.' But in success, luck was as
important as character: 'Really it's a great bit of luck. They
maybe is some men that are – that have got the brain and the
know-how maybe. But, I don't know, but if it's that or it's just
sheer luck.'[15] This notion of luck among the poorer families
clearly helped to mitigate the resentment they might have felt
that the better-off fishermen had their chances through birth.

The image of a successful skipper general in Buckie was of a
man of individual power. However egalitarian ashore, on the
boat his authority must be absolute, unquestioned: 'I'm a
different man from what I am at sea.' He had the instinct of a
hunter: 'It's in your blood.' The greatest satisfaction in fishing
was coming in with 'a good shot of herring – some of them
hadn't much and you had a big shot'. Skippers had to see their
success at work in terms of catch. They had to be men who
counted time like money; not merely 'sober, industrious', but
also 'go-ahead'. In another phrase typical of Buckie, Murray
Lockie said, 'It's born in them, born in them . . . fortunate

men. But it's not altogether fortunate. They're pushing men. Aye, they've the push.' Skippers with 'push' were commonly contrasted with deckhands who had 'something lacking in them . . . initiative', or with older skippers who had 'lost the urge' and 'hadnae the fire' any more. The Buckie image persists: at the fishquay today, the fishery officer, Richie Anderson from Findochty, believes that any 'go-ahead' deckhand can get a start as skipper of a boat of his own, and sees the key to success in a skipper as the 'extra something' in his character – above all, in his 'drive'.[16]

This 'drive' had to be combined with technical adaptability. 'The system of ownership imposed the task of technical thinking and action largely on the fishermen,' writes Malcolm Gray. All changes had to be 'made by the small groups of working fishermen, each responsible for its own boat and gear'. Although skippers tended to try to keep secret the discovery of a new piece of equipment or new grounds, information was usually teased out through quayside talk. Other fishermen would normally watch carefully to see whether an experiment succeeded, before deciding whether to follow. If they then followed as a group, the change would be easier, because the necessary ancillary services could be economically provided. There was thus again here a vital intertwining between individual competition and common needs and opinions. The outcome of the first experiments in the port counted most, and a manifest failure could have a lasting local impact. Peterhead, for example, was put off motor drifters for many years by the capsizing of the 'Olive Branch' off Yarmouth in 1936. When it was difficult to draw any clear conclusions, local opinion might fall back on moral justification. 'Our men have very strong ideas', John McGibbon wrote of Peterhead in the 1920s, 'of what is right and fair, and what would be . . . tempting providence and not fishing "fair".'

The qualities needed for individual success were moral virtues too. For Buckie they can be well summed up with the family story of another drifter skipper, William Cowie. The family pedigree of six boats spans four generations, from his grandfather to his sons. Each boat was step by step more valuable, the first costing a mere £65, the latest a full £140,000;

and the tone was set by the grandfather, the first to introduce the steam capstan to Buckie, and 'always a progressive fisher-man'. For William Cowie, the competitive exchange of in-formation in the group was the mainspring of progress. It would start when they were first taken on as boy cooks, and would examine each other's galley stoves for improvements:

Would you later on then talk about the nets with the other?
Oh yes. Well this is fishing. This is fishing. You see, you're always sounding your chum, you know, to see what he knows. Of course he's just doing the same with you. He's weighing you up and he's picking your brain. This is what makes a good fisherman. He's interested. You see, a good fisherman − for instance, you see, you work the net, and the seine net is in the stern of the boat, you see, there. If I was stepping over a boat I would stop and look at that boat's net to see what kind of net it was. You'd be counting in your mind how much floats he had in the top of the net. And what weight he had in the lower part of the net. This is all the things that contribute to the efficiency of the net.

Later on, he had been among those driven in the 1930s into serving as a trawlerman. He had returned with an intense dislike of wage-labour boats, with their suppression of initiat-ive: 'you couldn't use your own discretion.' The share sys-tem, by contrast, gave all the crew an interest in the boat's success, and above all it allowed enterprise and hard work to win the rewards they deserved. On a share-boat, if you proved yourself, you got ahead; if you did not, 'you'd nothing to grouse about'. And it eliminated discipline as a problem:

Do you remember any walk-offs or stoppages on a boat you were on?
No. As I say we never have that. You see, the thing is, you must work before you eat, with us.[17]

We have here the hard edge of the set of values which both generated the moral force and reflected the needs of herring steam capitalism in Buckie. Indeed, it would be difficult to imagine a more tightly-shaped example of a 'moral economy'. Nor are there merely accidental echoes, in the repeated emphasis on thrift, on work and on sobriety, of the classic Protestant ethic which Max Weber saw as the moral driving power behind the rise of capitalism; for Buckie in the early twentieth century was experiencing an emergence of small capitalist enterprises from within a merchant-dominated economy, which in some respects paralleled much earlier changes at the centre of the national economy. In Buckie's transformation too Protestantism clearly played a vital role. And it was a Protestantism again which not merely contributed to, but was in turn itself moulded by the emerging economy.

As with the other ports of the Scottish north-east, Buckie's strong attachment to religion was relatively new. The old parishes of the Church of Scotland reflected the earlier needs of the farming villages, and were only slowly adapted. As late as 1891, the effect of this long-standing neglect shows up in the uneven picture in Robert Howie's survey of *Churches and the Churchless in Scotland*; for while some smaller fishing stations – Boddam, Gardenstown, Macduff, Portsoy and Cullen – already had a little above the overall average of 36 per cent of the population belonging to the main presbyterian churches, both Fraserburgh and Peterhead with 24–25 per cent were still well below, and Portknockie, Inverallochy and Buckie with 14–18 per cent markedly so. It looks as if the change which began with the evangelical revival of 1859 took a full generation to work through. In the north-east the 1859 movement focused on the brief mission campaign which the Methodist curer-cooper James Turner launched in St Combs. After his health collapsed the work was carried on by Donald Ross's North East Coast Mission. He led his followers into the Open Brethren in the early 1870s, when the first 'undenominational' assemblies of the Church of Christ were also formed; while the Salvation Army's campaign began in the early 1880s. In this sustained succession of revivals the growing economic crisis was no doubt a major factor. But the sects grew very slowly at first. Howie noticed the Brethren and the Salvationists nowhere else along the coast but in Aberdeen, and the Peterhead Closed Brethren numbered a mere twenty as late as 1914. Their stronghold in Peterhead and Fraserburgh, Gardenstown, and the Buckie villages of Findochty and Portknockie, must have come only with the still more acute economic problems of the 1920s and the last great evangelical revival.

In the meantime, however, a very clear sign of the moral transformation which was being worked in the fishing communities came through the advance of the temperance movement. Around Fraserburgh, for example, although founded as early as 1833 it had been still ineffective in the 1860s. Yet by 1886 *Chambers Journal* could report that the formerly 'noisy, hard-drinking, indigent fishermen of the town' had given way to a 'sober, industrious, religiously inclined class of men, who in many instances have amassed and have at their credit in the bank large sums of money'. Neighbouring villages like Inverallochy and Cairnbulg, hitherto churchless, and St Combs, espoused temperance as a village cause, henceforth celebrating the annual mid-winter turn of the year with communal temperance walks, processions of young couples headed by a flute band which would tour the houses of village notables and supporters, serenading them with a 'standing beat'. Another indication is the spread of the friendly society lodges of the temperance order, the Rechabites. By the First World War there were 26 lodges in the Aberdeen district and 13 in Shetland, in contrast to a mere 8 in the vast Inverness district covering the whole north-west.[18]

In Buckie itself the parish church was inconveniently situated a mile away inland at Rathven. A second difficulty was the persistence of a substantial Roman Catholic minority, numbering a thousand in the eighteenth century, with the backing of the Dukes of Gordon. And there was also a powerful Episcopalian party within the parish church. As a result there were long struggles over the choice of ministers, and in 1715 and 1791 riots against their installation. This troubled church history helps to explain why in the 1890s Buckie had not only a particularly low level of formal church organisation, but also an unusual variety of denominations, including a higher proportion of presbyterians outside the established church than in any other coastal town. The Methodists had a congregation here in the early nineteenth century. But although 'at one time very strong in Buckie', these first Methodists had been defeated by 'the tippling propensity': so many members had been struck off the roll following drunken lapses, that the chapel had been forced to close by the 1840s. Shortly before, in 1837, Robert Shanks had arrived. His forty-seven years' of ministry for the Church of Scotland and from 1843 the Free Kirk came to be regarded as a turning point. When he first came to what was then still 'a mere straggling village', and he was a tall, strong young man, one of his prime pastoral duties had been regular visitations 'to the public houses to keep order amongst those who spent their gains in liquor'. He had been forced to be 'more a temperance lecturer than a preacher'; and he had to seek his congregation through open-air addresses. But by 1914 whole new districts of the town had been constructed, like Ianstown, without a single public bar; and even in the older district of Buckpool, where Catholicism probably had as strong a following as Calvinism, a parliamentary inquiry could be informed that drifter skippers, without a single exception, were 'all teetotallers'.

How directly Buckie was affected by the last great religious revival of the 1920s is uncertain. But by the inter-war decades it had taken on the 'deathlike stillness' that characterised an east-coast Sunday; and there can have been few if any of its fishing families without a religious attachment. All whom we interviewed had belonged to a church, and almost all attended with some regularity. Apart from the Roman Catholic congregation of 500, church attendance roughly reflected the pattern of social and economic standing. Thus the Episcopalian congregation consisted chiefly of townspeople and tradesmen; the better-off fisherfolk went to the various presbyterian churches; while the Salvationists, the two branches of the Brethren and the Church of Christ drew more on the poor.

These smaller sects had often won their strongest hold in marginal fishing communities which seemed, at least when they came, to be economically threatened. The Salvationists were especially active in Cullen and Portsoy, the Brethren in Gardenstown. They were in this sense religions of the disinherited, providing, for those who were losing hope in the present, a future in the world beyond. But it is important to recognise that no sharp distinctions were felt between the various groups with the one exception, to which we must return, of the Exclusive Brethren. There does not even appear to have been any important hostility between Roman Catholics and Protestants, and there were many families who attended both Church of Scotland and Methodist or Salvationist services, regardless of any difference in doctrine.

What did religious belief mean in the social and moral economy of Buckie? Perhaps most simply, it had brought sobriety. We have discussed earlier the vital contribution which temperance made to thrift, to the fishermen's ability to create the steam-drifter fleet. There were very few bars in Buckie in the 1930s – perhaps three. Half the men we interviewed, including all the former skippers, had been teetotal for most of their lives. George Garden put the local view: 'I would say it was a curse on a boat, drink.' Three people vividly recounted the conversion stories of their own fathers, handed down like family parables. One was Zetta Doran who had been told how as a ten-month-old toddler she had been sent into the pub to plead with her father, tugging at his clothes. 'That night he went down on his knees with the bottle. . . . I was brought up in a teetotal house.' Another girl was illegitimate, and had been brought up by a grandmother. Her father was converted by the 1921 revival, and she herself felt so strongly for teetotalism that when she worked as a maid in the Earl of Seafield's country house, she refused to wait at table: 'There was too much drink and all bad things going for me to do that. I wouldn't do it. No.'[19] Temperance was a matter of faith, not manners. Buckie's moral order was grounded in abstinence, self-control and thrift.

Equally fundamental was the belief in work. As John McGibbon wrote of the Peterhead fishermen that 'their religion has permeated everything they do, and their very daily labour has been transformed into an act of worship. *Laborare est orare* might well be the motto of our men.' This very belief in work, on the other hand, also put limits to the influence of religion. The Fraserburgh Fishery Officer noted in 1939 how a number of Brethren and Baptist fishermen 'do not believe in insurance of any kind. But only those who are independent of owners with other ideas can carry their scruples so far.' Their refusal to join trade unions or associations, or to borrow from mortgage societies or insure their own property could be tolerated. But when the Exclusive Brethren began to divide families by casting out non-members and disrupt free social relations in the communities, forbidding their girls to marry out, they met with mounting hostility. The crunch eventually came in 1961 when their American leader 'Big Jim' Taylor attempted to impose separate tables for non-members serving as crew on their boats. In Peterhead this provoked a strike: the men gathered on the pier before setting off for the East Anglian fishing, exchanging their anger at the new rule, and deciding unanimously to go to Yarmouth on the basis of one table only. Some of the Exclusives failed to man their boats, and missed their season; others chose to swallow their new principles; but the reputation of the sect never recovered. It is said that 2,000 of its 5,000 members in the north-east seceded; and its local humiliation was only confirmed by Taylor's subsequent personal downfall. Buckie too drew the line just at this point of interference with social relations with work. Murray Lockie, for example, refused to take on Exclusives as crew: 'brothers were leaving brothers in the boats and couldn't take a cup of tea with each other – I wouldn't carry them in the boats.' Willie Stewart remembered the wise advice of his grandfather, who had long before left the Open Brethren after hearing their preacher say, 'We're in the world, but we're not of the world.' His grandfather's belief, which can stand representative of Buckie, was: 'You've got to take part in the world.' He joined the Church of Christ.[20]

Buckie's commitment to individual achievement was again a key characteristic of its religion. There was – and remains – such a strong disapproval among Buckie skippers of traditional superstitions and beliefs in luck, that they may demonstrate their defiance by taking a minister out fishing, or even by deliberately choosing 'a number that added up to 13' for their boat's registration. Along the Moray Firth such superstitions are much more likely to be found surviving among poorer fishermen. On the other hand the Calvinist belief in predestination, in the pre-ordained salvation of a chosen few, although the official doctrine of the Church of Scotland and in a moderate form of the Brethren, was in very little evidence. The religion of the fishing communities was essentially an evangelical, open gospel, the creation of the successive missionary revivals.

The Christian symbolism of the 'poor fisherman' could indeed be claimed for themselves as a common possession. It is particularly interesting, therefore, that it was developed into a local notion of religious individualism: the 'worthy'. The worthy's claim to fame was almost the mirror image of the stern achievement of the go-ahead prosperous skipper. The term originally meant 'a distinguished or eminent person; especially a man of courage or of noble character', and in this sense was applied to the leaders and thinkers of the Protestant movement. But by the eighteenth century in England it had taken a significantly less-favourable twist as a jocular way of referring to anyone of 'marked personality'. But in the Scottish north-east the word, while again descending the social scale, kept its religious connotation. Here the worthy was often a poor eccentric, even a half-wit saint, whose real distinction was in his character and turn of phrase. Many worthies were local evangelical preachers, popular speakers in the style of the wandering mediaeval preaching friars who had preceded them. They spiced their sermons with a mixture of nautical and Biblical imagery, from 'The Heavenly Skipper' downwards. James Slater remembers one such Buckie fisherman George Wilson, known as Dodie Bainie, once declaiming to his audience the memorable – if obscure – phrase: 'There are nae labsters in the sleuchs (clefts) of the Rock o' Ages.'[21] The very recognition of such an unprivileged wit as a 'worthy, with the spark of sainthood in him', indicates the depth of Buckie's commitment to individualism. There was indeed here shelter for eccentricity; for the bid which failed. It was no mere path to this-worldly success.

It suggests too that Buckie's religion held a place for expressiveness as well as for self-control. This is the final point. For the conventional it was, no doubt, primarily a religion of restraint. We have already seen the mark of this in the severe role division between men and women in Buckie family life. No doubt where male heads of households were also elders of the kirk this further weighted an unequal situation. But there were important exceptions, for evangelical religion does allow a significant place for expressiveness, for love itself.

There is a warped reflection of this even in the absurdities of Taylor's downfall: for he was finally brought down by a confusion of religious and sexual emotionalism. The women of the Brethren, the sisters, had always dressed simply, without make-up; but in 1970 – the last year of his life – he began to urge them 'to throw away their foundation garments and wear their hair long under headscarves and flowing down their backs, as "proof of their affection for Christ".' During services, he liked men and women to embrace, even to caress. Finally, he was found after a mission meeting in Aberdeen by his host – Stanley McCallum, an ex-fisherman from Banffshire – being comforted in his exhaustion by a sister who lay in his bed, naked, 'serving him' by washing his feet and drying them with her hair. Despite Taylor's insistence that their love was pure, and her action scriptural, this was too much for McCallum, who insisted on exposing and challenging Taylor.

Before Taylor's insistence on separatism, the Exclusives were not known as 'narrow, joyless, severe and inward-looking'; their meetings were open occasions, and Brethren families often included members of other sects, with whom they shared many characteristics of small revivalist groups. But they always had a notable emphasis on the family. Originally, the sect operated exclusively on a family basis: it had a leader, but beyond this no formal ministry, no elders, and its services took place in the home. Children were especially cherished, and the Brethren believed in educating them leniently towards their strict standards. 'Big Jim has stressed time and again that his adult flock must grin and bear their children's tantrums.' And the Sunday breaking of bread is conceived at the same time as a domestic, family ceremony, and a moment of mystical passion, 'a veritable experience of Heaven to the participants', a union with God 'as Bride to Bridegroom'.

The Exclusives have always been a small sect. But one could find similar views in some other small religious groups in the area: in Peterhead, for example, 'the Love Family, a quaint sect who preach happiness through the Bible to accordion music and the beat of tambourines.' The very diversity of denominations, with people moving freely between them, makes it difficult for any particular church to become over-dominant. The idea of the 'worthy' reinforces freedom in expressiveness. It is as if religion had to offer its parallel for the experimentation which is essential to the continuing development of the fishing. In a tough world of painful work, bereavement and poverty, religion could give space for hope, for love. At the Salvation Army's open evening meeting of hymn-singing and testimonies in Peterhead, the old men will be 'on their feet, with the flush and hope of youth upon their faces, and the glad light dancing in their eyes as they sing their songs of praise . . . Surely here is the secret of happiness?' And for a few, from it could grow a real spirituality which allowed a very positive breaking of the community's conventions.[22]

It is not usually wise to end with an exception, but here it does indeed serve to prove the rule. When we think of the moral order in Buckie, we shall not forget that it had room for the old drifter skipper who, on his eightieth birthday night, sang for us a duet with his wife on the harmonium. He had been one of the town's most successful and respected drifter-men, and always known for his piety: he had an organ built into his boat, and would use it to broadcast hymns to the rest of the fleet – or play to himself when he lay in harbour away from home. He was also quite exceptional among Buckie skippers for the interest and share which he took with his wife in the work of the house. They were among the happiest, closest couples we met in the north-east communities. They sang together on the harmonium with a kind of strange interweaving, a 'half-fugue' which was first devised for hymn-singing by the mountain people of the American Appalachians, and must have reached the fishermen by way of one of the transatlantic revivals. The words made both a hymn – and a love song:

she	I will meet you
he	– in the morning
she	I will meet you
he	– in the morning
both	Just inside the Eastern Gate over there:
she	I will meet you
he	– in the morning
she	I will meet you
he	– in the morning
both	I will meet you in the morning over there.

Close-up: The Western Isles
14 The chiliasm of despair: Lewis

The Moray Firth marks only the beginning of the far north of Britain. Beyond it a final nub of mainland protrudes, a great brown moorland worn so thin that the granite breaks through its elbows, glistening silvery grey. Here the inland valleys have been utterly empty of people since the Highland Clearances. But the white-sanded coasts are clustered with crofting townships – and the sea's edge is really just the beginning of the crofting counties. To the north is Orkney, a full fifty-mile maze of richly farmed bright green low islands; beyond them the North Sea meeting the Atlantic, but before land is quite out of sight the browner, humpier outline of the Shetlands, with more townships again. Westward of the mainland the sea, the Minch, is sheltered by the great barrier of the Outer Hebrides, the 'Long Island' chain with the Barra Isles as its fragmented foot, and the joint mass of Harris and Lewis as its northern head: twisted, gleaming granite mountain with only a few townships at its scarce edges; but Lewis a low, dark moor whose sides are more densely stippled with the grey homes of crofters than any other part of the region. From Buckie westwards it is 150 miles to Lewis, and 250 miles to the northernmost of the Shetlands – as far as from London to Devon or to Cumberland.

The quarter of a million people of the crofting counties, having risen slowly to the end of the nineteenth century and since fallen, are today roughly equal to their numbers in the mid-eighteenth century: but then they were a full fifth of the whole population of Scotland. As late as 1914 Shetland and Lewis reported the largest numbers of fishermen of any Scottish registration district: over 6,000 (including non-residents) in Shetland and 4,000 in Lewis – in both mostly combining fishing with crofting. Despite falling numbers it

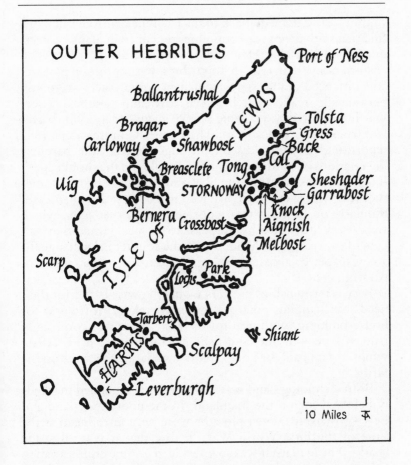

was a significant presence. Today the inshore waters close to Lewis and the Shetlands are the richest off the coast of Britain. Yet while the local fishing fleet in Shetland, although smaller than in the past, remains highly successful, activity by the Lewismen, despite their abundant natural resources, has declined so seriously that although a small fleet has recently been revived through government aid, in the early 1960s commercial fishing by the islanders had almost ceased completely. Why is this?

Historically, both Lewis and the Shetlands have shared a number of major economic and social disadvantages. Both were for long cut off from mainland markets, and from coal supplies. And if we go back to the late nineteenth century, we find that both their local economies remained in many respects quasi-feudal in character. Land was held by the crofters in custom rather than law, in 'townships' with common pasture, and unfenced arable strips which in some places were still periodically reallocated between township families. There was little currency available so that payment in kind, barter and truck were widespread. The Napier Commission's 1884 report singled out the 'discontent' engendered by the 'perplexing relations of traffic between the people and the shopkeeper'. It was perhaps worst in the Shetlands with the textile homeworkers who were normally paid in goods rather than cash. Similarly on Lewis it was reported in 1902 that eggs, which were 'very little eaten by the peasantry', were rather used 'as a coin of the realm . . . handed over the counter in exchange for a newspaper or a postage stamp . . . for tea, sugar, tobacco, paraffin, etc.'.

Between townships crofters would likewise barter for their needs, exchanging potatoes for mackerel, or driftwood for house-building, with peat for their fire. Rent was commonly paid in kind – in Shetland fishing tenures were paid in fish; while cottars paid for potato plots with labour services on the farms.

Both technology and material standards remained markedly below those on the mainland. In the poorer Shetland and Lewis townships, even ploughs were only introduced at the time of the First World War: 'before that it was all spade work'. The land itself was so infertile that some crofters had to cultivate in patches rather than in fields, heaping up soil and seaweed in 'lazy-beds' banked with turf. Crop yields were also reduced by lack of fencing, or of proper rotation. Crofters would use their scarce good arable to grow their vital subsistence crops, potatoes and oats, again and again. They were driven to this partly by the diminutive size of their holdings. The Napier Commission found that in four 'fairly representative' crofting parishes, with over 3,000 families in all, more than half were poor crofters with less land than could offer reasonable subsistence; and another quarter were landless cottars and squatters, 'without land and without regular access to local wages':

There are crowds of squatters who construct hovels, appropriate land, and possess and pasture stock, but pay no rent, obey no control, and scarcely recognise any allegiance or authority. These poor people support themselves by casual labour in the country, by the simpler kinds of fishing, and by wandering elsewhere in search of work.

Cottars and squatters were commonest of all on the Long Island and Lewis itself. Housing too remained especially primitive in Lewis. The 'black houses' once normal throughout the crofting region were again an outcome of material shortage: long houses, constructed of mortarless stone, peat-filled walls several feet thick, with roof rafters of driftwood and a thatch of barley straw tied down with heather. With wood so scarce, the rafters were rested on the inner edge of the wall, so that the rain soon seeped through and the family only kept dry at night by sleeping in their roofed-in box beds in the end room. In the middle room there would be a dresser, bench and chairs against the walls, and an open fire in the middle of the floor for cooking, its smoke drifting up without a chimney through the thatch. The soot-laden thatch eventually made good manure – and meanwhile kept the house warmer. In the third room, separated only by a partition, were the cattle, providing more warmth and manure from their byre.

It was the need for warmth, as well as the cost of light, which explained why – to the disapproval of mainland visitors – in winter both in Lewis and Shetland, 'the adult population remains up late at night, and lies in bed in the morning. The first meal is about midday.' Food was simple – mainly potatoes and fish – and also simply served, with a single dish – the 'trencher' in Shetland – in the centre of the table, and perhaps only one knife between the family too. Infants were breastfed and for this reason, despite insanitary conditions and the lack of professional medical assistance, there was an unusually low infant mortality among the crofting families.

There were some signs of changes by the end of the century, due both to slowly rising incomes and to increasing contact with the mainland. Children sent away to earn returned with ideas as well as cash. In 1916 a Lewis schoolmaster at Carloway recalled how when he first arrived in 1881, if he was asked to a local wedding:

> You would find very few knives on the table then. A fisherman would perhaps take out his knife and cut the bread and make the pieces for the young women. An improvement has set in, and only a few years ago I attended some of these marriage ceremonies and I found everyone sitting at a table with a knife and fork.

He might have noticed other signs of 'improvement'. Tea-drinking had become a basic part of crofting social life. Households had begun to buy sugar and jam, and at least for their men tobacco, shoes and some clothes. Some of these innovations were purchased at the mainland fishing. Alex McLeod from Back in Lewis remembers the brownish worsted tweed clothes his father bought in Buckie, which they called in the Gaelic 'clorbuckach' (Buckie cloth); while Norman Paterson's father was so

> very lucky in the fishing, we had a clock in the house ever since I remember – but I remember quite often people coming, especially in the dead of winter, coming to see what time it was.

And in the same way, the houses themselves began to change too:

> The crofter sends his sons and daughters to the large cities of the South and the Colonies, and if they prosper there they are mindful of and dutiful to their parents at home. They are the source from which the money now invested in stone and lime comes, for their desire to see their parents in greater comforts.

In most of the Hebrides and in Shetland the black houses gave way from the 1880s to 'white houses', stone-built, slate-roofed, with chimneys and separate byres. But in this respect Lewis proved notably conservative in its social habits. Many crofters preferred to improve their old houses by inserting chimneys and lining the inner walls with wood, rather than starting afresh. Even as late as 1947, black houses still made up 40 per cent of the housing of Lewis.[1]

More fundamentally, the 1880s had also marked the ending of the old semi-feudal social economy in both the northern and western isles. The Napier Commission had recommended measures to regularise the crofting township system, and to convert the crofters into self-sufficient, economically progressive small farmers. It advocated the enlargement of townships and resettlement on inland farms, if need be by compulsory purchase, and the division between them of the tracts of 'wild ground' to end the 'promiscuous use of pasture lands'. Land redistribution was to prove a very long process. But legislation was at once introduced giving a framework for township management, secure legal tenure, and compensation for improvements. Most important of all, a new standing Crofters Commission was set up to assess fair rents and insist on cash payment. All this brought the crofters both security, and substantial rent reductions. Nor could they now be legally bound to fish for a landlord. In Shetland, but much more slowly on Lewis, boat-ownership began to spread among the fishermen themselves. Local entrepreneurial initiative also developed quickly in Shetland. As in Lewis, the lingering of a semi-feudal economy had meant that the local business classes originated as merchants rather than as employing entrepreneurs. But again there was much less change in Lewis; and the contrast persists. The Lewis business class still consists chiefly of merchants. And Lewismen today, surrounded by apparent natural wealth in the resources of the sea, have the highest unemployment rate in Britain, even in the prosperous late 1960s and early 1970s running at between 20 and 30 per cent.[2] How can the contrast with Shetland, whose economic basis appears to have been so similar, be explained?

The answer lies deep-seated in the different local social cultures of Lewis and Shetland which have emerged through an essentially separate history. This is immediately apparent at the level of language. The Western Islanders speak Gaelic as their first language. This has both helped them to preserve a separate culture, and hindered their absorption into the mainland economy. The Shetland dialect was a cross between old Norse and English; and here an actively reciprocal relationship with the mainland not only of commercially minded local landowners but also of ordinary people, developed much earlier. Even in the 1870s, while Shetland young men and women would be earning as seafarers or as domestic servants on the mainland, Gaelic was reported as 'a check to the migration of both sexes' from the Western Isles. At times of catastrophe, as in the aftermath of the potato famine when 2,000 crossed the Atlantic from Lewis in ten years, language would be no barrier. But not until the later nineteenth century could a now bilingual younger generation develop regular patterns of seasonal migration to bring home cash earnings: enlistment in the Militia, the Naval Reserve or Lovat's Sea Scouts; summer yachting; winter gas-stoking and labouring in Glasgow; domestic service; or working as gutters and hired hands at the herring fishing. Above all, working at the fishing. A government report of 1906 on Lewis shows that while the sale of croft produce provided the average Lewis family with a net cash income of less than £3 in a whole year, those members sent out to follow the fishing brought home altogether to each household average earnings of over £30.

For Lewismen such a bonanza from the sea was a new and rather unexpected good fortune. It is a second important historical contrast that, unlike the Shetlanders whose seafaring traditions go back centuries, the Western Islanders are predominantly landsmen in origin. The nineteenth-century inhabitants of the Outer Hebrides were a population largely of relatively recent, and principally agricultural roots. The landowning class, until the eighteenth century conquest and pacification of the Scottish Highlands, had consisted of the hereditary military chiefs of paternalistic clans. By the end of the century, through persuasion and replacement, they had been converted to the philosophy of economic improvement, but this was carried out by the ruthless tactic of the Highland clearances. The inland population was driven out by force – if necessary, by burning their houses over their heads – to make way for sheep; and whole communities were resettled on generally less fertile land, close to the sea. Here it was intended that they should either supply labour for the thriving kelp (seaweed) industry; or, with some elementary instruction sometimes provided by the landowners, support themselves as crofter-fishermen. The advent of the potato also stimulated strong population growth, despite worse land resources; but it was principally the kelp which caused the population of the Western Isles in eighty years from the 1750s to more than double.

The crofters had thus been brought to the water's edge through force rather than freewill. Their landowners' attitudes hardly served to encourage material ambition in them. In 1820 the proprietor of Lewis, Lord Seaforth, set about clearing the Uig and Lochs districts for sheep, planning to move a thousand people to the more barren north end of the island. Some were given the grazing land of other townships, just roughly pegged out; others were settled on the waste land at Tong. They were told to build their own houses, and a road; and if the land looked unpromising – tenants 'must and ought to be content with whatever land we can give them'. The crofters can hardly have shed many tears for their landlords when in the 1820s both the kelp industry and the fishing collapsed, and the whole of the Long Island came into new ownership within a generation.

It did, however, teach them further scepticism about improvement, which subsequent economic vicissitudes rubbed in. The worst of these was the potato famine: without much doubt the nadir of their material hardship. It was to be followed by a slow improvement; but such memories die hard. Thus when the kelp industry revived in the 1900s it was said that during the summer £1 a day could be earned from picking kelp off the shore, but crofters would only 'play with this industry as they do with anything else of the kind', preferring to get their potato patches dug while leaving 'thousands of pounds' worth of weed rotting on the seashore'. Tangle had to be dried out on the dykes, and then burnt in August. But by then prices might have fallen; and the kelp industry's revival did not in fact prove long-lasting.[3] The home tweed-weaving industry first effectively organised in the 1900s which has since provided many crofts with an important supplementary income, has also similarly been dogged by disappointing price fluctuations.

It was essentially the same cycle of bitter experience, which held back the development of a self-sustaining local fishing industry. The potential of the Minch fishing had been recognised by east-coast fishermen as far back as the early seventeenth century, when the 'Fife Adventurers' were driven out in a series of attempts to set up a fortified colonial entrepot on the site of Stornoway. Later on the British Fisheries Society constructed facilities for Ullapool and Skye in the 1780s. These ventures failed partly because of the unreliability of the movements of the herring. But most crofting townships were far from a market, and lacked harbour, gear, or know-how. Official reports of 1841 and 1847 described many of the Long Island fishing boats as 'little better than the punts employed by anglers on the Thames' and the crofters as 'so poorly skilled and so ill provided with means' that they could not hope 'to pursue the occupation with effect'.[4]

In this a significant exception from the start was the small island of Scalpay off Harris, just south of Lewis, settled in the 1840s after clearances from Pabbay, Uist and Harris. Here the landowner had sent a fish-curer to start them fishing, and although he soon left a Scalpay man set up on his own as a herring curer in 1856. By the 1900s there were nine curing stations here. The islanders were forced to depend on fishing because of Scalpay's infertility. Of a hundred families in the 1880s, only forty had crofts, and even these could live off them for only two months a year. Rather than crofters who sometimes fished, the Scalpay people were thus fishing families some of whom had crofts. They combined local lobster and line-fishing with herring drifting, at first as hired hands, but by the 1920s with their own motor boats. After 1945 they turned to ring netting. Today with a fleet of eleven seiners, as well as many smaller boats, and three cargo vessels, Scalpay maintains a buoyant population of 500. The story of the similarly infertile Catholic island of Eriskay is comparable: 'the most active fishermen in Barra and the Uists' in the 1930s, with their own small motor boats, 'due possibly to the fact that their crofts are not very productive'. Again Eriskay, with its thriving co-operative, remains a rare centre of fishing activity on the west today.[5]

More generally there had been some advance from the 1860s

onwards. In the Western Isles the herring industry developed quite rapidly, partly through the intervention of east-coast men, but also with the founding of local curing enterprises. Castlebay on Barra and Stornoway on Lewis became major centres of activity. There were more than fifty Stornoway curers by the 1880s, profiting from the high-priced early summer herring, as well as the smaller trades in lobsters and dried or salted cod and ling. But as the Napier Commission pointed out forcibly, there was room for 'vast extension and development'.

Lack of good transport to markets was to remain one basic difficulty, even if improved by the extension of the Highland railheads to Kyle and Mallaig in the 1890s. Roads were also needed to the creeks: and above all harbours. On the whole west shore of Lewis there was a harbour only at Carloway. Many of the east-side villages, like Back, also had to launch their boats every day off the beach. The loan scheme to encourage bigger boats which had been introduced on Napier's recommendation hence proved of little value. A new harbour was built at Port Ness, and although even this could only take smallish boats the township became the second fishing station on Lewis. The other focus of activity was the cluster of villages close enough to use Stornoway's excellent harbour; though even here many men persisted in working from beaches or inadequate piers like at Sheshader, where the men had to re-launch and ballast their boats each time they set out.[6]

The problem could not really be solved economically while fishing remained a purely seasonal activity. While the men also needed to work on their crofts it would have made no sense for them to move; the more so while they relied on their women to bait lines and walk barefoot into the town with fresh butter and crowdie off the croft and a string of fish to sell 'round the doors . . . sixpence for a "gat" – the Gaelic word for fish'. Lack of an effective economic framework for fishing was one reason why, in the words of the Napier Commission, 'the intended fisherman has remained an indigent cultivator with an exhausted croft'.

Up to the 1880s the barter system was a further critical handicap. The Rev. Anderson Smith thought that one reason for 'the utter want of enterprise and self reliance of the bulk of the inhabitants' was the trap through which the local merchants held them:

> The system of the curers is to endeavour to keep them in debt, so that they may be obliged to fish for them the following year, and yet not to allow them so much credit as to be irretrievably involved.

As a consequence many of the salesmen would be struggling *not* to sell too much gear to their fishermen! And on their side a typical crew of eight, having run up a debt of £100, would treat the sum as 'purely fictitious. . . . The men, knowing they are greatly overcharged, retaliate by saying, "But we don't intend to pay" . . . They make no effort to extricate themselves from their financial difficulties, and when more credit is refused by one curer, threaten to bind themselves to another. . . . They hope for nothing better than their failure, that all standing debts may be written off.' The complex entanglement with which an antiquated merchant structure can throttle a developing local economy could hardly be better put. Such economic relationships, Eric Wolf remarks in his classic modern text on *Peasants*, represent the 'nadir' of the rental system. No wonder Lewismen who wanted cash were already setting off in increasing numbers each summer with their 'little canvas bags' to take berths as hired men on the east-coast boats: 'Only a few old men and young boys are left; and, indeed, no one will remain who can raise a few shillings to pay for his passage.'

This remained the pattern right into the twentieth century. Inshore work continued but was hardly pushed vigorously. Some Barra and Lewis crews bought the larger sailboats needed for open-sea herring drifting, but under a hundred Lewis crews had this courage. The local shipping registers show a significant progress towards fishermen-ownership of boats: from the 1890s with few exceptions the smaller boats were wholly theirs. But two-thirds of the first class sailboats at this stage were still owned by landsmen, most of whom were Stornoway merchants and curers. Although they included a few bankers, village shopkeepers and bakers, there was none of the Moray Firth's widespread investment in boat-ownership by landsmen, and a particular absence of part-shares. Boats were either owned outright by one or two landsmen; or by a fisherman, or sometimes a group of fishermen. Half the new registrations of first-class sailboats in 1910–14 were by fishermen outright; but the remainder were increasingly concentrated in the hands of a few Stornoway curers and merchants.

Still more striking is the failure of any Lewis crew, right through the boom years of the 1900s, to buy a steam drifter. The first local fisherman with even a share in a steam drifter was not recorded until 1915, and until 1919 there was not a single Lewis steam drifter fully owned by fishermen. Nor for that matter had the merchants been much quicker to move. Stornoway merchants and curers were quite active investors in large sailing merchant boats right up to the First World War, normally buying them secondhand from other ports. One cannot but suspect that in many cases they hoped to recoup more money from insurance than from trading, for *half* the ships registered from the 1890s to the First World War were either wrecked or lost at sea. Their first experiments with steam were very much in the same spirit: two Stornoway fish-curers bought old steam liners from the east coast in 1896, but both were wrecked in the Minch within months. Similarly, it was only when the first east-coast drifters were a decade old that Stornoway curers were prepared to risk putting their money into them. Two curers bought four old boats in 1911–14, working them with local crews but owning them outright. Nor were the curers much more adventurous with motor boats, although Murdo McLean, one of the two steam-drifter owners, did buy the first locally in 1913. But few followed before the early 1920s, and then it was the fishermen who put up the money themselves. The curers went on buying steam drifters, some as much as twenty years old, into the late 1920s.

One can see how, with local backing of this order, Lewis-men might prefer to work as hired hands on east-coast boats, picking the crumbs of the steam drifter boom. In 1906 2,000 hired men and 2,300 women fishworkers set out from Stornoway after the herring; but only nine Lewis sailboats were fit to

follow as far as East Anglia. On the eve of the First World War
the Provost of Stornoway told the North Sea fishing inquiry:

> There were some men who had boats, but they became
> disheartened with the boats and became hired men. . . .
> The pith is knocked out of the fishermen with their sail
> boats, so that they cannot compete with the steam drifters
> nowadays.[7]

This situation left the Lewis fishermen highly vulnerable to the
drastic recession which was to follow. Immediately after the
war there was a brief phase of high hopes for the local fishing
industry with the intervention of the Lancashire soap manu-
facturer turned business-philanthropist, Lord Leverhulme. In
the early summer he had bought the entire island from its
previous owners (since 1844), the Mathesons, who themselves
had failed to make any return on the considerable investment
they had made in developing their land. Leverhulme saw the
islanders' future instead in fishing, telling them on his first
triumphal visit in June 1918 that they were 'really, as far as the
harvest of the sea is concerned, what you may call the hub of
the universe. . . . You have got the wealth at the door waiting
to be harvested . . . and out of that we can pay the highest
wages.' Stornoway had the longest season of any fishing port:
but what was wanted was full-time fishing. There could be no
progress while the crofter-fisherman had 'to leave his drifter or
trawler in spring time to attend to his croft, and again in the
autumn to harvest . . . I call that amateur fishing!'

Late in 1918 he set up the Macline Drifters and Trawlers Co.
to buy and operate a fleet of ten motor drifters, aided by radio
and aeroplanes in fish-finding. Fresh catch would be frozen for
the home market, and the surplus canned – a new proposition.
Although Macline's quite quickly switched its headquarters to
Fleetwood, Leverhulme set about building the Stornoway
canning factory, and planned others for the smaller ports. He
bought out the existing Stornoway fishmeal factory, which
the local merchants had built in 1914. Most important of all, in
1919 he set up MacFisheries to provide an outlet for his catch.
With a share capital of £3 million, the new group rapidly built

up a chain of 400 shops, the biggest fishmongery ever known, with its soon-familiar neat, clean blue-grey fish counters. MacFisheries quickly proved a success, and in order to supply the chain Leverhulme bought out other large enterprises in the fishing industry, notably the Aberdeen Steam Fish and Trawling Company, and the big Yarmouth-based curing group of Bloomfields, which also had curing stations and kipperhouses in the Scottish north, including Stornoway. For the town itself Leverhulme proposed a radical new town plan, new housing and public buildings, gas and electricity, a light railway and an air service.

Some of the housing proposed, the gasworks and electricity station, and a dairy to provide pure milk were in fact built: but Leverhulme's vision of a new Lewis 'full of thriving and prosperous cities, towns and harbours, and of happy, rich, contented men and women,' was soon sinking in ruins. He had reckoned without two factors: the instability of fishing prices, and local resistance. By the end of 1920 fish prices had fallen drastically from their high wartime level. More generally, international recession had put the whole Leverhulme empire in crisis. By August 1921 the opening of the canning, ice and fishmeal factories was indefinitely suspended. Publicly Leverhulme put the blame on the opposition of a minority of landless men, who had persisted despite his warnings in raiding the remaining larger farms which he did not wish to see broken up. To emphasise this he persisted a little longer in his efforts to convert the small township of Obbe at the southern end of Harris into the fishing port of Leverburgh: but this was a still-more ill-judged scheme which left no more than a few melancholy traces on the barren rocky coastline. There was, at least in retrospect, a good deal more to be said for the judgment of some of the landless men. Lewismen had been pushed about by proprietors before. After one of Leverhulme's early idealistic speeches, 'a squatter from the Back district pointed out the uncertainty of the fishing and their determination to have a piece of the land they loved and fought for.'[8] With a croft, there was always something to fall back on.

In the lean years between the wars the scanty living which could be won from the crofts, supplemented by home weaving, was indeed a better prospect for most Lewismen. East-coast boats had less and less need for seasonal hired men. Their skippers would telegram to the local salesmen, who then 'sent word' that there were berths. Once hired men were known, skippers would telegram them direct: 'if anybody got a telegram with two or three vacancies that man would look out and get three men with him'. Similarly local girls who wanted to go gutting would form crews themselves 'at home, with friends: they put their heads together'. But from the 1920s word came less often. By 1938 although a thousand women still went gutting, only a hundred Lewismen were taken on as hired hands. Those with their own boats were little better off. Commercial line-fishing had all but ceased. The 'purely herring minded' crofter-fishermen around Stornoway had to make do with unreliable second-hand motor boats or still more antiquated steam drifters. Lobster fishing which needed only small boats was by 1934 'in point of value' the main Lewis fishery. Many of the Ness and Scalpay men had gone merchant seafaring instead. The hopelessness of the atmosphere is summed up in a letter of distress written by one Lewisman in 1924, who had returned from the war to find

> my boat is useless now for want of repair, I can't get to sea, and also my weaving house and loom was a wreck when I came back home, and is still like that, also my 24 lobster creels.

As in the past, many chose emigration as their only hope. Murdo Macfarlane – whose father had followed the herring, unlike him and his brothers – remembers how

> the Canadian Pacific Railway sent three – three – huge passenger boats to the Hebrides, to bring the youth away. Now in my days you see my mother used to out the milk in basins, and . . . when the milk thickened, she scooped the cream . . . (with) a shell from the shore, and – this is what happened to us, to this community, to the Hebrides. The cream was scooped off the thick milk. And we all left. I saw eleven people walking that morning across from this village to Stornoway – eleven people out of a small

village. . . . There were six in our family, and four of us
went across. . . . There was nobody left but the old
people.

A minority would eventually return with their savings to the
crofts – but not to fish. By 1938 only 350 fishermen were still
active in the Stornoway district on local herring boats; and
only 1,800 men could be described as fishermen or crofter-
fishermen – a mere third of the figure at the outbreak of the
First World War little more than two decades earlier. The
catch landed locally was still worth £100,000, drawing nearly
200 boats in season, but most of these boats were outsiders.
Meanwhile, unemployment in Ross and Cromarty as a whole
had reached the level of 58 per cent, the highest of any county
in Britain.

There seems little doubt that but for outside intervention,
after the Second World War further decline would have led to
the virtual extinction of the Lewis fishing industry. The
Herring Industry Board set up a fishmeal and oil factory, a
kippering plant and freezing facilities in Stornoway. In the
early 1950s, with better prospects, 600 fishermen were employed – but most were part-timers from the crofts. Scarcely
thirty steam or motor drifters were registered in the district.
Ten years later, from Stornoway itself a mere two or three
local boats remained active. Rescue came only through the
combined action of the Macaulay Trust, established by a
wealthy emigrant, which from 1959 offered to provide the
deposits for local men who wished to buy boats under the
government grant-and-loan schemes, and a government project for training a new generation of full-time fishermen. From
1965 the Highlands and Islands Development Board provided
its own further loans scheme, and a second training programme. Through these initiatives a small fleet of motor
boats equipped as light trawlers was built up, and a special
boat was maintained among them for the training of crews –
often drawn from former fishing families, but rarely with
experience of their own in the local fishery – to man each
new boat. Stornoway's modestly successful fleet of some
twenty-five boats today was thus reconstructed on new foundations.[9] It includes a few men, like Roddy McIver, skipper

of the *Golden Sheaf*, born in 1912 into a crofter-fishing family in Knock, who has persisted in fishing the Minch for fifty years, moving from sail to motor by the 1930s, and from drift nets to trawling in the mid-1960s. But such men are exceptional. While fishermen working out of Stornoway now generally live in the town, it has no fishermen's quarter: they live scattered. Today's Lewis fishermen have been created afresh, rather than come to fishing as part of a continuing tradition.

'Unsuccessful exertion is naturally succeeded by inert apathy,' Hugh Miller observed of the Lewismen in 1829. But this does not wholly explain the story of the Lewis fishing: for the islanders have responded to opportunities on the mainland and abroad as migrant workers. In understanding why they have been so slow to take up the local opportunities offered by fishing, we have also to take account of the impact on their culture of their treatment at the hands of the landowners: the historical making of the Lewis crofting communities.

The common people of the Highlands had been defeated by the British military before the clearances, and this was probably why in the late eighteenth century they only briefly resisted expulsion from their homes to make way for incoming sheep farmers. No doubt it was their sense of helplessness which made them take refuge in religion, responding to the great evangelistic campaigns of Calvinistic missionaries who toured the Highlands from the end of the eighteenth century, setting off waves of revivalism which reached their culmination in the 1830s and 1840s. With the translation of the Bible into Gaelic in 1801, religion could grow as a force from within the Highland communities, rather than merely be imposed on them from without by external clergy. Peregrinatory Gaelic schools were set up, led by independent catechists moving between the townships; local lay preachers emerged, providing the first internal leadership of the crofting community; and the great open-air gatherings for communion were begun, which became a tradition of the north-west. When – in the aftermath of the revival – the Established Church of Scotland split in half over the question of control of the appointment of parish clergy, the local lay preachers, 'the men' as they were significantly known, carried the Lewis population *en masse* over to the Free Kirk, which allowed congregations to choose their own ministers. A mere 500 out of 20,000 on the island stayed with the Auld Kirk. In 1843 for the first time the crofting majority stood up against the landlords – and won. The landowners kept hold of the endowments of the Church of Scotland, but at the cost of losing their authority over the communities. The crofters became morally a separate people.

It was in this way that the Free Kirk came to be as fundamental to the identity of the people of Lewis as Roman Catholicism has been to the nationalism of Poland or Ireland. When the Free Kirk itself split in the 1900s over a proposed reunion with a second secession from the Church of Scotland, and the United Free Kirk was formed (itself in turn to reunite with the established church in 1929), the people of Lewis stood firm, almost alone, to form the Gaelic-speaking Free Presbyterian Kirk, the 'Wee Frees'. For them the Church of Scotland minister stood principally for unjustified upper-class privilege. Lewis had a single landowner who, before the Leverhulme episode which ended with his presentation of part of the island to its inhabitants, had been little seen. The only other local representatives of the Anglo-Scottish gentry were visiting tenants who took leases of the lodges built by the Mathesons for the shooting season. They would bring most of their own servants, spoke no Gaelic and mixed little with the locals. But the Church of Scotland minister was very much present in his parishes, with his glebe, tithes and stipend, and worst of all his direct influence over the landlord and the factor, the landlord's agent. In Barvas the minister had the only horse plough, and a place on the moor 'protected for his own stock and his own cows, that the crofters didn't dare go near. . . . He ruled the roost. . . . He could by the stroke of his pen, he could tell you to move.' No wonder Lewis boys, believed ' "Jack's as good as his man" – Well, we got out of the minister's way so we wouldn't have to salute him.'

This class-based dislike was mutual. The Free Kirk clergy had come out as open supporters of the Highland land movement. In seeking to strengthen their own social base throughout the Scottish north, 'they identified the rump of the Auld Kirk with the interests of landlords and capitalist farmers'. Some stood as Land League candidates in local elections in the late 1880s. With the Park deer raid on Lewis in 1887, huge numbers of crofters invaded the forests and slaughtered 200 deer, then 'the deer were roasted and eaten amid scenes resembling a religious festival' in front of specially invited press reporters with the evident approval of Free Kirk supporters of the League. When it came to the post-1918 land raids the sympathies of the Free Kirk clergy were still, as the *Scotsman* reported, 'undoubtedly with the crofters', but by this date they were more hesitant in their attitudes to illegal activity and in some districts their influence was 'exerted to restrain them'. Thus on Lewis, while the minister was behind the raiders in Coll, in Gress he was 'not very supporting'; and in Melbost one of the elders who learned of the young men's plans warned them simply, 'You're going to suffer'; they should learn to take material hardship as 'a visitation – for our sins'.

The establishment knew little of such hesitations and their class fear of the Free Kirk can be seen in their response to the Ness 'church riot' of 1901. So fierce had been the split in the Free Kirk here on the reunion issue that the mainland police were brought in. It was reported that a crowd of anti-unionists, led allegedly by a squatter, Donald Murray, had forced their way into the church, barricaded its doors, and forced the local sheriff 'to quit the church after being mobbed'. The police, however, found that nobody in the townships could be persuaded to talk, whatever their view on the ecclesiastical dispute, so it could only be noted in the official file: 'There is no very definite evidence against anybody in these reports. The Islanders still appear to be in an excitable state of mind.'

Perhaps most excitable of all was the local doctor from Borve, ten miles from Ness, who demanded much stronger action. In his view,

the leading spirits in this movement have made no secret of their determination to defy and set at naught the authority of the Law Courts. Hitherto they boast that they have done so. . . . The layman presiding at one of their

meetings the Sabbath evening following the late riot
publicly thanked God in his prayers that they had won the
victory the previous night! Nay more, that very Sabbath
the Rev Mr Kennedy Park, the Interim Moderator . . .
administered the Sacrament to several of those who were
actively engaged in the riot.

The true ringleaders he believed were not religious men, but a
group of small shopkeepers, 'notorious' shebeeners; and before the trial their supporters –

a dozen young ruffians, with blackened faces, and supplied
with five bottles of whisky to fire up their passions,
actually came two miles on to the moor to way-lay and
maul the independent witnesses.

The ringleaders should receive 'exemplary punishment' forth-
with; and,

to avoid a further repetition of setting the law at defiance at
Ness, it is necessary to send a small military force there to
protect the Police. . . . The Ness lawbreakers openly
boast that the Government would never resort to such a
step! . . . The sooner the military appear on the scene the
better for all concerned.[10]

On Lewis, in short, church matters were equally questions of
community and class.

It is this which has given Calvinism its peculiar hold on the
Lewis communities. The kirk is effectively the forum of the
popular community. A socialist non-believer like Murdo
Macfarlane will attend church, and even act as leader of the
psalm-singing. Norman Macdonald of Tong remembers how
his father had gone to America in the 1920s for work, and
returned something of a rebel. When people passed on the way
to kirk on Wednesday afternoons he would stand at the croft
gate and shout, ' "What the hell do you think you are doing?
Why aren't you working?" . . . It took some courage to do
that'. But within eight years, after the death of one of his own
children had hit him, he was back in the kirk – and as an elder.

Church and community were too closely intertwined on the densely built Lewis townships for it to be easy to live for long outside the fold. Everyone was under the eye of the local elders. Members who had sinned, for drunkenness, for dancing or worst of all for bearing an illegitimate child, might even be obliged to stand outside the church bareheaded while the congregation filed in. Church and secular rituals and holidays still remain inseparable today. The church had no specific social organisations, like women's guilds or youth clubs. But the great social occasion of the year in each district was and still is the parish communion, when all work ceases from Wednesday evening until the following Tuesday. On the Wednesday the church would be prepared, and the houses cleaned too – often repapered if they had lined walls, for many came from outside to hear the preaching, and the houses would be full of visitors. And 'the women had to do all the starching then, because the men wore in those days stiff collars and cuffs'. From Thursday to Monday there were two services daily, at least for the men; including the Friday morning session, which consisted of a disputation by the visiting ministers and elders on a chosen Biblical text. The communion itself took place on Sunday afternoon. Each district still holds its communion on different weekends, so that there is a regular annual cycle which can be followed by the more enthusiastic kirk supporters.

Every Lewis Sabbath is in any case formidable in itself, with a total prohibition of work and play. In the past even fetching water from the well might be forbidden, and fishing was inconceivable. Even today Lewis has no buses, no air or ferry services on Sundays, and using the telephone may be strongly disapproved. In the rural districts, the crofting families meet twice at church, watched as they enter by the elders who receive their weekly offering. Inside are rows of plain brown deal pews, with a dais at one end where the elders sit at the sides, the precentor in between, and the minister in the high pulpit above. They stand for prayers, but otherwise sit. The long prayers and sermon convey a message of gloomy thankfulness to a severe God, that the crops do not stand rotting in the ground – for the poor weather is surely a visitation for our sins; that we live in an isle where the sword is at rest, where the gospel is understood in our own tongue, rather than among earthquakes or cannibals. But even this blessing is under threat. 'There are teenage girls in Stornoway who use the name of the Lord in vain on the public highway.' And beyond this there now looms the danger of a confederacy with hostile nations, perhaps even under the Antichrist himself – for once within the Common Market, how can we protect ourselves from the Papacy? Might we not yet have a United States of Europe, under the Presidency of 'The Man of Sin'? The congregation, further admonished for more homely vices, stands up suddenly for a prayer, and then sits for the last of the psalms, the precentor leading each line, followed by the women and then the men in a swelling dirge, an extraordinary entwining song of utter sadness and beauty. They rise for a final prayer, and then turn in absolute unity, surging down the aisle, silent, making for home with scarcely any conversation.[11] It would be hard to find anywhere else a Sabbath which weighs as heavily as that of Lewis.

Funerals also remain communal occasions. In the past, after a death, for the two days up to the burial 'the village went idle'. After the body had been washed by the women of the township, there would be a vigil of mourners for two nights in the house. The men then carried the body to the ceremony, leaving the women in the home. Every man that was able was expected to help carry the coffin, walking in pairs, sometimes several miles to a graveyard always well away from the church and often close to the sea:

> The menfolk, there's eight handles, they started at the top, and then they come down the bier you see, they changed hands till they were down to the last one, and then they went aside, so on till all the people went past and then you joined the tail end of them. Everybody helped to carry that was able. . . . And that was hard work on a rainy day. And then we had to dig the grave after getting there. But we were fortunate in having a good sandy dry soil . . . this is the Atlantic Ocean as near – well it's very wild in wintertime, you can hear that roar of growing sea.

The manner of burying, of sharing in carrying the bier, also continues in Lewis, a communal re-enactment of the equality of all before death.

Weddings were traditionally a more secular celebration. In the earlier phase of Highland Calvinistic evangelicism some of 'the men', with their long hair tied with 'bandana handkerchiefs', might have seemed to encourage unconventional social behaviour through their chiliastic millennial fervour. But the Free Kirk ministry seems to have been imbued from the start with a rigid and extremely severe Puritanism, and set about to extinguish the 'various worldly and pernicious customs and amusements' of the crofters. Among these customs wedding and courting practices were prime targets. Even the ordinary *ceilidh*, the traditional winter social gathering in the crofters' homes, came under severe criticism. In Lewis it was purified to the point of becoming a 'means of recreation and instruction' which an official report could compare with urban evening classes. Ceilidhs were normally held,

> where the head of the house is an intelligent, communi-
> cative man, or where there are a large number of
> daughters. To such a house or houses young men and
> women repair in large numbers after nightfall. Here old
> tales are rehearsed and songs sung, or the public questions
> of the time are discussed.

Norman Paterson, whose father was a crofter-missionary, remembers how in wintertime at ceilidhs in his home there was some singing, but,

> they generally repeated their experiences – in places where
> they'd been at. The girls when they were at the fishing and
> the men when they were sailing, when they called in New
> York . . . or Quebec . . . or Australia, they'd be telling
> stories – telling their experiences. And the religious people
> always talked about the sermons they heard and the
> communions they'd been on, and the people they had
> seen and what they said. And some of them that could
> read, they would repeat what they read in a book,
> what Augustine said . . . and what Napoleon and what
> Spurgeon said. . . . And outside of that they discussed the

weather, they discussed the animals, the plights of animals, and – how they had good crops, and – where could they get a cow . . . and who was going to get married. . . .[12]

It was above all the crofters' traditional dances, worldly songs and poetry, and the courting custom of 'bundling' in bed, which came under attack from the new moral leaders. To a very considerable extent they succeeded. The secular musical tradition was driven underground, and largely disappeared through most of Lewis. And if bundling was not eradicated, there was certainly an exceptionally low illegitimacy rate on the island – usually under 2 per cent in the 1890s, contrasting with 6 per cent on the mainland, and twice that in some rural counties in the north-east of Scotland.

Most of this must have been due to restraint, although concealment also played some part. There were times away at the gutting whose consequences could be covered by a quick marriage. And here and there pleasures continued at home: like at a crossroads between townships, where 'there was a bridge with a concrete surface . . . and the bridge was a great place for dancing in those days, somebody would have an accordion you see.' Weddings continued to provide a similar opportunity for adults. In the 1870s Anderson Smith described two-day weddings when there would be wild dancing in a barn, a huge pile of straw at one end into which couples might disappear, peat torches, jigs to the fiddle, songs by the girls, choruses, and energetic beating of time; and when the 'bedding' of bride and bridegroom had been witnessed, since bundling was 'still universal' in Lewis, 'most of the dancers take home their partners and court them in bed until morning'. Goodrich Freer describes similar scenes at weddings in the 1900s, when after the minister and elders had left the wedding supper it was

> no uncommon thing for the guests to hang plaids over
> door and window to deaden sound, and screen the festive
> lights, and (taking turns to watch outside) to draw the
> fiddle from its hiding-place (probably too the whisky
> bottle), and clearing the house for a dance, to 'play at'
> bringing back the old times when, under a more congenial
> faith, the world was young and hearts were merry.

Bringing out the hidden whisky was itself a more general habit. Some had become imbued with Puritanism to the point when they believed they had to get drunk 'before they can enjoy themselves'. Drunkards were a familiar sight in Stornoway and in the 1920s a number of illegal shebeens were prosecuted for operating in the town. More serious and widespread, however, was and is the extent of covert alcoholism in Lewis generally.[13]

The significance of such indulgences was not so much in their prevalence – which would be difficult to estimate and could easily be exaggerated – but in their secrecy. For this was highly symptomatic of the moral order which had been constructed with the kirk in the townships. Out of sight, it was a different matter. Even on the island this was the convention with ceasing work for funerals. Within the village, 'there wasn't a turn done. . . . Outside the village you could work.' Bundling likewise was a known and common, yet covert, socially secret breach of morality. More generally, as migrant workers Lewismen were not expected to be tee-totallers; and in fact many of those who crossed to America returned with markedly new social and political views. Women fishworkers too, as migrant female groups for once free from the supervision of the male elder, took on a special spontaneity, which still returns in the memory, especially when they talk about it together. This was how many were able to meet future husbands and marry 'for love' into another community. One woman, whose three sisters chose to go away to domestic service, recalled insisting on the gutting: 'I was the black sheep of the family. . . . We used to enjoy it – I was longing to go.' But in the townships, even when Puritanism was not felt inwardly, dissent must not be openly expressed. As one crofter-fisherman's son born in the 1900s, himself a seaman before he became a crofter-weaver, put it: 'They're afraid of one another, more or less, I think that's what keeps them strict.'[14]

It was a lesson learnt from childhood. Lewis children were not fully incorporated into the moral order until adulthood. They did not attend kirk; their families could not afford to provide them with Sunday clothes. They had the run of the countryside, especially in summer, when some were able to go to help look after the cattle on the summer shielings, rough pastures higher on the moor, where they would live in little stone bothies with only the supervision of a few of the older women. And in some families the relative licence of innocence could come close to the open mocking of religion. A Stornoway girl, Margaret McLeod, daughter of a merchant seaman brought up in her grandmother's home, remembered:

> there was an old trunk in my granny's room and when my brother was small he used to get great fun out of delving into it you know, lifting the lid and delving into it, and it was creaking you see, and she's – oh, she was horrified at making a noise like that on Sunday. . . . My mother was a Godly woman, she would never allow us to do anything like that on Sunday. . . . 'The Lord will put judgement on us'. . . . She was always on about the creaking lid and so my brother said to her this day, 'Why are you not putting oil on it then?'

But generally children soon imbibed the attitudes of adults – and their devices. Donald John Macdonald lived as a child next door to

> the elder o' the kirk, and we were all scared to death of him. And as soon as he came from the kirk we never went outside our wall, hiding here before he would see us. . . . But when he was in kirk, oh dear, we were always over in his house along with their boys. . . . There was always one or two of us lookout.

The means by which children were taught the community's values varied quite considerably between families, from a gentle leniency, or parental authority requiring only a reprimand, to an ex-soldier crofter-father who would lash his son 'with a rope's end'. But it is noticeable from our interviews that the use of corporal punishment was considerably more widespread than in the north-east or still more than in Shetland, and resorted to quite regularly in two-thirds of the homes. An atmosphere of strictness, at least within the house, was standard; and many children were distinctly afraid of one or other parent. All this undoubtedly inhibited open affection and intimacy between parents and children; nor was it encouraged by the values of the Free Kirk, whose ministers were liable to look on any form of love but the love of God, even love between parents and children, as a form of human failing. There were of course children who adored their parents. Alex McLeod remembers how he first went out with his father in a sailboat at the age of eight, barefoot, but 'I felt like the king with two crowns on.' But respect and gratitude convey the commonest feelings – and respect most of all. Within the Lewis crofting family children were rarely encouraged to discuss issues with adults. If their elders were talking, and they were not sent away, they were not expected to join in: 'Oh no, no, no. Oh the birch was out for that.'[15]

This attitude to children was part of – and indeed derived from – a more general rigidity in the structure of authority of the family, a deference to the word of the male head of the household, which made for intolerance of criticism and argument, and so of social unconventionality and individuality. This comes out particularly in the situation of women, which clearly rests on the cultural moral order rather than the constraints of the economic system.

The pressure of the economy is towards a flexibility of roles and considerable responsibility and independence among the women. A high proportion of men are away for months on end as migrant workers. And on the island, although weaving is unlike elsewhere exclusively men's work, women used to bait lines, dry and sell fish for the inshoremen, and continue to work alongside men on the crofts, sometimes also marketing part of the produce. But it does not appear that this led to a partnership form of marriage, in which the wife took a critical part in crucial financial decisions. The shipping registers do not show women taking up shares in boats. On the crofts, despite the men's absence, women were only recognised as formally responsible for the farming enterprise on one-fifth of the holdings. They might not be the formal tenants in such cases either, for a male tenant was normally preferred, even when succession came through a married daughter or to a widow.[16]

It seems rather that the effect of the increasingly migrant pattern of the Lewismen was to leave their women with a growing burden of labour, without any commensurate increase in their social standing. Already by the 1870s it was noticed that both seeding and harvesting were 'carried on mostly by the women and children, including sickling and hand-thrashing.' Women seemed 'possessed of far greater energy than men', and could be seen digging vigorously while 'the lazy worse-half does nothing but fill and empty his everlasting pipe'. The men would cut peat; and where there were ploughs, they used them. But in general, according to a government report of 1902, 'the labour required for the cultivation of the land falls to a large extent to the women'. And everywhere they could be seen carrying: seaweed from the shore for manure, corn from the harvest to the store, peat from the moor to the croft, all on their backs, knitting as they went.

The women's outside labour was in no way complemented by assistance from the men. In the families of nine-tenths of those whom we interviewed the father gave no help in the house, apart from sometimes disciplining children. 'The men in Lewis are far too lazy and they leave too much to the women to do,' remarked a medical officer during the First World War: 'the men would sit and see the fire go out and they would not go for peats.' Abstinence from housework, and also other women's tasks, was inculcated from boyhood.

> We helped with herding the cattle, but boys as a rule
> would sort of – they were insulted . . . you see to wash
> dishes, or do any washing clothes. That fell to the
> girls. . . . The boys never carried a cradle of peats. . . .
> Out here I seldom if ever seen a man carrying a cradle of
> peats on his back . . . unless of course some houses where
> there were no women. But the women I'd say had the
> biggest load – had the biggest heaviest end of the stick to
> carry.

While men were telling us their life stories, wives would not comment, but frequently disappeared with an air of tacit disapproval to a back part of the house, from which they might be summoned out to produce a cup of tea. But when they found a turn to speak themselves in confidence, they often expressed resentment against the men of the island in no uncertain terms. 'The men – were attended upon hand and foot.' They were 'no use at all': 'Lewis menfolk are spoiled.' Margaret McLeod summed it up with a vignette of her seacaptain grandfather. He was:

> a terror. He used to shout. And he was always sitting in the window gazing out to sea, you see with longing. But of course he was in the habit of shouting at the crew, so these captains will be shouting and swearing. . . . I can still see him sitting there gazing out to sea, my poor granny was sitting – in those days she seemed to me to be a slave, you know. Had to do his bidding and everything he said, he wanted.[17]

The combination of authoritarianism within the family in the subjugation – following St Paul – of women as well as children, and the severe values which the male elders sought to impose on the community, certainly achieved outward conformity in the Lewis townships. But it carried a double price. Firstly, because the community's values set such a high standard, many, perhaps most people either knew from their covert transgressions or feared from temptation that they could not live up to them. One clear sign of this was that while with scarcely an exception the crofting families were attached to the churches, only a small minority of the population, less than a tenth in the 1890s, put themselves forward for church membership. Calvinism, with its doctrine of the elect, the chosen people who know that they are destined to be saved, may have been a spur to Swiss enterprise, or a 'most blessed and comfortable doctrine' in Elizabethan England, but it had acquired another, much more disheartening, meaning for the people of the Western Isles. Goodrich Freer thought 'the depression of the Lewis people is intellectual rather than physical'; and other observers today find that the doctrine of predestination still 'weighs very heavily' with them. For most, it implies a contemplation of personal unworthiness. Even for the saved, it may bring little joy, so deeply imbued is the sense of individual inadequacy. One women was converted during the Second World War:

> One day I went to church and I was converted through the Minister's text that day. I can truly say that because I started praying in earnest. . . . What did it feel like? Very depressing at first, till I came to experience Christ helping me. That day after coming home from church I was praying in my own bedroom, that's how I met Christ. . . . I was crying. Crying with joy, I was then, see?

This inner repression and sense of inadequacy combine with a strong disapproval, both in kirk and community, of any who openly step out of line – even if they step ahead. For this is the second price: a valuing of conformity at the expense of individuality, which stifles at the same time both deviance and enterprise. For the preacher, indeed, any human creativity is a potential threat to the divine purpose:

> What does it do? It inflates man's ego, it inflates man – makes him a master creator. So much so that he can command the Creator, whereas what God has told us in his Word – is this: that it is for Him to command, for us to obey.

'This is a very conforming community', Norman Macdonald observes: 'People are afraid of being different, of seeming to try to be different.' They disapprove of working too hard, because too many worldly goods are a bad thing. In the past people were unwilling to reap or sow too much ahead of those on other crofts. When the agent came round for the east-coast hired hands in the 1930s, he had to wait and wait for the first person to sign on: 'Nobody wanted to be first. It might look as if they wanted to be noticed, or had a special arrangement with the skipper.' He tells in his autobiographical novel *Calum Tod* of how in a race 'he contrived to come fifth, when he could have come second. . . . He did not want the limelight.' It is all summed up in the memory of his great-grandfather, born in Tong in the mid-1850s, who grew to be the most successful man in the township; one of 'the more enterprising crofters'. He had his own boat, which he took with a local crew to the east-coast fishing. His was the best croft in the township, producing the most meal. But he was fated to die a young man. He was killed when his cart loaded with grain overturned on him: as the township observed, 'crushed by the weight of his worldly goods'.[18]

Successful fishermen need a different spirit from this: skippers above all. The moral order of Lewis did not foster the man with 'drive' and 'fire' like that of Buckie; and the bearers of its religious values were the 'elders' of the law, rather than the individualistic 'worthies' of the north-east. But most crofter-fishermen carried the ethic of the township to the fishing. Anderson Smith noted how 'the skippers of the Lewis boats have not the absolute control thereof, but more the position of chairmen.' Ill-at-ease as leaders, for many it was easier to work as hired hands in outsiders' boats, not only for economic but also for cultural reasons.

Among those who persisted a rather different balance of values seems often to be found. Alex McLeod's father was one of a small minority of fishermen in Lewis in the 1900s with both a small inshore boat and a sailing drifter. Luck came into the fishing, he believed: 'some people were very unfortunate although they would try their utmost. . . . Others were very lucky.' But with success, 'individuality creeps in here. A fellow that was diligent and made efforts to prosecute the fishing . . . quite often that happens if there's a go-ahead – he's better off.' In Roddy McIver of the *Golden Sheaf* one can sense a similar shift towards the values of the east-coast men – alongside whom he has worked as a lone Lewisman for years. He describes (in a characteristic Lewis phrase) the share system as making fishing 'the only industry run as a form of communism'; but in his view crew should have labour shares only. A skipper is in a much clearer position as sole owner. Success as a skipper is partly a matter of experience, but he also emphasises the constant need to be changing; and persistence. His is not one of those Stornoway boats today which will be home for tea on Thursdays. He fishes to the last possible time. Unlike many local boats he tries to avoid the uncompetitive fish market in Stornoway, with its lower prices, preferring the extra journey to land his fish on the mainland west coast. And he cares passionately about the price they fetch. So much so that he will not ask what he got until the morning: 'I wouldn't sleep otherwise, I'd be so angry at it.'[19]

In those two small islands among the Outer Hebrides, Scalpay and Eriskay, which have persisted successfully as fishing communities, it is again striking how this is associated with a somewhat different balance of attitudes. Goodrich Freer found the Eriskay people in the 1900s 'altogether brighter and more intelligent than their neighbours in Uist, possibly owing to the greater independence of their lives'. In the 1930s their willingness to experiment with ring netting and winter trawling in the Minch met with the strong disapproval of the other, less-active fishermen of the Barra Isles and Uist. There is a similar contrast between the conventions of Scalpay and nearby Lewis. Scalpay people see themselves as 'quicker' and remember even between the wars more of a spirit of competitiveness, watching each other. Today material competition, and knowing each other's catches, is certainly part of the atmosphere. Some of the fishermen's recollections ring like those from the north-east. In Angus McDonald's family as they changed boats they transferred the name, so as 'to keep the name on the boat' – and one notes also how one of their earlier boats had been named 'Economy'. Kenneth Morrison, a strongly religious fisherman, told me that when he fished, he fished for money: 'God says, if you don't work, you do not eat.' Still more striking was his certainty that men had a choice in their own fate: 'You've a will, to make your own life.' This is hardly the tone of predestinarian Lewis Calvinism, though in other points of view he is very much a Free Kirk man. One can sense another moral world too, when Norrie McLeod explains how a good skipper must not only be 'keen and intelligent', and well equipped, but must be prepared to try new things – 'to speculate'.

In all this, one important factor may be that although the Scalpay islanders are with few exceptions Free Kirk supporters, before 1945 there was no minister or church on the island: before that its families would sail each Sunday across to church in Tarbert. It may be that this allowed a little more tolerance for individuality. And there are signs of a variation in family relationships too which may be equally significant. In some homes the dominance of men over women and the strictness of child-rearing closely repeats the Lewis pattern; but families can also be found in which roles were more flexible, and men would look after children and sometimes cook. One Scalpay fisherman described his happiest times as coming home to help wash and dry his children and put them to bed: 'I shared her work because she shared mine.'[20] There seems also a less thorough suppression of sexuality. More of the old tradition of song and poetry has survived; and today teenagers make a kind of monkey parade (in old cars, if they have them) down the island's single narrow track of road on a summer evening, while *Titbits* is on sale openly in the store. On Scalpay, unlike most of the Western Isles, men and women will take turns in weaving at the loom.

All this can be exaggerated. As a whole Scalpay holds strongly to the God-fearing values of the Free Kirk, and in most ways its culture closely matches the Lewis pattern. But it is as if, first forced by necessity, aided maybe by a slight distancing of the kirk, the balance had been shifted just sufficiently to give space for enterprise within the community. Its achievement is indeed remarkable: for the township has consistently thrown up not only generations of fishermen prepared to persist, adapt and 'speculate', but its own entrepreneurs too, fish-curers and merchant ship-owners working the Hebridean cargo trades. It has required special qualities to survive on its unpromising rocky outcrop.

In Lewis an only slightly different culture has tipped the subtle balance between community and individuality in another direction: for here too is a moral order of special qualities, born historically of suffering and survival, and handing down through the generations of its people a rare endurance. It was a local culture, a moral order, which gave its people both weakness and peculiar strength.

The weakness was in a system of values so overwhelmingly discouraging to individual initiative. It was at bottom this, rather than structural economic disadvantages, real though those were, which stifled the local fishing industry when for a full century outsiders have been able to make money at it. The moral order of Lewis is pervasive, and the discouragement, the sense of despair which it generates, have not only disheartened its would-be fishermen, but its local business class too.

Up to the 1880s Lewis businessmen had been predominantly merchants, partly due to the survival of a semi-feudal economy. But they seem to have been unable to break out of this role subsequently. Some did make ventures, which turned out to be mistimed. A group of Stornoway merchants had combined to open a fish factory in 1914 – but the war followed; and the enthusiasm with which they bought eight steam drifters following the advent of Leverhulme in 1918 also proved misjudged. The willingness of the banks to back local enterprise in the years before the First World War was also reduced by the spectacular bankruptcy in 1909 of Aeneas Mackay Mackenzie, who from the late 1870s had been Stornoway's leading speculator in merchant shipping, branching out as a shipbuilder and curer, opening a carding mill to supply the Harris tweed weavers in 1903, and even boasting of a yacht named *Forward Ho!* It looks as if as with the crofters, economic setbacks served to reinforce existing philosophies.

With the Stornoway merchants, however, a further twist was given by the dimension of class. The town merchants and their families, while being clearly within the moral community of the Lewis Free Kirk, nevertheless saw themselves as on a different social level from the crofters. The merchants could be picked out easily in the Stornoway streets, 'lounging gentlemen . . . trim and well-dressed', and in their social life preferred to mingle with the professionals on the island, setting themselves apart from the people of the townships. One finds in the comments to official inquiries on the social economy of the island again and again, from both merchants and professional men, a tone in which predestinarian despair fuses with social disdain. During the First World War, for example, John Wedderspoon the county sanitary inspector was prepared even to argue against building improved housing:

I do not think it would be wise to seek a way out of it. . . .
These black houses reared hardy men. There is nothing
wrong with the houses if you lead a healthy life in
them. . . . We are spoiling the Hebrides. . . . They are
lying on their backs waiting for you to *feed* them now. . . .

I would prefer to leave the people to work out their own salvation . . .

In the same disparaging spirit, the local Fishery officer wrote from Stornoway in December 1919 that the withdrawal of out-of-work donation from ex-servicemen had not really created much of a problem:

> The complainants . . . if they are fishermen at all . . . only fish during the summer months, and would not in any case be fishing at present . . . They speak about being left destitute . . . but . . . I am inclined to agree . . . that there was no such thing as poverty in Lewis. . . . With regard to the statement that their boats and gear had rotted when away, I doubt if they ever had any.

By the mid 1930s it was difficult to deny that there were economic problems; but local professional and business leaders were no less negative in their attitudes. The minister of Leverburgh 'would advise nobody to put their money into fishing boats' because local people would never work with the 'energy' of east-coast driftermen. Norman McIver the Stornoway curer regarded development as a 'very difficult' question, 'mainly because of the lack of energy on the part of Lewis men'. He believed 'that whoever provided the capital would not see their money back, he personally would not advance one penny.'[21]

The Lewis business class remain ultra-cautious, and continue to see justification for their despondency in the failings of their own people. It took direct outside intervention to revive the fishing fleet. Local crews, often sons of crofter-fishermen, have come forward to man it. But meanwhile local merchants have preferred to see the factory space which was also built in the same period through government initiative, to stimulate local development, stand empty. It was a Norwegian firm which successfully moved into fishmeal and fish-oil production in Stornoway in the mid-1970s. When local businessmen did eventually launch a Lewis Development Fund in 1971, it was proposed that loans should be made on the basis of 'character rather than security'. Little has come out of it; for the old moral order prevails.

It is strongest, as it always was, in the rural townships, where one may still see, despite the marks of agrarian decay and an ageing population, its firm basis in the experience of common economic activity – the joint landholding of the common pastures, joint sheep-shearing, harvesting, house-building and so on. It is still the duty of the elected township officers to arrange the times for gathering the sheep for clipping, weaning, casting, counting and dipping; and they also organise fence repairs and heather burning. In the past they also took responsibility for road repair, the allocation of peats, and, because there were no fences, appointed boys to mind the cattle. There was also more informal co-operation in many other ways. At the peat-cutting parties would work at each crofter's bank in succession; at the harvest neighbours would give help to those behind at any particular stage in the work – cutting, binding or stooking – before passing on to the next. On these occasions the day would end with a common meal: 'they tried their best to kill a wether if there was any do on, huge pot of soup. For that day. A huge pot of soup. And that satisfied everybody. And plenty of potatoes, very good table potatoes.'

There was also a sharing of equipment, for example for ploughing. 'It was a communal life really, and that was – a necessity, an economic necessity. . . . For instance two houses, a horse in each house: they combined of course, they ploughed.' A similar attitude followed with the produce of their work. 'Oh if you were short of anything, go to your neighbour. That still exists. . . . "I haven't got any onions", say, go along to the next house – the same with them, they – (it's) still communal business here.'

Help was especially given to older people in the community with little land – but who were 'very independent. And if anybody lent them or gave them anything it was kept secret, they weren't to hear it.' Katie Barr, whose father was a crofter and relief lighthouse-keeper with a small fishing boat at Breasclete on the west side of Lewis, scarcely remembers any fish being sold. A lot was given to households without a man –

spinsters or war widows. 'It was primitive communism of the best kind.' Similarly the Grimsby trawlers working off their coastline, in return for eggs and potatoes from the crofters, would land fish on the pier for anybody in the township to pick up: no money was involved on either side. An equally striking instance of this communality is in Murdo Mac-farlane's account of the cutting of seaweed for manure at Melbost:

> The whole village went to the cutting seaweed when the tide went out. And, we all took to the sickles first, cutting the seaweed. Then half, half the people then took to the creels – in order to get the seaweed up to the rocks before the tide would come in. . . . But – this is what happened. We counted all our houses: every household was counted. Assuming there was twenty or thirty houses, that meant thirty piles. Now, the oldest man was picked out. He was sent up to the rocks to where we were going to make the piles, and he showed you where you were going to dump your creel. . . . Now, when we have salvaged all the seaweed – from the incoming tide – the old man would pick somebody out, out of the crowd, and he says, 'You go down there and keep your back to the piles.' And he would say, 'Who does this belong to – who gets this one?' Nobody could pick his own. Nobody could pick his own. Now, assuming there was the house where somebody was sick, his pile was there too. You see, how the communal life which was necessary for survival – it really helped to keep the compassionate aspect of our age alive and sharp.[22]

Here in sharp opposition are both the strength and weakness of the social economy of the townships. It survives as a communal system at the margin of an individualistic capitalist economy from which others – like the Grimsby trawlermen – are making money. While within a socialist economy their values might have been used positively, here they serve to exacerbate economic stagnation. But socially, one can but share the just pride with which Lewis people describe them.

They have shown too a remarkable strength in defending

their way of life. We have already seen how the capture of the
kirk marked their first victory against the landowning class.
Closely linked to the kirk was the story of schooling. The early
nineteenth-century travelling Gaelic schools, which would
spend perhaps three years in a township and then move on,
teaching reading and religion, could evoke an almost evangelical enthusiasm in the whole population. It was reported
from Barvas in 1828 that:

> The emulation excited here, and still maintained in
> vigorous activity, is really wonderful. With very few
> exceptions, all the married and the aged attend as much as
> they can. It would be needless to dwell on the peculiar
> gratification afforded by such a scene and by the animating
> spectacle of husband and wife attending together, the latter
> coming forward to say her lesson, holding at the same time
> an infant in her arms . . .

From the secession in the 1840s until legislation brought Board
Schools in the 1870s, the Free Kirk's own schools became the
backbone of local schooling. They were then superseded; but
the crofters continued to take a notably independent attitude to
the School Boards – and rightly, for the Lewis boards were
undeniably mean and cheese-paring, underpaying their staff,
failing to maintain sanitary buildings, and giving scant attention to the views of crofting parents. The crofters protested
against the board's exaction of daily peat supplies from the
children, and eventually won this point. They threatened to
withdraw their children if music was taught on secular rather
than religious lines (that is with rather than without instruments). In Back and Arnol in 1884–5 the Board Schools were
so disliked that parents set up Adventure Schools on the lines
of the old Gaelic school, and as a result the Back Board School
teacher was forced to resign. This militancy in the face of the
Board continued: in 1927 for example, the parents of Gress
township staged a school strike in support of their demand for
a bus to take their children to Back school, declaring they had
'every respect for the law of this country, but we want from
the same law justice to protect the lives of our children'. The
schools not only continued to provide for a minority within

the community one ladder to distinction in the wider world, but also through locally born teachers returning to the community a tradition of leadership within it. It was the township teachers who in the 1930s formed the backbone of the growing Labour Party organisation on Lewis, and the main platform speakers of the excited, idealistic campaign of 1935, in which the local 'crofter-socialist' Malcolm MacMillan was elected as first Labour member for the Western Isles, to make it – for thirty-five years – one of the very few rural socialist constituencies in Scotland.[23]

Lewismen have been less persistent in trade-union organisation. The local women fish-gutters, although unionised, were prepared to strike: 'we were on strike half a dozen times – we never struck until there was a glut of herring.' The hired men had formed the Highland Fishermen's Union for their largely unsuccessful campaign of 1913. They claimed over a thousand Lewis members; but with a banker treasurer, gentleman secretary and six clerical vice-presidents, it took on a communal rather than a class tone. Between the wars unionisation would have been hopeless. Lewis's present trade-union organisation of crofter-weavers, dockers and some skilled trades effectively dates from the 1940s. The inter-war depression also explained why the Agricultural Co-operatives formed on at least seven Lewis townships, part of a wider Highland movement dating from 1908–9, proved short-lived.[24]

Rather than in these forms which were characteristic of the urban working-class movement in Britain, it was through rallying on the issue of the land that the islanders followed their religious success with an economic counter-attack on the Highland ruling class. From the 1880s they began a highly effective campaign, combining land raids and occupations with political pressure for legislation and administrative moves, which eventually was to lead to the dismantling of the large sheep farms in the crofting districts, and their reorganisation into townships of small crofts. The crofters were helped by the fact that in many parts of the Highlands and Hebrides the landowners had become largely absentees, keener on deer-shooting than on sheep farms; and also – at least initially – by the backing of radical mainland political sympathy. A crucial figure in making this link was John Murdoch, a treasury civil servant who on his retirement to Inverness in 1873 founded the weekly *Highlander* to raise a wider awareness of the land issue. Thus while the occasional outbursts of protest in the 1870s against attempted evictions, like the 1874 riot in Bernera on Lewis, were ignored by the urban national press, the movement of the 1880s succeeded in winning the backing of the Liberal Party, and through that the crucial legislation which finally ended economic feudalism in the north. The Highland Land Law Reform Association was formed in 1883, in London, but it soon secured a strong following in the townships after mass meetings of the hired men at the east-coast fishing. Within a year it had 5,000 subscribing members among the crofters, and in the 1885 election four of its candidates swept out the old landed MPs, including Lewis's own Matheson. Renamed the Highland Land League in 1886, it went on to capture the north-west Highland county councils in the first local elections on a democratic franchise at the end of 1889, and reelect its candidates to Parliament in 1892.

By then, however, it had become little more than a wing of the Liberal Party. With its failure to win any strong legislation for land redistribution, active backing among the crofters dried up. Nor was the reformed Highland Land League of the 1900s, run by Glasgow-based socialists independent of the Liberals, more successful in recovering a crofting membership. John Maclean and Tom Johnston came up to visit the Lewis land raiders, and described their action as 'the highland equivalent of strikes . . . components of the same general crisis of capitalism'; but the crofters had by this date become fully disillusioned with politics. It had proved more effective to demand the land through direct action.

For more than forty years, from the early 1880s until the 1920s, the crofting population of the western Highlands and the Hebrides waged an incessantly erupting campaign of land seizure and agitation. The storm centre shifted: in the 1880s it was Skye, in the 1900s the Barra Isles, from 1918 above all Lewis. But the disturbances were always widespread, and punctuated by incidents of high drama – the imprisonment of landless crofters and tumultuous welcomes on their return, the invasion of sheep islands by night, the destruction of fences and dykes and telephone wires, the threat of boycott, torch-light processions and bonfires on the moors.

Its first peak was before the 1886 Crofters Act, and culmin-ated in the despatch of a gunboat and a force of 3,000 marines to put down the disturbances in Skye. The Crofters Act greatly eased the grievances of those with land, but failed to help the landless; so the seizures continued. Some were in grand style, like the raid on the Aignish farm east of Storno-way by a thousand men 'in line abreast with pipes playing and flags flying'. But later raids were more often the acts of smaller groups of younger men like the six who were imprisoned in 1909 for raiding and staking out plots on Dalbeg Farm at Shawbost on Lewis. They were, according to a display in the school museum there today, 'desperately land hungry . . . second sons, sons, that is who were not heirs to crofts. . . . Arrested, tried and imprisoned in Inverness, denied an inch of their country's soil, all but the first nonetheless fought in the First World War.'

Such repeated pressure eventually secured improved legis-lation in 1911. But the procedures were complex, and with landowners remaining hostile progress remained slow. There were already signs of mounting impatience, especially from Lewis which had only just reached its peak population and was now by far the most crowded part of the west. At the end of 1913 cottars occupied the farm of Reef declaring that they had been asking for it for five years: 'The only reply we get now is "that our applications are under consideration". . . . We have suffered long enough as we are and though we were to suffer in another way we would hardly be worse off than we were.'

The Scottish Under-Secretary rightly noted the action at Reef as 'a symptom and a warning'. The First World War intervened. But even during the war some raiding continued; and the men returned from it more determined than ever. It was recognised by Lloyd George's government that a land programme was essential to avoid serious disturbances when the Highland soldiers returned home and the 1919 Land Settlement (Scotland) Act at last gave the Board of Agriculture really effective powers backed by nearly £3 million for land redistribution. They were forced to use these powers – as they had feared – by a wave of land seizures 'on a larger scale and of a more determined nature' than any since the 1880s. In the peak year of 1920 altogether 47 farms were threatened, and 16 taken by raiders; and the crisis was not over until 1924. The crofters had emerged victorious. By the late 1920s, with nearly 3,000 new holdings and 1,500 enlarged since 1911, they had won back over half a million acres from the old landed class. Redistribution was to continue at a slower pace into the 1950s, but already they had achieved most of what they demanded. In Skye, landlessness was virtually eliminated; in Harris and North Uist there was extensive resettlement; and in the most crowded areas of the Long Island, South Uist, the Barra Isles and Lewis, almost every farm of any size was broken up and divided among those who needed land.[25]

The crofters had won, in short, a social revolution in reverse. And their most dramatic victory was on Lewis itself, for here they had been faced by the opposition of their new proprietor and autocratic ambassador of industrial capitalism, Lord Leverhulme. To him crofting seemed an obsolete way of life in a modern economy, an obstacle to his plans for development. He was determined to resist its further extension. Probably the majority of the population welcomed Leverhulme's positive plans, including many of the raiders themselves. As Murdo Macfarlane put it, his developments were providing wages, 'and day work was such a novel thing in my young days that we had a Gaelic word for it, the day work, for day wages . . .' When Leverhulme challenged the townships in 1920–21 to declare whether or not they were behind him, their meetings were almost unanimous in his support. But however much the Lewis community wanted development, they were not prepared to abandon the crofting culture which was basic to their way of life, or to stand actively in the way of those prepared to break the law for land. The land raiders were the sons of their neighbours and kin, if not their own, and they could draw on their community's own past approval in giving moral justification for their actions. And the people of Lewis as a whole could not see the need for conflict between crofting and development.

Leverhulme could not understand this: and his obstinacy brought a headlong clash. In March 1919 the first Tong farm was invaded and pegged out as crofts; then at Coll, a large field was staked out, and raiders drove the farmer's cattle out on to the moor, bringing in their own in their place; and at Gress thirty men drove out the sheep, brought on their own, and began digging and planting potatoes. By the end of the summer 16 of the 22 farms on Lewis had been occupied, at least temporarily. Some raids were symbolic, farmhands just standing by while the plough horses were unyoked; others went on to the construction of small huts. 'We fought for this land in France, and if necessary we will die for it in Lewis' was their slogan. At first the raiders hoped to persuade Leverhulme of the justice of their cause. When his fundamental hostility was realised, there was a lull in the land seizures, and most raiders withdrew. But at Coll and Gress they refused to be shaken:

> We will defy him. We must have the land because we were promised the land and we fought for the land. We made a living before Lord Leverhulme came to the island, and we will make a living after he has gone.

Late in 1920 the government intervened seeking a compromise, and persuaded them to withdraw temporarily; but when they saw that they might have to wait indefinitely for their land, they seized it again in the spring of 1921, unharnessing the farm horses and reoccupying the land for the second time. Leverhulme could have had them legally ejected, but he feared the hostile publicity this would make on the mainland; and the raiders would not have been frightened by imprisonment. As Alec Graham remembered: 'No. We didn't care at that time whether there was legal action or not, no. We just wanted the land and – if we didn't get it well, we had just come out of the war and we were – fit for anything as you might say.' Leverhulme threw in his hand and within weeks left Lewis to its fate.

The price has been stagnation, which leaves their culture today under threat of extinction. But one can only admire the tenacious solidarity of a people who, two hundred years after their defeat at Culloden and the first Highland clearances, have still maintained their way of life. The rain-sodden land is theirs; and they hold to the faith. 'Whom He did predestinate, to them He also called, and whom He called, them He also justified; and them He justified, them He also glorified.'[26] The crofters of Lewis remain a morally separate people.

Close-up: Shetland
15 A choice of destiny

Fate hangs heavily over the western crofts. Its shadow to the north seems perceptibly lighter. Shetlanders will talk more freely, enjoying and quite often seeking out discussion. 'You probably don't go to church yourself. I always think if it can't do you any good, it can't do you any harm. You can always sit an hour, whether you listen to the minister or not, you can always sit an hour and meditate,' one of Shetland's leading skippers told me. And at sea – when East Anglian smacksmen might be singing at the helm, or Hull or Aberdeen trawlermen putting back whisky – he thought it was 'the kind of life that they led' which would make Shetland fishermen reflect on man's place in the universe, and what they had made of it with their own lives.

> You know, a fisherman has a lot of time when he's steaming about the sea, when he's not fishing . . . He has a lot of time to think and he has a lot of time to stand up – if he's in the wheel-house – and look at nature and commune with nature and think what all this is about. And sometimes he gets in a situation, bad weather, that makes him think of all the things he's done wrong . . .

Shetlanders – men, women and children – live as if they have real choices to make. Whether religious or not, they tend to hold their own particular opinions on the meaning of life. The future of their islands remains open, worth debate. Even before the oil boom, there was work to be had in the islands, an air of modest prosperity – and a choice of whether to stay or to leave. A visitor coming from the north-west would immediately sense how the pace at the quay was much quicker. For almost twenty years, the Shetlands have been the only Scottish region with full employment.

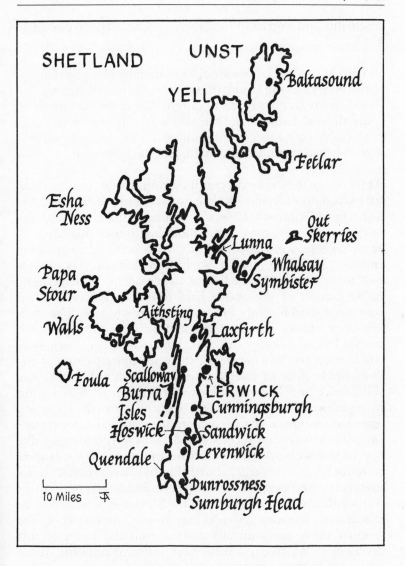

SHETLAND

UNST

YELL

Baltasound

Fetlar

Esha
Ness

Out
Skerries

Lunna

Whalsay
Symbister

Papa
Stour

Aithsting

Walls

Laxfirth

Foula

Scalloway
Burra
Isles

LERWICK
Cunningsburgh

Hoswick

Sandwick

Quendale

Levenwick

Dunrossness
Sumburgh Head

10 Miles

Before the oil, that prosperity rested on the recovery of
Shetland's fishing industry. But fish are as abundant around
the Western Isles as off the Shetlands. How can such differences in economic fortune and in outlook be explained? A
hundred years ago they seemed very much on a level. The

Highland and Agricultural Society of Scotland reported in 1878:

> The two archipelagoes are alike in their insular position, in the very rude and comfortless nature of their ill-lighted, and, we regret to say, dirty cabins. The crops they grow are almost identical, and the men who cultivate them resemble each other in combining . . . the occupations of the husbandman, the shepherd, and the fisherman.

At this stage they shared a common primitive technology and bare standard of living. As late as 1920, only the most fertile districts – Dunrossness in the southern mainland and the northern isle of Unst – were ploughed rather than dug by spade. These were also the only areas with adequate crop rotation. Even here 'runrig' – which in Shetland was a fossil-ised form of the old mediaeval strip system, with periodic redistribution of the arable land found only rarely – had continued until recently in some of the townships. The shallow open 'stanks' left the land nowhere well enough drained, and for lack of fencing cattle were kept tethered or watched by children on the 'town-maells', the open inner pasture of the households close to their cottages. Life was still tied to the subsistence line: 'a good sillock and taatie year, was a good marrying year'.[1] Up to the 1880s in both regions the economy operated within a semi-feudal framework, and Shetland's agriculture was then reconstituted as a crofting system like that of the Western Isles. But from this point onwards their fortunes begin to diverge, at first slightly, but eventually quite markedly. And even in 1878 observers had begun to pick out some differences: the poverty of the Shetlands appeared to be less drastic, the men more willing to migrate for work, the women more economically active. And the roots of this divergence, which explain the very different response of the two areas to their opportunities from the 1880s onwards, go back much further. We have seen how the people of Lewis became trapped within a consciousness moulded by genera-tions of history. The Shetlanders have also been made a separate people by their history; but it is a distinctly different story.

The Shetlands were captured and settled by Vikings in the ninth century and remained part of the Kingdom of Norway until 1469. Although the Shetlanders were bilingual by the early seventeenth century, their dialect today still includes several hundred Norse words. The Norse tradition provides an important sense of identity, even though some Shetland 'traditions' are in fact quite recent. Thus the great annual celebration of the passing of mid-winter, Up-Helly-a, when 'guizers' with placards and flaming torches process through Lerwick's streets to set fire to a Viking galley, only dates from the 1890s. It was a romantic improvement of the common Scottish New Year custom of tar-barrel burning by masked youths.

Nor can there be a more than tenuous connection between contemporary Shetland egalitarianism and the old Norse local assemblies and the principle of tenure by 'udal' law. The udallers held their small strips (as against the larger common pastures) by freehold, and customarily divided their land between all heirs in each generation. But they made their last public stand in 1577 when their protests secured the dismissal of the king's rapacious 'foud' or chamberlain, Lawrence Bruce. For the 300 years which followed they preserved little more than the dwindling memory of a juster past, which at no point – in contrast to the Lewismen – drove them to active rebellion. In the 1880s the Napier Commission found that the fencing off of parts of the 'scattald', the rough higher pasture, which as common land would not in fact have been subject to udal tenure, was 'regarded as a grievous injustice by the small occupiers in Shetland, and is associated in the popular mind with the supersession of the primitive udal tenures of the county by the feudal institutions of the southern kingdom'. In effect the memory served principally to justify the later customs of common tenure which had by then evolved.

At sea, on the other hand, it is undoubtedly true that late nineteenth century Shetlanders, unlike Lewismen, drew on the strength of boat-handling skills and seafaring traditions handed down from the Vikings in the early middle ages. The 'sexaering' of the sagas became the Shetland 'sixereen', a six-oared open undecked rowboat; and like the typical local rowboat or yawl today, it had a prow at both ends, derived from the Viking long-boat. It was from these little, open sixereens that the Shetlanders, from the late eighteenth to the mid-nineteenth centuries, conducted the heroic ocean 'haaf' fishing. They would venture forty miles or more out into the open Atlantic on the banks of the continental shelf, the undecked boat continuously bailed in rough water as the oarsmen drove its light frame through the spray. The haaf fishermen had learnt to tell the direction of home without compasses by sensing the underswell, the 'moder-dye', as the sea met the land. Along with such skills, old nautical terms were handed down too. Here the characteristic fishermen's taboos were reinforced by the linguistic divide between popular Norse tradition and the new Scottish culture. At sea the use of the old words took on the power of 'sainin', protecting their boats and catches from evil. 'That's the old Norse words you see; the same – as the sea. Just they had the language, the sea language, aboard the Viking boats. You know that?'[2]

As close to Bergen as to Aberdeen, many Shetlanders think of themselves as belonging to the Scandinavian as much as the British world, and their sense of themselves as heirs to a distant Norse tradition is a vital part of their self-understanding, the particularity of their culture, their attachment to the 'Aald Rock' which they have taken as their home. But the manner in which the greater part of these earlier traditions were ended is as important as those elements of them which may have survived. From the twelfth century Shetland had been administered directly by the Norwegian crown through the 'foud', rather than forming part of the patrimony of a great aristocratic estate. The foud appointed 'underfouds' in each parish, and the Shetlands evolved their own elected officers, a 'lawman' and parish 'lawrightmen', who adjudicated and negotiated the collection of customary taxes and fines on behalf of the local population. In contrast to both mainland Scotland and Norway, Shetland therefore escaped feudalism proper. After the transfer of the islands to Scotland, minor Scottish lairds came north to seek quick money, some as fouds. Although failing to get rich themselves, they succeeded in destroying the old system and creating in its place a pattern of fragmentary estates, most too small to allow a decent living for a laird from unimproved agricultural rents alone. Shetland lairds, in short, would have had to become improvers of one kind or another if they were to keep the roof on the 'haa-house'. In the seventeenth century most of them failed to find a way, but from the early eighteenth century they were bought out by a new breed of merchant-lairds prepared to exploit the sea as ruthlessly as the land. While the techniques they used were in part feudalistic, these new men were nevertheless undoubtedly entrepreneurs, opening the way for generations of successors in Shetland, and fusing much earlier than in most of Britain the local upper class into a single landowning and business elite.

Shetland crofters must have fished for subsistence for centuries. In the eighteenth century their small plots could provide for a family for little more than half the year. Even from 1780 to 1850 it has been calculated that there was on average one famine year in every four, and although destitution did not reach the level of Ireland or the Western Isles in the 1840s, there were families who lived without oatmeal or bread for months on end. Fish proved their salvation. But long before this, fishing had also been developed commercially. From at least 1400 Hanseatic merchants were buying regularly in Shetland. When they were finally expelled by the British government, in 1707, the local merchant-lairds quickly stepped into their place, taking over the organisation of the trade with Germany and accepting payment of rents for the crofts in fish.

Rent paid in this form very soon hardened into a system of fishing tenures, which forced the fishermen to sell all their catch to the landowner, at a price he fixed retrospectively. Gradually, as the pressure of growing population led to further splitting of the small crofts, the open-ocean haaf fishing became a mainstay of the Shetland economy. The fishermen ventured further and further out, seeking better grounds, driven by their need to make ends meet. In return for their fish they would be advanced food and clothing and fishing gear, remaining most often still in debt at the annual settlement after the season. 'They just took the price Mr Bruce fixed. . . . When they landed the fish they did not know what they were to get.' They were still worse off when the first half of the catch had to be given free to the landlord in return for supplying the sixereens which – as in the past – were imported pre-fabricated from Norway and assembled on the estate; although there was probably always a significant proportion of these small boats owned by the haaf fishermen themselves.

In order to be closer to the more distant grounds, some landowners also developed haaf stations for their estates nearer the edges of the island group. Here the men would live during the week through the summer season in small thatched 'lodges', drying cod and ling on a stony beach which, with factors weighing fish, men melting livers or attending to their gear, and 'yet others busy cooking', was 'like a great ship, for not one woman was to be seen'. The men rowed out once or twice a week to the grounds, taking a day to reach them, baiting and shooting their lines, hauling and gutting, until they could return with a full load of catch. Some had a peatfire and pot in the boat's bows, but others would carry 'no food but a little meal and water, and when they came ashore they would be so bad that they would have to help each other out of the boat. . . . Well then, they had no warm fire to come to, and they had to turn into a small thing of a hut, and put on a little of fish or pottage, and many a time death was created through the want of both food and raiment', one old Lunna fisherman complained in the 1880s. 'He had been a slave both night and day, and now he was fit for nothing more.'

The haaf fishing continued strongly right into the 1880s. Only then – especially after the shock of the July 1881 disaster, when 58 men were lost in open sixereens in a single sudden gale – did it succumb, rather rapidly, to easier and safer ways of earning a living. But meanwhile the world had changed about it.

For Shetland the period of the Napoleonic Wars marked a crucial turning point. Thousands of men were drawn, or forcibly pressed, into service with the navy; from the late eighteenth century east-coast whalers were calling regularly at Lerwick to pick up crews; and as merchantmen too Shetlanders were soon to be 'found in British ships all over the world'. They returned with wider experience, and sometimes a nest-egg of savings which could be put into the starting of a country shop. Equally important was the rise of a group of much more substantial family firms in Lerwick and a few other centres. During the Napoleonic Wars local merchants took over as export agents – making good side profits from smuggling – and moved into ship-owning. By the 1820s, when the Shetland Bank and the first Hay's firm were founded, they had begun ship-building, and also lauched substantial new enterprises in the fishing.

Despite the longstanding use of Lerwick as a base by the Dutch, the landowners had no more than tentatively experimented with herring fishing, from open boats. Now led by the town merchants, in the 1830s Shetland enjoyed a striking – if brief – herring boom. A local fleet of 500 boats was built up, including 200 larger half-decked boats, half belonging to the single firm of Hay and Ogilvy. The collapse of the boom when the elusive shoals moved offshore brought down the firm with it; but reformed as Hay and Company in 1844 they continued as substantial boat-builders, as also as operators in the new cod smack fishery.

The sixereens caught cod with long lines on the sea bottom, and the rowboat's manoeuvrability was regarded as essential to this technique. But cod could also be caught in mid-water by handlines operated from sailing smacks. From the 1820s a fleet of ten specialist firms built up a fleet of such smacks, eventually reaching a hundred: substantial decked boats with crews of up to fifteen who split and salted the catch abroad, returning only three times during the March to August season so that the cod could be cured. From working off the islands they gradually moved further away to the Faroe Bank, Rockall and Iceland. The shore-owners supplied and maintained the boats, in return for half the catch; the men provided lines and food for themselves. On the grounds, 'work went on night and day', the men kept going with coffee laced with brandy 'to act as an opiate' to the 'crowd of blood-splashed, half-frozen automatons with gashed and salt-scarred hands'.[3] It was a high-pressure commercial fishery which cut men off from their families and drove them to the limits, but its high earnings attracted younger men. At its peak in the 1860s its crews numbered a thousand, although still well short of the numbers at the haaf fishing; and it then fell away rapidly as the herring revived. The last Shetland cod smack was sold to Faroe in the 1900s.

This growing diversification of the local economy generated pressure for the ending of the old form of monopoly which the merchant-lairds exercised through fishing tenures. When the Crofters' Commission came to Shetland in the 1880s old men took the chance to vent the grievances of earlier decades. On Whalsay the Bruces of Symbister had bound Thomas Hutchinson to fish for them in the 1820s, and fined him £3 for going away to sea. Others were fined for selling saltfish to Lerwick merchants. George Irvine remembered how when his brother had gone to the Greenland whale fishing, 'they were summoned to Symbister and told they would have to leave the place or turn out the son who went to Greenland' – so that son had left home for ever. Sometimes landowners gave way in the face of collective protest. On Fetlar, according to James Laurenson:

> the men had had a meeting among theirselves, and they said, 'Now men look here. There's plenty of money to be made at the Greenland whaling fishing. And we're going with – we'll have to see what we can do. We'll have to – we could tell the landlord he could take his land, and keep it and we're going – to where we can make more money.' So they agreed on that. And most of the island set out for Brough Lodge. That's where the laird, Nicolson lived. And my grandad . . . was the youngest man there . . . he was seventeen years of age, a boy. And they gathered around the castle of Brough. And they sent word for Gifford, who was Sir Arthur's man of business, they sent in for Gifford to come out. And he said, 'Men what's to do?' What does this mean?' he said. 'Well you go in and tell Sir Arthur we're gathered here today to tell him that we're not going to fish for him, we're going to the Greenland fishing for the month of May.' So he went in. And he wasna very long in. Come out again, he said, 'I've delivered your message. And I'm to – I have to tell you from Sir Arthur Nicholson, "Go where you like. And leave me in peace. Go home peacefully to your homes and go where you like. But you have to pay the rent".' So they said, 'All right', and they gave a cheer among theirselves for him to hear it, 'Hip hip hooray'. So that he could hear it inside the castle. And he looked out of the sitting room

door with a white face, and they all waved to him as they passed. And that was the end of (the fishing tenures). After that they paid their rent.

The laird of Fetlar unfortunately had the last word. There were about a thousand people on the island then. But after transferring from rent in kind to cash, Sir Arthur Nicolson

found out that he wasn't making a lot of money from the rents. He would like more. So what he did – you see all the far dykes don't you? You see all these. Well he evicted about forty or fifty crofters off the rich land. And brought in sheep, black-faced sheep and cattle from the Highlands of Scotland, and kept sheep and cattle. And he did think he made more cash out of this. And so he would.

These Shetland lairds were in fact caught in a dilemma. Some of them had large estates, but their incomes were by mainland standards low. They had little chance of figuring in national upper-class society. They therefore wished all the more to feel honoured locally, patriarchal benefactors appreciated by the people. Even in the 1900s Bruce of Symbister kept no horse and gig on Whalsay, but walked about the island on foot like his crofting tenants. When a Bruce family maid married a crofter, her mistress made her a surprise high tea and danced with her in the kitchen. Grierson of Quendale, on deciding to take over direct marketing of fish himself, 'read out a statement to his tenantry at large, in the schoolroom'. They justified ways of exploiting tenants, which had become by national standards unacceptable, in the same spirit. The Bruces of Sumburgh, father and son, told the 1872 Truck Commission and the Napier Commission a decade later how it was mutually beneficial to bind men to fish to them, and exact part of their rent in labour services. Without being able to oblige men to bring in his peats, potatoes and hay in the busy summer time, a proprietor 'could get no labourers, and therefore he could not reside in the country amongst his tenants'. As he saw it, the most prosperous districts are those under the direct management of the landlord. Many of the fishermen in this country (as, indeed, many of the poorer classes everywhere) are unable, from want of thrift and care, to manage their own matters in a satisfactory manner, and require to be thought for and acted for and generally treated like children.

In the last decades of their power the lairds resorted to a variety of tactics. Some began to look towards clearances. But for most of them, income from fishing tenants remained crucial. Several estates experimented with free tenures at higher rents, but in the principal fishing areas the 'period of freedom' had ended by the 1870s, for the Sumburgh and Quendale estates were back under the merchant-laird system, while both Burra and Whalsay were leased to Hay and Company who also operated on the basis of fishing tenures. Some landowners demanded rents for the right to fish, 'boat teind', although they had constructed no piers or harbour; or 'liberty-money', for permission to fish with somebody else. Such charges were no less resented. As 72-year-old Thomas Sutherland of Levenwick put it in 1889:

> Formerly we had to pay teinds, cow-money, boat-money, liberty and everything 'at dey could lay apo'wis, an' if we didna pay it we would have to go, an' when we complained 'at we couldna pay it dey told wis 'a dey wid come an 'peck' w'is, whatever dey meant by'at I dunna ken, but I suppose dey were ta come an' peck awa everything we had.[4]

In the end the Crofters' Act forced the lairds back to reliance on straightforward rental income.

Meanwhile crofting family income had climbed slowly through the nineteenth century. Men brought home cash from migratory work as well as fishing; while women were earning increasingly from the home knitting industry, which went back to the eighteenth century, but had been especially stimulated by the introduction of steamers and a parcel post service from the 1840s. The first regular all-the-year steamer service was started in 1858, and this also had an immediate impact on the returns from agriculture.

Within four years the weekly number of cattle and ponies sent south had reached more than was shipped in a year in the 1820s. The Shetland Agricultural Society was formed, and the more active landlords began to build steadings and put in drains, introduce farm carts, machinery, and new sheep breeds. By the later nineteenth century there were 'in several districts farms . . . of which the Lothians would not be ashamed'. They also began to encourage the abolition of runrig. But for the scab epidemics which decimated the local sheep stock, no doubt the very survival of many crofting communities would have been threatened with clearances like those of the Highlands. But it was only from the 1870s that the clearance of crofts from the better pastures and fencing with stone dykes for sheep farming began in earnest. In the twenty years to 1881 the population of the islands fell drastically by a quarter, drained by emigration. But then the Crofters' Act put a stop to further clearances.

The lairds had thus moved too late for their own interests. They were left a system of smallholdings – 95 per cent under 15 acres in 1938 – at reduced rents, and a largely passive role in estate management. From this point onwards their role as local social leaders was to fade away. Small-scale agricultural improvement certainly continued with their encouragement, and patronage of local shows. The scattalds became better managed, crofters began vegetable-growing and poultry-keeping, and in ten or more districts set up marketing co-operatives, sixty or more members strong. The force behind change was now the crofters themselves, at last in a position to benefit from their own improvements.

The new spirit could be seen especially in the crofters' housing. In the early nineteenth century a form of black house had been usual in Shetland as in the Western Isles, although even then a Poor Law Commissioner noted signs of difference:

> There is a barrenness and desolation about the misery of a Harris house that is tenfold more depressing. It is a poor house and an empty one – a decaying, mouldy shell,

without pretence of a kernel. Whereas in Shetland there is
usually a certain fullness. There are bulky sea-chests, with
smaller ones on top of them; chairs, with generally an
effort at an easy one; a wooden bench, a table, beds,
spades, fishing-rods, baskets and a score of other little
things, which help . . . to make it a domus. The very
teapot, in Zetland always to be found at the fireside, speaks
of home and woman, and reminds one of the sobriety of
the people . . .

One of the complaints to the Crofting Commission was that
the lairds, unlike many mainland landowners, had never built
any housing for their tenants. But after 1886 the crofters
rapidly set about their own reconstruction. By the 1900s there
were 1,500 three- to five-room houses in the islands, and black
houses had disappeared from all but the remotest parts such as
Foula. 'The bulk of the crofters in Shetland are what you might
call handymen; they buy the material, the wood and the
cement, and put up the house themselves', a school board
chairman told the Royal Commission of Scottish Housing in
1913. Another witness, the Baptist minister in Dunrossness,
said that 'since I came to the place, thirteen years ago, I should
say two-thirds of the whole of the houses have been taken
down and re-erected'. They had done so without any encouragement from their landlord: indeed, to the contrary.

I know that when Mr Bruce was alive I talked over the
matter many times with him, and he was of the opinion
that these houses would bring an increase in consumption
[tuberculosis]. . . . You could almost say that the old
house ventilated itself; at night you could feel the wind
blowing through them and the drops of water in them. In
the old houses they used the high-backed chairs, and when
you were seated in one of these chairs you practically had a
little house of your own. The new house is hermetically
sealed.

Shetland crofters had certainly not moved into a life of luxury.
Larger families had to crowd several children into one box
bed, with perhaps 'a bed in alang wi' the fire, for the small

uns'. For washing they would go to the stream or light 'a fire to wash wi' at the loch'. Their diet was 'mainly potatoe soup and fish and sometimes mutton', sometimes all eating from 'a big earthenware dish, and the potatoes would go on that, then the fish would be laid on the edge. . . . When we were youngsters, they only use a knife and fork if we had some stranger in.' At breakfast they had porridge and milk and home-baked bannocks 'wi' what we called "fresh butter". . . . We were never hungry and it was a good living.' A special late summer delicacy was 'piltocks' caught from the rocks – 'I don't think you could have a better taste of fish than that. That's how we like it, but that fried young coalfish, the older he got and the coarser-like, he wasn't so good to eat. The younger he was the better he was.' The Whalsay fishermen would fit themselves out well for sea too:

> At hirsting, when you were tyin' up your tatties and gotten in your corn, . . . you go across there to the mainland . . . and then every boat would buy a fat cow and you would kill her, and salt her down in the barrel, and that's what you get for your breakfast when you went to the fishin' in the summer. . . . They didna look for the thin, lean flesh then, they had to have some fat on it before they thought it was right.

If the crofter was indeed by the end of the First World War 'a contented man, in fairly good circumstances, whose wants are few', he owed it principally to his own efforts – and to seizing the chance he had been given through the Crofters' Act, when 'that fellow from – Liverpool – the – Gladstone – he clipped all their wings'.[5]

The gradual withdrawal of the lairds from their earlier direct concern in the fishing did not immediately leave the Shetland crofter-fishermen as free family boat-owners like the communities on the north-east Scottish mainland. At first they were succeeded by the merchant firms which were operating the commercial herring and Faroe cod fisheries. These firms proved equally adept at holding the fishermen to successive binding annual engagements to sell to them only, trapping them in a cycle of advances for gear and recurrent debt, as the lairds had through fishing tenures. By 1867 four-fifths of the haaf catch was being sold by nineteen merchants and two of them had nearly a quarter of the haaf boats under their control. As with the lairds, moreover, the price was only fixed well after the end of the season, when the fisherman had no bargaining power because he had already delivered his catch.

Small merchants continued to work in this way into the mid-twentieth century, especially in the less fertile north-west whose herring fishing failed after 1905. Housing here was noticeably less improved. The merchant with his garage and pier was one of the few local employers, so that 'if there's anything in the nature of "an outside job" . . . it is to be found at "da shop"'. As the only source of credit, more generally shops were able to insist on underpayment through bartering both with the fishermen and with the women knitters. One woman shopkeeper told a parliamentary Truck Committee in 1908 quite frankly, 'I would never take work again from a woman who asked for money except I knew she wanted it for something special.' Lerwick's chief police constable regarded the law against truck as unenforceable: 'In the small islands', a factory inspector reported in 1905, 'they take what is given them . . . If money is given, the payment is at a lower rate.'

There was nevertheless by this date a widening gap between the experience of such districts, and the steady advance of the fishing communities close to the best markets, Lerwick on the east side and its small rival Scalloway on the west. Here a new relationship between the fishermen and the local business classes was emerging, which was to culminate in the resurgence of the post-Second World War years.

Throughout, a key part in Shetland's survival has been played by locally rooted families of entrepreneurs. Of the early nineteenth-century Lerwick firms, Hay and Company remained active and their diminishing fleet of eight boats was still the largest under a single owner in the 1930s. Garriock and Company, founded in 1839, had three descendants active in the 1900s, one a Lerwick ship's chandler and agent, two Scalloway curers and merchants. Another local dynasty was founded by Joseph Leask, mid-nineteenth century agent for the Greenland whale fishing, whose office would be 'besieged by men eager to engage': he was also fish-curer, boat-owner and supplier, owner of Leasks Docks, dealer in coal and salt.[6] In the north of Shetland there was another longstanding entrepreneurial family in the Sandisons of Unst.

The evidence of the local shipping registers shows, however, that landsmen owning boats wholly or in part were drawn from a strikingly wide social spectrum. Curers, chandlers and agents predominate; but there were also merchants of other kinds, coopers, carpenters and clerks, an auctioneer and a dentist, a miller, a factor and farmers. Although concentrated in Lerwick and Scalloway, many lived elsewhere – including one last laird, R. H. Bruce, who was putting up loans for motor boats just before 1914. And while some parts of Shetland had 'virtually no native entrepreneurs',[7] there was certainly room to build up new businesses elsewhere. James Shearer of Whalsay first appeared as an insurance agent in the 1900s, and besides his boat-ownership and curing on the island he set up herring stations elsewhere, started the first Shetland ice factory just after the Second World War, and ended as provost of Lerwick. On Whalsay he has been succeeded by a west-side man, John Tait, who turned from teaching in the 1960s to set up a knitwear business and build fish-processing factories and cold stores at Symbister. Similarly in Scalloway the leading owner of the 1900s, the fish-curer William Rae Duncan, had by the 1930s been succeeded by the motor-boat builder and engineer John Moore.

In Lerwick itself two particularly interesting new adventurers were John Brown and John Robertson. Brown had started as an apprentice blacksmith in his father's shop, developing boat metalwork as his speciality. In the 1870s he took the big step of erecting a steam hammer. His Freefield Engineering Works, close to Hay's Dock, became the focus of an industrial quarter at the north end of the town: he built tenements and shops for his workers, and launched into boat-ownership and herring and white-fish curing on a substantial scale. One of his employees who set up independently subsequently became Shetland's leading expert in fishing-boat motor engines, and started the first motor garage on the islands in 1911. Brown, who died in the First World War, was bought out by John Robertson, who added wartime salvage work to the enterprise, and was among the leaders of steam and motor-boat ownership in Shetland. His business suffered badly in the depression years, although the reformed company was still active in the 1950s. Robertson seems to have been an imaginative, controversial public figure: in 1914 the 'outstanding personality' of the younger generation, and in 1938 as a county councillor trying to press forward plans to set up a Shetland ice factory, so that trawlers could be supplied and base their operations on Lerwick. The Scottish Fishery Board noted sarcastically that his schemes 'usually err on the side of optimism'. Probably the most ambitious was the great plan of 1919, backed in that hopeful year by the Zetland County Council for a company managed by Robertson which would construct docks and shipyards, operate a large-scale fishing fleet out of Scalloway, and build 'a model town for the workers at Laxfirth . . . on the most modern lines', with swimming baths and football grounds, co-operative shops and a cinema, and smallholdings for casual workers. 'There will be no smoky factory chimneys, as the whole power will be electrical.'[8] Launched at what proved an impossible economic moment, Robertson's scheme got nowhere. It was none the less significant that Shetland should have produced its own native would-be Leverhulme.

There were also business families in Lerwick whose founders, such as John Mair of Peterhead and James Mitchell of Fraserburgh, were settlers from the Scottish mainland. Mair was one of the first local steam-drifter owners, while Mitchell was acting for a fleet of a hundred boats from different mainland and island stations at the turn of the century.

They were part of a wider movement towards closer contact and more active influence from the Scottish north-east which went back to the late 1870s. It was then that Wick and Moray Firth fishermen began to come to Shetland for a late winter white-fishing season; and their success helped to persuade the islanders to switch from their open sixereens to decked sailboats. More important, experiments with larger boats also proved that a herring fishery was again viable in Shetland. A spectacular revival followed, with mainland curers and crews rapidly moving in. The Shetland herring fishery had its own pattern, with a break between the fishing of the Atlantic herring on the west side from May and the North Sea herring off the east-side grounds in late summer. By the peak of the revival in 1884, there were 930 boats operating from altogether over a hundred curing stations on the islands.

The Shetlanders themselves began with astonishing rapidity to desert their sixereens and acquire decked sailboats for use both in the summer herring season and in the new winter white-fishing season, which – with catch sent to Aberdeen by steamer – was developing simultaneously. No doubt a strong additional incentive was the new standard of engagement, with prices negotiated *before* boats started fishing, which the Scottish curers brought with them. It was a crucial step in the path to economic emancipation. But the crofter-fishermen, unlike the fishing communities of the north-east, had not yet been able to build up the savings needed to buy boats. The shipping registers of the 1880s and 1890s show that half the new first-class sailboats were fully owned by landsmen, worked by crews on the old half-catch basis. The remaining boats were share-owned, shore-owners normally participating alongside fishermen. There were no skipper-owners before the 1890s. By 1885 there were 342 decked Shetland boats: a transformation within five years of the local fleet. It had been brought about by a combined response from all levels of the community.

The advance was abruptly checked when here as elsewhere the herring industry went into crisis in the mid-1880s. This brought one major long-term advantage, for selling fish by public auction was at last introduced to Shetland in 1894. But meanwhile the number of larger boats at work declined. The Fishing Board was told in 1893 that only a tenth of Shetland's 2,800 fishermen worked full-time. Their fortunes only began to pick up from just before 1900 with the revival of the herring industry, rising to its all-time peak landings in Shetland in 1905, drawing altogether 1,700 boats. There was by this time a fleet of 400 first-class local sailboats. After this it tailed away again. But there was some compensation in the steadier growth of local white-fishing, and together they provided work in Shetland for 6,000 fishermen, well over half of whom were incomers for the season only, in 1913.

Despite the scale of this activity off the islands, the Shetlanders were slow to switch from their sailboats to steam drifters – even if ahead of the Lewismen. The first five locally registered steam drifters appeared in 1907–8, two owned by J. Mair from Peterhead, but another two by local fishermen. But they were not successful enough for others to follow. In 1913 the *Shetland News* was asking why the example of the 1880s could not be followed. 'Why should English drifting companies and Scottish private drifter owners come here every year and take away certainly not less than three fourths of the whole Shetland catch?' Somebody should start a drifter company: 'Let the subscription list be open to all, so that people of small means have a chance as well as those better off. . . . "Shetland for Shetlanders" should be our motto.'[9]

There were, however, good grounds for hesitancy in switching to steam drifters, especially among the small men. It implied a drastic leap forward in capital investment, and with it a loss of the independence which was slowly being won. By 1935 two-thirds and by 1950 85 per cent of the first-class boats were owned by the men who worked them. In this respect steam-drifter ownership would have marked a step backwards; and working for shore-owners on the half-catch system implied a much more active control than that exercised by landsmen in the north-east ports. J. Mair, for example, brought in ten different skippers as master of his first steam drifter, the *Content*, from 1907 until 1924; while another boat bought by Hay's in 1915 was to be operated by 14 skippers in 31 years. A second difficulty was that steam drifting implied a full-time commitment to herring fishing, including an absence from the islands for at least three months each year, at a moment when locally the herring fishery was again contracting, and a safer basis had been found for full-time work in fishing by combining a summer herring season with winter white-fishing. For this the expensive steam drifter was uneconomic; and hence, from 1909 onwards, led by the Scalloway and Burra fishermen, the Shetlanders moved rapidly instead into motor-boat ownership. There were fifteen in the local fleet by the outbreak of the First World War, and more than sixty by 1920, mostly bought in the north-east ports, but a number built locally, for example in Burra. It was motor fishing which enabled the Shetland fishing communities to survive the lean inter-war years.

By the First World War, distinctive fishing communities had evolved in Shetland. This marked a break with the earlier pattern of seasonal fishing by a dispersed crofting population. The principal nuclei were three, all in the central area: Lerwick, Burra and Whalsay. Of these the first was an oddity, for few Shetlanders belonged to it. The burgh of Lerwick had no crofter-fishermen of its own, and although the crofters on the bays to the south as far as Sandwick and Levenwick were active herring fishermen into the 1900s, their response to the subsequent falling away of the fishery was to abandon it almost entirely. From the late 1890s, however, migrants from some of the smaller Moray Firth villages had moved with their families into Lerwick to pursue their traditional inshore line-fishing with the advantages of a good harbour and access to market.

Socially the 'Scotties' remain even today a rather separate community, keeping their north-eastern ways of speech; while on their side the townsmen tend to look down on them somewhat, if affectionately. Their standard of living was originally certainly unenviable. Until a council estate was eventually built they lived in the congested, insanitary wooden huts at the industrial north end of the town where they had settled, surrounded by 'fish offal and refuse of every description'. Their families also had to contend with the process of baiting the 'small lines' in their homes – 'fancy a woman with maybe four or five children, young children, two or three crying, had their eyes on the line, goes and looks after the child, then come back to the line again . . . back and forward, back and forth . . .' Small-line fishing clearly carried social disadvantages; but it was this technique, introduced by the 'Scotties', which was taken up by Burra and Whalsay.

The Burra Isles are the largest of numerous small islands in the sheltered sea off Scalloway. Well placed between its market and the west-side grounds, in the late nineteenth century the Burra fishermen were the most prosperous in Shetland, supporting a growing population of almost 900. They would work their big herring sailboats for the summer, and then lay them up in the voe and turn to small-line haddock fishing from fourareens. It was Burra herring men who bought Shetland's first lugger in 1876, and took the first sailboats to the Western Isles and English herring drifting. After 1908 they also led in replacing their fourareens with dual-purpose motor boats. From the 1890s many of them took to full-time work at sea, turned their backs on the land, and moved from their crofts to build a dense cluster of small houses above Hamnavoe harbour, the first 'true fishing village in Shetland'.

They showed too a new willingness to work in combination, founding a small co-operative for marketing haddocks in winter, with a manager and gutting shed in Scalloway, and later establishing along with Scalloway an independent link with the Glasgow market. Burra fishermen were also largely responsible for one of Shetland's rare incidents of collective protest, in the Scalloway 'riot' of 1906. The cause was the opening, against expressed local wishes, of the herring season in the first week of April, by east-coast curers. When the Lossiemouth and Yarmouth drifters were spotted, the Burra boats chased them into Scalloway, and a crowd of a hundred remonstrated with them, threw some herring into the sea, and obstructed further sales until forcibly dispersed by a police charge. Although they then retreated, five Burra men and the Shetland Fishermen's Association secretary – a Lerwick curer – were subsequently charged with riotous behaviour.

The hardest months for Burra fishermen followed the summer season. Their herring drifters carried a crew of eight, but the haddock rowboats took only four – 'so four men had to find something to do. . . . You either had to go in the Merchant Service or go down to East Anglia.' This meant that there was always some diversity in individual work patterns. Some took to whaling for Norwegian companies in the Arctic and later the Antarctic. Others followed Lerwick's 'Scotties' and their Moray Firth cousins into experiments in seine netting: there were nearly thirty Shetland seiners at work in 1928. But a satisfactory technique for seining on rocky bottoms had yet to be found, and only a few persisted. Other Burra men hired steam or motor drifters on a half-catch basis from Lerwick to follow the East Anglian season. But few local boats were fit enough for this – only eleven went in 1930.

Several tried enlisting with north-east steam drifters, although even if they got a berth it did not always bring much return:

> I got the chance on a Buckie boat . . . that came down here for the summer fishing. I'd bin two year married, 1932 . . . I went aboard a boat and asked them if they could take me for the East Anglian fishing. 'Fair enough'. He said he would send me a telegram when I was to come. Now I had to pay my own fare on the steamer, the mail boat, 17/6d I paid to take me to Aberdeen. I paid £1 on the bus to take me to Buckie. Then I went aboard and when I came aboard he gave me a packet of Woodbines and a case of matches, I'd got me grip. And I was away ten or twelve weeks and I came home £5 in debt . . . No, I never paid that back . . . So that's how I came home. So I started going to the line [the haddock fishing], to keep things going.

Those were the worst years Jimmy Henry remembers:

> a hard life, no money in the purse . . . well, it was terrible. Fish and potatoes mostly. Christmas time the children would hang up their stocking. Apple and orange, perhaps, not much. We got no money at all. My wife – she made a jumper, a Fair Isle jumper, and a man who had the shop, he bought the jumper from her and gave her a line, that she could go and take stuff to the value of the money. To keep her going . . . We had what you call a pass book. I went down to the shop and I got stuff and he mark it down and mark it down.
>
> When I started up in the fishing, if I'd £5 I'd give it to him, if I'd £10 I'd give it to him; you see there was no much rent here so you paid no rent – five bob. Well I give it to him. And one time I went down and I only had £5 and still I was a good bit in debt in the book. And he said, 'This is a bad shot. Yes, this is a bad shot.' Says, 'We'll have to carry on.' And he helped you for five years, before I got it paid off – and he said, 'Thank you very much.' A better man – that man helpit me all of my life.

His difficulties were typical. An investigation of thirty-one Burra boats in 1937 showed that they carried an average debt of almost £300 each.[10] The island's population began to fall again, as men and women left to look for work; but with unemployment in the whole of Shetland running at 41 per cent, the choice was between leaving home altogether, or hanging on. And sufficient of the Burra crews did hang on.

Whalsay's fortunes went through much the same cycle, although the patterns of fishing, as well as the character of the community, were different. Whalsay was equally well placed, this time between the grounds of the east side and Lerwick's harbour. But although its population rose to over a thousand in 1911, the Whalsay people remained crofter-fishermen in scattered hamlets, so that between the wars they could fall back more easily on the resources of their relatively fertile small crofts. Partly because the harbour at Symbister could not take larger boats, they had concentrated on the white fishing, working at the haddock handlines from November to February and the halibut from March to May. These were marketed fresh in Aberdeen, although for a time Whalsay tried to develop a trade in smoked haddocks. By 1935 it was said that only seven Whalsay herring drifters were still at the summer herring fishing. A few joined east-coast boats. 'The bulk of the young men, however, are in the Merchant Service. There is a continual trickle of emigration.'[11] Once again, however, there were sufficient fishermen remaining in the community to take the new chances which were to come after the Second World War.

New chances were certainly needed: for the 1930s marked the lowest ebb of Shetland's economy. The 1931 census showed a startling drop in the working population from 14,000 to 9,000 in twenty years. The entire population was now 25,000, shrinking more slowly, and there were no doubt a good many merchantmen away at sea uncounted, but the sharp contraction of the local workforce meant that decline was bound to go on – as it did, into the 1950s. The number of local fishermen, including crofter-fishermen, fell from a peak of 3,000 in the early 1900s to 1,000 in 1930, and a mere 600 by the mid-decade. The total local fishing fleet which had numbered over

800 at the turn of the century was down to 300 – and of these over half were still sailboats. The active first-class boats totalled little more than fifty. The purchasing of new boats had almost come to a standstill. Only a sharp turn of fortune could have saved the Shetland fleet.

The impact of the Second World War, with the intensifying of activity in the islands, direct government intervention in the economy, and post-war reconstruction aid, brought about such a change. In 1945 the Herring Industry Board launched a special scheme in support of the Shetland fishery, constructing a quick-freezing plant and cold store in Lerwick which was intended to stabilise local prices at a higher level. The first Shetland ice factory was opened under local initiative. At the same time the government grant and loan scheme for boat-buying was introduced and 1947 saw the launching, with part backing from a local shopkeeper, of the *Enterprise*, 'the first large fishing boat to be built in the islands since the early years of the century'.

The effect was a transformation – if not exactly in the way the planners had anticipated. The Shetlanders re-equipped themselves with a fleet of dual-purpose diesel motor boats for drift netting and seining, reaching 300 by the 1960s. But the long-term revival of the herring industry proved impossible due to the failing from the 1950s of the herring stocks, and although with higher prices a small fresh herring fishery remained viable, the last curing stations in Whalsay and Lerwick closed around 1960. The main growth of local earnings instead came from the introduction – just before 1945 – of the Moray Firth technique of fly-dragging with seine nets; and to a much lesser extent from a small-boat shell fishery.

These changes, especially government boat financing and the end of profits from the migrant herring fleets, undercut the old role of the local business classes in the fishing industry so quickly, that by the late 1950s only one large fish sales firm was left in Lerwick. To get better prices, over half the local catch was being sent to Aberdeen. A special report insisted that 'a plan for ACTION' was needed if an independent local fishery was to be sustained. Shetland again found local entrepreneurs with the imagination to respond to the changing situation.

The key was through developing work for women, in or near their homes. While the Lewis tweed industry was languishing, Shetland home-knitting boomed under the 'dynamic' leadership of A. I. Tulloch's Lerwick firm, who 'created a world fashion almost singlehandedly. At one point they were sending out a million mail order coupons each year for Shetland woollens.' And parallel with this, starting in 1959 with Ice-Atlantic in Scalloway, other initiatives resulted in the setting up of a series of local factories for filleting and freezing white fish, thus both saving freight charges and providing new work for women. Within five years, nearly three-quarters of Shetland's catch was being processed locally. The fish factories proved the linchpin of the sustained revival of the fishing communities – which went on to include not only Burra, Whalsay and Lerwick, but also the isolated Skerries beyond Whalsay, and to a small extent even the northern islands of Unst and Yell. Local processing kept the profits from transforming cheap catch to expensive shop produce within the islands; and it recaptured the dual economic role of men and women which had operated in the crofting-knitting-fishing economy of the past.

The grant and loan scheme freed the fishermen at last from the local merchants. The local boats were within a short period almost all owned by the fishermen themselves. They moved forward with a certain wariness, which given the vicissitudes of the past is hardly surprising. 'The Shetland men are very cautious, you know. They want to wait until a thing is proved,' one Burra skipper commented recently to a visiting researcher. But, with the added help since 1965 of the Highlands and Islands Development Board, they certainly have continued to advance technologically. From the 1960s most boats moved on from the intership radios to position-finders, radar, sonar and echo-sounders – enabling a more active hunting and finding of fish; the old nets were replaced by stronger nylon, hand-hauling by power blocks; and the first crews went on to pair trawling, and from 1967 purse seining. And in this last phase Whalsay has edged significantly ahead of Burra. The Whalsay community seems to have been especially galvanised by the post-war reconstruction spirit, already in 1949 'one of the most progressive places' with its own local

Development Council, its new houses and co-operative store. Subsequent years have seen – besides many more houses, a golf course, yacht slipway and so on – the opening of fish factories (in part through co-operative subscription), a net factory and a crofting co-operative. And Whalsay's first purse seiner was the third in Britain. Today the island, with a full-time fleet of 23 boats, including 6 new purse seiners, can in fact boast a higher investment per head in new fishing plant then any other community in the north.[12]

The new fishing demands men who move quicker than any fishermen in the past. How have the people of these small, cut-off islands – as far from the economic power centres of London directors' board-rooms as Milan or Prague – wrought their own technological revolution, leaving the Lewismen once again behind?

The answer lies, I believe, in the peculiar fusion of communality with individualism which makes up the Shetland spirit. This is not too easily characterised, partly from its very nature. Shetland fishermen tend to think out their own standpoint, and this makes for a considerable variety of attitudes. There are thus some men whose views have a very similar ring to those of the north-east. For Robbie Watt, a successful fisherman had to be 'ambitious. Ambition. You've got to be ambitious'. He is a Lerwick 'Scottie'. But in Burra too, Jimmy Henry put it down to 'Drive. Drive . . . Keep going – see, some of the men, when bin two days at sea and would no bother to stay, nae good. You had to keep going.' One finds also that sense of the hunter, and delight in a good catch: 'When you got a good shot of fish, or a good haul of herring, that's what I enjoyed the most. Your first net when you're hauling her up in the morning, you could see the herring sparkling in the net . . . flashing away in the moonbeam.'

Other attitudes, however, are more special to Shetland itself. One is an affirmation of sceptical rationalism, quite often explicitly contrasted with an admittedly superstitious past. Some of the older generation were: 'ridiculous. You couldna mention a mouse or a cat, . . . They would put a knife in the mast if they wanted wind, . . . Terrible – but I didna believe in that at any time at all . . .' Former taboos might even be challenged almost deliberately: 'I had ministers out with me several times . . . I didna believe it.' Shetland fishermen recognise the element of luck in fishing, but like to play it down: luck there was 'right enough, but I would say that a lot depends on your skill'. Especially they emphasise the use of the mind, the intelligence. 'There is no stigma attached to independent experimentation that fails, but there is stigma attached to following others habitually.' Failure to take advantage of resources, and wastefulness are disapproved. A man to be admired was 'a *serious* fisherman, very keen'; the quality above all needed in a successful skipper to be 'quick-thinking and have good ideas'.

Closely linked to this is the subtle way in which creativity, and the authority which skippers need to carry through their ideas, is so handled that it does not rupture the firmly egalitarian foundations on which these small face-to-face societies are bedded. Open rivalry, open boasting or harsh criticism, would be disruptive. Shetlanders have learnt to hide a good many of their innermost feelings more shrewdly than their open and humorous – if slightly cynical – friendliness would immediately suggest. This is true both at work and at home. Most of the boat's crew will normally be related to each other, and the formal authority of the skipper is deliberately played down: 'If one of the group of brothers is the skipper, it is always the eldest who is in legal charge of the vessel and foreman in the fishing operation.' Moreover at sea, although the skipper, isolated in the wheelhouse, inevitably holds the key information and makes most of the suggestions concerning fishing tactics, 'in theory, decisions involve the whole crew, owners and non-owners alike, in consultation and consensus. . . . The skipper never gives orders; instead he makes suggestions in an off-hand, understated way.' As a Whalsay skipper summed it up to a recent investigator, 'You saw for yourself, we do everything equally. I always ask them, and I always listen.' Ashore, while 'Everyone likes to come in top man', success is more likely to nurse inner self-esteem than to feed outward display. On the contrary, with a versatility that 'speaks of real egalitarianism', the skipper will be alongside the others hauling peats with a tractor, 'turning his acre of hay with a wooden handrake', painting his house, or out in a tiny boat with a handline or 'ferrying some sheep to a summer grazing on a holm.'[13]

More generally, competition is generated, encouraged, yet at the same time kept within distinct limits. Whalsay people delight in 'celebrating distinctiveness', the anthropologist Anthony Cohen has observed, and it is a 'continuous if restrained competitiveness which frames the observation of local behaviour'. In this spirit, at sea crews compete, yet at the same time exchange a good deal of information between each other, as far as possible to the exclusion of outsiders. Differences are also celebrated between communities, through numerous nicknames like 'Burra haddocks' and 'Scallwa smaa drink'. The local regattas provide annual occasions for straightforward sporting competition between crews. But work itself could also be made into a kind of game.

Hansie Smith of Burra's father 'had a pretty good crew, really had drive in them'; and he used to pitch them regularly against another local boat. 'They were racing all the time, one with the other.' Neither crew was prepared to break the Sabbath, but they would rise on Sunday night – all the bigger boats were anchored out in the harbour at Hamnavoe – and within six minutes they would be pulling the 'wee boat' down the beach into the water to get out into the big boat. Then, they began to get up earlier, at a quarter to twelve: taking some food, creeping down to the beach and *carrying* the wee boat down so as not to make any noise grating on the pebbles, which people might hear – and be ready on the big boat to sail dead on midnight. Walter Duncan also remembers how they might decide to take an extra line for each man on the fourareens: and then 'the women would say, "Your men had four pieces each, no wonder they got more fish". So the women were competitive too.' And, it seems, in much the same spirit in their own work. James Laurenson remembers how the Fetlar women spinners would come together for a 'kemp session of work-competitions who could spin most . . . Well we called that "kemping" with one another, sort of racing them. Same as two boats would be racing one another, they would be kemping.'[14]

It was no accident that the same attitudes could be found amongst women as men: for the place where Shetlanders learnt to reason, to value individuality and creativity as well as community and equality, was in the family, as children. We have already noticed the exceptional 'progressiveness' of child-rearing in the Shetlands. By the end of the nineteenth century families were smaller than those of Lewis – a fact which itself could well reflect the relative independence of Shetland women, and the recognition of their role in work as well as motherhood. But there could be no doubting their skill as mothers. For infants, partly because breast-feeding remained standard, the local death rate was the lowest in Britain.[15]

Gentleness and closeness did not end, as was common elsewhere in Britain, with infancy. Shetland children were brought up to be independent, but at the same time valued members of the family. There was none of the strict insistence on bedtimes or subordinated silence at mealtimes which were so common in most parts of the country. They were allowed to roam about freely at play – 'you would come in any time . . . They never bothered, as long as you were dry, d'you see?'; but they were also made welcome in adult company. At the table they could talk, indeed might be encouraged to do so, for some families regarded meals as 'a special time for talking'. At night in winter, especially when there visitors, they would sit up late round the fire, listening to stories or fiddle tunes, while the men and women worked at knitting and kishie-making. One fisherman-seaman's girl remembered with special delight the smell of his scented tobacco. 'I loved to snuggle down beside him. . . . And I could never go to bed when kishie was making until he rocked me in the kishie and of course he sang to me and rocked me.' Another, daughter of a Dunrossness crofter-fisherman, recalled her father's storytelling:

> In the winter evenings there was nothing I liked better than
> to sit and hear him and one of his friends, fishermen
> friends, come in you see, and sit and chat. . . . And of
> course, there was usually a couple coming along and the
> woman would bring her knitting, and I would be edging

my way round to where the storytelling was going on. We as children went to bed when the older people went to bed.

Shetlanders would – and still do – make children welcome at communal social occasions too. Children often came to dances. Laura Malcolmson remembers how her father, a fisherman, would play the accordion when 'we danced in – maybe in the barn. All the village would come.' When the American sociologist Erving Goffman took work as a waiter in Shetland in the 1950s, he was surprised how children were allowed to scamper about 'playing tag' during group singing at socials, or cut across the floor chasing each other between dancing couples, 'corrected only if they threatened to disrupt radically the adult activity'. Different age groups would also dance together: a woman of seventy, for example, with a boy of ten.

At Christmas and New Year it was the children who led the celebrations, 'guizing' for sweets or pennies from house to house – 'and you usually had a melodion or a fiddle, if anybody could play the fiddle, and you'd dance to those.' The next day 'the old men used to start Christmas at about eight or nine o'clock in the morning . . . out with their bottles, Christmas day, going from house to house.' Scottish Calvinism has never succeeded in suppressing the old popular Nativity holiday in Shetland.

No doubt the ready inclusion of children in social life was encouraged by the early contribution of both girls and boys to the work on the crofts. 'We did all the field spreading [of manure] and the building and the combing and drying the hay, oh yes, the children always did it. From the age of maybe six years old you were always doing some little job,' Laura Malcolmson remembered. 'We shared the work. Mother said would we go to hay today. Well we would all go you see. All work.' Andy Flaws as a boy was minding cattle 'tethered out in the fields, and the sheep, maybe in the wintertime', taking out hay to feed them in bad weather, and also 'starting to handle horses . . . I can remember me distinctly on the hill and even taking them from the fields when I was eight.'[16]

These work parties, both outside and at home on winter evenings, were made up of all generations, old and young: and this was a second important point. For responsibilities were spread, both for work and for child-rearing, beyond the nuclear family. On the crofts it was very common for parents to share the house or live adjacent to a grandparent, aunt or uncle, who would help bring up the child. Work and play here too were intertwined. While adults were making and mending on winter evenings, the 'younger ones tried to do some lessons between listening to ghost stories' and so forth. The stories might in themselves be an important way of learning. Magnus Anderson, haaf fisherman's son, might be out in the day playing at sailing boats in the loch, but at night he was magnetised by his grandfather's stories about the small-boat fishing:

> I liked to hear 'im tellin' it, because it was very interesting and very exciting them makin' the land with bad weather, you see; comin' into this tight bay . . . You just learnt with the old men just the same as a schoolteacher and youngsters so when you come to go to sea, nobody was equal to you then. Because you had gotten all the schooling you needed. In fact, you were better teached by the old men as the teacher in school.

No wonder when many Shetland children started school they felt it a 'prison'. Here rote learning was imposed in the ubiquitous Board School style, backed by the 'tawse' or strap as on mainland Scotland. Even to speak in their native Shetland dialect was to run the risk of this savage penalty.

Strapping at school came as all the more of a shock because it was in such marked contrast to the handling of discipline in the Shetland home. Here, as nowhere else in Britain, corporal punishment of any kind was regarded as undesirable and more often than not avoided. The evidence of our interviews suggest that less than a quarter of children were ever struck by their parents, very few of these with any frequency, and then just – 'a little – oh, no, not – not to be hurtful'. But 'mostly they didn't put upon the bairns': 'very seldom do you see the hand being laid on them.' Much more often, 'they just spoke to us and told us what to do', 'explained', 'lecture you'; 'reminding you . . . that you had gone from the straight a bit and you have to mend your ways'. 'I think slapping bairns is awfully bad. You make them gentle, keep them gentle,' explained one crofter's daughter of how she had brought up her own boys:

> I think if you slap a bairn even when he's very little, suppose he scratches your face and you give him a slap on the hands, he'll do that to you . . . You just grow up as you're trained. And you can get a lot out of bairns, especially if you're kindly to them. 'Live the idea more than the fear', you see.

Gentleness, example, explanation, conscience and mutual consideration are the keynotes. Whether this philosophy may be based on longstanding Shetland tradition must remain an open question, for lack of any firm evidence. But it does seem likely that it had become easier for Shetland parents to bring up their children in this way as family size had declined from the late nineteenth century. The mean number of children in the families of our informants is four; and it is noticeable that while corporal punishment is scarcely ever recalled in families of one to four children, in those of six or more it occurs more often than not.

These habits of reasoning and explanation, inculcated in Shetlanders from childhood, sank deep into their conscious-ness, becoming instincts of speech which spring to mind as they tell their life stories. They remember how effectively some of their parents could convey their feelings – like the Burra fisherman who obeyed his mother as a child because 'by the way that she spoke, I knew I was hurting her and I didna like it'; or Magnus Anderson, Whalsay crofter-fisherman born in 1887, who believed he should treat his own children as he had been brought up himself:

> Na, they didna believe strappin' you – na, they just spoke gently the way, and I think it was just as good. And we had five, and I never gave one of them a pick yet, no, no I never touched them. I just thought it, as it would do no good . . . thought it might mak them more awkward . . . No, I never touched the youngsters in my life, no, no. I

was frightened . . . I would make hurt them too sore.
They was youngsters, you see, I didna know, understand
what pressures they could stand, you see – and if I was
doin' it too much or – it would have bothered me, so I
never touched them.

I think they did as well. Yes, I think they just did as well
after they grow up and they come t'theyselves, they gan all
right.

This understanding of children as independent persons,
with individual needs, who had to be encouraged rather than
drilled to find their own way in the world, led children
towards an adult world in which distinctions between age
groups and between men and women, in terms of work and
authority, were far from rigid. The customs of childhood and
adulthood were mutually reinforcing. As parents were gentle
with their children, so, it was noticed by the laird of Sumburgh, 'as a rule young Shetlanders are very kind to their
parents and consider it no hardship to support them.'[17] But
equally fundamental to attitudes were relationships between
men and women.

Shetland men and women were economically mutually dependent – and knew it. The season's work on the croft would
begin in March.

On a fine day we were getting out the manure from the
byre and put onto the fields. And then it was all turning of
the – we'd no ploughs, used to turn it all by hand. And it
would take about five weeks altogether.

And then you were free again until August when you're
cutting the hay. And by the middle of October you'd be
cutting the corn, gathered it all into the croft, gathered the
potatoes, which had to be done by hand of course. And
take up the turnips. Then you're free . . .

In all this work the women would take part, and although
there were strong traditions of men's work and women's
work, due to the coming and going of the men and the
arbitrary sex balance on different crofts, there were few tasks

which could not at times be undertaken by either of them. In particular, the women were neither spared the distant work nor the heavy work: they would be up on the hills looking after lambs, build haystacks, drive stock to market, join in sheep-shearing and dipping, and at one time even in carrying 'sea-chests to the ports. I myself have walked to Lerwick with a heavy trunk on my back, that is twenty miles from here.' The whole system, and their part in it, was well summed up in the toughest task on the croft, the annual digging of the arable: 'Delving was family team work. Two, three or four men and women, or young men only, stood side by side and turned the earth with their spades, edging along with rhythmic unity of movement', stamping their spades into the ground at one time, pausing, turning and breaking the soil together, and so on all day. 'All this ground doon here, you can see all the rigs, there were no ploughs, you just turn it w'a spade three o' you – three on a pit, as we call it. . . . You wouldna believe what three folk could turn ower in a day!'

But in Shetland, in marked contrast to Lewis, this full participation of the women in the hard work and responsibility of the croft, brought them recognised social standing. Not only informally, as Peter Jamieson noted, 'the women have a big say in the running of the crofts'; but still more striking was the high proportion, nearly one-third, of the farms and crofts, which the census recorded as being formally run by women. In this respect Shetland was quite distinct from the normal British pattern. And the social reality of this arrangement comes across vividly in the hearings before the Crofting Commission: for the witnesses who came forward to complain of being forced into signing unjust agreements by the lairds were often women, acting – and being exploited – as heads of their house. Mrs John Smith, for example, could not read, and was forced to sign an agreement by the estate clerk before it was read aloud to her: 'and when I came to hear it read I saw the snare into which we had fallen. I was put off my sleep for nights about it.'[18]

This flexibility in the outside work was mirrored within. Again there were traditional male and female roles, but it is equally striking how much sharing there was despite them. Among the Lerwick 'Scotties' especially there were some

homes with a softer version of the Lewis or north-east pattern:
'a fisherman was nae help in the hoose. . . . When he came
hame he was looked after like he was a long-lost lover.
Everything was almost *served up* to him.' But in general,
Shetland men helped with their children, and with domestic
tasks such as washing up and firelighting, as well as decorat-
ing, repairs and improvements. But many went a good deal
further. 'All the sailors can wash clothes better than any
woman,' commented one crofter-seaman's daughter; 'some
of the fishermen did a lot of baking.' Laura Malcolmson's
father cooked, 'and I know quite a lot of men of his age who
did the same.' Magnus Anderson 'had an old uncle there, he
could bake that bannocks, that scones, and he could knit, he
could make this guernseys and stockins and yer inside-wear,
he could do a' that. If it was the wrang wool, he could card it
and spin it . . .'

Sometimes such attitudes were reinforced by explicit feminist sympathies. Laura Malcolmson's father again was 'awful
keen to give women the vote. And yes, Mrs Pankhurst – oh he
just admired this wife.' But more generally, an important
factor must have been the independent contribution to the
household budget which Shetland women made. Principally
through knitting and farming they made up 43 per cent of the
local workforce, markedly more than elsewhere. The knitters
were even unionised in the Shetland Home Knitters Association in the 1940s, a very unusual step for home workers. They
gained social self-confidence, even a sense of solidarity, from
customary work-groups of women on the crofts at an evening
'cairdin', sometimes ending in a dance with the young men.
Unmarried girls could experience still greater independence
by going away gutting:

> I was free – because once you were off with the fishing in
> the year your time was your own and you'd nobody to
> say, well do this, you see – you were just with the girls;
> and you would go to the theatre, you could go to dances or
> anywhere . . .

From the 1880s, as the haaf fishing with long lines baited at sea
gave way to the haddock fishing from small lines baited at

home, Shetland women in the fishing communities took on a
further task which increased their men's dependence on them.
Herring drift nets also required mending. 'Oh yes, everybody
was involved, women, men an'll . . . They mended the nets
during the winter . . . And that lines were all brought inside
the house.' George Hunter of Burra summed it up:

> The women never got their heads up. They probably had a
> cradle on the floor and lines to bait and nets to mend, a
> croft to look after, cows to milk, bread to bake – women
> played a big part, a major part in the whole thing. Women
> made all the difference. . . . It had to be a communal
> effort. There was no other way a crofter-fisherman could
> survive, except you had a good wife. No other way. She
> was fifty per cent of the effort.

It was clearly a tough life which does not bear romanticisa-
tion; and certainly not one in which there were no strong social
divisions of roles between the sexes. But there was also in
Shetland just enough sharing in work, and just enough of a
balance in power between the sexes, to help towards a genuine
mutual appreciation of the other's contribution as well as a
degree of flexibility in apportioning common tasks. The sea
itself remained almost exclusively a male world: although even
here exceptions could sometimes be made. From the 1890s a
few fishing boats were owned by women, like the Burra
Friends, registered in 1911 under the names of Johanna Goodlad, wife of the boat's skipper, and two other Hamnavoe
wives. And Whalsay can even remember, with distinct
admiration, a Shetland woman yachtmaster, who taught
navigation in the 1960s and early 1970s, Jeanette Williamson:
'She went to the fishing with a boat for a whole week,
sometime . . . She was awfu' interested in the sea, she was very
clever . . . very, very brilliant and everyone that ever she
taught, passed . . .' Johnny Irvine remembers how he was on
his brother-in-law's boat,

> and she came to learn from us. And she said, 'This is the
> first time I've seen a Decca', she said, 'How does it work?
> . . . How do you read it?' Well, I started pointing this out

to her – and it took me weeks to get into this. And she took
out a packet of fags and she wrote it down. She said 'Is this
the reading?' and I said 'Yes'; she said 'I see' – she just saw
it, just in a blink . . . I got it worked out ultimately, told
them here we were – but that took me weeks to get into it.
She'd just pick up the book and write down the readings
just in a blink![19]

One cannot help feeling that Whalsay is one of the few places
where such a conversation could have happened aboard a
fishing boat. There too, women have their assigned social
place; but in the last analysis, Shetlanders see and weigh each
other up as individuals.

They are individuals whose lives are acted out within a strong
communal framework, certainly. But here again, despite basic
similarities in township agricultural organisation, social egali-
tatarianism and ceremonies, there are distinctions between the
community in Shetland and Lewis which help to explain its
different character.

Like Lewismen, Shetlanders saw their communities as con-
sisting essentially of equals. While recognising that '"The
ragged sleeve keeps the hand back" – if people's poor they take
a back seat, regardless of what their personal qualities are' –
they were prepared to openly show their resentment when
those 'a step up', whether merchants, ministers or lairds,
showed themselves 'aloof':

> I remember meeting one of the lairds (of Unst) and his
> wife when I was a young man. I raised my cap to both of
> them and said, 'Good morning'. He said 'Good morning',
> but he didna raise his cap. So next time I met him I didna
> raise it.

When the laird of Whalsay put up for the first county council
elections in 1890, the response of the crofters was a characteristic turning of the blind eye: only 9 out of 82 electors turned
out to vote for him. As Sinclair Mowat put it, 'my cap went
on to stop'.

In Shetland communities too there were patterns of mutual

aid. Cottars would be given potato land, children sent with fresh fish to an old widow. 'If you were finished your job first you would go and help your neighbour . . . with the hay and the corn and with lifting the potatoes.' This was especially 'if some old body were left by herself or a pair of old people left by themselves. Some of the young ones of the district would go there, and work the croft . . . They would gather together half-a-dozen young fellows and go and cut their peats for them. . . . I've worked many a long day just for nothing.' And in the same spirit, 'if you were building your house, I would help you, if I was building my house you'd help me.' House-building called for more systematic teamwork – 'those of us who weren't qualified for building stones, we'd go and carry stones, and bring them in for the older men to use. And we helped in that way.'

Generally, however, such acts had a more spontaneous character in Shetland. Shetlanders do not speak of them, like Lewis people, as collectively organised forms of 'primitive communism'. This also reflected a looser form of social organisation. In Lewis the communities were tight settlements, each village one agricultural township, almost all belonging to one estate and one kirk. In Shetland the settlement pattern had been loose and irregular, 'with a predominance of hamlets, called "towns", "farms", "rooms" or "townships",' scattered along the sea coast and inland valleys. It was not possible to organise a neat agricultural system, because hamlets would have some common pasture of their own, but often share the rough hill pasture with other groups of crofts. Thus although the townships from the 1880s were formally organised around the hamlets, they also had to be worked as part of a wider grouping, which might more nearly represent the social sense of community. Whalsay for example is clearly regarded as a single community, yet divided into separate townships. And while the island now has a single estate and kirk, in many other parts of Shetland there are arbitrary parish boundaries, rival churches and fragmented estates. As a consequence, power in the community is spread, and decisions made by a whole series of different groups, rather than by chosen township officers or elders of the kirk. 'They just speak together.'[20]

The more dispersed Shetland settlements reduce the unified power of opinion, of gossip, leaving more space for individuals to make their own way in life. But in particular their relatively diffuse organisation gave less of a structure for men, through the township committee and the kirk, to assert a social dominance over women. The absence of public houses in most districts has a similar influence. The social life of the Shetland community focussed primarily on the group of croft homes in the hamlet, where 'the door was open' and neighbours would drop in to work or talk together. This placed women on a social basis much nearer to men: they would call on each other like the men, hold their own work parties, become similarly known in the community as storytellers. And they clearly have a social standing, and confidence, today, which contrasts markedly with the situation of women in Lewis. They are in the habit of being taken seriously as persons in their own right.

The difference in attitude, as opposed to behaviour, comes out particularly clearly in regard to courting and sexual relationships between young people. As in Lewis, young couples courted secretly in bed, and despite a late age of marriage this did not often lead to intercourse itself, for the level of illegitimacy was low: 'a girl and a boy would go to bed together as they might for a walk'. But self-control was left to the conscience of the young people, rather than imposed through severe communal censure. If anyone was to be blamed, it was the man who had evaded the responsibility of paternity, and not repaired his offence through marriage. The mother was not made to suffer in his stead. As a Shetland doctor reported, when illegitimacy did occur, 'in no case have I ever found the children neglected or the mothers harshly treated. The people take the philosophic view, "It's da Lord's will, and we can gae nae further".'

Their way was to trust; and to celebrate when things turned out well. In an egalitarian community, choice of spouse was in any case less of a cause for acute parental anxiety. Thus bundling was not merely ignored, but accepted openly. A dance, or a 'flatchie carding' of young women, might end with straw mattresses spread on the floor; and 'this was a signal for boys to come in and spend the night rolling around with girls, jumping and rolling over them.' When courting then led to a decision to marry by the couple, the 'bridegroom-elect' only had to go

> spurring for the bride . . . just to go and ask the father. . . . And all that he had to take with him was a good bottle of Scotch whisky. . . . And of course he would be welcomed then in the house, and was sitting in the but end, and after a time the wife of the house would go and set about tea . . . and when the table's about to be set the young man, he'll go to his coat and take out this bottle of whisky ar.d set it in the middle of the table, and say nothing. And the father would say, 'Now bairns, set you in around. And boy, set thee in among us' – and that showed that he was accepted into the family. That was the words that were spoken.

The wedding itself would be a celebration of the whole community. It is symptomatic that while in Lewis the rite of passage which probably mattered most, summed up communal values in the most powerful symbolism, was the funeral, in Shetland it was the wedding. In both places customs have formally much in common. But in Shetland the carrying of the coffin to the cemetery by the men alone had been come to be seen in many districts by the mid-nineteenth century less as a hallowed task than as an unpleasant duty, calling for the compensation of a stiff drink; and there are a good many Shetland stories about disorderly funerals. They are not a tradition regarded with much pride. With weddings, on the other hand, while Lewis celebrations could often only be conducted as semi-secret illicit orgies, in Shetland they remain the most highly valued of traditional ceremonies. Weddings were open celebrations of sexual exuberance, from the gunshots before the church service to the dancing in the barn all night and often longer, when all age groups joined in, and the bride would dance in turn with each man present. Neighbours would help to prepare for the feast, bringing down sheep to a house where 'they'd maybe a dozen old men in there to help cook this mutton ready for the wedding'. There was 'plenty of drink' too; and after the feast the dancing, the young people continuing into the next day with brief spells of sleep. 'They behaved themselves. Yes, yes' – at least most of them. For the old custom of guests sharing 'the lang bed' had not altogether disappeared:

> If it's coming on a snowstorm the people couldna – maybe there was no roads to go to their houses . . . when they looked at the weather used to say, 'Well, you're here for the night. You can't go home just now. You'll have to stay with us.' They'll spread out a lot of straw, and that's what they call a long bed – have you ever heard about them? Well they laid a lot of straw, anybody, with coats or anything could lay down, and then you could take your partner whenever you liked and squat down among this straw there, they'll come with another lot to put on the top of you. See that's what they called the long bed.
>
> And very often you know, supposing – well I might as well tell you the whole story mightn't I? Supposing anything happened – they would be having the drinking you know, that most men was – was, when they got – they were a sort of virile race – maybe some of those girls would get into trouble latterly. Then you had to be taken before the session to get church privileges, to get the communion. And the head [elder] would stand up, stand up and say to the minister, 'Now, be merciful to the young people. They were at a wedding . . .' So they would take a comparatively lenient view . . .

Shetland's Calvinism, in short, had bitten less deeply than that of Lewis. And here was another difference between the two regions, undoubtedly of fundamental importance. Historically, organised religion has never had the full impact in Shetland which it has had throughout most of Britain. Neither the mediaeval Catholic church, nor the Church of Scotland after the Reformation, could find the resources to provide effectively for such an impoverished, scattered population. Many of the islands had no church at all before the eighteenth century. Subsequently, Shetland escaped the experience of mass conversion by Calvinist missionaries. The work of crofter-fishermen evangelists, like Sinclair Thomson of Dunrossness and John Inkster of Burra, instead brought Baptists and Methodists a following in some districts from the 1800s: indeed Shetland became Methodism's strongest Scottish district. In the 1840s the new Free Kirk won little support outside Unst; and afterwards, by improving its parochial arrangements, the Church of Scotland recovered some of the ground it had lost in the split.

The result was a situation in which there was often religious choice; and whatever their official doctrines – for of the main groups, only the Methodists were not Calvinist – the kind of puritanism experienced in Lewis made a relatively slight impact. The much higher proportion of full church members itself bore evidence of less exacting standards. Shetland women would return cheerfully from a prayer meeting to sing, 'with great volubility, . . . the eloquence of *da dear cratur*, the minister'. Attempts to suppress pleasures such as dancing, card-playing and fiddle music made little headway. Good fiddlers were symbols of a strong community; islands like Burra and Whalsay had their own bands of fiddles, accordion and later guitar, to set the company dancing to the traditional reels; and by the end of the nineteenth century 'the minister danced as well'.[21]

Temperance made more headway. It was said in the 1860s that some districts previously noted for drunkenness had become more 'solemn'. By 1900 the temperance order of Rechabites had 24 Shetland branches, and Lerwick itself was officially 'dry' from 1923 until 1946. But since drink remained on sale from wholesalers a group could club together to buy a crate, and 'along the market, you'd see a congregation of men, two or three dozen men, all standing around drinking big bottles of beer'. Some grocers would also quietly serve a glass to a lone drinker at the back of the shop; and there were shebeens in the town too – 'this place was dry for a long, long time but you could still get a drink.' Outside Lerwick the most fervent teetotallers were a minority in Burra. Whalsay was more typical, temperate rather than fanatical. 'They just had a bottle for Christmas, a bottle of whisky . . . and once that was finished, it was finished till next Christmas.' There was no bar on the island, no drinking on its boats: but 'they're a rare one, that's teetotal still, and it was the same then.'

Most Shetlanders believed that pleasure had its proper place in life, whatever the kirk said; and with a characteristic twist of humour, many kept a cynical watch on the doings of a world of rival spirits, 'da trow's hill we call it . . . I know there was a lot of hard drinking in the old days.' One retired drifterman-seaman born in the 1890s, a fiddler himself, wrote out for us in his shaky old hand:

> Some reckoned they had seen what was known as 'Trows'. I heard once at one time about a man in Walls fishing 'sillocks', coalfish. You know, on his way back home again he passed a 'knowe' or small hill, he was satisfied the noise of music came from within the Hill. This man sat down his fish and thought he would go in and have a dance with the so called 'Trows'. The story goes that he did not reach his home until a year later, his people mourned him as dead. When he was asked why he was been so long away, well, he said, he only stayed until the reel finished. Some reel *eh*.[22]

A second favourite theme in the Shetland oral tradition was the ghost story in which social oppressors and evil-doers rose from the dead, haunted by the knowledge of their own wickedness. But the repentance won from the restless consciences of evicting and short-changing factors was less likely to be wrung from the crofters' social enemies in this world. And part of the weakness of the kirk, and resistance to it, sprang from its entanglement with the local ruling class. 'The laird and the minister they worked together. The minister, he preached that you had to do what the laird told you to do,' Robbie Bairnson remembered of the south mainland. On Whalsay letters had even been discovered subsequently which showed the minister acting as 'a spy for the laird', reporting 'that these men was going so-and-so and would be able to pay a bit more rent and all this. That was the minister, he'd been employed by the laird, one of his henchmen.' The established church no longer has any rivals on Whalsay, but the apathy

suggested by scant attendance may be in part a reaction to the
use of religion as an instrument of class control.

Nevertheless it was also a moral reaction. Johnny Irvine
'hardly attended in my life', nor did his father,

> No, he did not. I'll tell you what made me father against
> the church. Because you had them taking people before the
> church session . . . like if your wife was going to have a
> baby when you married . . . just minor offences, you'd be
> taken before the elders maybe in the church, Sunday, and
> you had to sit in front of the whole congregation. And that
> put his back up against the church . . .
>
> Another thing: it was a year that there was a fish famine,
> in Whalsay, and this old man was down at the shore and he
> saw a lot of fish . . . piltocks and poddies. . . . And he
> went and got a net . . . and filled all the holes around with
> this fish and . . . told everybody that they were to go
> down and take up this fish. It was on a Sunday. . . .
>
> The people were hungry: there had been a tattie famine
> and a corn famine and a fish famine afterwards. And he
> was taken before the church session . . . for this, this crime
> that he had committed. And the minister – or the chief
> elder – asked if he had anything to say for himself and he
> says, 'Yes, the Lord says to Peter that he was to put his nets
> over the right side of the boat. Well, I put my pock [net on
> a stick] over the right side of the geo [crevice].' So that was
> all that [he] said.
>
> It was things like that that put his back up against the
> church.

Certainly it would be false to suggest, especially of this
earlier time, that there were few devout Shetlanders. Magnus
Anderson recalled Whalsay Sundays in the 1890s, when 'you
could play aroond', but 'we all had to be kind o'good that day.
The old folk was very religious – yes, they believed in the kirk,
the minister, a' that.' There was an old men's choir in the kirk.
One uncle would come each Sunday to read the sermon in the
Christian Herald, 'readin' all this Christian sermon at our
house, he would every week.' And when Magnus was out near
to his grandfather's croft 'just to play aboot the banks and that

like – whenever I went near that hoose, I could hear him readin'
this Bible – me auld grandfather, wi'tha' strong voice, you
could hear the roar from Braga's Bank!'

But it was a religious atmosphere better characterised by
dissent than enthusiasm. The essential moral point which
Shetlanders seem to have taken from their Protestantism was a
profound belief in the need for each individual to seek his or
her own salvation. Of the fishing communities, Burra comes
closest to the feeling of the north-east, with its strong Baptist
chapel, its 'peerie kirk', an undenominational wooden hut
built by the fishermen down by the shore, challenging the
'muckle kirk' of the United Frees higher up, its Methodists,
and even for a time a small group of Brethren. But Burra
people make up their own minds. Church was a place for
thinking, not passively accepting what the minister said.
'Who's right and who's wrong? . . . As far as going to church,
I agree, but I don't need anyone telling me what to do. I know
myself what to do. You know the same.'[23]

Closely linked to the Shetlanders' belief in independent
thinking has been their support for self-education. Formal
education here was a direct legacy of Protestantism, for
schooling was first introduced by the kirk. But provision
remained very patchy into the nineteenth century. This meant
that the high rate of literacy, already over 90 per cent in 1826,
was as much due to self-help as to formal schooling. Even in
the 1870s, before there was a 'recognised school' on the island,
Whalsay parents clubbed together to pay an old man 1/6d a
quarter for teaching their children in an iron-roofed hut which
they built for him.

He was a little man like that, he was my father's uncle, and
he taught himself and he could read and write, and the
people used to send the kids to that school . . . He'd teach
in this village this time and go to another village and teach
in somebody's barn, and he'd teach them.

Such informal education was soon to give way to the more
comprehensive, if rigid, Board School system. But the Shetlanders' belief in self-education continued to be shown by the
number of parents who began teaching their children to read

before they started school, and also, in a more particular way, by their social recognition of local 'crofter-scholars' who might have earlier been community teachers.

There are stories of men like Robertson of Nissetter in the north mainland, freethinker, follower of Herbert Spencer, with his library of science and philosophy, whose croft, after the day's work outside, 'became a veritable "university", as the crofter expounded the famous "First principles" to the keen youngsters'; or of another crofter-scholar whose wife insisted on using the 'big buik', Kant's *Critique of Pure Reason*, to prop up her spinning wheel. Today best-known of them all is Laurence Williamson of Gardie on Yell, born in 1855, who died in 1936. His only income came from selling two or three bottles of milk a day from his tiny croft. He slept in an outhouse bunk in his half-repaired house, and his coat was ragged, 'often kept in place by a bit of string round the middle'. But he was a figure of substance at the meetings of the Literary and Debating Society formed in Mid Yell in 1906; and an acknowledged expert on local history and stories, dialect and folklore. His interests went beyond this: he was an enthusiast for Greek and Renaissance scholarship, for poetry, for Tolstoy and Ibsen – a man with a passion for intellectual conversation, who was reputed to have once stood for six hours after a regatta, debating anthropology and archaeology with a visiting Edinburgh professor. He read political theory too, including Marx – with whom he disagreed, but recognised as a 'powerful and original thinker'.

The Shetland crofter-scholars have their parallels in the Gaelic tradition-bearers among the crofters of the north-west, and also in the 'worthies' of the north-east, but they differ from both in their much wider interests. They stand not just for cultural tradition or religious morality, but also attempt to grapple with the new political and philosophical problems of the present. Nor should a figure like Laurence Williamson be seen as altogether exceptional in the breadth of his intellectual interests. His reputation was in fact due in part to the very way in which he was able to express the experience of that whole generation which had lived through the dramatic social transformations of the late nineteenth century. 'We stand in a great transition time, such as has not been seen since the end of the

Middle Ages,' he wrote in 1913. It was the same sense which stimulated the remarkable strength of Shetland interest in Marxism at the same time. Herring fishermen could then be found, it was said, who on the boats would 'pore over a well-thumbed paper-covered copy of Edward Aveling's *The Student's Marx*'; and Lerwick town had a flourishing branch of the Marxist SDF (Social Democratic Federation) which was two hundred strong by 1914.

Shetlanders remain great thinkers, and great readers. Their library circulation rate today is the highest in Britain. Independent thinking, self-education and reading all spring in part from the form of Protestantism which developed among them: but these have led a significant minority beyond that religious tradition, to open rationalism and secular anti-authoritarianism. As one crofter-fishermen and seaman put it, 'I just started thinking for myself and I couldn't see – read the Bible and thought some of it rather far-fetched . . .' And then one day he discovered Omar Khayyam: 'and when I first read his *Rubaiyat*' saw in a flash – 'I think that's something like myself . . . I'm a kind of a free thinker or a rationalist . . . I think you'll probably find in a dictionary a free thinker is one who rejects authority and religion. Well – I agree with that.'[24]

At the turn of the century it seemed increasingly likely that this independent-mindedness would generate a radical political movement in the islands. There were signs of a growing willingness to speak out, and perhaps even for collective action. The exposure of the Shetland truck system through the 1872 inquiry first restimulated widespread political discussion. It did not, however, lead to any agitation for reform. Nor did the Shetlanders organise land raids to counter the clearances which their lairds had begun. Even in the 1890s the attempt to form a Crofters Defence League met with little support. There were a few signs of revolt in this period, almost all against the Bruces of Sumburgh: the Hoswick men who defied their claim to a share of a shoal of whales driven ashore in 1888, the Cunningsburgh crofters' fight against a scattald enclosure and the Levenwick electoral boycott against the laird in 1890–2. This was also when a dispute between fishermen and curers brought false rumours of 'disturbances' and the needless dispatch of a gunboat to Whalsay. But the response of Shetland crofter-fishermen to class injustice was more characteristically through evasive devices and individual wit.

Just because of the opportunity which they gave for self-expression by the Shetland people, the very hearings before the visiting Crofting Commissioners in the autumn of 1889 made a sensational turning point in the social life of the islands. 'It is not often we get a chance of making our complaints made known,' said John Halcrow, crofter, to the full house in Dunrossness parish church. 'We have been under tacksmasters and factors for forty years.' As witness after witness made their telling points against the islands' ruling class, the audience roared with approving laughter and applause. And those in other districts waited expectantly to read the reports of the hearings in the local newspaper, and learn 'how the laird of Sumburgh had come out. They were particularly pleased that some interesting stories had been well published, and that it was becoming a lively time generally for lairds.'

Ordinary Shetlanders seized the hearings, in fact, as an opportunity to set straight the record of the past, as much as to determine the future: to reaffirm that their own values, the values of the common people of the township ought to be weighed equally with those of lairds and governments. And that included their regional speech; and the respect they felt for women. Two moments, especially, stand out from the reports. One was in the hearing at Aithsting, when a very old crofter, 78-year-old Peter White, faced the commissioners. What did this aged man have to say to them? Simply that they should hear his will, that his will should be set down with due dignity as part of the record of their proceedings. He called on his daughter to hear him read it aloud in court: 'She has stayed with me, and done everything she could for me, so I am to will it to her.'

And the second moment, equally difficult to imagine anywhere else, was at the Cunningsburgh hearing, when a Shetland woman crofter succeeded in crumpling the laird's solicitor with her mockery of his 'superior' accent. He had begun his cross-examination of widow Smith, of Gott:

'Was your husband a *mason* on the estate?'
'Was he *mentioned* on the estate?'
'Was he *mason* on the estate?'
'Is it *stane-mason* you mean? You should speak your words proper- an' dan a person understaand you . . .'

The court burst into 'great laughter'. The solicitor, who was Bruce's agent, tried to get her back to the question he wanted answered, about rent – but she brushed him aside this time,

'Never ant him, I must get through with my story'.

And she did indeed tell her story: about how the Bruces had forced her to sell her cow, to pay the doctor's bill.

Words without actions cannot bring about change: but once Shetlanders had seen the strength they could show in public protest, crofters, fishermen and town workers all began to move forward. In Lerwick trade unionism began to spread among the skilled men. The first Labour town councillors were elected in 1905, with the help of the new Lerwick Co-operative Society. Some of the crofting townships also began to form small co-operatives; Whalsay set up a club doctor for its boats, and Burra its haddock marketing co-operative. Shetland now had the largest branch of the Marxist SDF in Scotland, organising regular outdoor meetings, selling its journal *Justice* and the socialist *Clarion*, sending out cycling missions to the rural townships. The older generation still carried bitter memories 'of the lairds and what they'd done to the crofting folk'; while the young, facing the competition of steam fishing, harboured real fears of domination by 'huge rings and syndicates'. It looked as if the future would see an intensifying class conflict.

It did not turn out that way. The reforms of the 1880s had set both crofters and fishermen on the way to independence. The drastic unemployment and out-migration of younger men in the inter-war years undercut the basis for an organised working class movement. No local Labour Party was formed until 1924. It collapsed in four years. Reformed only in 1937, it disappeared again after three years.

By 1943, when a lasting Labour Party branch was finally

established, trade unionism had also revived. The organisation of the scattered women home knitters marked a specially significant advance, and from 1938 onwards a labour group has been a presence in the county and town councils. Throughout this period too Shetlanders had sustained their appetite for political ideas. Crofter-fishermen who became merchantmen in the 1930s, for example, could still be found reading philosophy and psychology, picking up a second-hand copy of Plato's *Republic* for the voyage, or arguing about Freud, Darwin and Marx 'while painting the ship's side'. That political liveliness has been shown again more recently in the initially very determined and creative response of the Shetland County Council to the North Sea oil companies, for which it succeeded in obtaining special legislation; and more recently in sponsoring the Shetland Fishing Plan, a far-seeing proposal for future conservation and development of the sea's potential.[25] Equally notable has been the criticism of the council's handling of the oil companies and pressure for more independent radical alternatives through the breakaway Democratic Group of councillors of 1973 and the Shetland Movement formed in 1978 with its aim for increased local self-government.

Whether the islands' politics can provide sufficient answers for Shetland's future remains an open question. The political consciousness of the islanders has remained essentially popular, rather than class-based. It rests, like the post-war economic revival in the islands' fortunes, on a belief in both individualism and community: above all in independence. The balance of effects between communal solidarity and individualism is delicate. There is very little to be said, in terms of mere economic rationality, for a way of life based on fishing from a windswept, infertile cluster of islands out in the north Atlantic. Without the cultural distinctiveness and isolation which gives Shetlanders such a strong sense of community and attachment to their homeland, the islands would have been more likely almost totally depopulated through the individualistic logic of migration. And even today, in the new era of oil, despite a now-rising population the future of the Shetland community must hang uncertainly in the balance. Shetland's fishing now faces a double threat. On the one hand are the multi-national oil companies, with immense financial

resources to draw off local labour whenever they require it and
to buy the power to exploit the sea-bed as they find necessary.
On the other are the rival fishing fleets of the Common Market
countries seeking their own access to its fishing grounds, and
making the destruction of the sea's basic resources an increasing danger. To survive a future of this kind the Shetlanders
will need collective action as well as individualism.

We can only say for certain that their culture has so far
served them well. While Lewis has languished, in Shetland a
different consciousness, also historically moulded, has
allowed its chances to be seized. Shetland has not merely
survived: it has flourished – and without abandoning its own
special spirit. This in a sense represents a secular maturing of
Protestant individualism in its most absolute and logical form:
a freethinking faith that men and women can choose their own
destinies. But the very creativity of that individualism springs
from a threefold rooting: firstly, in an egalitarian belief in the
worth of ordinary people – of men, women and children;
secondly, in the gentleness and understanding with which
children are brought up, and the acceptance, even celebration,
of difference among adults; and finally, in a defiant pride in the
distinctiveness of their own common culture, values and
speech.

16 Ahead

Though the prospects are better for some than for others, all the various ways of life in fishing must face constantly the threat of extinction in a world of recurrent economic change. The danger to them is both external and internal.

The parcelling of the sea which has taken place over the last thirty years, and the still more recent allocation of catch through international negotiation, marks the end of an epoch. The distinctive history of fishing has rested on the freedom of the sea, modified only by a marginal restriction of inshore waters to local communities, and by the assumption that the sea's resources were boundless. Long after the land had become divided up under the exclusive control of private individuals, the sea remained an open resource. Peasants who have lost their land have lost the linchpin of their way of life, the means to farm in the future. Fishermen who lost their boats to other owners were not excluded from the sea. So long as there were fish they could find, catch and sell, they had a future. This legal framework, little questioned until now, provided the essential context for the survival of the small entrepreneur in a free market; and it was reinforced by longstanding government intervention, in providing subsidies (bounties, boat loans, harbour construction), regulation and naval protection. But such assumptions are no longer acceptable in view of the now incontrovertible evidence of the disastrous consequences of over-fishing. The hidden politics have been forced out into the open. If Britain's fishing communities are to recapture any control over their own destinies, they will need to learn very quickly from the example of others: from the determination of the Bretons in protecting communal interest through collective action which has forced Paris politicians to take notice of their needs, or the success of the Faroese in building a thriving industry on the basis of government conservation and support policies.[1] In the meantime, whether they are to have *any* future is a question now hanging in the balance, dependent on horse deals over the tables in Brussels.

Equally vital is the delicate equilibrium between solidarity and individualism which they still need, if they are to survive without stagnation. Fishing has been at most times a relatively poorly paid occupation in return for exceptionally long hours and uncomfortable, dangerous working conditions. As late as the 1960s, a 90-hour week was normal on the trawlers, and death rates have remained very high. At the end of the 1970s, they were ten times as high as in the coal mines, and fifty times more than in manufacturing industry: 205 fishermen, 1 per cent of the workforce, were killed at sea between 1974 and 1978. A cohesive local sense of involvement in the industry is essential to maintain a labour force in which sons follow fathers to sea, as to the pits, rather than choose easier rewards in other local work, or migrate to search for different opportunities. Economically and socially, fishing communities only survive at all because the internal bonding through neighbours and family, together with a sense of separateness – moral, social and physical, often moulded by a common history of oppression and struggle – combine to set them apart from the wider society. These values are continually under pressure from outside, and are undoubtedly vulnerable. Sometimes they have given way under frontal attack, as in the Aberdeen case. In other instances they have succumbed to more subtle pressures, like the intrusion of government-built roads and consumer goods brought with welfare subsidies which have so effectively destroyed the economy of many of the Newfoundland outports since the 1950s, leaving their young men to choose only between unemployment and migration – even though the fish are still there, in abundance. And any new technological development may bring with it insidious social assumptions which if not consciously resisted could be equally threatening. The men of the Scottish herring ports kept their own boats in the past only because, when they were first offered steam drifters, they were unwilling to work them as wage-earners for company owners. Similarly, when the purse seiners came to Shetland, they were worked on a Norwegian system with an elaborate division of roles, and a literally built-in hierarchy of authority symbolised by the captain's separate cabin accommodation. But the first successful Shetland purse seiner was owned on a share basis and operated with flexible and overlapping work roles just as other Shetland boats today, and on many of their purse seiners 'significantly the skipper never uses his cabin, preferring to sleep below with the other owners and crew'. Such a *conscious* reassertion of the community's own values must be essential if they are to be maintained.

On the other hand, if such cohesiveness is pushed too far towards a dominating conformism, it can stifle the possibility of any individual initiative for change. In the most extreme cases, a cohesive solidarity can maintain an outdated way of life long after its time against all apparent odds. In the isolated outports of Newfoundland, many until twenty years ago accessible to the nearest town only by several days by ship or – when the sea was iced over – by dog-sleigh, cod continued to be caught by tidal traps, and sun and wind-dried for the market, in a fishery fundamentally the same as when it was begun in the sixteenth century. Only the tightest bonds could have held the very existence of settlements to such a bitter, barren coast. But the egalitarianism, and disapproval of mutual aggression and exploitation, also inhibited experiment, ambition and leadership of any kind. A missionary on the coast wrote in 1906 that: 'The strenuous man, if perchance he comes their way, wins no admiration. They cannot understand pushfulness and ambitions.' Sixty years later another visitor – this time an anthropologist – described how even on the boats there was no leadership, and co-ordinated effort was only possible because each man knew what to do. In the spring hauls, 'all men shout orders and suggestions, to which no one pays attention, and effort is finally consolidated by one of several work songs, each man singing and hauling according to the rhythm of the tune.'[2]

Even today, cod trapping is extensively pursued, and Newfoundland fishermen can persist at a level of technology which remains extraordinarily basic. In June 1980 one of us visited Bauline, north of St John's; a cluster of wooden houses clutching to a steep mountainside as it falls into the open Atlantic. A crowd of men were busy at work landing salmon from small open motor boats. They face regular hundred-mile-an-hour winds and immense seas. Yet they have not even the protection of a harbour for their boats: just a landing ramp between the rocks, from which the fishermen push off, jumping in as their boat strikes the water; and every time they come in with catch it takes a winch and a dozen men to drag them to safety.

There are no examples of survival in Britain as extreme as those to be found in the Newfoundland outports, for in Britain even the remotest islands are less isolated. The closest to this is Lewis: a community held together through the twentieth century by the shadow of its own history.

The trawling ports represent the opposite solution to this dilemma. Economically the concentrated ownership of the fleets ensured that capital resources could be marshalled to provide the changing facilities needed to supply and service the boats, and market their catch. Through this power trawl-owners were also able to create a workforce, either by cannibalising other fishing communities, or by drawing on the city poor. This process underlines the vulnerability of community and family values to economic change. Fishermen who had been family boat-owners, petty entrepreneurs in a community of equals, found themselves reduced to wage-earners, proletarian labourers, one of the lowest sections of a city working class. And while socially, their new solidarity and separateness as wage-earning fishermen helped to provide a continuing workforce for the companies, economic decisions could now be made independently by a separate small group of owners, belonging to the wider business classes. This was the capitalist solution: but it does not end here. The community's economic fate is now out of its own hands. Its industrial base can be destroyed at one blow by company take-overs, transfers or sell-outs. Its ecological resources can be fished to extinction too. Yarmouth was killed by both. And the case of Aberdeen shows what can happen when the economic logic of company capitalism is able to break through the restrictions, first of the traditional moral order, and finally of communal solidarity, consuming its own workforce.

Politicians in the west in recent years have increasingly portrayed our choices as between the 'freedom' of large-scale

monopoly capitalism and the rigid social and economic control of socialist societies. Our research suggests that an alternative way forward, based on social egalitarianism on the one
hand and more diffused access to capital and resources on the
other, might be as economically effective as it is socially
appealing.

We have shown in this book how the social outcome of
technology is not predetermined. It can be used to create, or to
destroy: which, is open to choice. The latest technology does
not invariably lead towards an inexorable concentration of
economic power. The way in which it is utilised in modern
fishing is paralleled by the booming 'high technology cottage
industry' producing shoes, ceramics, motor cycles and
machine tools which emerged in the 1970s in north-central
Italy, or the de-centralised artificial textiles industry of Lyons
in which diffused artisanal innovation made the region as a
whole into a giant 'laboratory for experimentation with new
fibres'. We can see similar precedents in our own earlier
industrial history: in Sheffield cutlery, for instance, or the
Midland bicycle-makers of the turn of this century.[3] Britain
today, the first 'workshop of the world' of a hundred years
past now facing de-industrialisation, desperately needs to find
new roads forward: to foster all the true creativity which it can
for its future. Ultimately, like the question of resources, this
has to be seen as a political issue. But to be met, it will require
the recovery of a broader political vision than is offered within
the short-term perspectives of present-day party politics.

The past moulds the future: whether we like it or not, the
slate cannot be wiped entirely clean, and to pretend so is to
stumble forward in unnecessary ignorance. That moulding
takes place partly through the community and partly through
the family. Hence the history of women and children is as
central as that of men. And while history cannot provide neat
recipes, for every case is in its own way particular and unique,
there are surely lessons to be drawn from the story of Buckie in
the 1900s, and still more of Shetland: both societies which
found room to value individuality as part of their sense of
community. Of the two, the example of Shetland is the most
relevant today: for it is secular, and rooted in the nature of the
family. It suggests that it may not only be proper, but vitally

worthwhile, for adults to treat children, and men to treat women, as equal, responsible persons. And it is surely on such a foundation that we must set about the rebuilding of our own community.

If the past constrains us, it nevertheless also presents us with a simple choice: to accept or to challenge what we have been given by history. Like the fishing communities in their struggle for survival, we are all caught within the contradictions of an increasingly exploitative and in too many ways senseless world. Let us at least make sure that future generations are allowed the freedom to make that choice.

Note on methods and sources

In writing this book we have drawn, both in seeking our evidence and in constructing our interpretation, on the approaches of both social history, sociology and anthropology.

For our sources we have used a wide range of both published and unpublished material. The most relevant is indicated in the bibliography and notes which follow, and in greater length in the original manuscript, which we have deposited in the library of the University of Aberdeen. It is worth noting that among the recently published works which have been most important to us, we would especially pick out those by Tunstall, Hunter, Gray and Ennew – a sociologist, social historian, economic historian and anthropologist respectively. On the particular communities on which we have focused, there are no other publications to single out for East Anglia, Lancashire, or the Scottish north-east. For Shetland, however, there have been two substantial studies of fishing history by historical geographers, Hance Smith and Goodlad, and valuable recent research by Byron on Burra and Cohen on Whalsay, sociologist and anthropologist; while two earlier anthropologists, Vallee and Owen, also contributed to our understanding of the Western Isles. For fishing communities outside Britain we have drawn almost wholly on anthropologists and ethnologists. Less directly, we should wish to mention the influence of two powerful historical studies by sociologists, Carter and Moore, in fields close to our own.

The conventional historical manuscript evidence requires little comment. By far the largest single collection is in the Scottish Record Office, but we have also consulted documents of many different types held in the communities and elsewhere. We have again made a substantial use of national and local newspapers and printed official reports. One general conclusion which emerges is that any research too heavily based on either of these latter sources would be seriously defective. For example, the reporting by newspapers of disputes in the fishing industry has been extraordinarily irregular. Many strikes were too brief to be mentioned in local weeklies while even the most protracted might be ignored by national daily papers. Thus *The Times*, while regularly devoting several column inches to reports on fishing as a gentlemanly sport, gave no news whatever of the Hull and Grimsby strikes of the 1880s, or even of the Fleetwood strike with which our book opens.

The danger of trusting official statistics is perhaps more serious because of their deceptively superficial neatness. In fact many of the different series produced are incompatible. The 1911 census, by excluding local men fishing in other regions, only recorded 60 per cent of East Anglian fishermen. On the other hand, the more convincing figures produced by the Fishery Boards can include the double-counting of men and boats who worked in more than one port during the year. The 1913 figures, for example, give Shetland the largest steam fleet in Scotland, while in truth nearly all were visitors from elsewhere. Other official figures, like those of fish landings, can be still more arbitrary – often concocted, as oral evidence reveals, through mere guesswork by fishery officers who had no opportunity to visit the stations they were supposed to record.

We have, like many of the authors mentioned above, also depended very significantly for our evidence and interpretations on the communities themselves, both through observation and interviews. Tony Wailey is himself from Marshside; we have all worked at sea for varying periods, and as visitors participated in the social life of the communities. The ethnographer's notebook has been one of our tools. So has the interview: with some 160 men and women, both active and retired, including skippers, deckhands and enginemen from all sections of the industry, fishworkers and their families, and also merchants, salesmen and trawler-owners. These interviews were carried out between 1970 and 1980. Our methods have varied: for the East Anglian project a schedule of questions was followed systematically and every interview recorded, while for the Lancashire and Scottish interviews, notes alone were taken in roughly a quarter of cases when tape recording seemed inappropriate, and a rather more flexible 'strategic' approach to the developing focus of inquiry was used.

The strengths and limitations of the oral history interview are discussed at length in Paul Thompson's *The Voice of the Past*. We shall limit outselves here to a few points bearing directly on this study. Firstly, we have sought to ensure a range of informants in order to provide a variety of perspective in each community. In particular, we have everywhere interviewed women as well as men, and deckhands as well as skippers. This was not always easy because in many places skippers are invariably the informants suggested. Secondly, while our interviews are in this limited sense representative, they certainly do not offer a formal sample. This is why our findings are not set out here in tables. Thirdly, we should emphasise how the actual words used by people to us, their particular choice of phrases, has helped us to pinpoint attitudes in ways which would have entirely escaped the old-fashioned questionnaire survey.

The strength of oral history for a book like this is, of course, just that it does allow people to speak of their own lives in their own words. But it allows more than this. Through combining oral and documentary sources the historian can reach interpretations which neither, separately, would suggest. An account of Aberdeen from interviews alone would reveal the extent of family dislocation, but few precise details about industrial conflict. A study of newspapers would allow the reconstruction of the narrative of local strikes. But because these were reported primarily – reflecting the assumptions of the journalists of the day – as wage disputes, it was only when two forms of evidence were juxtaposed that it became apparent that a central issue had been the trawlermen's struggle to maintain a home life.

A second crucial step is to take the study of each separate community out of isolation. When a community is studied on its own, and especially when the extent of change is ignored, it may seem possible to accept the tautological explanations offered by functionalism, or even the crude one-way path suggested by the 'traditional' versus 'modern' contrast. But once different communities are compared it becomes clear that many routes are possible, and the choice between them needs to be seen against the interaction of economic and social structures and attitudes, both internal and external. For worthwhile comparison what is required is sufficient in common and sufficient difference. Fishing communities are particularly valuable in presenting sharply different social systems operating within a common technological world and an international market.

We have used the word 'choice' deliberately. It will be evident that we have brought a number of theoretical approaches to this study: in particular, on the one hand the framework offered by Marxism (and in particular some of the more recent ideas developed from Gramsci, and the theory of under-development), and on the other the counter-suggestions which have come from Weber, and more recently from the feminist movement. Not that it is necessary to view these perspectives as irremediably antagonistic: for we would insist, with Weber, that it is not our aim 'to substitute for a one-sided materialistic an equally one-sided spiritualistic causal interpretation of culture and history'. There is nothing to be gained from choosing between such crude polarities. What is needed is a subtler understanding of their mutual interaction. And as part of this much more attention needs to be given to the role of women and children in change, and to the social process of the forming of personality and attitudes, from infancy through to adulthood, both within the community and in the family. The lack of a trustworthy general theory on this point especially means that the conclusions which we draw can only be tentative.[1] But of one thing we are confident. The structures which shape the lives of communities and individuals are never so closed as to leave no space for the choices and actions which make life stories and make history. That is the final reason why we have wanted to offer here not only our own interpretations, but the voices of the people of the communities themselves.

List of informants

Fleetwood

H. Farrer (deckhand, mate and inshoreman); B. McGlachan (deckhand); J. MacIntyre (skipper); A. Williams (trimmer); R. Wilson (deckhand and inshoreman); G. Wright (inshoreman); R. Wright (inshoreman and deckhand); W. Wright (manager, Wyre Fishermen's Co-operative).

Marshside

C. Abrams (fisherman and historian); J. Ball (fisherman); B. Hargreaves (boat-builder's daughter); J. Hargreaves (upholsterer); T. Rigby (fisherman); P. 'Will' Rimmer (fisherman); H. Penn Wright (fisherman); Pluck Wright (fisherman's wife).

East Anglia★

William Balls; Edward Botwright; Mr Burrell; Harold Cook; Thomas Crisp; H. Harvey; Frederick Knights; Walter Mussett; Richard Reade; M. Sheales; Sidney Watts; Percy Westrup; Charles Wright.

★ For East Anglia, only informants cited are listed here. Tapes and transcripts of these and the Scottish interviews are held at the University of Essex.

Buckie

George Murray 'Lockie'; Zetta Doran; Mr and Mrs Flett; Bella Jappy; George and Jean Murray 'Stone'; William Cowie; Mr and Mrs William Stewart, Ianstown; George Garden; William Geddes; Joch and Lass Bruce; Alec Smith; Mr Coull; Daisy Geddes; William Stewart; John and Elsie Farquhar; Richard Anderson; Mr McNab; John Mackenzie; Mr and Mrs Henderson, Portsoy; James and Helen Slater, Portsoy.

Fraserburgh

Fred Stephen; William Whyte; Christian and James Marshall; Joe Crawford; William McKay; James Duthie; Andrew Noble; Andrew Ritchie; Lord Saltoun; Maria Gatt.

Peterhead

Peter Buchan; Bob Bruce; Bill Buchan; George Strachan; Alex Summers; John Buchan.

Lewis

Donald John Macdonald; Norman Paterson; John Morrison; Alex McLeod; Kathleen and Hugh Finlayson; William Sutherland; Katie Barr; Jessie Martin; Margaret McLeod; Mrs C. A. McLeod; Murdo Macfarlane; Alec Graham; Donald Graham; Norman Macdonald; Roddy McIver; Angus McLeod; Peter McLeod; Donald McInnes.

Scalpay

Christine Ferguson; Angus Macdonald; Norrie McLeod; Kenneth Morrison; Christina Morrison.

Barra and Vatersay

Kate Gillies; Peter Campbell; Mary Haggerty; Nan Mackinnon; Donald Campbell; Mary and Calum Johnston.

Shetland

Robert and Catherine Bairnson; Peter Henry; Mrs Laurenson; Miss Peterson; Mrs Malcolmson; William Robertson; Sinclair Mowat; Peter Moar; James Laurenson; John Graham; Mura May Burgess; Jemima Burgess; Margaret Henderson; Mrs Jacobson; Elizabeth Johnson; Dr Thomas Manson; Barbara Reid; Andrew Flaws; Andrew Moar; Robert Polson; Peter Robertson; Hugh Cuming; Magnus and Helen Anderson; John Irvine; Jimmy Henry; George Hunter; Walter Duncan; Robert Watt; Jessie Watt; Robert Irvine; Hans Smith; Alex Morrison; Edward Simpson.

Aberdeen

Bill Holland; Ted Porter; George and Edith Glasgow; Bill Mitchell Garthdee; John Fizpatrick; Mrs Norton; Mrs Lindsay; Mr and Mrs George Connell; William Mitchell; George Leiper; Robert Lees; Bert and Edith Williamson; Jeannie and Grace Craig; Richard Irvin; Dr John Leiper.

Newhaven and Granton

Mr and Mrs Ian Mitchell; W. M. Liston.

Abbreviations

AFP	*Aberdeen Free Press*
APJ	*Aberdeen Press and Journal*
BO	*Buchan Observer*
EE	*Evening Express* (Aberdeen)
F	*Fisherman*
FN	*Fishing News*
FFTOA	Fleetwood Fishing Trawler Owners Association
GH	*Glasgow Herald*
MLG	*Ministry of Labour Gazette*
NSA	*New Statistical Account*
NSFU	National Sailors and Firemen's Union of Great Britain and Ireland commonly known as National Union of Seamen
NUBF	National Union of British Fishermen
PP	Parliamentary Papers
SJS	*Scottish Journal of Sociology*
SRO	Scottish Record Office
TGWU	Transport and General Workers Union
TSA	*Third Statistical Account*

Notes

1   Fishing – a way of life?

1 Dyson, 16.

2   Fishing communities and the developing exploitation of the sea's resources

We owe the details on north Yorkshire in this chapter, and also some of the information on the introduction of steam trawling, to Peter Frank.

1 R. Gough, *Camden's Britannia*, 1806, III, 323; *Whitby Gazette*, 31 January 1885.
2 March, vol. 2, 45; Winstanley, 147; Evans, 183–6.
3 F. Buckland, Fisheries Inspector, *Encyclopaedia Britannica*, Edinburgh, 1879, IX, 249.
4 John Dawson of Newbiggin: PP 1878–9 XVII, 367.
5 PP 1882 XVII, 674; Sam Larner, c. 1959, 'Singing the Fishing, A Radio Ballad', Argo Record Company RG 502; Eperon, 1; Anson (1932), 164.
6 PP 1914 XXXI, 786; PP 1866 XVII, 123; Mackenzie, 514; Leather, 68–9; PP 1914 XXX, 493; PP 1913 XXIV, 296.
7 Miller, 12, 32, 36–7; *FN*, 2 May 1914; Anson (1930), 211; *Banffshire Advertiser* (Buckie), 27 March 1913.
8 *FN*, 12 October 1935; *APJ*, 14 September 1923; *FN*, 19 February 1921, 16 December 1933; Herring Industry Board, Third Report, 7.

3   Trade unionism and industrial conflict

1 PP 1892, 596; Wood, 83 (cf. Mitford); Rule, 401; PP 1882 XVII, 674, 768, 747.

2 Interview 3175, 25; *F*, May and October 1891; Webb Trade Union Collection, LSE, Section A, Volume XLI; Edwards (1979).

3 NSFU Executive minutes, Modern Records Centre, Warwick University: 13 April 1912.

4 *Anarchy* 86, 110; TGWU biennial reports; S. R. W. Moore; Leiper; interview 3187, 3; Eperon, 8.

5 In Faroe wage bargaining associations go back to the 1900s and in Iceland to the 1890s; preference for union members was introduced in 1938. But among Newfoundland and Nova Scotia share fishermen trade unionism was held illegal because they were classed as co-venturers.

6 SRO FS; PP 1852–3 XC, 460–3, 1860 XXXIV, 635; *Chambers Journal*, 15 May 1886, 307.

7 PP 1914 XXXI, 926–7.

8 *FN*, 7 April 1913; Gray, 161; *FN*, 21 April–23 May 1913; interview 3117, 1; *Banffshire Advertiser* (Buckie), 1 May 1913.

9 NSFU minutes, 11 January 1921.

10 *FN*, 19 June 1920; Anson (1932), 106; *FN*, 26 February 1921, 25 April 1925, 2 May 1931, 10 June 1933.

11 Interview 3139, 18; *FN*, 13–20 June 1936; SRO AF 62/1355, 1121. The only evidence of subsequent unionisation on herring boats is the TGWU's brief post-war recruitment of a 'fairly substantial' East Anglian membership (1948 report, 131).

12 Cf. Byron (1974), 147–61; Cohen (1977), 186–92; Andersen and Wadel, 99, 107; Scase and Goffee, 59–60, 67.

13 *The Times*, 1–2 April 1975.

4   Strike – the Fleetwood trawlers, 1920

1 *Fleetwood Chronicle*, 13 February 1920; interview 11; Tunstall (1962), 30.

2 *Fleetwood Chronicle*, 27 February 1920; *West Lancashire Gazette*, 23 and 27 February 1920.

3 *Fleetwood Chronicle*, 19 and 26 March 1920.

4 *West Lancashire Gazette*, 3 March 1920; *Fleetwood Chronicle*, 5 March 1920; W. W. Rostow, *The Stages of Economic Growth*, Cambridge, 1960, 60.

5 PP 1935 X, 341.

5   Community: life in the inshore village of Marshside

1 Interviews 1, 4, 8; *Southport Independent*, 16 May 1862; interview 2.
2 Census manuscripts for Marshside, 1851–71.
3 Interviews 7, 2, 8.
4 *Southport Visitor*, 20 May 1913; interviews 7, 8; Levi, 32.
5 Interview 1; North Meols Fishermen's Provident Association minutes, Southport General Library; Society of Rechabites records for Marshside, Churchtown Office, 1876–1919.
6 Hosker, 11; *Primitive Methodist Centenary Handbook*, Marshside, 1909, 9; S. Chaplin, *Durham Mining Villages*, University of Durham, 1973, 10.
7 Interview 5.
8 *Southport Directory*, Southport, 1902, 21; baptismal register, Marshside Chapel, 1861–1901; *Southport Guardian*, 27 May 1913.
9 Barron; Jackson, 11; Alderman Austin, *Southport Visitor*, 10 May 1913; Morecambe Fishermen's Association minutes, History Department, Lancaster University.
10 *Southport Visitor*, 22 May 1913; interview 6.
11 E. P. Thompson, *The Making of the English Working Class*, Harmondsworth, 1968, 326; *Manchester Guardian*, 24 May 1913; *Southport Visitor*, 27 June 1913; Matheson, 40.

6   The old ethic and the new – inshore village within a trawler port

1 Kelsall, 158–9; Johnston, 409; Ward, 11, 23; Rothwell (1975), 286.
2 Rothwell (1974), 7; *MLG*, 11 (1932), 82–3.
3 *Ownership of Trawlers*, FFTOA, Fleetwood 1927; interview 13.
4 Interview 14; Sutton, 273; interviews 16, 14.
5 Interview 15; *Fleetwood Chronicle*, 26 March 1920, 17 December 1926, 16 April 1928; *West Lancashire Gazette*, 18 November 1928.
6 Interview 14; Diary of Wyre Fishermen's Co-operative, 1927–35, Victoria Street, Fleetwood, 14 April 1927.
7 As Eric Hobsbawm remarks, 'though small-scale production renews itself at every stage of capitalist development to some extent, it does and did so on a decreasing scale and in increasing dependence on large-scale enterprise', *Labouring Men*, 1964, 279.

8 Interview 8; Wyre Fishermen's Diary, 9 October 1927; interview 6.

9 *MLG*, 11 (1932), 83; *The German Ideology*, 1965, 59.

7   The aftermath of defeat: The paradox of rebellion and organisation

1 *MLG*, 29 (1921), 26.

2 Tunstall (1962), 218; interviews 11, 9, 10, 13.

3 Kelsall, 162; interviews 12, 13; M. Service, *Report of Working Group on Indiscipline in the Fishing Industry*, 1975, 7.

4 Priestley, 362; interview 12; *Fleetwood Chronicle*, 16 July 1920, 22 January and 3 and 21 May 1926; Tunstall (1962), 175; interview 11.

5 Kelsall, 103; *Fleetwood Chronicle*, 22 November 1935; Duncan (1963), 343–4; *Fleetwood Chronicle*, 21 May 1926, 5 April 1935; TGWU General Committee Meeting minutes, Dock Street Fleetwood, 1 March and 6 July 1936, 28 September 1938.

6 A. Gramsci, *Collected Works*, Turin, 1949, III, 9.

8   The nemesis of steam capitalism

1 *Guardian*, 19 September 1979. Despite Aberdeen's oil boom, an insignificant number of fishermen have taken work in the new industry; nor is there any direct connection between the rise of oil and its decline as a fish landing port from 1970 (Hunt; Mackay and Moir).

2 Gray (1978), 166–80; Pyper.

3 SRO AF 56/1381; *FN* 19 October, 9 November 1935.

4 *FN*, 1 August 1913; interviews 3186, 1–3; 3187, 1–2.

5 Gray (1978), 180; *FN*, 4 September 1926; Richard Irvin and Sons, accounts and minutes; *TSA*, IV, 180; interview 3178, 61.

6 *FN*, 26 September 1913, 25 June 1921, 8 February 1936; interview 3174, 76; *TSA*, IV, 505.

7 *TSA*, IV, 196; *The Times*, 21 July 1969; interview 3175, 9.

8 Interviews 3178, 58, 65; 3170, 5–6, 21, 24; 3172, 14; 3171, 8.

9 SRO AF/1381; interview 3180, 9; *TSA*, IV, 192–6; Greenwood, 137ff.

10 SRO AF/1381; interview 3172, 7–8; *FN*, 28 March 1931, 14 February 1925; interviews 3171, 9–10; 3181, 6–7; 3175, 7; 3180, 9–11. For non-drinkers, to work on trawlers was 'just a torment,

they wanted drink, they were always after you for drink' (interview 3151, 1–3).

11 *FN*, 16 January 1926, 24 September 1927; *EE*, 16 and 18 November 1977; interviews, 3182, 16, 19; 3183, 1.

12 SRO AF 62/2187/1; *FN*, 28 October 1922, 24 July 1926; interview 3178, 6.

13 *FN*, 1 August 1914, 5 June and 25 September 1920; interviews 3183, 1; 3184, 1; 3172, 21; 3180, 6–8; 3182, 11; 3180, 13; 3172, 21.

14 Interviews 3174, 75, 79, 90; 3181, 3–6, 19–20; 3170, 11; 3172, 20.

15 *F*, March-September 1891; J. H. Smith, recording with Duncan, Scottish Labour History Society; *AFP*, 15–18 April 1913; SRO FS4/964; *FN*, 18–25 July 1914.

16 Interview 3178, 56; *FN*, 28 April 1923; SRO AF 56/778.

17 *FN*, 28 January, 11 and 25 February 1922; 13 and 20 January 1923; SRO AF56/778; *Fish Trades Gazette*, 17 March 1923; *Daily Mail*, 9 April 1923.

18 *FN*, 28 April 1923; *Scotsman*, 31 March, 5 and 9 April 1923; *Glasgow Herald*, 4 April 1923; *Dundee Advertiser*, 3 April 1923.

19 Gray (1978), 177; *FN*, 27 June 1914, 30 August and 6 September 1919; *AFP*, 4 September 1919.

20 *FN*, 1 November 1919, 31 July, 6 and 20 November 1919, 7 January 1922, 10 August 1935, 13 February 1937; interview 3187, 3.

9   The penetration of capital and the family boat

1 Howden; *It's Men's Lives*, Humberside Voice, 1966.

2 Gray (1967); Gray (1963); James Mitchell and Sons, accounts, Shetland county archive.

3 Scase and Goffee, 21 (cf. on Italy, Berger).

4 PP 1902 XV, 716; J. Duncan, 827, 833; *Banffshire Advertiser* (Buckie), 27 March 1913.

5 *FN*, 17 October 1913; interview 3070, 3; PP 1914 XXXI, 807, 885, 945, 802, 879.

6 PP 1914 XXXI, 888, 791; McGibbon, 203; Anson (1932), 193; *FN*, 3 November 1923, 3 May 1924; PP 1933–4 XII, 12, 22.

7 Richard Irvin and Sons, Aberdeen, Company minutes, 21 March 1911, 30 September 1912, 21 April 1931; balance sheets and assets.

8 PP 1914 XXXI, 906, 761–2, 808.

9 Interview 3154, 1–2; Byron (1974), 69, 184, 300; Löfgren (1972), 97; Brox (1963): cf. Wadel (1972), 110–11; and in a muted form in small business ashore, Scase and Goffee, 59–60.

10   Women in the fishing

1 Frank (1976); interview 3139, 5, 24, 34.
2 *FN*, 21 March 1925; interview 3176, 24; *FN*, 21 April 1913; Gorman, 23, 94–5.
3 Buchan, 6; interview 3139, 2, 18; *BO*, 12 December 1939; SRO FS 4/964; *FN*, 20 June 1914, 17 October 1931; interviews 3139, 14–16, 30; 3126, 2; *FN*, 31 December 1938.
4 SRO AF 56/1431; *FN*, 28 March 1914, 10 July 1920; PP 1906 XV, 727, 733; PP 1914 XXIX, 553; PP 1905 X, 485; *FN*, 16 May 1931; interview 3139, 18; Buchan, 9.
5 Paine, 178; Jorion, 31; Berggreen (1977, etc.); Löfgren (1979). Women are taken on as crew in Sardinia when no men are available (Mondardini, 127); and there are cases of women fishermen both in County Down, Northern Ireland (like the *She Cruiser*, coaxed by a local midwife and crewed by women who had no male earner in the family – information from Anthony Buckley) and Eire (first woman skipper at Helvik, Waterford – *Guardian*, 12 May 1982).
6 Tunstall (1962), 162; Butcher (1980), 60; Recher; Loti; information from Asbjørn Aase; Firestone, 69, 74.
7 Walter Scott (1977 edn), 246–7; Norbeck, 49; Firth, 80, 133, 144 (cf. Gulati); Christensen; Mead, 253; Persson; information from Anmarie Brockman, Birgitta Frykman and Sven Ek; Ek; on Iceland, information from Marie Johnson; Henningen; Tolosana; Lloyd.
8 Robert Goffee and Richard Scase, *Guardian*, 11 April 1980; Scase and Goffee; Forman, 114; Faris, 74–5, 87.
9 Out Skerries, information from Rex Clarke (cf. Fox, 99); Jorion; Brox (1964).

11   Luck: longshoremen, smacksmen and driftermen

1 Slater (1979), 38.
2 Interview 3003, 13. Interviews cited in this chapter are taken from sixty conducted by Trevor Lummis as Senior Research

Officer on the project on 'The Family and Community Life of East Anglian Fishermen' at the University of Essex, directed by Paul Thompson and funded by the Social Science Research Council. For the full findings, see the final report of the project, Lummis (1978) and Lummis (1981). All the informants started work as fishermen before 1914 and some as early as the 1880s. The chapter intentionally focuses on the pre-1914 period, although some of the incidents recounted took place subsequently. We are deeply appreciative of the co-operation, time and hospitality during our fieldwork which all of them gave to us.

3 Interviews 3003, 30–1; 3050, 6; 3001, 21–2.

4 Herubel, 278; interviews 3021, 28; 3014, 17.

5 Interviews, 3011, 46–8; 3005, 12–3.

6 Poggie and Gersuny; Mullen; interview 3047, 21–2; Mather, 178.

7 Interview 3014, 37: on class, see Lummis (1977); interview 3011, 45.

8 Mullen, 219; interviews 3015, 29; 3021, 54; 3014, 21; 3017, 18 and 3019, 71; 3027, 44–5.

12   The Protestant ethic, the family and the economy

1 Clark, 151; Butcher (1979), 117–120; interview 3151, 8; *Fraserburgh Herald*, 20–7 December 1921; Slater (1970), and (1979), 40–3.

2 Autograph book of Hilda Shedd, Sonia Jackson; William Owen of Maentrog, interview 186, 42–4; Marshall, 70, 78; interview 3107, 2.

3 Hugh Miller, 33–5; McIver, 201–2; McGibbon, 73–5; Flinn et al.; Smout; Cramond, 34, 48, 73;

4 Greven, 12–22, 52, 81, 269–76; for a fuller discussion of these points see Thompson (1982).

5 Interviews 118, 41; 134, 10, 22; Charles Booth, *Life and Labour of the People in London,* 1892–1903, I, 160; interview 208, 14, 32; E. H. Cooper, *The Twentieth Century Child,* 1905, 107–8.

6 Löfgren (1974) and (1978).

7 The project on 'Upper and Middle Class Families in the Early 20th Century' was funded by the Social Science Research Council, and Thea Vigne was its Research Officer; the final report was written by Paul Thompson.

8 *Etiquette for Every Day,* 1902, 297.

9 Bernstein; on Fiskebäck, information from Ole Lisberg Jensen;

Wadel (1972), 119 (cf. Brox (1963)); David Miller; Weber (1948),
321; on child-rearing in Sweden, Löfgren (1974), (1978), etc.; and
in Norway, Christiansen, Wadel (1972), 119, Park.

13   The moral order of free enterprise: Buckie

1 Hutcheson, 262; PP 1893–4 XIX, 31; Hutcheson, 64; *TSA*, X,
   100, 266–7; *Guardian*, 7 January 1980; Anson (1932), 214; PP 1905
   XIII, 735.
2 *FN*, 19 November 1938, 10–31 October 1931; interviews 3154,
   3–4; 3132, 4–5; 3101, 1.
3 Hutcheson, 20; *NSA*, XIII, 257; Slater (1979), 24–5; interview
   3117, 12; Buchan, 12.
4 *NSA*, XIII, 231; *Chambers Journal*, 22 May 1886, 329; interviews
   3130, 21; 3139, 10; McGibbon, 31; interview 3117, 29; Bertram,
   450 (requoted Anson (1930), 142, and *EE*, 11 November 1977);
   TSA, XVII, 143, VII, 74.
5 Hugh Miller, 43; *FN*, 20 February 1914; Cramond, 73; *EE*, 11
   November 1977.
6 McGibbon, 13, 54; Slater (1979), 14; SRO AF 56/1039.
7 Interviews 3103, 3; 3117, 2; 3109, 2; 3104, 5; 3118, 4; 3108, 6;
   3117, 1–3; 3101, 10; SRO AF/56/771; interview 3104, 3–4.
8 John Murray, *Handbook for Travellers in Scotland*, 1875, 352;
   interview 2020 (b. 1886), 1, 4, 38; Melvin, 10, 38.
9 PP 1914 XXXI, 871; *Banffshire Advertiser* (Buckie), 1 May 1913;
   FN, 9 May 1913.
10 PP 1914 XXXI, 870; interview 3105, 6.
11 Interviews 3110, 6; 3117, 11; Anson (1932), 186, and (1930), 202;
   FN, 19 September 1913.
12 *FN*, 19 June 1920; interviews 3108, 2, 5; 3103, 3; 3105, 5; *EE*, 8
   November 1977.
13 SRO AF 56/1039; interviews 3101, 9; 3110, 8; 3102, 2; 3108, 4,
   3104, 2.
14 Interviews 3139, 6 (from Rosehearty); 3105, 4; 3117, 6–8; 3114,
   3–4; 3113, 2–3; 3111, 4; 3117, 7.
15 Interviews 3101, 13; 3105, 6; 3108, 1–2; 3103, 7–8.
16 Interviews 3103, 9; 3105, 3; 3110, 8; 3101, 8; 3120, 1–3; 3123, 5.
17 Gray (1967), 206–7; Noble; McGibbon, 70–1; interview 3107,
   1–3.
18 Howie; Adams; Cordiner; *Chambers Journal*, 22 May 1886, 328;
   SRO FS.

19 Hutcheson, 44ff; *FN*, 22 March 1919; PP 1914 XXXI, 874; Anson (1932), 92; interviews 3110, 4; 3102, 9.

20 McGibbon, 80; SRO AF 62/1437; Adams; interviews 3136, 3; 3101, 14; 3108, 4.

21 *Guardian*, 7 January 1980; *Shorter Oxford English Dictionary*; Slater (1976), 6, and interview 3111, 3 (cf. 3117, 23; *EE*, 8 November 1977).

22 Wilson, 334–9; Adams, 10–15, 111, 22 (cf. interviews 3137 and 3153); McGibbon, 127.

14   The chiliasm of despair: Lewis

1 PP 1884 XXXII, 26, 47–8; PP 1902 LXXXIII, 383; PP 1908 LIX, 289; Owen; interview 233, 20; PP 1884 XXXII, 14, 43–4; Hope, III, 447; PP 1917–18 XIV, 462, 568, 575, 466; interviews 290, 6; 233, 18; Geddes, 78.

2 The official average of 22.15 per cent for 1964–75 must be an underestimate: Ennew, 48. The current official rate fluctuates around 30 per cent.

3 Royal Highland, 135–8; PP 1906 CIV, 717–9 (with two working in the fishing in each household); Hunter, 45; PP 1914 XXXII, 229.

4 Mackenzie; Dunlop; PP 1846 XXIII, 16; Hunter, 55.

5 Scalpay, PP 1884 XXXIV, 1174; SRO AF/256, AF/1039; interviews 3321, 3322; Martin, 200–1; Eriskay, Goodrich-Freer, 182ff; Scottish Economic Committee; AF 1030.

6 Hunter, 109; PP 1884 XXXII, 53, XXXIV, 1032; PP 1900 XIII, 114–122; Gray (1973).

7 Interview 3304, 25; PP 1884 XXXII, 16; W. A. Smith, 39–44, 70–1; Wolf, 55; PP 1914 XXI, 835–6.

8 Nicolson, 57, 86ff, 147, 161ff; *FN* 21–8 June 1919.

9 Interview 3314, 1; SRO AF 1030, AF 56/799 (John Mackay of Timsgarry); interview 3308, 7–9; Geddes, 306; AF 56/1243; Ennew, 34–8.

10 Hugh Miller, 8; interviews 233, 22; 290, 38–9; Ian Carter, Ruskin History Workshop, 1 December 1979; Ennew, 24; *Scotsman*, 1 July 1919; interviews 3310, 5; 3309, 15; 3308, 15–17; SRO AF 67/56.

11 Interviews 3312, 1; 294, 25–8; Ennew, 67–71; Uig Free Kirk, 11 July 1971.

12 Interview 233, 15; Vallee (1955); *Stornoway Gazette*, 'The Men', 12 June 1924; Geddes, 211; PP 1902 LXXXIII, 384; interview 233, 34–5.

13 Smout; interview 288, 49; W. A. Smith, 79–89; Goodrich-Freer, 323; Beckwith, 171; interview 3304, 28; *Stornoway Gazette*, 6 March 1924; Whittet; Dight.

14 Interviews 233, 15; 3301, 1; 3303, 1; 3307, 13.

15 Interviews 233, 28; 3304, 31; 3307, 12–13; 3306, 22; 290, 9; 3307, 23.

16 PP 1912–13 CXX; Barvas Rent Books, Stornoway public library; Ennew, 17–19; Mewett (1980), 200–6 (for three villages, 1910–37, 33 men and 6 women succeed).

17 W. A. Smith, 74, 90; PP 1902 LXXXIII, 383–4; Scottish Housing Commission *Evidence*, I, 443; interviews 233, 7–9; 294, 19; 3306, 8; 3310, 20; 3316, 2; 3304, 25, 67; cf. Ennew, 8, Caird and Moisley.

18 Goodrich-Freer, 325; interview 3312, 2; Nancy Pawson and Revd Murdo McRitchie, 'The Last Stronghold of Protestantism', BBC TV 21 January 1979; interview 3312, 1–2; Macdonald, 44.

19 W. A. Smith, 47; interviews 290, 40; 3313, 1–4.

20 Goodrich-Freer, SRO AF 56/1030; interviews 3321, 1–2; 3323, 1; 3322, 2; 3323, 2; information from Morag McLeod.

21 Goodrich-Freer, 361; Scottish Housing Commission *Evidence*, I, 321; SRO AF 62/1694, AF 56/1030; cf. Caird and Moisley.

22 Interviews 3307, 8–9; 3308, 1–2; 3302, 1; cf. 3310, 20, 3309, 12, Owen, 43.

23 Paterson; Educational Institute of Scotland, *Proceedings*, 1911–12, *Report by Special Commission on the Conditions under which the work of Education is carried on in the Island of Lewis*, Edinburgh 1912; *Stornoway Gazette*, 21 January 1927; interview 3308, 24–8. Macmillan is remembered as a crofter-socialist, although he was an Edinburgh graduate and his father an engineer.

24 Webb Trade Union Collection, Section C, Vol. 88, V, London School of Economics; interviews 3303, 1; 3311, 1; 3304, 55; SRO FS.

25 Hunter, 175, 194, 200; Shawbost School Museum; PP 1921 VIII, 87; PP 1928 XI.

26 Interviews 3308, 7–8; 3309, 17; Nicolson, 123ff, 152; Hunter, 199–202; Revd Murdo McRitchie, BBC TV, 21 January 1979.

15   A choice of destiny

1 Interview 3208, 12; Royal Highland, 135; *Shetland Times*, 17 February 1906.

2 PP 1884 XXXII, 28; interview 207, 77; Shaw; B. Smith (1979).

3 *Shetland Times*, 31 August 1889; Ployen, 38–9; Halcrow, 70; Goodlad (1971); H. D. Smith (1972) *Shetland Times*, 12 October 1889; Royal Highland, 135–8; Halcrow, 100–2, 124.

4 *Shetland Times*, 5 October 1889; interviews 207, 80; 3205, 98; PP 1872 XXXV, 239, 245; PP 1884 XXXII, 217, XXXIV, 1226; *Shetland Times*, 31 August, 7 and 28 September 1889. Shetland had five estates of over 20,000 acres and none over 50,000, a very low proportion for Scotland; and no resident landowner with an income of over £3000, the criterion for John Bateman, *Great Landowners of Great Britain*, 1883.

5 Heineberg; Graham; Cowie; MacGillivray; Cohen (1979); Scottish Housing Commission *Evidence*, I, 483, 572, 491; interviews 3205, 101, 93–5; 157, 13; 3205, 5; 174, 44.

6 Jamieson, 41; PP 1908 LIX, 16, 268; Manson, 21, 66, 177–8.

7 Yell: Caird and Coull, 4 (in 1961–3 unemployment here ranged from 18 to 46 per cent).

8 Manson, 167–8; *FN*, 6 June 1914, 10 May 1919; SRO AF 56/1266.

9 *Shetland News*, 20 September 1913.

10 PP 1917–18 XIV, 550; interview 3210, 4–5; on Burra, Byron (1974); H. D. Smith (1973); Goodlad, 219, 222; PP 1914 XXXI, 754; *Shetland Times*, 7 April and 12 May 1906; interview 3208, 8; *FN*, 16 May 1931; interview 3207, 9–10, 4–5; *Shetland News*, 3 February 1938.

11 Goodlad, 222; A. P. Cohen (1977, etc.); PP 1872 XXXV, 238, 241; *Manson's Shetland Almanac*, Lerwick, 1935.

12 Shetland Development Council, *Report on the Fisheries of Shetland*, Lerwick, 1958, 8, 10–11; *Guardian*, 2 April 1980; A. F. Cohen, 9; Jamieson, 33; A. P. Cohen (1977b) and (1978). The pessimism of Goodlad (1972) thus proved unfounded.

13 Interviews, 3210, 29; 3207, 9; 3206, 30, 10; 3208, 13; A. F. Cohen, 15, 12; Byron (1975), 154–7; interview 3204, 16; A. P. Cohen (1977a), 186–92, (1979), 261.

14 A. P. Cohen (1977b), 4, 7; interviews 3213, 2; 207, 77–8.

15 Hope et al., III, 488. The mean number of children in the families in which our informants were reared was four, as opposed to six in Lewis. Family size has since fallen in both areas, but remains higher in Lewis (cf. Ennew, 79).

16 Interviews 3205, 22; 3219, 6; 159, 16–20; 164, 8; Goffman, 229, 273; interviews 159, 18; 3206, 24; 164, 8; 3223, 8.

17 Shetland Folk Society, 'Daily Round in Shetland Sixty Years Ago', c. 1970; interviews 3205, 91–2, 115, 97; 157, 20; 156, 27; 3214, 1; 3206, 29; 3219, 5; 3218, 3; 166, 11; 207, 20; 159, 34; 3207, 18; PP 1884 XXXII, 217.

18 Interview 171, 30; Livingstone, 171, 97; interview 3205, 105; Jamieson, 39; PP 1912–13 CXX; *Shetland Times*, 9 November 1889.
19 Interviews 3211, 13; 159, 15; 164, 4, 27, 44; 3205, 104; PP 1914 XXXII, 135; interviews 3206, 16–17, 12; 3208, 11.
20 Interviews 164, 30; 171, 20, 14; 207, 42; 174, 37; 157, 34; 3207, 5; 3202, 7; Heineberg, 51; interview 3204, 59.
21 Boyd, 122; Smout; Hope, III, 484; interviews 158, 73; 207, 69, 70–1; 3202, 22; 3206, 21; Cowie, 99; interview 166, 26.
22 Reid, 31; interviews 3210, 17; 3205, 95; 3204, 19; but cf. the growing contemporary problem, J. W. G. Wills in Button, 32; Livingstone, 153; interview 3203, 10.
23 Interviews 157, 39; 3206, 27–8; 3205, 102–4; 3207, 18.
24 Interview 3202, 13; Jamieson, 109–10; Johnson, 88, 175; interview 157, 30–1.
25 *EE*, 15 April 1892; *Shetland Times*, 23 April and 7 May 1892, 7–14 September and 26 October 1889; Peter Jamieson papers, Shetland record office; interview 3210, 27; Jamieson, 154; Coull, Goodlad and Sheves.

16   Ahead

1 West. The Shetland Plan and the TGWU proposals (*Fishing, the Way Forward*, 1980) are for local development plans within the Common Market, for which there is some support in Brussels; but they could only be fully developed with the independent control of resources secured by Faroe, Norway, Iceland and Canada.
2 Byron (1974), 147ff; Revd J. Lumsden, *The Skipper Parson on the Bays and Barrens of Newfoundland*, Toronto, 1906, 97; Faris, 103.
3 Charles Sabel and Jonathan Zeitlin, 'Historical Alternatives to Mass Production', working paper, October 1981.

Note on method and sources

1 Weber (1930), 183. For a fuller discussion of theoretical issues, Thompson (1982).

Select bibliography

Place of publication of books is London unless otherwise stated.

Adams, Norman, *Goodbye, Beloved Brethren*, Aberdeen, 1972.

Aflalo, F. G., *The Sea Fishing Industry of England and Wales*, Stanford, 1904.

Andersen, R., 'The "Count" and the "Share": offshore fishermen and changing incentives', in R. J. Preston (ed.), *Proceedings of the Fourth Annual Congress (1977) of the Canadian Ethnological Society*, Ottawa, 1978, 27–43.

Andersen, R. (ed.), *North Atlantic Maritime Cultures; Anthropological Essays on Changing Adaptions*, The Hague, 1979.

Andersen, Raoul and Wadel, C. (eds), *North Atlantic Fishermen*, St John's, Newfoundland, 1972.

Anderson, Michael, *Approaches to the History of the Western Family 1500–1914*, 1980.

Anson, P. F., *Fishing Boats and Fisher Folk on the East Coast of Scotland*, 1930.

Anson, P. F., *Fishermen and Fishing Ways*, 1932.

Aubert, V. (ed.), *The Hidden Society*, Ottawa, 1965.

Aubert, V. and Arner, O., 'On the Social Structure of the Ship', *Acta Sociologica*, 3 (1977).

Baks, C. and Postel-Coster, E., 'Fishing Communities on the Scottish East Coast', in M. E. Smith (1977).

Barron, J., *A History of the Ribble Navigation from Preston to the Sea*, Preston, 1938.

Barry III, H., Child, I. L. and Bacon, M. K., 'Relation of Child Training to Subsistence Economy', *American Anthropologist*, 61 (1959), 51–63.

Beckwith, Lillian, *The Sea for Breakfast*, 1961.

Berger, S., 'The Uses of the Traditional Sector in Italy: Why Declining Classes Survive', in F. Bechhofer and B. Elliott (eds), *The Petite Bourgeoisie: Comparative Studies of the Uneasy Stratum*, 1981.

Berggreen, Brit, 'Maritim etnologi, sjofartssamfunn og kvinner', *Dugnad*, 2 (1977), 7–16.

Berggreen, B., 'Kvinner i maritime naeringar', *Syn og Segn*, 3 (1979), 163–76.

Berggreen, B., 'Kystens kvinner–kystens bønder', *Norges kultur-historie*, V (1980), 75–92.

Berggreen, B., 'Skipet som hjem: kvinner og barn på langfatt', manuscript.

Bernstein, Basil, 'A Socio-Linguistic Approach to Socialisation: with Some Reference to Educability', *Human Context*, 2 (1970), 18–46.

Bertram, James, *The Harvest of the Sea: A Contribution to the Natural and Economic History of the British Food Fishes*, 1865.

Black, W. A., 'The Labrador Floater Fishery', *Annals of the Association of American Geographers*, 1960, 267–95.

Bochel, M., *'Dear Gremista', the Story of Nairn Fisher Girls at the Gutting*, National Museum of Antiquities, Edinburgh, 1979.

Boswell, David, *Sea Fishing Apprentices of Grimsby*, Grimsby Public Libraries, 1974.

Boyd, K. M., *Scottish Church Attitudes to Sex, Marriage and the Family, 1850–1914*, Edinburgh, 1980.

Brown, G. W. and Harris, T., *Social Origins of Depression: A Study of Psychiatric Disorder in Women*, 1978.

Brox, Ottar, 'Three Types of North Norwegian Entrepreneurship', in F. Barth (ed.), *The Role of the Entrepreneur in Social Change in Northern Norway*, Bergen, 1963.

Brox, O., 'Natural Conditions, Inheritance and Marriage in a North Norwegian Fjord', *Folk*, 6,1 (1964), 35–45.

Buchan, Margaret, 'Social Organisation of Fisher-girls', conference paper, Aberdeen, June 1977.

Buckley, K. D., *Trade Unionism in Aberdeen*, Edinburgh, 1955.

Butcher, David, *The Driftermen*, Reading, 1979.

Butcher, D., *The Trawlermen*, Reading, 1980.

Button, John, *The Shetland Way of Oil*, Sandwick, 1976.

Byron, R. F., 'Burra Fishermen: The Social Organisation of Work in a Shetland Community', London, PhD, 1974.

Byron, R. F., 'Economic Functions of Kinship Values in Family Businesses: Fishing Crews in North Atlantic Communities', *Sociology and Social Research*, 60 (1975) 147–60.

Caird, J. B., and Coull, J. R., *Report on the Survey of the Island of Yell*, Lerwick, 1964.

Caird, J. B. and Moisley, H. A., 'Leadership and Innovation in the Crofting Communities of the Outer Hebrides', *Sociological Review*, 9 (1961), 85–102.

Carter, Ian, *Farm Life in Northeast Scotland 1840–1914*, 1979.

Carwardine, R., *Transatlantic Revivalism: Popular Evangelicism in Britain and America, 1790–1865*, 1978.

Christensen, J. B., 'Motor Power and Woman Power: Technological and Economic Change among the Fanti Fishermen of Ghana', in M. E. Smith (1977).

Christiansen, A. L. G., 'Barndomsminner som kilder', *Tidsskrift for samfunnsforsning*, 5–6 (1979), 631–8.

Church, Roy, 'Family and Failure', in B. Supple (ed.), *Essays in British Business History*, Oxford, 1977.

Clark, David, *Between Pulpit and Pew: Folk Religion in a North Yorkshire Fishing Village*, Cambridge, 1982.

Cluer, Andrew, *Walkin' the Mat*, Aberdeen, 1976.

Cohen, A. F., *A Pilot Study of Technological Change and Authority Structure in a Shetland Fishery*, SSRC Final Report HR 2612, 1974.

Cohen, Anthony P., 'For a Political Ethnography of Everyday life: Sketches from Whalsay, Shetland', *Ethnos* 4 (1977a), 186–92 (a).

Cohen, A. P., '"The Same-But Different": The Allocation of Identity in Whalsay, Shetland', paper to 4th International Seminar on Marginal Regions, Aberdeen 1977 (b).

Cohen, A. P., 'Oil and the Cultural Account: Reflections on a Shetland Community', *SJS*, 3 (1978), 132–41.

Cohen, A. P., 'The Whalsay Croft: Traditional Work and Customary Identity in Modern Times', in S. Wallman (ed.), *Social Anthropology of Work*, 1979, 249–67.

Collier, Adam, *The Crofting Problem*, 1945.

Cordiner, James, *Fragments from the Past*, 1961.

Coull, J. R., 'Fishing in the North East of Scotland before 1800', *Scottish Studies*, 13 (1969).

Coull, J. R., *Crofter-Fishermen in Norway and Scotland*, Aberdeen, 1971.

Coull, J. R., *The Fisheries of Europe: An Economic Geography*, 1972.

Coull, J. R., Goodlad, J. H. and Sheves, G. T., *The Fisheries in the Shetland Area, A Study in Conservation and Development*, White Fish Authority, Edinburgh, 1979.

Cowie, Robert, *Shetland Descriptive and Historical*, Aberdeen, 1871, 1896, etc.

Cramond, William, *Illegitimacy in Banffshire*, Banff, 1888.

Cutting, C. L., *Fish Saving: A History of Fish Processing from Ancient to Modern Times*, 1955.

Czerkawska, Catherine, *Fisherfolk of Carrick*, Glasgow, 1975.

Dight, S. E., *Scottish Drinking Habits*, 1976.

Duncan, Joseph, 'Capitalism and the Scots Fishermen', *Socialist Review*, 2, 1 (1909).

Duncan, P., 'Conflict and Co-operation amongst Trawlermen', *British Journal of Industrial Relations*, 1 (1963): 331–47.

Dunlop, Jean, *The British Fisheries Society, 1786–1893*, Edinburgh, 1978.

Dyson, John, *Business in Great Waters: the Story of British Fishermen*, 1977.

Edwards, P. J., 'Humberside Fishermen 1880–1938, Aspects of a Labour History,' paper 1979.

Edwards, P. J. and Marshall, J., 'Sources of Conflict and Community in the Trawling Industries of Hull and Grimsby between the Wars', *Oral History*, 5, 1 (1977), 97–121.

Ek, Sven B., *Borstahusen- ett fiskeläges uppgång och fall*, Landskrona, 1980.

Elégoët, Fañch, *L'homme et la mer*, Plouguerneau, 1979.

Ennew, Judith, *The Western Isles Today*, Cambridge, 1980.

Eperon, Arthur, *Adam was a Fisherman*, 1961.

Evans, George Ewart, *The Days That We Have Seen*, 1975.

Faris, James, *Cat Harbour: A Newfoundland Fishing Settlement*, St John's, 1966.

Festing, Sally, *Fishermen, A Community Living from the Sea*, Newton Abbot, 1977.

Firestone, Melvin, *Brothers and Rivals: Patrilocality in Savage Cove*, St John's, 1967.

Firth, Raymond, *Malay Fishermen: Their Peasant Economy*, 1946.

Flinn M. W. et al., *Scottish Population History from the 17th Century to the 1930s*, Cambridge, 1977.

Forman, Shepherd, *The Raft Fishermen*, 1970 (Brazil).

Fox, Robin, *The Tory Islanders: A People of the Celtic Fringe*, 1978.

Frank, Peter, 'Women's Work in the Yorkshire Inshore Fishing Industry', *Oral History*, 4, 1 (1976), 57–72.

Frank, Peter, 'Fisherfolk: A Social History of the Yorkshire Inshore Fishing Community', manuscript 1978.

Geddes, Arthur, *The Isles of Lewis and Harris*, Edinburgh, 1955.

Geistdoerfer, Aliette, 'Connaissances, techniques et patrimoine maritime', *Etudes rurales*, 65 (1977), 47–8.

Goffman, Erving, 'Communication Conduct in an Island Community', Chicago, PhD, 1953.

Goodlad, C. A., *Shetland Fishing Saga*, Lerwick, 1971.

Goodlad, C. A., 'Old and Trusted, New and Unknown: Technological confrontation in the Shetland herring industry', in Andersen and Wadel (1972), 61–81.

Goodrich-Freer, A., *Outer Isles*, 1902.

Gorman, John, *To Build Jerusalem: A Photographic Remembrance of British Working Class Life, 1875–1950*, 1980.

Graham, John, 'Social Changes during the Last Quinquennium', paper 1969.

Gray, Malcolm, 'Fishing Villages 1750–1880', in British Association, *The North-East of Scotland*, Aberdeen, 1963.

Gray, M., 'Organisation and Growth in the East-Coast Herring Fishery, 1800–1885', in P. Payne (ed.), *Studies in Scottish Business History*, 1967, 187–216.

Gray, M., 'Crofting and Fishing in the North-west Highlands', *Northern Scotland*, 1 (1973), 89–114.

Gray, M., 'The Fishing Industry', in D. Ommand (ed.), *The Moray Book*, 1976.

Gray, M., *The Fishing Industries of Scotland, 1790–1914: a study in regional adaptation*, Oxford, 1978.

Greenwood, Walter, *How the Other Man Lives*, 1939.

Greven, Philip, *The Protestant Temperament: Patterns of Child-Rearing, Religious Experience and the Self in Early America*, New York, 1977.

Gulati, Leela, *Profiles in Female Poverty: A Study of Five Poor Working Women in Kerala*, Oxford, 1982.

Halcrow, Capt. A., *The Sail Fishermen of Shetland and their Norse and Dutch Forerunners*, Lerwick, 1950.

Heineberg, Heinz (trans. Anne Menzies), *Changes in the Economic-Geographical Structure of the Shetland Islands*, Inverness, 1973.

Henderson, Tom, 'The Half Deckers: A Story of Success and Failure', in J. Graham and J. Tait (eds), *Shetland Folk Book*, VII, Lerwick, 1981, 12–21.

Henningen, Marie-Luisa Rey, 'Galicia, State of Women', *Spare Rib*, 70 (1978), 27–9.

Herubel, M. A., *Sea Fisheries, Their Treasures and Toilers*, 1912.

Highet, John, 'Scottish Religious Adherence', *British Journal of Sociology*, 4 (1953), 149–76.

Horobin, G. W., 'Community and Occupation in the Hull Fishing Industry', *British Journal of Sociology* 8 (1957), 343–55.

Hosker, A., *The Fishing Industry of North Meols*, Birkdale, 1953.

Hope, E. W., Mackenzie, W. L. et al., *Report on the Physical Welfare of Mothers and Children*, Dunfermline, 1917.

Howden, Peter, 'The Hull Fishermen and Worker's Control', *Anarchy*, 86 (1968).

Howie, Revd Robert, *The Churches and the Churchless in Scotland*, Glasgow, 1893.

Hunt, Deirdre, 'The Sociology of Development: Its Relevance to Aberdeen', *SJS* 1 (1976): 137–54.

Hunter, James, *The Making of the Crofting Community*, Edinburgh, 1976.

Hutcheson, George, *Days of Yore: or, Buckie and District in the Past*, Buckie, 1887.

Innis, H. A., *The Cod Fisheries: The History of an International Economy*, New Haven, 1940.

Jackson, A. E., *Accretion in the Ribble Estuary*, Southport, 1936.

Jamieson, Peter, *Letters on Shetland*, Edinburgh, 1949.

Jenkins, J. T., *The Sea Fisheries*, 1920.

Johnson, L., *Laurence Williamson of Mid Yell*, Lerwick, 1971.

Johnston, J., 'Sea Fisheries of Lancashire', *Victoria County History, Lancashire*, 2, 1908.

Jorion, Paul, 'L'ordre moral dans une petite île de Bretagne', *Etudes rurales*, 67 (1977), 35–45.

Kanter, R. M., 'Families, Family Processes, and Economic Life: Towards Systematic Analysis of Social Historical Research', *American Journal of Sociology*, 84, Supplement, 'Turning Points: Historical and Sociological Essays on the Family'; 316–39.

Kasdan, Leonard, 'Family Structure, Migration and the Entrepreneur', *Comparative Studies in Society and History*, VII (1965), 345–57.

Kelsall, R. K., 'The White Fish Industry, Fleetwood', in M. P. Fogarty (ed.), *Further Studies in Industrial Organisation*, 1948.

Leather, John, *The Northseamen, the Story of the Fishermen, Yachtsmen and Shipbuilders of the Colne and Blackwater Rivers*, Lavenham, 1971.

Leiper, J., 'Medical Services in Fishing Fleets', in J. S. Grant, L. G. Norman and R. M. Heggie, *Medical Services in Transport*, 1966.

Levi, L., 'The Economic Condition of Fishermen', *Fisheries Exhibition Literature*, IV, 1 (1884), 149–76.

Levi, L., *Wages and Earnings of the Working Classes*, 1885.

Leyton, E., *The One Blood: Kinship and Class in an Irish Village*, St John's, 1975.

Livingstone, W. P., *Shetland and the Shetlanders*, 1947.

Lloyd, Theodora, 'The Libbers of Llanon', *Western Mail*, 30 June 1978.

Löfgren, Orvar, 'Resource Management and Family Firms: Swedish West Coast Fishermen', in Andersen and Wadel (1972), 83–109.

Löfgren, O., 'Family and Household among Scandinavian Peasants: An Exploratory Essay', *Ethnologia Scandinavica*, 1974, 17–52.

Löfgren, O., 'Maritime Hunters in Industrial Society: The Transformation of a Swedish Fishing Community 1800–1970', English summary to *Fångstmän in industrisamhället*, Lund, 1977.

Löfgren, O., 'The Potato People: Household Economy and Family Patterns among the Rural Proletariat in Nineteenth Century Sweden', in S. Akerman, H. C. Johansen and D. Gaunt (eds), *Chance and Change, Social and Economic Studies in Historical Demography in the Baltic area*, Odense, 1978, 95–106.

Löfgren, O., 'Marine Ecotypes in Preindustrial Sweden: a Comparative Discussion of Swedish Peasant Fishermen', in Andersen (1979).

Löfgren, O., 'The Making of a Fisherman: the Social Context of Socialisation in a Swedish Fishing Community', mimeograph, n.d.

Loti, Pierre, *An Iceland Fisherman*, 1888.

Lummis, Trevor, 'The Occupational Community of East Anglian Fishermen', *British Journal of Sociology*, 28, 1 (1977), 51–74.

Lummis, T., *The Family and Community Life of East Anglian Fishermen*, SSRC final report HR 2656, 1978.

Lummis, T., 'The East Anglian Fishermen, 1880–1914', Essex, PhD 1981.

McClelland, David C., *The Achieving Society*, New York, 1961.

Macdonald, Norman, *Calum Tod*, Inverness, 1976.

Macfarlane, Alan, *The Origins of English Individualism: The Family, Property and Social Transition*, Oxford, 1978.

Macfarlane, N. C., *The 'Men' of the Lews*, 1924.

McGibbon, John, *The Fisherfolk of Buchan: A True Story of Peterhead*, 1922.

MacGillivray, J., 'Agriculture in Shetland', *Scottish Journal of Agriculture*, III (1920), 414–28.

McIver, Revd D., *An Old Time Fishing Town: Eyemouth*, Greenock, 1906.

Mackay, G. A. and Moir, A. C., *North Sea Oil and the Aberdeen Economy*, Aberdeen, 1980.

Mackenzie, W. C., *History of the Outer Hebrides*, 1903.

Mackinlay, D., *The Island of Lews and its Fishermen-Crofters*, 1878.

Manson, Thomas, *Lerwick in the Last Half Century*, Lerwick, 1923.

March, E. J., *Inshore Craft of Great Britain in the Days of Sail and Oar*, Newton Abbot, 1978.

Marshall, Gordon, *Presbyteries and Profits: Calvinism and the development of capitalism in Scotland*, Oxford, 1980.

Martin, Angus, *The Ring-Net Fishermen*, Edinburgh, 1981.

Mather, E. J., *Nor'ard of the Dogger*, 1887.

Matheson, Colin, *Wales and the Sea Fisheries*, Cardiff, 1929.

Mead, Margaret, *Sex and Temperament in Three Primitive Societies*, New York, 1935.

Melvin, W. R., *Caller Herring: An Original Operatic Drama of Scottish Fisherfolk*, Aberdeen, 1913.

Mewett, Peter G., 'Occupational Pluralism in Crofting: The Influence of Non-croft Work on the Patterns of Agriculture in the Isle of Lewis since about 1950', *Scottish Journal of Sociology*, 2, 1 (1977), 31–49.

Mewett, P. G., 'Social Change and Migration from Lewis', Aberdeen, PhD, 1980.

Miller, David, 'Presbyterianism and "Modernization" in Ulster', *Past and Present*, 80 (1978), 66–90.

Miller, Hugh, *Letters on the Herring Fishing in the Moray Firth*, Inverness, 1829.

Mitchell, A. R., 'European Fisheries in Early Modern History', in E. E. Rich and C. Wilson (eds), *Cambridge Economic History of Europe*, V, 1977, 134–84.

Mitford, William, *Lovely She Goes!*, 1969.

Mondardini, Gabriella, *Villaggi di Pescatori in Sardegna*, Sassari, 1981.

Moore, Robert, *Pitmen, Preachers and Politics: The Effects of Methodism in a Durham Mining Community*, 1974.

Moore, S. R. W., 'The Morality and Morbidity of Deep Sea Fishermen Sailing from Grimsby in One Year', *British Journal of Industrial Medicine*, 26 (1969), 25–46.

Mullen, Patrick B., 'The Function of Magic Folk Belief among Texas Coastal Fishermen', *Journal of American Folklore*, 82 (1969), 214–25.

New Statistical Account of Scotland, Edinburgh 1845 *(NSA)*.

Nicolson, Nigel, *Lord of the Isles: Lord Leverhulme in the Hebrides*, 1960.

Noall, Cyril, *Cornish Seines and Seiners: A History of the Pilchard Industry*, Truro, 1972.

Noble, Andrew, 'Fishing Recollections in North East Scotland', conference paper, Edinburgh, 1977.

Norbeck, Edward, *Takashima, a Japanese Fishing Community*, Salt Lake City, 1954.

Owen, Trevor, 'Some Aspects of the Social Life of a Crofting Community in North Uist', Edinburgh, PhD, 1953.

Paine, Robert, *Coast Lapp Society II*, Tromsø, 1965.

Park, George, 'Sons and Lovers', *Ethnology*, 1, 2 (1962), 412–23.

Paterson, Kenneth M., 'History of Education in the Island of Lewis with Particular Reference to the 19th Century', Glasgow, MEd 1970.

Persson, Yvonne, 'Evaluations and Roles at the Island of Ockerö', *Fataburen*, 1977.

Ployen, Christian (trans. C. Spence), *Reminiscences of a Voyage to Shetland, Orkney and Scotland in the summer of 1839*, Lerwick, 1894.

Poggie, J. J. Jnr and Gersuny, C., 'Risk and Ritual: An Interpretation of Fishermen's Folklore in a New England Community', *Journal of American Folklore*, 85 (1972), 66–72.

Priestley, J. B., *English Journey*, 1934.

Pyper, William, *History of a Great Industry: 21 Years of Trawling*, Dundee, 1903.

Recher, Jean, *Le Grand Métier: Journal d'un capitaine de pêche de Fécamp*, Paris, 1977.

Reid, J. T., *Art Rambles in Shetland*, Edinburgh, 1869.

Rothwell, Catherine, *The Port*, Fleetwood, 1974.

Rothwell, C., 'A History of Fleetwood on Wyre 1884–1934', Fleetwood FLA, 1975.

Royal Highland and Agricultural Society of Scotland, *Report on the Present State of Agriculture of Scotland*, Edinburgh, 1878.

Rule, John, 'The Smacksmen of the North Sea: Labour Recruitment and Exploitation in British Deep Sea Fishing, 1850–90', *International Review of Social History*, 21 (1976), 383–411.

Scase, R. and Goffee, R., *The Real World of the Small Business Owner*, 1980.

Schilling, R. S. F., 'Trawler Fishing, An Extreme Occupation', *Proceedings of the Royal Society of Medicine*, 59 (1966).

Scott, Joan W. and Tilly, Louise A., 'Women's Work and the Family in 19th Century Europe', *Comparative Studies in Society and History*, XVII (1975), 36–64.

Scott, Sir Walter, *The Antiquary*, Edinburgh, 1819.

Scottish Economic Committee, *The Highlands and Islands of Scotland*, 1938.

Shaw, Frances, *The Northern and Western Isles of Scotland: Their Economy and Society in the 17th century*, Edinburgh, 1980.

Sider, G. M., 'The Ties that Bind: Culture and Agriculture, Property and Propriety in the Newfoundland Village Fishery', *Social History*, 5 (1980), 1–39.

Slater, James, *The Voyage*, Lytham St Annes, 1970.

Slater, James, *Revival Reminiscences*, 1976.

Slater, James, *A Seafaring Saga*, Fleetwood, 1979.

Smith, Brian, 'Shetland Archives and Sources of Shetland History', *History Workshop*, 4 (1977), 203–17.

Smith, Brian, '"Lairds" and "Improvement" in 17th and 18th century Shetland', in T. Devine (ed.), *Lairds and Improvement in the Scotland of the Enlightenment*, Glasgow, 1979, 11–20.

Smith, Hance D., 'The Historical Geography of Trade in the Shetland Islands, 1500–1914', Aberdeen, PhD, 1972.

Smith, H. D., 'The Development of Shetland Fisheries and Fishing Communities', in P. H. Fricke (ed.), *Seafarer and Community*, 1973.

Smith, M. E. (ed.), *Those Who Live from the Sea*, St Paul, 1977.

Smith, Revd W. Anderson, *Lewsiana: or Life in the Outer Hebrides*, 1875.

Smout, T. C., 'Aspects of Sexual Behaviour in 19th Century Scotland', in A. A. Maclaren (ed.), *Social Class in Scotland, Past and Present*, Edinburgh, 1976.

Stoklund, Bjarne, 'Okologisk tilpasning i et Dansk osamfund', in A. Daum and O. Löfgren, *Ekologi och Kultur*, Copenhagen, 1971, 35–40.

Sutton, J., 'Early Fleetwood 1835–1847', Lancaster, MLitt, 1972.

Third Statistical Account (H. Mackenzie et al eds.), Edinburgh 1951 etc. (*TSA*).

Thompson, Paul, *The Edwardians, The Remaking of British Society*, 1975.

Thompson, Paul, *The Voice of the Past: Oral History*, Oxford, 1978.

Thompson, Paul, 'Life Histories and the Analysis of Social Change', in Daniel Bertaux (ed.), *Biography and Society; the Life History Approach in the Social Sciences*, 1981, 289–306.

Thompson, Paul, 'Family, Economy and Ideology: the Role of Women and Children in Change', paper, World Congress of Sociology, Mexico City, 1982.

Thomson, David B., *The Seine Net: Its Origins, Evolution and Use*, 1969.

Tolosana, Carmelo Lison, *Antropologia social de Galicia*, Madrid, 1971.

Tunstall, Jeremy, *The Fishermen: The Sociology of an Extreme Occupation*, 1962.

Tunstall, Jeremy, *Fish: An Antiquated Industry*, 1968.

Vallee, F. G., 'Social Structure and Organisation in a Hebridean Community' (Barra), Edinburgh, PhD, 1954.

Vallee, F. G., 'Burial and Mourning Customs in a Hebridean Community', *Journal of the Royal Anthropological Institute*, 85 (1955), 119–30.

Wadel, Cato, 'Capitalisation and Ownership: the Persistence of Fishermen-Ownership in the Norwegian Herring Industry', in Andersen and Wadel (1972), 104–19.

Wadel, Cato, *Capital Management under Extreme Uncertainty*, Tromsø, 1973.

Wallace, F. W., *Blue Water: A Tale of the Deep Sea Fishermen*, 1914 (Nova Scotia).

Ward, W., *A Short History of the Trawling Industry of Fleetwood*, Fleetwood, 1974.

Weber, Max (trans. T. Parsons), *The Protestant Ethic and the Spirit of Capitalism*, 1930.

Weber, Max, 'The Protestant Sects and the Spirit of Capitalism', in H. H. Gerth and C. W. Mills, *From Max Weber: Essays in Sociology*, 1948, 302–22.

West, John F., *Faroe: The Emergence of a Nation*, 1972.

Whitaker, Ian, 'Seafarer and Community: Aspects of Organisation in Maritime Communities', paper Cardiff (UWIST) 1972.

White Fish Authority, *The Fisheries of the European Community*, Edinburgh, 1977.

Whittet, M. M., 'Epidemiology of Alcoholism in the Highlands and Islands', *Health Bulletin*, XXVIII, 4 (1970), 1–6.

Wills, J. W. G., 'Of Laird and Tenant – A Study of the Social and Economic Geography of Shetland in the 18th and early 19th Centuries, based on the Garth and Gardie Estate Manuscripts', Edinburgh, PhD, 1975.

Wilson, Bryan, *Patterns of Sectarianism: Organisation and Ideology in Social and Religious Movements*, 1967.

Winstanley, Michael, *Life in Kent at the Turn of the Century*, Folkestone, 1978.

Wolf, Eric, *Peasants*, Englewood Cliffs, 1966.

Wood, Walter, *North Sea Fishers and Fighters*, 1911.

Parliamentary papers

1843 XXIX, etc.	Annual Reports of Commissioners for British Fisheries (i.e. Scottish) and from 1873 of Fishery Board for Scotland.
1866 XVII–XVIII	Report of Royal Commission into Sea Fisheries of the United Kingdom.
1872 XXXV	Second Report of Commission into Truck System (Shetland).
1878–9 XVII	Report on Sea Fisheries of England and Wales (modes of fishing).
1882 XVII	Report of Committee on Relations between Owners, Masters and Crews of Fishing Vessels.
1884 XXXII–XXXVI	Report of Royal Commission into the Condition of the Crofters and Cottars in the Highlands of Scotland (Napier).
1884–5 XVI	Report of Royal Commission into use of the trawl net.
1887 XXI, etc.	Annual Reports on Sea Fisheries of England and Wales.
1892 XXXV	Evidence before Royal Commission on Labour.
1893–4 XV	Report of Select Committee on Sea Fisheries.

1901 X, etc.	Annual Reports of Women Inspectors of Factories.
1902 LXXXIII	Report by Crofters' Commission on Social Condition of the People of Lewis.
1905 XIII	Report of Departmental Committee on the Sea Fisheries of Sutherland.
1908 LIX	Report of the Truck Committee.
1912–13 XLII	Report of Highlands and Islands Medical Services Committee.
1913 XXIV	Report of Committee on Applications of Devon and Cornwall Fisheries Committees for Grants Assisting Fishermen to Install Motor Power.
1914 XXX	Report of Departmental Committee on Inshore Fisheries.
1914 XXXI	Report of Scottish Departmental Committee on North Sea Fishing Industry.
1914 XXXII	Report on Home Industries in the Highlands and Islands.
1917–18 XIV	Report of Royal Commission on Housing of the Industrial Population of Scotland (also *Evidence*, Edinburgh 1921).
1928 XI	Report of Committee on Land Settlement in Scotland.
1933–4 XII	First Report of Sea-Fish Commission: The Herring Industry.
1935–6 X	Second Report of Sea-Fish Commission: The White Fish Industry.
1945–6 XII	Inquiry into Stoppage of Work in the Trawler Fishing Industry.
1960–1 XV	Report of Committee of Inquiry into the Fishing Industry.
1970–1 XVII	Report on the Regulation of Scottish Inshore Fisheries.

Index

Aberdeen, 10–12, 18–19, 37, 54–60, 69, 102,
  110–45, 152, 160–2, 169, 172, 176, 230–1,
  240, 246, 255–7, 277, 308, 325, 330, 360,
  362, 367, 376
Accidents, 21, 57, 123–4, 171–2, 195, 360
Africa, 111, 177
Apprentices, 20–2, 51–2, 141

Barra Isles, 14, 24, 31, 170, 272–4, 294
Belgium, 111
Boatbuilding, 19, 61, 111, 150–2, 229, 231,
  245, 248, 297, 315, 331
Boatowners, 15, 19, 25, 30, 35–49, 52, 61–3,
  67, 71–3, 83, 90–3, 99, 102–6, 113–17,
  120–2, 128–9, 133, 136–44, 149–66, 178–9,
  185, 189, 197, 227–8, 243–9, 253, 269,
  274–5, 290, 296–7, 315–16, 321–6, 330–2,
  343, 359, 362
Brazil, 179
Buckie district, 14, 32–5, 44, 62–6, 160–2,
  171, 207, 211–13, 222–3, 227–63, 268, 294,
  329, 363

Caithness, 29, 59, 66
Canada, 24, 41, 178, 286, 374
Children, 5, 76, 80, 131–3, 143, 167, 175–6,
  180–1, 214, 223, 231–41, 262, 267, 288–91,
  296, 301, 327, 336–40, 345, 352, 363–4, 383
Chile, 41
Clyde, 12, 16, 28, 66
Co-operatives, 92–7, 229, 248, 329, 333, 356
Cornwall, 26, 35, 46, 204, 231
Cromarty, 29, 211

Denmark, 41, 44, 178
Devon, 16–18, 20, 26
Dorset, 12, 25–6
Drifting, 16, 21, 25, 28, 30–41, 44–6, 58–67,
  117, 152–62, 168–72, 175, 181, 189–204,
  228–38, 243–9, 253–5, 260, 263, 272–8,
  293–4, 297, 315, 324–9
Drink, 19–22, 57, 105, 121, 124–7, 130–1,
  211–12, 233, 288, 349–50
Dundee, 55

EEC, 42, 68, 285, 358, 360, 384
Engineers, 53–4, 58, 60, 71–4, 99, 108,
  118–20, 134–6, 143, 157, 251

Essex, 16, 24, 27, 186–7, 194
Eyemouth, 212

Family, 5, 83, 119, 130, 141–5, 149ff, 175–81,
  208–9, 214–33, 227, 232–50, 262, 300, 334,
  338, 345, 360
Faroe, 25, 42, 129, 203, 315, 359, 374
Fife, 14, 55, 272
Fish stocks, 11–13, 23–4, 27–9, 40–2, 331
Fleetwood, 4–7, 11, 18, 43, 55–7, 68–74, 86,
  90–109, 133, 182, 276, 366
France, 11, 41, 68, 111, 174–80, 215, 359, 363
Fraserburgh district, 30–1, 34, 38, 58, 60,
  63–7, 152, 155, 158–61, 169, 171, 205–6,
  211, 227, 230, 236, 242–6, 256–9, 324

Germany, 18, 28, 30, 41, 113, 137–41, 154,
  313
Grimsby, 11, 16–23, 44, 50–60, 68, 71, 95,
  102, 112, 119, 127, 141, 161, 169, 176, 183,
  196, 300, 366

Harris, 14, 26, 272, 277, 294–5, 305, 319
Holland, 28, 30, 41, 86
Hours, 20, 51–2, 57–8, 124, 360
Housing, 14–15, 35, 83, 94–5, 111, 115, 158,
  172, 179, 227, 230–1, 239, 245–6, 249,
  266–9, 297, 310, 319–20, 324, 327, 338, 345
Hull, 4–7, 11–12, 16–21, 37, 43, 50–8, 71, 102,
  107, 112, 119, 127, 141, 175–6, 308, 366
Husbands, 5, 130–3, 144, 175–80, 213–14,
  232–40, 250–2, 262–3, 285–92, 296, 336–43,
  346–7

Iceland, 11, 18, 42, 102, 149, 178, 315
Illegitimacy, 212–14, 233–4, 287, 346
Ireland, 10, 30, 34, 95, 163, 313, 378
Italy, 363, 378

Japan, 41, 163, 177

Kent, 13–20, 27, 55

Lancashire, 27, 86, 90, 93
Land, owners of; lairds, 15, 151–2, 179, 219,
  227, 242–3, 266–72, 276–7, 280–1, 290,
  301–6, 310–23, 341, 344, 350, 354–6, 383
Leith district, 13, 28, 30, 34, 55, 161

Lewis, 10–12, 31, 33–5, 59–67, 95, 119, 151,
    170–1, 213, 222–3, 231, 236, 243, 264–307,
    311–13, 326, 329, 342–8, 358, 362, 365, 383
Line-fishing, 12, 16, 26, 31, 64, 111–12, 131,
    229–30, 240, 272–3, 311–15, 324–5, 328–30,
    335, 338, 342–3
London, 13, 20, 50, 112, 187
Lossiemouth, 30, 39, 44, 63, 171, 230, 328
Lowestoft, 18, 20, 32, 34, 44, 50, 57, 62, 64,
    95, 119, 149, 152, 175–6, 181–204, 228, 231

Macduff distict, 10, 14, 33, 58, 66, 158, 162,
    207, 235, 256–8
Marketing, merchants and salesmen, 11–17,
    21, 27, 30–1, 37–9, 63–5, 75–7, 92–6, 103,
    110–16, 129, 139, 141, 153–5, 158–64, 167,
    177–8, 229, 243–4, 265, 269, 274–5, 294,
    313–18, 321–5, 331
Malaysia, 173, 177, 179
Marshside, 27, 68, 75–93, 96
Marx, Karl, 6, 98, 210, 353–7, 368
Migration, 9–12, 34–5, 118–19, 178, 182, 252,
    280, 283, 286–91, 318, 327
Moray Firth, 14–15, 24, 63, 110, 118, 137,
    152, 167, 182, 204–7, 227ff, 324, 327–8, 331

Newfoundland, 12, 24, 42, 50, 149, 163,
    173–9, 203, 360–2, 374
New Guinea, 177
Norfolk, 10, 14, 27, 184, 204
Northumberland, 20, 34, 174
Norway, 11–12, 25, 28–9, 41–6, 111, 138,
    163, 166, 173–80, 203, 221–3, 311–14, 360

Orkney, 31, 33

Peru, 41
Peterhead district, 12, 31–4, 62–6, 155,
    158–62, 169, 170, 206, 211–12, 227, 230–1,
    235–7, 244, 248, 254–6, 259–63, 324, 326
Processing curers, 11–12, 21, 28–31, 34,
    75–81, 110–14, 150–5, 160, 167–74, 179,
    227, 232, 241, 272–7, 296–8, 302, 322–4,
    331–2

Religion, 5, 21, 65–6, 84, 97, 115, 131–2,
    182–3, 188, 194, 201–14, 220–1, 228, 250,
    255–63, 280–96, 301, 306–8, 345–54, 358
Ring netting, 16, 28, 59
Russia, 41, 173

Seine fishing, 7, 13, 16, 44–6, 174, 230, 328,
    331–3, 360
Share system, 15, 19, 50–2, 58, 61–2, 77, 99,
    118, 128, 150, 157, 161, 165, 185, 188–9,
    196–8, 231, 243–6, 255, 294

Shetland, 4, 7, 10–14, 29–34, 44–6, 65, 67,
    151, 154–5, 160, 165, 171, 179, 213, 218,
    222–3, 230–3, 257, 264–70, 308–66, 383
Shields district, 17–19, 55, 57, 60, 119, 134,
    169
Skippers, 19–21, 35, 38, 43, 50–7, 61–74,
    99–102, 107, 115, 118–26, 129, 132–3, 138,
    141–3, 150, 174, 188–9, 200–2, 211, 231–2,
    237–8, 241, 244–5, 248–9, 252–5, 259–60,
    279, 294–5, 308, 325–6, 333–4, 361
Spain, 11, 41, 174, 178–9
State loans, 25, 35, 38–40, 43, 163–4, 273,
    279, 331, 359
Suffolk, 10, 14, 184–6
Superstition, 105, 131, 182–202, 253, 260,
    333–4, 350
Sweden, 24, 28, 43, 114, 165, 173–4, 177–9,
    203, 218, 221

Temperance, 82, 115, 126, 154, 207, 211–12,
    233, 257–9, 288, 349
Trade unionism, 4, 22, 43, 49, 53–74, 88, 99,
    106–8, 120, 134–43, 168–72, 243–4, 247–8,
    255, 302, 328, 342, 356–7, 374
Trawling, 4–7, 10–11, 15–23, 37, 40–3, 46,
    49–58, 64, 70–4, 79, 84, 88–92, 94–145,
    149–51, 155, 175–6, 181, 185–9, 195–6, 230,
    255, 276, 279, 324, 332, 362

USA, 41, 193–4, 215, 263, 283, 286

Wages, 19–22, 38, 49–58, 66, 70–4, 81, 87,
    99–100, 118, 120, 135–7, 142, 150, 156–7,
    170–2, 188, 196, 231, 247, 360
Wales, 18, 55–6, 84, 88, 97, 178
Weber, Max, 207–14, 223, 256, 368
Whaling, 12, 314, 316, 328
Wick, 29, 30–2, 60, 63, 211, 324
Wives, 5, 110, 130–3, 143–4, 164, 167,
    175–80, 213–14, 232–40, 250–2, 262–8,
    290–2, 296, 332, 335–7, 340–3, 346
Women fishermen, 173–5, 343, 378;
    fishsellers, 77, 167, 177, 234–5, 272;
    fishworkers, 60, 63, 66–7, 76–81, 96–7,
    111, 134–5, 167–74, 179, 231–2, 278, 288,
    302, 327, 332, 342; networkers, 96, 168,
    173–4, 234, 241, 343

Yarmouth, 10–11, 20–2, 28–9, 32, 34, 41, 44,
    50–5, 62–6, 119, 133, 141, 149, 152, 158,
    168–71, 176, 181–205, 233, 254, 260, 277,
    308, 329, 362
Yorkshire, North, 3, 9–12, 18, 34, 55, 121,
    167, 204